Selves in Time and Place

Identities, Experience, and History in Nepal

edited by
Debra Skinner, Alfred Pach III,
and Dorothy Holland

ROWMAN & LITTLEFIELD PUBLISHERS, INC.
Lanham • Boulder • New York • Oxford

ROWMAN & LITTLEFIELD PUBLISHERS, INC.

Published in the United States of America
by Rowman & Littlefield Publishers, Inc.
4720 Boston Way, Lanham, Maryland 20706

12 Hid's Copse Road
Cumnor Hill, Oxford OX2 9JJ, England

British Library Cataloguing in Publication Information Available

Library of Congress Cataloging-in-Publication Data

Selves in time and place : identities, experience, and history in
   Nepal / edited by Debra Skinner, Alfred Pach III, and Dorothy
   Holland.
        p.   cm.
   Includes bibliographical references and index.
   ISBN 0-8476-8598-5 (hardcover : alk. paper). — ISBN 0-8476-8599-3
(pbk. : alk. paper)
      1. Ethnopsychology—Nepal. 2. Nepalese—Psychology. 3. Nepalese
—Social conditions. 4. Nepalese—Ethnic identity. 5. Nepal—Social
conditions. I. Skinner, Debra, 1953– . II. Pach, Alfred III,
1949– . III. Holland, Dorothy.
   GN635.N425S45   1998
   155.8'491495—dc21   98-18244
                                                            CIP

Printed in the United States of America

♾™ The paper used in this publication meets the minimum requirements of American
National Standard for Information Sciences—Permanence of Paper for Printed Library
Materials, ANSI Z39.48–1984.

To Stan Mumford

January '99

To Joan & Wally Lonergan

in memory and appreciation
of Stan's contribution to Asian Studies.
His chapter is short but contains
an important spiritual legacy

With warm Friendship,

Maria Mumford

Contents

Note on Transcription

Words in the various languages (e.g., Nepali, Tibetan, Gurung, Tamang, Newari, Sherpa) spoken by the groups represented in these chapters have been transcribed in line with common conventions for those languages (e.g., Turner 1931 for Nepali). Except for problematic terms (e.g., *man*), words are italicized only the first time they appear in each chapter. Proper names and terms familiar to English speakers appear in the text without diacritics or italics.

Preface

The impetus for this volume arose out of a session organized by Alfred Pach, entitled "Psychological Approaches to Persons, Society, and Culture in Nepal," for the 19th Annual Conference on South Asia in Madison, Wisconsin in 1990. That session provided a forum for discussion of the theme of this volume: selves in time and place. Given that Nepal had just undergone a major political revolution, the topic of sociopolitical change was very much in the foreground. Those of us present had done our research in Nepal during the Panchayat era (1962–1990), a time of one-party government. We were certainly cognizant of local and national politics; however, with some notable exceptions, we had not always explicitly located our ethnographies of persons and selves within a political context (see Mary Des Chene's recent article, "Ethnography in the Janajati-yug," in *Studies in Nepali History and Society* 1(1):97–161, 1996, for a critique of ethnography during the Panchayat period). The 1990 People's Movement and 1991 elections, which restored a multi-party system of democracy, made it clear that persons and groups could not be viewed apart from the political landscape. Voices that had been muted under the Panchayat government were seeking representation in Nepal's changing sociopolitical arena. Individuals and groups were transforming themselves into political actors and vying for certain representations and positions within a multiethnic state intent on nation building and economic development. Likewise, outside the overt political arena, power hierarchies were more openly contested. Tensions between various groups, resistances to the dominant Brahman-Chetri national culture, and critical commentaries, although never totally absent in Nepal's history, became more explicit during this time of political change.

The theoretical focus in anthropology that had turned to examinations of practice, power, resistance, and history also worked to redirect our attention to people's agency within a full range of contexts, from the power relations and discursive practices of the household to those of local and nation-state politics. New ethnographies of the person were emerging that located persons in history, exploring the ways in which they fashioned selves in specific sites and with cultural resources that were themselves infused with institutional histories. Thus, movements both in anthropology and Nepal led many of us who were doing research in psychological anthropology to reformulate notions of self, identity, and experience as being located and produced within historical and sociopolitical events.

Contributors to this volume were asked to organize their essays around the theme of persons-in-history/history-in-persons, and to examine, through grounded ethnographic studies, the ways in which persons form and are formed by specific practices and discourses within larger sociocultural and historical processes. Our goal was not to impose on the authors particular definitions of the person, self, or experience, or any one theoretical perspective on the processes of their construction. Rather, we asked that contributors draw upon their long history of ethnographic research in Nepal for cases that provided views of the ways in which people formulated notions of themselves and their experiences in dialogic relations within and against material and social conditions. Contributors responded with richly detailed studies that trace out the social and historical interpenetrations of selves and experience in Nepal. They represent the people with whom they worked not as isolated ethnic groups or social categories, such as "Newars" or "women," but as people involved in a nexus of social and political relationships that are not easily bounded. They explore the actual ways in which specific practices and discourses form selves and position subjects, and the processes by which people contest, appropriate, or resist certain identities and subject positions. As such, this volume makes a contribution to the theoretical discussion of persons-in-history/history-in-persons and to the ethnographic record of Nepal.

We would like to thank our colleagues who provided useful suggestions and stimulating comments throughout the long course of this project. They are individually acknowledged in the chapters. Special thanks goes to Miki Kersgard for her help in formatting this text. We would also like to acknowledge our receipt of a University Research Council Grant from the University of North Carolina at Chapel Hill, which helped offset some costs of publication.

Introduction _____

Chapter 1 _____

Selves in Time and Place: An Introduction

Debra Skinner, Dorothy Holland, and Alfred Pach III

Anthropology for many years has been concerned with exploring the forms
that selves, identities, and experiences take in different cultural places.
This anthropological work on culture and the self has made it absolutely
clear that there exists an enormous variety of discourses, practices, concepts, means,
and modalities of the self.[1] Our aim in this introduction is not to recount this
immense body of work, but to indicate how the essays in this volume build upon
it to move to a new ethnography of personhood and an emerging "practice theory"
of self. This orientation locates persons in history and history in persons, focusing
on the ways in which individuals and groups fashion and are fashioned by social,
political, and cultural discourses and practices in historically specific times and
places. The diversity of peoples within Nepal's boundaries, recent political
transformations, rekindled efforts at nation building, and media-encouraged
cultural flows make Nepal an especially rich locale for examination of these
processes.

The contributions to this volume present detailed ethnographic accounts of
people's struggles to constitute themselves as particular kinds of actors and persons vis-à-vis others within and against powerful sociopolitical and cultural worlds.
This perspective situates the study of selves in local practice where structure,
activity, and selves come together (Dirks et al. 1994; Holland and Lave forthcoming; Fajans 1997; Ortner 1989:11–18; Turner 1994). Persons are considered as

persons-in-activity. They are agents, but their agency is not freewheeling or un-mediated. They are cast by themselves and others in discursive and practical genres, and are circumscribed by material and social conditions, institutional structures, and their own embodied and social histories, but these are not only constraints. They also serve as resources for self-making, and the outcomes of these efforts of self-reformulation are never inevitable. In heteroglossic worlds where there are multiple voices and contested positions, where struggles are occurring on a num-ber of levels, where societies are in flux from mass migrations and transnational cultural flows, selves too are not fixed. People, perhaps especially in situations of rapid change—as Levy points out (this volume), are involved in the constant process of reworking objectifications and senses of themselves vis-à-vis others, forging identities from available resources in the flow of activity within histori-cally specific sites.

Contributors to this volume do not hold one theoretical vision of how selves are constituted, nor do they adhere to the same definitions of self, identity, or experience,[2] but they do share an emphasis on history, power, and practice, and on the struggles of individuals and groups to forge self-understandings within local relationships and larger sociohistorical and political contexts. Drawing on in-depth ethnographic cases, the authors emphasize the specific cultural discourses and practices of self-making. They treat these discourses and practices not as indicators of essential features of Newar or Gurung or Sherpa selves or culture, but rather as the media or artifacts around which socially and historically posi-tioned persons construct their subjectivities. These media are themselves viewed as infused with power relations and institutional constraints, but are nonetheless culturally produced and reproduced, and thus are not fixed. They are "living tools" that figure selves in dialogic and open-ended ways. Thus, the selves depicted in the essays are selves in practice, not selves who have forever internalized homo-geneous, static, cultural codes nor selves who are totally determined or buffeted about by powerful discourses. Several of the chapters also share a focus on the plurality of sites of the self; that is, the recognition that the loci of self-production or self-process are many and even competing.

In this introductory chapter, we emphasize the contribution of the essays in this volume to an emerging practice theory of the self. In our portrayal of the chapters, we coeditors do not seek to substitute our interpretations for the au-thors'. They have clearly articulated a variety of theoretical perspectives for the ways in which they see selves and persons forming within and against sociohistorical and cultural worlds. They also make other crucial points that go beyond what we attempt to elucidate here. We want to offer, however, a view of how certain themes and processes noted within and across the chapters advance an understanding of the ways in which persons are constituted in history and history in persons as this happens in specific sites and activities, with the aid and constriction of cultural artifacts.

New Ethnographies of Selves in Practice

The authors' concerns with selves in process, sites of the self, and culturally produced artifacts that are the languages and practices of the self locate this volume among new ethnographies of personhood and in emerging accounts of persons-in-history/history-in-persons (for reviews, see Holland and Lave forthcoming; Holland et al. in press). Before the 1970s, most inquiries into the relationship between culture and the self were oriented either toward uncovering aspects of "the self" that were universal or "natural" or toward examining culturally specific concepts that shaped selves in profoundly different ways. Since this universal self was species specific, history and power were not considered necessary ingredients to its formation. Nor were relations of power and history considered crucial to analyses of culturally specific selves and the collective meaning systems that produced them. Instead the culturally specific self was often described in the ethnographic present, removed from time and change. This self was envisioned as stable, enduring, and manifesting the core values of what were assumed to be pervasive cultures—asserting a kind of double essentialism of self and culture. The culturally specific self—created by the end of childhood (or shortly thereafter) through rituals and other socializing practices that distilled cultural principles for the neophyte—persisted through time, regardless of change in social and material conditions.

Roughly two decades ago, these views were disrupted. Anthropology entered a period of intensive critical examination of its relations with its subjects. The discipline came under sustained criticism from within; critics reflected upon the collaboration of anthropologists with colonial powers (e.g., Asad 1973), for example, and upon the tendency of anthropological fieldwork to focus myopically on males and male activities (e.g., Reiter 1975; Weiner 1976). Somewhat later, following these early seminal critiques, anthropologists began asking related questions about their representation of others. What messages were conveyed by anthropological writing practices? Clifford (1988), Fabian (1983) and others harshly judged devices such as the ethnographic present (the use of the present tense) to describe peoples who were actually studied during a particular historical period. Such usage suspended the Samoans, or whomever, in time, removed them from history, and treated them as though they were simply pliable specimens of science.

In a move critical to our discussion here, anthropologists also, along with some psychologists (e.g., Henriques, Hollway, Urwin, Venn, and Walkerdine 1984), adopted Foucault's work, especially his formulation of power/knowledge, as an impetus for critical reflection. Foucault's histories of post-Enlightenment disciplines depicted social and psychological sciences as constructing, rather than objectively studying, their subjects.

In anthropology these critical stances have had a number of ramifications. For one, "culture," that is, anthropological descriptions of cultures, came under scrutiny and were seen to be suspiciously entangled with systems of power/knowledge, such as Foucault (1980a, 1980b) described. Feminists rigorously critiqued past representations of culture as well, claiming that anthropologists had often put forward a patriarchal and thus myopic account of other lifeways. Twenty years of detailed and persuasive feminist scrutiny have made it impossible to ignore the importance of gender in *all* societies and to avoid the recognition that what males may take to be important and sacrosanct may well be experienced in quite different ways by females. Clearly a person's social position—defined by gender, race, class, and any other social division that is structurally significant—potentially affects one's perspective on cultural institutions and the ardor of one's subscription to the values and interpretations that are promoted in rituals and other socially produced cultural forms.

We cannot here review at length the implications of this critical disruption for studies of selves and cultures, but suffice it to say that anthropology is much more reticent to treat the cultural discourses and practices of a group of people as though they were indicators of an underlying cultural logic or essence equally compelling to all those raised in its folds. As for the self per se, discourse or discursive theory, as Foucauldian understandings are sometimes called, has provoked a new concept of selves as socially constructed. The discourses and categories dominant in a society, the argument goes, are imposed upon persons, both interpersonally and institutionally. Eventually the imposition comes to be self-administered. Selves, in short, are socially constructed through the mediation of powerful discourses and their artifacts. The "subject" of the self is always open to the power of the discourses and practices that describe it. What this view has done is make the socially positioning power of discourses a fundamental part of the social constitution of the self. In its extreme form, however, the social constructivist perspective may regard selves as ephemeral, lacking embodiment of cultural forms, continually positioned by first this discourse, then that one, lacking the ability to orchestrate or author the self in and against these discourses.

The contributions in this volume represent an emerging direction in the anthropological study of the self and subjectivity. These newer inquiries build upon the insights of the critical disruption, placing selves in history and noting the power of cultural discourses and practices to position, and so socially shape others (see also, Kondo 1990). But, in addition, they recognize that people are more than constructed subjects. Although they may be powerfully positioned by discursive practices, they are also agents involved in co-producing and resisting dominant discourses, and in creating worlds and selves alternative to those posited by dominant ones. Power, history, agency, and practice become the interrelated components of a theoretical refiguring of the relationship between culture and self (Holland et al. in press; Ortner 1984). Selves are viewed as grounded in history, mediated by cultural discourses and practices, and yet makers of history, of culture, of selves. This is an approach that takes social constructivism seriously, yet tempers its extreme versions with accounts of people's activities and struggles.

Living Personal Trajectories

We have divided the volume into three sections: personal trajectories, cultural productions of identity, and politicized selves.[3] The essays in the first group focus on the struggles and creative responses of individuals as they act within sociocultural constraints. Contributors examine people's actions, narratives, and songs as the symbolic means whereby they (re)produce and contest the social order and their place in it. These accounts avoid a simplistic portrayal of people's actions and resistance as freewheeling agency. Instead, they offer a complex and nuanced account of how people struggle and make hard choices in ambiguous worlds, with outcomes that are open-ended and often unresolved. For example, in Des Chene's richly textured story of the lives and relationships of Bhauju and Jethi, two Gurung women, we view their attempt to redefine themselves within and against the Gurung culturally figured world of marriage, inheritance, and domestic authority, where *ijjat* (honor, prestige, deference) is a powerful cultural model for proper behavior and evaluation. Bhauju, in more pain than Jethi, conformed to the figured world of honor, accepting the suffering and subjugation that contingent circumstances and her social position as a daughter-in-law and then widow brought about as a socially legitimate and honorable way to maintain her reputation and integrity. Both she and Jethi were actively trying to better their positions by advancing certain claims and rallying social support, but as Des Chene points out, they were less involved in a conscious fashioning of self than in doing what they could given untoward events and the central tensions of Gurung social life.

Skinner and Holland's account of emerging femininities in a multi-caste community in Nepal's middle hills takes a more developmental approach to the formation of self-understandings, examining the sites, activities, and media in and through which girls and young women produce—orchestrate in Bakhtin's terms—gendered self-understandings over their lifetimes. Some activities, such as gossip and scoldings, encourage girls to think and act in accordance with the dominant Brahmanical model of what it is to be a "good Hindu woman." Yet these girls experience hardships in their social world even while carrying out the expectations associated with this social location. These hardships engender a sense of anger and resentment at the relatively disadvantageous position that women's versus men's life paths accord them. Through the cultural media of Tij songs, long a resource for women's critical commentary (Holland and Skinner 1995), these girls have constructed a more political critique and a novel femininity around the notion of an "educated woman," an identity alternative to that given by the Brahmanical model. In this chapter, we see how subjectivities, agency, and cultural worlds co-develop and are shaped through engagement with cultural forms in the flow of activity within historically specific sites. Tij songs become a mediating device for identity formation and the means by which alternative worlds and novel views of self are imagined and engaged.

Narratives also serve as media for the construction of cultural worlds and notions of self that subvert the dominant caste order. The lower-caste Newars in Parish's chapter recount tales of caste hierarchy and origin that contest Brahmanical views by positing alternative moral bases to the purity and pollution model underlying the caste system. Parish discusses the narratives of these low-caste actors as a means by which they constitute and sustain a critical consciousness in counterpoint to the dominant model of caste. Similar to Tij songs, these narratives are cultural forms that actors use to create and explore imaginary worlds and alternative visions of self and society. They become a means, and their telling a "space," to author new selves. Although the women who practice Tij may return to the domestic world that configures them as relatively powerless compared to men, and the untouchable narrators may return to practices that reinforce their impurity vis-à-vis the higher castes, they return to these worlds with altered subjectivities. Through the media of songs and narratives, these actors have opened their thought to new figured worlds and selves. For a time they come to "disinhabit" the boundaries of everyday life, and this opening brings with it the power to transform selves.

For persons with severe behavioral disorders ("madness"), narratives of suffering make claims about the meaning of their behaviors and, in the process, accord them social identities and positions in the family and community. Drawing upon his research in a Jaisi Brahman village, Pach examines narrative accounts of disordered behavior. These accounts, given by various family and community members, utilize similar cultural models of causation and include histories of social tensions and injustices, but they vary from person to person, reflecting the aims of the particular narrator. Explanations of the sufferer's condition and its cause become grounds for dispute as narrators stake out moral positions and material resources vis-à-vis the sufferer. The stories position both the sufferer and the narrator. How the story of madness is told, the authority attributed to the narrative, and who has the power to enforce an authorized viewpoint hold importance for the sufferer's inclusion or exclusion from family and community life, and for his or her social identity. This case demonstrates how family and community histories and relations become tied to the sufferer's identity through narrative forms.

These chapters with their focus on personal trajectories exemplify components of a practice-based approach to selves. They are grounded in nuanced accounts of people's lives. They share a sensitivity for the importance of plural sites of self-making and work otherwise to illuminate the heterogeneities of cultures that persons draw upon in responding to, producing, and contesting the meanings of events and experiences. They take seriously the mediational processes of the self, insist on embodiment, and give culturally specific discourses and practices a pivotal role in constituting the self. As a whole these essays avoid the errors of essentialism, recognizing that powerful discourses continually shape and reshape human subjectivities, yet they also stress human agency, exploring the ways in which individuals and groups inhabit and co-develop spaces and sentiments, and fashion and are fashioned by social, religious, and political discourses and practices. Subjectivity in these works is seen as developing within the interplay between the social and embodied sources of the self, in what we might call "the self-in-practice" or to use a label inspired by Bakhtin (1981; see also Holland et al. in press), the "space of authoring." The self-in-practice occupies that interface between intimate discourse, inner speaking, and bodily practice formed in the past, and the discourses and practices to which people are exposed, willingly or not, in the present. It authors or orchestrates these sites of the self.

Producing Practices and Media of Identity

The second set of essays focuses on cultural productions of identities and selves, examining the discourses and practices that mediate experience. In a number of societies, for example, codes of honor underlie various social hierarchies. In the Nepal context, honor/prestige (ijjat) is important across many ethnic groups for the status and reputation of one's self and kin. Des Chene's graphic saga demonstrated that ijjat was a compelling force for Bhauju and others in Gurung society. McHugh, in her study also set in a Gurung community, focuses on a cultural model of honor that is highly salient for Gurungs' sense of social worth and personal well-being and frequently evoked as a guiding principle that motivates actions and evaluations of self and others. She describes how ijjat is associated with key social practices related to marriage, hospitality, and everyday gender relations. Yet the meanings and practices of honor are not static. As people enter new social and economic circumstances in their migrations to urban areas and as new forms of prestige emerge—forms based on the display and consumption of consumer goods and the investment in prestigious schooling for one's children—new meanings of honor are produced and contested. Honor remains a powerful foundation of Gurung discourses of personhood and morality, but the content or bases of honor in an increasingly transnational setting are currently being reworked.

Liechty, too, focuses on the transformation in meanings of status and social class identities that a rapidly growing consumer culture has brought about. Distinctive consumer goods are now part of a social currency in Kathmandu that individuals can and must use in order to successfully claim middle-class status. Older codes and markers of status have been disrupted by this consumer logic, where display and consumption are key communicative domains of social status and middle-class identity. As consumer goods become more widely available and as individuals from a number of ethnic groups and castes become able to afford them, the stakes for claims to higher social positions increase. Interviews with middle-class individuals living in Kathmandu indicate they are caught up in the competition to maintain their status in this new consumer field. Their "play" in this field brings with it pressure to consume, and they express feelings of insecurity and anxiety in their ability to keep up with ever increasing demands. Liechty's analysis clearly demonstrates the identity struggles taking place within this discourse of consumerism—a discourse that is linked to Nepal's broader rhetoric of economic development and democracy. In this cultural world, we find middle-class identities, desire for goods, and loyalty to the ideas of development and capitalism forming together. As Liechty notes, for some individuals, consumption not only becomes a claim to middle-class status, but a moral and patriotic duty to build and participate in a modern nation-state.

Tibetans who live in the Gyasumdo region of Nepal enter another discursive space as they take part in a set of well-defined ritual and teaching practices designed to transform their identities. Tibetan Buddhist culture in this area has evolved in dialogic encounters with non-Buddhist shamanic traditions. The Nyingma lamas are in a struggle to win over the laity from certain shamanic practices that they claim to be inferior and immoral. Through a series of rituals and commentaries, these Tibetan lamas promote the Buddhist path and guide the laity to "higher," more moral, more reflexive states of being, away from the "lower" practices associated with *samsāra* (conditions of earthy existence). Mumford's complex examination of these practices focuses on the power of discourse and mediating devices to effect transformations in selves. By participating in certain rituals, laypersons experience a move from the lowest level of everyday bodily and material concerns to a second higher level—the spiritual plane of good deeds, faith, and knowledge. Lamas use demon exorcisms and the Tibetan death rite as teaching devices to move persons to the third and highest level—to global consciousness, the level of the bodhisattva. Mumford draws upon Bakhtin's notion of dialogism to describe how these rites and their meanings have evolved through encounters between shamanic practices and Mahayana Buddhism. The lamas consciously incorporate meanings and images of the former tradition in their efforts at transmuting them to Buddhist ideals. The mediating devices of rituals and commentary work to bring about other worlds of existence and other subjectivities as figured within these worlds. Like the low-caste narrators in Parish's account and the women celebrating Tij in Skinner and Holland's chapter, the laity may return to the everyday world that situates them in material concerns and practices, but they return with an altered subjectivity and a vision of other worlds and existences.

March's chapter examines another Buddhist group in Nepal, the Tamang, and their constructions of selves. In these constructions, female bodies are not only relied upon as representations of physical existence but as sites of consciousness and awareness. March explores how meanings of femaleness (as opposed to maleness) and gendered bodies circumscribe a Tamang landscape of personal and social identities. Female bodily images in songs become metaphors for spiritual values and symbols of Tamang sociality. In addition to finding aspects of women's self-identities "embodied" in these images, the author argues that the same images also shape men's experiences and expressions of their lives, particularly in coming to terms with human suffering. Whether called *dukha* in Nepali-speaking groups or *gyurba* in Tamang-speaking societies, this experience of hardship or suffering permeates the ambivalent and often unequal position of women within Nepal. March describes how suffering, or gyurba, is central to female-embodied experiences and representations in Tamang religious practices and gender relations. She describes how women's bodies are not only sources of productivity and prosperity, but are also "sites for suffering" as social exchanges, ritual practices, birth and marriage are fraught with pain, uncertainty, and loss. March portrays the critical role that women play in the reproduction of offspring, household relations, ties to divinities, and the aesthetic sensibilities centered around female identity central to Tamang cultural values and religious imagery. Gender in this analysis is presented as a socially and culturally constituted performative accomplishment.

Although many of the cases presented here are centered primarily on one or another of Nepal's many named ethnic groups (e.g., Tamang, Gurung, Tibetan, Sherpa, Hod, Newar), the authors take care to avoid the impression that these groups are bounded and isolated entities. In the multi-ethnic context of Nepal, ethnic identities are constantly reconstituted in dialogue with others. Ghimire's chapter explicitly examines how the Hod (known also as Satar) have endeavored to maintain their identity as Hod within a social milieu populated by many other castes and ethnic groups. The Hod have made a conscious, political attempt to assert their ethnic identity as they collectively resist incorporation in the local Hindu caste system and the inferior ritual and moral level it would accord them. Through two primary marriage forms—one that reinforces matrilineal bonds by extending the personal names of the matrikin to newborn children and the other that allows the Hod to recruit children of mixed or illicit unions into their fold and bestow on them their sense of social identity—the Hod are able to maintain their identity as Hod. Employing such adaptable practices, they can accommodate inequalities in economic and gender relations and breaches of moral behavior that would otherwise threaten their sense of unity. As Hod representative bodies adjudicate and legislate the meaning of breaches in marital practices and establish policies regarding cultural practices (e.g., responses to brideprice inflation), they produce what Adams (1997) has called a "strategic essentialism," in their efforts to recreate and legitimate a collective identity.

Making Politicized Selves

The final set of essays by Ortner, Enslin, and Lewis continues this exploration of the making of politicized selves and identities through examining historical and political events that lead to contestations among groups over identities and control. Ortner demonstrates the need for an interwoven cultural and political analysis to understand the complex transformations and continuities in shamanic ritual practices and meanings among Sherpas in the Solu region of Nepal. She begins by asking why Sherpa shamanism declined under the impact of Buddhist monastic disapproval. This is the starting point for a critique of the ways in which shamanism has been depicted and a critique of certain styles of argumentation. Shamanism has been interpreted in the ethnographic literature as embodying a relational orientation, as opposed to a more individualistic orientation embodied in Buddhism or modernity or both. This interpretation rests on and produces binary and "essentialist" categories that preclude an understanding of the multi-centered elements and shifts in the politics and meanings in ritual practices that have occurred. Ortner argues that we should follow the lead of feminist and postmodern theorists to question such binary oppositions and the modernization narrative that embeds them. She draws upon ethnographic and historical materials to show how shamanism could be analytically rendered as either individualistic or relational, and moreover, how these categories were as much a part of the politics of labeling as they were labels for real processes in Sherpa society. Ortner questions the notion of a "decline" in shamanism among Sherpas by exploring this process across a number of cultural and political fields. She shows that the notion of a decline in this practice rests upon analytical and historical interpretations fraught with incorrect assumptions about the homogeneity in the meaning and practice of shamanism for Sherpas, who are also assumed to experience a unified subjectivity within an unbounded and "universal" locality. Exploring the multiple meanings and possibilities for the absence (or survival) of shamanism, the author leads us to reexamine the questions we have asked. Instead of looking for essences of Buddhism and shamanism, Ortner focuses on how relationalism may be variously construed in a political field of shifting alignments where people construct multiple histories.

The contradictions and emerging divisions in Nepal are perhaps most evident in current discourses on politics and gender. As women increasingly enter the political arena, divisions surface not only between men and women, but also between women along class, caste, and ethnic lines. Critical commentaries on gender and politics by women throughout Nepal and women's groups such as the *Nārī Jāgarān Samiti* (Women's Awareness Organization) in Chitwan described by Enslin (this volume), and more informal Tij song groups (Holland and Skinner 1995; Skinner and Holland, this volume), undergird transformative female identities and participation in Nepali society. For many years, Tij songfests have been sites of the cultural production of social critique and have provided spaces for women's authoring of new visions of self and society. Enslin examines these types of songs and poetry in rural Chitwan and their extension into new sites where women author themselves as educated, middle-class activists for women's rights. As political activists, they have joined others in appropriating the rhetoric of development and progress with its emphasis on acquiring the forms of cultural capital that mark the middle class. This discourse divides people into the educated and the uneducated, and the modern and the backward. For middle-class Bahun and Chetri women, advancement of women comes through education, development of the country, and modernity. Even as they call for women's unity against injustices and create an imagined community of women united by their struggles in the lyrics of their songs, in other aspects of their songs and related activities, they reproduce social divisions and so distance themselves from lower-caste, lower-class women. Enslin also critiques the "middleness" that middle-class women are in, caught in a contradictory position in which they both seek to enter the public sphere of salaried employment and education, yet remain situated between social classes and dependent on males in domestic and political arenas. Although Enslin examines women's songs for their creation of a middle-class identity, she weaves through her analysis accounts of women's suffering that results from forms of violence enacted against them. This serves to remind us that resistance should not be romantically portrayed as unleashed creativity and agency, but rather consists of ambiguous activities still subject to domination and tied to identity struggles. Enslin chronicles stories of women's pain and suffering to temper representations of women as though they were completely autonomous agents who pay no price for their actions of resistance.

The final chapter analyzes a seemingly innocent and informative children's reader, *Jhī Macā*, or "Our Children," as a cultural resource used in struggles to re-establish Newar ethnicity in a multi-ethnic and increasing transnational context. Chittadhar Hridaya, a native resident of Kathmandu and one of the great literary figures of modern Nepal, published *Jhī Macā* in 1947, with the intention that this book both guide Newar parents in their home teaching and serve as a first reader for their children. This reader remains one of the most popular short works written in Newari. Chittadhar's short vignettes touch upon every significant area of Newar life, depicting much of the sensory experience and cultural imagery of childhood in Newar Buddhist families and neighborhoods in Kathmandu. Lewis explores how the author, utilizing a form difficult to assail, teaches children numbers, the names of months, deities and kin terms, and script—all in Newari terminology and cultural forms that had been forcibly restricted from use in public. In a children's text, Chittadhar inscribed an agile and "disguised" (Scott 1990) form of resistance that promoted a Newar cultural identity while it undercut its authorized repression by Rana and Shah state-supported forms of Brahman-Chetri cultural hegemony.

In his afterword, Robert Levy provides another perspective on the essays in this volume, locating them in the time and place of anthropology as a discipline. He begins by tracing anthropology's changing perspectives on agency: concepts of persons have transformed from persons as radically shaped by culture to the equally agentless view of the Foucauldian emphasis on power/knowledge to our perspective here on persons as actors in and against cultural systems. Some of this vacillation has come, of course, from the general theoretical orientations dominant in different eras in anthropology's history, but Levy attributes part of it to the changing social and material conditions that encourage reflexive self- and identity talk (e.g., Nepal now), a symbolic mastery of who one is, or, alternatively, an out-of-awareness habitus of self (Tahiti in the 1960s). Levy compares the material and social conditions that have defined Nepal in the last twenty years and contrasts the Nepal of this historical period with the Tahiti of the early 1960s, to argue that some periods and places are more conducive to and increase the visibility of the processes of self-making and self-authoring that this volume emphasizes.

In summary, the essays in this volume explore how people—positioned by gender, ethnicity, caste, and locale, and constrained by powerfully compelling cultural worlds—nonetheless use cultural resources in creative ways to produce new self-understandings in response to changing material and social circumstances, altered media of identity, and political practices to reposition themselves and their groups. Through ethnographic cases, the authors examine how subjectivities, agency, and cultural worlds co-develop and are shaped through engagement with cultural forms; and they portray the appropriation and dialogic interchange of multiple voices for self and group formation. As such, these essays add to the anthropological literature on Nepal and South Asia and to recent discussions of South Asian subjectivities (e.g., Adams 1996; Ewing 1997; Kumar 1994; Parish 1994, 1996). These ethnographically grounded and complex accounts of the mutual constitution of selves and society also reach beyond geographical boundaries to more theoretical ground as they examine specific processes of self-formation in time and place, critique analytic categories central to anthropologies of the self and South Asia, and demonstrate the complexity and ambiguity of self-understandings as these are formed in and against daily practices and dominant discourses.

Notes

1. For reviews, see Harris (1989), Marsella, DeVos, and Hsu (1985), LeVine (1982:291–304), Shweder and Bourne (1984), White (1992), and Whittaker (1992).

2. The concepts "individual," "self," "identity," and "person" have been defined and distinguished by several authors as belonging to different fields of inquiry and traditions. Reviews of these traditions can be found in Fogelson (1979), Harris (1989), Ito (1987), and White (1992). Although various contributors may draw upon certain of these distinctions, we did not attempt to impose hard and fast definitions of these terms across chapters. Our emphasis is more on how all of these concepts are relational and formed in historically situated activities.

3. Most of the chapters reflect the themes of all three sections. The chapters are allocated to the sections based on their predominant emphasis.

References

Adams, Vincanne. 1996. Tigers of the Snow and Other Virtual Sherpas: An Ethnography of Himalayan Encounters. Princeton: Princeton University Press.
———. 1997. Dreams of a Final Sherpa. American Anthropologist 99(1):85–99.
Asad, Talal, ed. 1973. Anthropology and the Colonial Encounter. London: Ithaca Press.
Bakhtin, Mikhail M. 1981. The Dialogic Imagination. M. Holquist, ed. Austin: University of Texas Press.
Clifford, James. 1988. The Predicament of Culture: Twentieth-Century Ethnography, Literature, and Art. Cambridge, MA: Harvard University Press.
Dirks, Nicholas B., Geoff Eley, and Sherry B. Ortner. 1994. Introduction. *In* Culture/Power/History: A Reader in Contemporary Social Theory. Nicholas B. Dirks, Geoff Eley, and Sherry B. Ortner, eds. Pp. 3–45. Princeton: Princeton University Press.
Ewing, Katherine P. 1997. Arguing Sainthood: Modernity, Psychoanalysis, and Islam. Durham: Duke University Press.

Fabian, Johannes. 1983. Time and the Other: How Anthropology Makes Its Object. New York: Columbia University Press.

Fajans, Jane. 1997. They Make Themselves: Work and Play Among the Baining of Papua New Guinea. Chicago: University of Chicago Press.

Fogelson, Raymond D. 1979. Person, Self, and Identity: Some Anthropological Retrospects, Circumspects, and Prospects. *In* Psychosocial Theories of the Self. Benjamin Lee, ed. Pp. 67–109. New York: Plenum Press.

Foucault, Michel. 1980a. The History of Sexuality. Vol. 1. New York: Vintage.

———. 1980b. Power/Knowledge: Selected Interviews and Other Writings, 1972–1977. C. Gordon, ed. and C. Gordon, L. Marshall, J. Mepham, and K. Soper, trans. New York: Pantheon Books.

Harris, Grace Gredys. 1989. Concepts of Individual, Self, Person in Description and Analysis. American Anthropologist 91(3):599–612.

Henriques, Julian, Wendy Hollway, Cathy Urwin, Couze Venn, and Valerie Walkerdine. 1984. Changing the Subject: Psychology, Social Regulation and Subjectivity. London: Methuen.

Holland, Dorothy, William Lachicotte, Debra Skinner, and Carole Cain. In press. Identity and Agency in Cultural Worlds. Cambridge, MA: Harvard University Press.

Holland, Dorothy, and Jean Lave. Forthcoming. Introduction. *In* History in Person: Enduring Struggles and the Practice of Identity. Dorothy Holland and Jean Lave, eds.

Holland, Dorothy, and Debra Skinner. 1995. Contested Ritual, Contested Femininities: (Re)forming Self and Society in a Nepali Women's Festival. American Ethnologist 22 (2):279–305.

Ito, Karen L. 1987. Emotions, Proper Behavior (*hana pono*) and Hawaiian Concepts of Self, Person, and Individual. *In* Contemporary Issues in Mental Health Research in the Pacific Islands. A. B. Robillard and A. J. Marsella, eds. Pp. 45–71. Honolulu: University of Hawaii, Social Science Research Institute.

Kondo, Dorinne K. 1990. Crafting Selves: Power, Gender, and Discourses of Identity in a Japanese Workplace. Chicago: University of Chicago Press.

Kumar, Nita. 1994. Women as Subjects: South Asian Histories. Charlottesville: University of Virginia Press.

LeVine, Robert A. 1982. Culture, Behavior, and Personality: An Introduction to the Comparative Study of Psychosocial Adaptation. Chicago: Aldine.

Marsella, A., G. DeVos, and F. L. Hsu, eds. 1985. Culture and Self: Asian and Western Perspectives. New York: Tavistock.

Ortner, Sherry. 1984. Theory in Anthropology Since the Sixties. Comparative Studies in Society and History 26(1):126–166.

———. 1989. High Religion: A Cultural and Political History of Sherpa Buddhism. Princeton: Princeton University Press.

Parish, Steven M. 1994. Moral Knowing in a Hindu Sacred City: An Exploration of Mind, Emotion, and Self. New York: Columbia University Press.

———.1996. Hierarchy and Its Discontents: Culture and the Politics of Consciousness in Caste Society. Philadelphia: University of Pennsylvania Press.

Reiter, Rayna Rapp, ed. 1975. Toward an Anthropology of Women. New York: Monthly Review Press.

Scott, James C. 1990. Domination and the Arts of Resistance: Hidden Transcripts. New Haven: Yale University Press.

Shweder, Richard A., and Edmund J. Bourne. 1984. Does the Concept of the Person Vary Cross-Culturally? *In* Culture Theory: Essays on Mind, Self, and Emotion. Richard A. Shweder and Robert A. LeVine, eds. Pp. 158–199. Cambridge: Cambridge University Press.

Turner, Stephen. 1994. The Social Theory of Practices: Tradition, Tacit Knowledge, and Presuppositions. Chicago: University of Chicago Press.

Weiner, Annette B. 1976. Women of Value, Men of Renown: New Perspectives in Trobriand Exchange. Austin: University of Texas Press.

White, Geoffrey M. 1992. Ethnopsychology. *In* New Directions in Psychological Anthropology. Theodore Schwartz, Geoffrey M. White, and Catherine A. Lutz, eds. Pp. 21–46. Cambridge: Cambridge University Press.

Whittaker, Elvi. 1992. The Birth of the Anthropological Self and Its Career. Ethos 20(2):191–219.

Part One _____

Personal Trajectories

Chapter 2

Fate, Domestic Authority, and Women's Wills

Mary Des Chene

First Impressions

My first impression of Bhauju remains very clear in memory. I first saw her one early morning. She stood, illuminated by predawn light, gazing out over the flagstoned courtyard across the great river gorge toward the farther hills and mountains. I was struck by her great beauty and poise—her self-possession as it seemed to me then. She looked over to me in time. "Bahini,"[1] she said in soft greeting, raising one hand to her forehead. Then she picked up a bamboo basket, took down a sickle from the porch rafters[2] and quietly departed the courtyard, off to cut many pounds of cold, wet grass for the buffalo.

This clear, simple first impression has never been erased, but to it have been added many complex overlays. Bhauju was the wife of the eldest son of the family with whom I lived in a large Gurung village in west central Nepal.[3] We came to know one another slowly, and sometimes surreptitiously, as both mundane daily happenings and extraordinary events involved us in one another's lives. Doing research on other matters, I nonetheless was at times immersed in what I came to think of as "The Saga of Bhauju." I now know that when I first saw her she gazed toward her *māita*, her natal home, but I did not know that—nor much else—then.

The trials that Bhauju endured during the time I lived in her household, and the complex responses of others taught me much of what I know about Gurung styles of managing reputation and negotiating anger. I learned at the same time about depths of friendship among women not readily evident without being immersed in difficult times together. Besides the personal concerns for my daily companions which will be evident here, it was about these topics that, at the time, I understood myself to be learning from Bhauju's saga. With the aid of time and distance, I have come to think this story also speaks to concerns less culturally specific and perhaps more profound. I now find that it teaches me about the ongoing project of assessing one's possibilities in life against the backdrop of one's position in a complex local world, and my current understanding of this story leaves me dissatisfied with the social scientific language that might make sense of it.

Selves, it is now commonplace to observe, are crafted in the crucible of daily life. Who we understand ourselves, socially, to be, and who we imagine we might become affects our perceptions and our choices in the present.[4] And yet, except perhaps for anthropologists, some devotees of spiritual traditions, and a few cultural traditions that elaborate discourses of the self, I wonder how many of us think and therefore act on a daily basis in terms of "crafting selves"? It seems more common to think, "What can I do now," or "What should I do now?" These two questions point to what in anthropology we might describe as social structural constraints and to culturally shaped moral sensibilities. Bhauju's saga has made me believe that how people pose such questions to themselves ought to have a greater role in shaping theoretical language,[5] and thus I first tell my version of that story, and then return to what it might teach those whose story it is not.

While Bhauju will always be, in my mind, the central character, this paper is in fact about two women, Bhauju and her husband's eldest sister, Jethi.[6] In demeanor and in situation, they appeared to have little in common. Bhauju was quiet, deferential; Jethi assertive, voluble. Bhauju was in the often unfavorable position of daughter-in-law, Jethi the eldest and favored daughter of the household. Yet they also had two great commonalities. First, each was engaged in a struggle to redefine herself, sometimes transgressing social expectations to do so. Second, all that transpired between and around them took place against a single backdrop: a steady decline in the reputation of their household. Bhauju's trials and Jethi's actions were ingredient to this decline, while the reputation of the household had, at the same time, a bearing on their fortunes and on the choices they made. It is thus only by examining their lives in this specific social context that their conflicting efforts to forge new identities for themselves can be understood.

A Host of Circumstances

I had been living with Bhauju's household for several weeks before our first encounter. Bhauju had been in town, several day's walk away, undergoing treatment for her tuberculosis. It was the only time she would have such treatment in the two years for which I know the details of her daily life. Bhauju herself was, in a sense, a newcomer. She had briefly lived in the household as a new bride some ten years before, but through most of her marriage she had been in India where her husband worked as a peon in a government office. During those years in India she had borne four children. The two eldest, a boy and a girl, died at the ages of six and seven, within fifteen days of one another from a disease for which Bhauju knew no name. Her two living children, Nani, a daughter nearly two, and Babu,[7] still an infant, returned with her from India.

Around the time of Nani's birth, Bhauju's husband contracted tuberculosis, and sometime thereafter she, in turn, contracted it from him. Just six months before our first meeting he had brought his family back to live in his parents' house. After visiting briefly, he returned to his work in India. And so Bhauju was, on our first encounter, a long-married woman but a newly arrived daughter-in-law—the only daughter-in-law—among a household of relative strangers. She was thus, in many ways, back where she had been years before, yet older now, unwell, carrying sorrow, and without the buffer that a husband's presence might afford in her in-laws' house.

I learned all these details of Bhauju's past only slowly. At first I simply knew that her husband worked in India while she lived here with her children. Having gone to study Gurkha soldiery, the main form of migratory labor, I found such a situation unexceptional. I knew many women whose husbands were abroad. Indeed it was some time before I learned that Bhauju was, like me, a newcomer.

Bhauju's children were the joy of the household. Throughout the day they circulated among their great-grandmother, grandmother, and two paternal aunts, Jethi and Kanchi,[8] with whom they also slept at night. I first saw this, naively, simply as an example of the virtues of an extended family for child care. Only gradually, and as other things made me watch more closely, did I realize that the children were rarely in the company of their mother. Indeed, I slowly came to see that they were actively kept away from her. Bhauju would often say, when Nani begged to be carried, that she was too old and her back too sore. It was a long time before I learned that this was the sacrifice of a woman who did not want her child to learn, by being snatched from her arms, that others thought poorly of her mother. What Bhauju never knew about, and I never told her, were the criticisms of Bhauju whispered nightly into her young daughter's ear by her aunts.

Bhauju had begun to decide, she told me much later, that her *kismat*—her fate—would not be kind. Marriage, migration, and childbirth had marked Bhauju's transition to adulthood. Like other young women with children, she described herself as "*baccāko āmā*" (the mother of a baby). This identity entails marriage and a husband, and it entails being a daughter-in-law, but it is talked about by women in other ways: having a baby on one's hip, being peed on in the night, and knowing, with other women, the joys and trials of being a mother in a place where the health of infants is precarious. Unlike other women with young children, however, Bhauju spoke of herself this way only in the past tense. In her view she had passed quickly through the time of young motherhood and was now in decline—*buḍhī bhayo* (old). To be young in years yet feel oneself to be old, to have given birth to four children but have only two, and those kept away from one, and to be married ten years yet be treated as a new daughter-in-law, all these circumstances combined appeared to Bhauju as marks of a cruel fate slowly unfolding. "When my children died," she said to me, "I too began to die...Still, we women must try to live."

Of Bhauju herself, it took me some time to acquire any more sense than that afforded by my first impressions. Her silence I took for serenity, knowing nothing of her history. Her careful attention to appearance and her fine clothes, when I thought about them at all, I took to signify a degree of wealth and perhaps a certain vanity, for I thought her beautiful and imagined that she thought the same. I could not have guessed that she wore her best skirt to cut grass so that it would not disappear while she was gone, nor that Bhauju thought of herself as an old woman. It was a long time before I learned that she treated her body with care less out of vanity than because she sensed its decline, and as a means of affirming an identity other than the one attributed to her by members of her household—that of a laborer. Her apparent serenity I learned to understand as the carefully practiced deference of a newly arrived daughter-in-law escaping into silence.

Her grace in speech and action, like her physical appearance, were means, I now think, of preserving a different sense of herself, and a constant, visible critique of the treatment she received—meeting disrespect with respect, gracelessness with grace. I learned this and much more over the months to follow. I counted myself naive for not having seen all this from the outset, but without knowing Bhauju's history or understanding the challenges being put forth by Jethi, I could never have read all the statements being made in the course of perfunctory daily tasks.

I came to know Jethi much more quickly, or so it seemed at first. She was outgoing, quick-witted, and fun to be around. She quickly took me over as her responsibility. Jethi ran a "hotel" as she called it, just down the path from the house, which was situated at the lower edge of the village. Her hotel was a small thatch hut from which she dispensed homemade liquor (*raksī*) and a few store-bought goods. It was also a place where the porters of tourists might cook their own food and take shelter. In the back were two cots where Jethi, her younger sister, Kanchi, and Bhauju's two children slept at night. Someone had to protect the goods in the hotel, Jethi explained to me. In turn, the children's presence protected the reputations of the two sisters, particularly when porters were present.

Jethi spent much of her time at her hotel, selling tea to occasional village visitors, weaving carpets on a loom set up by the door, and overseeing the children. Through the open door she could see the path to the water source for the hamlet, and so she carried on many shouted conversations with women as they proceeded to and from that busy spot. She also cooked for me there. On most days I would visit morning and evening and have my meal with Jethi and little Nani, Bhauju's daughter. We were often joined by Kanchi, and sometimes by other family members. After supper other neighbors often joined us there, and we had many pleasant, and for me informative, conversations around the fire in Jethi's hotel. But as crises occurred and relationships soured, this hearth became the site of family conferences and Jethi's plan making. I was thus privy to many discussions of Bhauju's future and subject to many efforts to gain my allegiance to Jethi's point of view. After supper conversations remained informative, but were less often pleasant as events transpired.

As with Bhauju, I first took the way things were, and how they appeared, to be circumstances of long standing. Eventually I learned that the hotel was a new venture, embarked upon in anticipation of Bhauju's return to the household. Gradually, I learned that Jethi's apparent popularity with the women in nearby households was not so universal as it appeared from the friendly public conversations I heard take place between path and hotel. Much later I learned that the piece of land where Jethi's hotel was built had been wrested from her father after great argument. It was her first public claim to authority in the household.

After a few months women who had befriended me began to say quietly that I should not "walk with" Jethi too much. In fact, we rarely walked anywhere together, but I knew enough by then to take this as a warning about reputation: that those with whom one associated would be taken as a guide to one's own character.[9] I was also learning that actions counted for much more than words in the judgment of a person's character.[10] Perhaps, I thought, Jethi's entrepreneurial spirit is seen as inappropriate. Are other women trying to keep her "in her place?" At this point I had little sense of a relationship between Bhauju and Jethi, for I saw Bhauju mainly at the house, and Jethi mainly at her hotel, where Bhauju did not visit. And, as it turned out, I knew little of Jethi's past and present endeavors. I could not see that their apparently quite separate daily lives had everything to do with one another.

What I would learn over time was that Jethi took the opportunity of Bhauju's return to redefine her place in the household. No longer would she do agricultural labor. The addition of Bhauju's labor to the household was crucial to such a stance, which was nonetheless taken as a sign of noncooperativeness, and a radical challenge to parental authority, by observant neighbors.[11] By opting out of agricultural labor, Jethi removed herself from a primary site of sociality and a main means of inter-household cooperation, for much agricultural labor is done communally. Her argument was that she would instead contribute cash to the household, through her "hotel" business and the sale of carpets. Jethi's longer-term plan, as it turned out, was to become economically independent and leave the village, preferably for Kathmandu. The notion of a single individual being economically independent is not one that makes sense in a Gurung context, thus no one guessed this carefully guarded secret until events made it unavoidably clear. In the meantime the public faces turned toward Jethi were friendly, but privately her usurpation of her father's authority within the household met with disapproval. Fewer local customers at her hotel was, initially, the only outward sign.

Bhauju's Daily Round

It is not a secret that, in many parts of the world, women do an inordinate share of daily labor. *Which* women is, however, less often remarked upon. One of the overriding facts of Bhauju's life was the distribution of labor, not across genders but within her own. Within the household there were, excluding myself, five women. Bujai, nearing ninety, watched the children, and kept chickens away from drying grain while warming herself in the sun, but was otherwise exempt from labor. Aamaa,[12] in her sixties and healthy, if thin, was still well within the age when many women cut wood and grass, and sowed, weeded, reaped, and hauled loads from the fields. But with two adult daughters and a daughter-in-law in the house, she preferred to confine her work to the preparation of meals, watching the children and other tasks around the house. Thus the bulk of the agricultural labor fell, potentially, to Jethi, Kanchi, and Bhauju.[13]

In practice it was to Bhauju that the bulk of daily work devolved. Her routine went much like the following, day after day. She rose from her spot on the floor, quite far from the fire, about four in the morning. Her first task was to make three or four trips to fill the great brass jars with water for the day. While at the water source, she found a moment for a daily *pūjā* (worship). The next task was to plaster the porch which ran along the front of the house. Taking clay from a pile she would later replenish from a site far above the village, she mixed it with water and, with an old rag, produced a fresh floor coating for the day's activities. This finished, she would feed and milk the buffalo (sometimes one, sometimes two). It was then time to go inside and start the fire, where she would place the milk to boil and set a kettle alongside so that tea could be prepared by Aamaa. As others then arose, she applied a fresh clay coating to the floor around the fire. Sometimes she would have a cup of tea at this point, sometimes it was not yet prepared when she left. Now she departed to cut grass for the buffalo. It was at this moment, well into her morning, that I had first encountered Bhauju. The rest of the day varied by need and season—collecting wood or clay, grinding grain at the water mill and hauling the flour to the house, weeding, harvesting, winnowing, washing clothes.

In such a daily routine one would often descend and climb several thousand feet in a day. The loads of grass, wood, and grain that Bhauju commonly carried in a *doko* (basket) on her back weighed from sixty to eighty pounds, by the reckoning of my own back. She ate, like others, two meals a day, midmorning and evening, with an afternoon snack between. But Bhauju's food, doled out by Aamaa, came last and was most scanty. She was rarely given meat or milk, even when the rest of the household ate it. Under this regime, Bhauju's tuberculosis seemed to worsen. She looked drawn, and she coughed.

Bhauju's daily routine is not an atypical one; many Gurung women work hard from morning till night. Indeed, on top of the activities outlined above, many must cook for their households and care for their young children. Yet Bhauju's daily routine was the subject of much gossip and thoroughgoing disapproval by all the women who knew the family well enough to be aware of it.[14] Bhauju's increasingly obvious ill health was one reason for this approbation. Even in a poorer household, it was said, a daughter-in-law would be given easier tasks and not be made to carry loads in such condition. Bhauju's heavy manual labor was frequently contrasted to Jethi's sedentary routine; it was evident that there were other options. The bulk of the criticism, however, had to do with the manner in which Bhauju was made to do her work: in solitude.

Women's labor is eminently social in a Gurung village. Major projects, like sowing and reaping are achieved through organized labor sharing within hamlets, involving both men and women.[15] Daily tasks are carried out by the women of each household for that household, yet they are done socially. Several women will go together to get water. Friends coordinate trips to the mill. Wood and grass cutting are often also excursions with friends, and no one would do either alone except out of dire necessity. Yet Bhauju was forbidden to join such groups. Once beyond the vicinity of the house, of course she sometimes did, and it was during these trips that other women learned in some detail of her circumstances. Kanchi, Jethi's younger sister was, however, frequently sent out to ensure that this did not happen, and Kancha, Jethi's youngest brother,[16] was also a source of information. If news of Bhauju socializing while working reached the house, she faced an evening of sustained criticism by Aamaa, Baba, and often Jethi, who would yell at her for gossiping about them and for her lack of appreciation for the food and shelter she and her children were given. That talk would flow was, of course, precisely the motive for attempts to keep Bhauju away from such groups in the first place. But this restriction, contrary to common practice and to women's sense of their rights and of a key source of pleasure in life, produced just the gossip it was meant to foreclose.

Women Watching (Out for) One Another

Here it is necessary to introduce one peculiarity of Bhauju's household. Gurung kinship reckoning is patrilineal, marriage after residence is patrilocal, and cross-cousin marriages, especially matrilateral ones, are preferred. When joint households split, often when sons are married adults, brothers frequently build adjacent houses. Thus in large villages, hamlets tend to coincide quite closely with patrilineages, and many inmarried women are of the same clan as one another. This situation aids the cooperative arrangements among households for they are formally united through patrilineal relations, and informally related through women's clan ties. Bhauju's household was the sole exception to this pattern within its hamlet.

Bujai (Jethi's father's mother), had grown up in that hamlet and moved at marriage, as per custom, to her husband's house in a distant part of the village. But at the death of her father, as sole surviving child, she inherited the house and moved back with her husband and children. Thus the clan relations were reversed in this case. Bhauju's husband and his family belonged to the clan of most of the inmarried women of the hamlet, while Bhauju was, by birth, a member of the clan of the men of the hamlet and their children.

The point of this excursion into Gurung kinship is twofold. First, the inmarried women of the hamlet owed allegiance to Bhauju's household as members of the same clan. They had a number of ritual obligations to the household, and relations should have been, and in times past I was told had been, especially close and cooperative. Moreover, the conduct of the household members rebounded on their own reputations in a particularly forceful way, for if they were stingy or uncooperative, it was members of their own clan who were behaving poorly. The second consequence of this chance of inheritance was that Bhauju, unlike all other inmarried women, was in the relation of sister or daughter to the other adult men of the hamlet, as members of the same clan.[17] They thus owed to her the solicitude and aid appropriate to this relationship. Their wives, as members of their married households, had the further responsibility of seeing to the welfare of their husband's clan sister. Thus the women of the hamlet had a special interest in Bhauju's welfare, in Jethi's conduct, and in the reputation of the household.

Neither Bhauju's circumstances nor Jethi's behavior met with their approval, but for many months I was puzzled by what seemed a dissonance between private talk and public behavior. Privately I heard scathing criticism of the conduct of household members. Empathy for Bhauju, and sometimes empathy for Jethi's father, who was perceived to be publicly humiliated by Jethi's usurpation of household decision making, was frequently voiced. Some women spoke of their anger over the treatment of Bhauju; household members were said to be no longer Gurung at all—as evidenced by their conduct—a grave indictment. I was even urged by a number of women to move out.[18] No one, they said, should have to endure such disharmony. Yet the public faces turned toward household members remained friendly, Jethi's shouted pathside conversations continued daily, and cooperative labor exchanges remained operative. I began to understand that to make a rift public is avoided at all costs. Everyone might know, but if it is not publicly stated, the breach may yet be mended, whereas a public breach produces further disharmony (cf. Brenneis 1984).

What took longer to understand was how women's skill at taking care of one another was at work. It was only by maintaining the public appearance of harmony that Bhauju could be helped, for a formal breach would cut off access. Indeed, those who voiced the strongest disapproval maintained the most compelling appearance that nothing was amiss, and had the most interactions with the household. They were thus more free to come and go from the house, and Bhauju was less heavily censured if seen pausing by their courtyards or cutting grass in proximity to them. That these women brought extra food to the forest for Bhauju, hid her clothes in their houses, and provided moral support, went unnoticed despite the careful scrutiny to which she was subjected.

It is a common sight in the hills of Nepal to see women carrying heavy baskets on their backs through field and forest, and along village paths. I first saw just that, and only gradually came to see much more in the travels of a group of women I was coming to know. Those who have lived for years together read yet more knowledgeably the social significance of who walks with whom, and who does what labor where. I made the mistake of imagining the daily routines I first encountered, like those of Jethi and Bhauju, to be quite timeless ones. But even as I learned they were the result of recent circumstances, they were becoming routine. When after seven months I left for a visit home, both Jethi and Bhauju had for some months been settled into the daily routines I have described. The implications of those routines, and the likelihood of conflict resulting from their entanglement—Jethi's sedentary routine depended precisely on Bhauju's peripatetic one—was just then becoming evident to me. Of course, what precisely would happen I could not foresee, but trouble seemed to loom ahead.

Changing Fortunes

I was away for several months. When I returned there was, of course, news, but things seemed much the same in the household. I brought Bhauju pictures of her and her children, and one night soon after my return she came late in the evening to see them.[19] She looked at them with evident pleasure, naming *chorā, chorī* (son, daughter) with a catch in her voice, but then handed them back. "They're for you, take them," I said. "No, Bahini," she said, "you keep them and I will come and look at them sometimes." Prior to my departure Bhauju had commented to me only in the most oblique of terms about her situation in the household. Now she stared long at me assessing, I think, whether she could trust in my discretion. Finally she said in a low, low voice, "If I take them, they will take them away from me." And after this, a flood of stories about the disappearance of her best skirts and other things, came forth. She told and told, of small hardships, of having no place of her own. The key to her one trunk had, she said, been taken from her and was now kept by Aamaa. I kept the pictures, and adjusted my vision once again.

Change, and with it conflict, came quickly. Within a few months of my return Bhauju's health (although, as it happened, not her tuberculosis), finally brought about a change from her daily round. Bhauju's right hand and forearm became, over several weeks, swollen beyond recognition. She carried on her work in this condition for weeks, but finally, nearly delirious with pain, it was evident that she could not carry on with her daily labor. Kanchi was despatched in her place, fetching water and grass, the minimum for the day's requirements. For several days Bhauju lay on the bed furthest from the hearth, moaning quietly, lapsing in and out of sleep. No one could diagnose the cause. Neighboring women speculated that a grass cut infection was the source, but privately I was told that it was only in her weakened state that it could become so severe. I took this to be a reference to her tuberculosis but was quickly corrected. It was the state of her souls (*plah*) and her *sae*[20] that were meant.

I had tried unsuccessfully in the past to take Bhauju to town to be treated for her tuberculosis. Since my return I had renewed those efforts, to no avail. With the onset of this new health problem, I feared that soon she would not be able to walk, but despite my offer to pay, departure was continually delayed. Finally Aamaa had explained to me that they could not do without Bhauju's labor even for a few days. My reply that they might soon have to do without it altogether had no effect but to increase ill feeling. Now it seemed that both prophecies were coming to pass: Bhauju could no longer walk to town, but neither could she work. Thus an impasse and a crisis were simultaneously reached. On the third day I stayed nearby to watch and try to feed Bhauju, working on transcriptions in my small loft room. It was a day of *sim-sim pānī*, a light steady rain falling from low clouds, mountains hidden, sounds muted yet distinct. As it turned out, it was the lull before the storm.

Around four o'clock I heard Kanchi return and deposit her load of grass by the buffalo shed below. As I prepared to come down to check on Bhauju and make sure she was not sent out to feed the buffalo, I heard Kanchi, instead, ascending the ladder. She came, shaking rain from herself, and pulled an envelope from her skirts. Looking pensive, she handed it to me and asked me what it said. As Kanchi watched me, I read, in the blunt shorthand language of telegrams, that Jetha, Kanchi's eldest brother, Bhauju's husband, had "expired," and that his wife was to be sent forthwith to India. I looked at Kanchi peering anxiously at me and I thought of Bhauju lying, semiconscious, below. Rain pattered gently in the long silence. Finally, I spoke:

M: X, that's your oldest brother's name isn't it? It's about him.
K: Is Jetha all right?
M: You know that he's been ill don't you?
K: Yes, is it worse?
M: It got worse, and now...
K: No!
M: Yes, Bahini, it says...three weeks ago...
K: Jetha's dead isn't he?
M: Yes, Bahini, three weeks ago...he died three weeks ago.

She sat stunned beside me, finally saying amid her tears that she could not tell her mother and grandmother. We made no mention of Bhauju. Finally she went below and, like me, forced to give the news, she did. I soon heard keening from below and went down.

Bhauju had risen from her sickbed. Clutched in her good hand was the photo of her husband that usually adorned the *pūjā* place. Kneeling, photo pressed to her forehead, she was crying and at once singing, in the staccato lament of Gurung women's mourning songs. She sang of her sorrow, of her pitiful condition. Not only ill, not only alone in her in-law's house, not only a mother deprived of the affection of her children, now she was, moreover, a widow. Life is over, yet life will go on, she sang. "What is to become of me now?"[21] Aamaa, Bujai, and Kanchi sobbed in the corner. Jethi soon arrived and sobbed louder than anyone. Hearing the commotion, and recognizing the sounds of mourning, women from nearby houses soon began to arrive, shawls tightly pulled over their heads and joined in the crying and singing even while urging Bhauju and the others to stop. Bhauju's children wailed in bewilderment and held tightly to me.

Neighboring men also began to arrive, sitting in the courtyard and examining the telegram, which I was called to interpret. After a long discussion of the word "expired" they accepted the news and promptly began to debate the likelihood of a pension being forthcoming. Baba, father of the now deceased Jetha, arrived home and heard the news. He sat in stony silence staring at the cold hearth, joining in neither group.

After several hours I was drawn away to a nearby house. There the women of the hamlet, except those of the immediate family, gradually congregated and discussed Bhauju's fate. All agreed that her life would become yet worse. Now there would be no income from India to compensate for her presence, and no worry of a son or brother's disapproval of maltreatment. But above all, these women who frequently took risks to make Bhauju's life better in small ways said to me, over and over, "Now your Bhauju's bangles will have to be broken. We will have to do it. You'll cry when you break her bangles. It's too sad. Our hearts will break." Saying this, or something much like it, they would sob uncontrollably.

I knew that a widow could no longer wear the red bangles that signify married status. But so much else, besides the imminent loss of bangles, seemed more important. Bhauju appeared to be seriously ill; now she was widowed with all that portended. This focus on bangles seemed to me petty, or perhaps, I thought, a displacement of grief. Or perhaps bangles are an especially evocative symbol of all that being married means to a woman. I was soon to revise my opinion by joining in the making of a widow.

Making a Widow

Many Gurung men, serving as soldiers, have died abroad. The armies that recruit them provide Hindu *pandits* (priests) to perform rituals, including those of death. Like a soldier abroad, Jetha had been cremated and Hindu ritual observances performed.[22] From a Gurung point of view, his body had been taken care of, but it remained to care for his soul. He must be made to realize his state, be prepared for his journey and, finally, guided to the land (or "village," as most people said) of the dead. Thus all funeral rites except those concerned with preparation and disposal of the corpse are carried out at home, wherever and whenever a person may have died. The day the news arrived was counted, for these ritual purposes, as the day of death. So it was that, after a day of spreading the news to scattered kin, the lamps that would bring Jetha to his former home were to be lit. First, Bhauju would be stripped of all symbols of marriage.

On this day I awoke to find on the porch an old woman in the process of slicing Bhauju's swollen hand with a rusty razor blade. Over my protestations she made three long slits on thumb and palm. As I explained about rust and infection, she explained that the pus must be let out. But all that came was blood, and as we debated, Bhauju's eyes rolled back and she fell into a coma. For two hours she lay unconscious, pulse alternating from pounding to barely perceptible. It seemed she might follow her husband to the village of the dead. But at last we roused her and fed her hot milk. Thereafter she lapsed in and out of consciousness, finally dozing on the porch. By noon the porch was needed for the funerary rituals, and Bhauju, bundled in a blanket, was carried inside and laid by the cold hearth. So began the making of a widow.

Later in the afternoon the lama called into the house that it was time to "make my little sister a widow."[23] Bhauju was sleeping, but the women who sat watch beside her shook her awake and pulled her into a sitting position. She could not sit unaided and was barely conscious. Her face was slapped to revive her and she was held in a sitting position. We surrounded her, so no one could see her. None of the other women of the household was present, all were in the courtyard, but the house was full of neighbors and relatives. It was those of us who had become Bhauju's quiet supporters who gathered around her, half a dozen women from nearby houses and myself. All cried, but everyone except me also evinced a strong resolve to carry through with what must be done. Following curt orders, I took off Bhauju's red *colo* (blouse) which she could wear no more, removed her *pote* (wedding necklace) from around her neck, and dressed her in an old T-shirt, turned inside-out.[24] Then the other women began beating at the bangles on Bhauju's wrists. Those on her swollen arm were so tight they cut her flesh. I had tried to remove them days before when she lay sick, but with a soft smile she had refused, saying that she must always wear them to honor her husband. We wept and they beat at Bhauju's arm while she again lost consciousness and I propped her up. Finally the last glass shards fell to the floor. A wife had died; a widow was born.

Bhauju was then carried outside where we loosened her hair and poured water over her head in the cold fall weather. She moaned, but did not regain consciousness. Her part in the ritual over, we took her inside and tried to warm her. As we sat around her, wondering if she would live, I no longer thought that the talk of bangles was an oblique way of referring to her other, more serious troubles. For the breaking of the bangles was, in the doing, not a "mere" symbol of becoming a widow; it was the act itself. At least it was so for those who performed it; Bhauju thankfully remembered little of the ordeal. Still, when she awoke late that night she looked first to her arms and said: "No bangles. It's finished then."

"What Is to Become of Me Now?"

A week later preparations for the main funeral ceremony were in full swing. Jethi had left for the capital, Kathmandu, to get money that, so women whispered to me, she had acquired for her business by selling Bhauju's wedding gold. Whether this was true I never ascertained, but it was "true" for all intents and purposes, for it was what people now believed. If so, it was instead to be spent on her brother's funeral, and people remarked on the appropriateness of this karmic retribution.

A Gurung *pae* (funeral) is a large event, entailing much expense and requiring much labor. Besides its significance for the deceased, it is also a realignment and reaffirmation of social ties now transformed by absence. Careful track is kept of attendance and contributions, and not to attend a pae or contribute appropriately, is one way to publicly mark a breach of relations. Some distant relatives and powerful village families took advantage of the chance to break their ties with this increasingly ill-mannered and unfortunate household. Close kin and neighbors, however, whatever their sentiments, were not willing to create a public breach. Nonetheless, Jetha's father was forced to make rounds requesting assistance, a most unusual occurrence. This, women explained to me, was a way to make public their disapproval without overt statement of it. The message, of course, was lost on no one.

Bhauju remained very weak and ill. Yet one morning I did not find her on the bed that was now hers. From neighbors I learned that she had been sent to grind rice flour in preparation for the ceremonies. I quickly followed, for I knew the weight of a basket of flour (80 to 100 pounds) and did not think Bhauju could carry it back up the long steep hill. Grinding flour takes many hours and though she had left in the darkness, it was not yet finished, giving us our first chance to talk privately since the news of her husband's death had arrived. As soon as I arrived, Bhauju began to talk. "I have been quiet, like a good daughter-in-law," she said, "but now I am *khatam*" (finished). She now faced life as a widowed daughter-in-law. The thought of their son's return could no longer, even theoretically, temper her treatment by household members. There was no life to anticipate different from the one she had been leading. Even the solace of caring for her children had already been taken from her.[25]

Bhauju explained all this to me as part of her kismat, her fate. She did not know why she was destined to suffer, but it was clear to her as she assessed her situation, that she was so destined. It was at this time that she looked back to the death of her two older children as the moment when her fate had turned, as she said, to ash. She saw only two possible futures for herself. She could stay and soon die from her diseases and hard work. If she did this she would at least have the pleasure of watching her children for some time. Or she could try to make a life outside the hills in a town where she would not be forced to do such demanding labor. The most likely way to make such a life, she said, would be to remarry. She thought herself old and undesirable, not a good candidate as a wife, but thought that if she had the reputed pension she might have better hope, likening it to a dowry. She told me then what others had already said: that her husband had had a lover in India and that it was from this woman that he had contracted tuberculosis and then passed it on to her. He had not written to her in over a year and this, she said, proved that he had no longer loved her.[26] Given all this, she reasoned, it would be all right to use some of his money as a means to a better life. At least half, she said, she would put in a bank for the children when they were older. But if she left the household, she must leave her children. This was the irreconcilable dilemma with which Bhauju struggled during the weeks after her husband's death.

All this we discussed under cover of the rushing stream and grinding grain. Then, when it was finished, we loaded the ḍoko, and I crouched to place the tumpline on my forehead. At first Bhauju protested, but as I looked up at her, and then up the path toward the house, she quickly envisioned the end of the journey, back in the courtyard. Cracking the first grin I had seen on her face in a long while, she acquiesced, saying only "we will go slowly." With many pounds of flour on my back we did, indeed, go slowly—slowly enough for many to see and more to hear of our little journey. My slow walk was taken, as intended, as a clear public statement, yet not an overt one, of my disapproval of Bhauju's treatment by her household. Back in the courtyard I could, and did meet sharp queries from Jethi and Aamaa with the simple assertion that I worried for Bhauju's health and so went to carry the load. Many people over the following days remarked to me with a smile that I was "learning to be Gurung." Certainly I was learning to negotiate Gurung women's worlds, though always without the risks incurred by others.

Jethi Makes a Bid for Independence

Jethi had often spoken to me of her eldest brother. She clearly held him in great affection, and she often displayed to me the gifts he had brought her. When he died she mourned deeply. But at the same time, like Bhauju, she looked to her future. As the men's debates went on about whether or not a pension would be forthcoming from the Government of India, Jethi was never far away. Indeed, she encouraged them to come to her hotel, where she provided free tea and raksī. Within a few days Jethi was declaring that her brother had intended the pension for her. He had, she claimed, made out papers to transfer it to her, but had died before they were properly filed. She would go to India and get them.

These declarations were met with shock and derision by turns. In her presence the men merely said, "It is a long way. Do you know Hindi?" and the like. Out of her presence they said, "She's become a lāhure" (a soldier). That is to say, she acts like a man and, moreover, a man who has knowledge of the wider world. Spontaneous skits by former soldiers rendered the spectacle of Jethi, cast now as an out-of-place hill woman, stammering in ungrammatical Hindi-Nepali patois in front of an unimpressed Indian government clerk. These performances met with roars of laughter, not least from Jethi's father, whose laughter shored up his declining position with the other men who saw him becoming subservient to his daughter within the household hierarchy.[27] In Jethi's presence, however, he did not say no to her plan, but rather said that she would need a male companion and should take her brother, Saila,[28] along.

A Public Breach

Debates and funerary rites continued apace. Funerary rites (though not debates) at last concluded, but not without a final turn of events, taken to be the death knell for Bhauju. Among those attending were Bhauju's relatives. The final event of the pae is a complex exchange of gifts among affines, meant to publicly mark the continuance of relations among those who were connected through the deceased. This proceeded in the courtyard and all, including Bhauju's mother, distributed their gifts. But as others made their distributions and as speeches affirming close ties were made, Bhauju's mother began to speak from her seat, softly first and then more loudly. Finally she rose and entered the circle where Jetha's relatives sat. Shaking her fist she decried the treatment that Bhauju had received in this house, listing her grievances, one by one.

This outburst was met momentarily with stunned silence, then Bhauju's other relatives and the inmarried women of the hamlet (i.e., of the same clan as Bhauju's husband) tried to drown out her words. People tried to drag her away, but she stood her ground. Bhauju fled, sobbing, into the house. The rest of the family began to pace the courtyard, up the steps and along the porch, and back down again, saying nothing. Finally Aamaa, then Jethi began to deny the charges, one by one. They proclaimed their love and affection for Bhauju, the care they rendered to her because of her illness, and their desire that she stay in their household now that she was a widow. Jethi briefly changed her tune, saying once, "If you want her, take her. Take her back to her māita. We don't want her." But then she returned to the earlier denials.

At last Bhauju's mother was dragged out of the courtyard by the women who had broken Bhauju's bangles. Damage control began, as Bhauju's other relatives, with her elder brother as spokesman, and the rest periodically chiming in, denied all that had been said. They explained that Bhauju's mother had been drinking and knew not what she said. "Our ears can't hear, our hearts can't understand this talk," said Bhauju's brother. "It never happened," he declared. The family listened but did not respond. At this juncture Bhauju burst from the house and, to my astonishment, began to recite her lineage. She explained how she was the product of a *rodhī*[29] union, that her mother had not brought her up, but rather she had been taken in by her father's first wife and raised as one of her own. This woman (also present) was her true mother. She then proceeded to deny all that her mother had said, averring the fine treatment she received in the household and her desire to continue to live there. I could only read this performance as a desperate act of self-preservation.

At this juncture I too was practically dragged from the courtyard. "Come," commanded a friend, "this is not talk to be heard." This woman, who lived next door, was quite closely related to Bhauju by marriage ties within their natal families. She was widely agreed to be among the kindest and most generous people in the village. She had supported Bhauju throughout all her troubles at great risk to her relations with the rest of the household, yet managed to remain on good terms with Jethi and the others as well, not only publicly, but in their estimation. Thus trusted, she had been able to help Bhauju substantially. This delicate negotiation of opinions and knowledge over months was regarded as an extraordinary feat by the other neighboring women who observed its daily execution.

When we arrived at her house she was shaking. I thought she might be crying for Bhauju, but on taking a closer look I saw she was shaking with anger. Dragging me up to the attic, a relatively private place, she thrust wool and carding tools at me and sat at the loom where we often wove and chatted. Pounding the loom, she began fiercely to weave, her angry speech punctuated by the flying shuttle. She began by denouncing Bhauju's mother as vehemently as the mother had just denounced the members of my household. Still I thought she was angry because of the repercussions for Bhauju, and I said so. "No! I hope I never see her again. I hope she dies. She is nobody. I will never speak to her again," she said of Bhauju's mother. I was initially baffled by her passion and by the position she took. But as she spoke further, I heard her genuine despair at such a public breach of relations, at ill will publicly expressed. When she dragged me from the courtyard, she meant precisely what she said. Hearing such talk, she explained a bit impatiently to her sometimes dull-witted student, will make your sae shrink. You will get those thoughts inside you and become the same. So too for everyone else. Bhauju's mother had placed everyone in danger.[30] She then explained how hard it was for her to endure, with friendly face, daily interactions with those in the house below. She placed herself in danger by doing so, she said, but it was necessary for the sake of Bhauju. Now her mother ("her own mother!") had come along and destroyed everything. "Bhauju's life was bad before, now it will be unbearable," she finished in a low voice. Then she began to sob. It dawned on me that she had, quite literally, come back to save me from ill effects, just as she always showed up when I sat in the courtyards of those she considered to be witches and found pretense to take me away. And I learned one more lesson about the risks women may take for one another.

India, Land of Pensions

At this juncture it seemed that, surely, nothing more could happen. Bhauju would have to leave the household. She told me this, with finality, that very evening. But in doing so she would have to leave her children. This was unbearable, but better than having them witness her death. She was convinced she would not survive if she stayed. Between the health of her body and the health of her dharma, she said, she could not last long there. Later that same evening we sat, in silence, in the main room of the house. All family members were present and still fuming over Bhauju's mother's statements earlier in the day. Bhauju lay on the far bed, hidden by darkness. Into the house walked a man I had never seen before and sat down on the cot by the fire. This was Maila,[31] the second-eldest son, returned from India. He had not been home in five years. His entrance went unremarked.

When tea was brewed he began to speak. He described Jetha's death, in a hospital, of tuberculosis. He described how he had taken care of the cremation and of Jetha's belongings, and itemized the money he had spent. At this point Aamaa gave him food. He took his plate, walked into the gloom at the far end of the room, and began to feed Bhauju the meat he had just been given. I saw where he stood in the unfolding drama.[32]

Like Bhauju, Maila was the offspring of a rodhī union. His mother had died when he was quite young, and he was sent to shepherd, and was rarely at the house of his father. He had followed his elder brother to India five years before, living with him (and with Bhauju prior to her return) and working there. He had had no further contact with his family. Relations were outwardly civil, but it was clear that there were no ties of sentiment between them.

After feeding Bhauju, Maila came to me—as yet we had not met—and asked me to read the papers he had brought with him. Evidently he had made some stops along the way, being brought up to date on events at the house, including my presence and my allegiances. The papers I read stated that someone from the household must work a further four years in order for a pension to be received. As I began to read this out Maila, with a quick jut of his lower lip indicated Bhauju on the far bed. I quickly revised my reading: Jetha's wife must complete the period in order to receive a pension. Further inspection of the papers revealed that the pension beneficiary was indeed Bhauju. There was no mention of Jethi.

Long negotiations followed Maila's sudden arrival. I will not recount them all here. Jethi continued to claim that the pension was intended for her. Privately she muttered that Maila had destroyed the relevant papers. She made plans to go to India. The skits continued, still out of her sight, and now out of sight of her father as well. With Maila in the house Bhauju was not sent out to work. He continued to feed her most of the milk and meat he was given, under the disapproving eye of Aamaa. There was no hold on him in this household, he explained to me. But they needed him to arrange the pension which they hoped to keep for themselves. It was fitting, he concluded, that he feed Bhauju their meat. Maila, a man of few words—at least in this situation—said no more. By the end of a month Bhauju's hand and arm were again recognizable, and she took up her daily round, but a somewhat less onerous one, perhaps because of Maila's presence. He saw to it that Kanchi continued to do some of the labor that usually fell to Bhauju.

Bhauju's enduring dilemma was her children. She could leave with Maila and return to India. But without her children, she said, she would be cut in two. In the end there were several trips to India. Jethi left first, about two months after the funeral. Publicly her father supported her action, though privately he had urged her, to no avail, to wait. Other men had convinced him that a woman could not do this male business. From her rather mournful letter it seems that the soldiers' skits were not too far off the mark. She returned, somewhat chastened, and resumed weaving carpets. Maila and Bhauju were now to go, but their departure was continually delayed and the children were closely watched. One by one, however, Bhauju's clothes and belongings found their way into other women's locked trunks. Finally food for the journey was prepared late at night in other houses. Maila and Bhauju left for India without the knowledge of other members of the household, but also without the children. Two weeks later Jethi and Saila followed. Stories of shouting matches between Jethi and Bhauju at the home of a village man residing in India trickled back to the hills. Then Maila reappeared, alone. He had come, he stated publicly, to take the children "for a visit." With Jethi and Bhauju away, Kanchi had become both the main laborer of the household and the main caretaker of the children. "I am," she said, "a mother and daughter-in-law anyway; perhaps I should get married." She smiled at her own joke, but looked tired as she said it. Maila returned to India without the children. All three—Bhauju, Jethi, and Maila—remained there at the time of my departure.[33]

Fittingly, the saga of Bhauju has no neat conclusion, for the struggles I have recounted did not end here. Bhauju did escape the household, but she left without her children. Jethi asserted her independence in clear terms, traveling to India in search of the means to support herself. Ironically, Jethi and Bhauju now live in the same town, not too far from the village where so much passed between them. Jethi eventually returned home and resumed her hotel and carpet business. But a few years later she married a man from a nearby town and moved there. She bore a son, but evidently she continued her quest for financial independence, for the last news I heard of Jethi was that her business dealings had gotten her into trouble with the law, and that she faced a jail sentence.

Bhauju too returned to Nepal. Maila stayed to work for his brother's, now Bhauju's pension. Bhauju, when I last heard, was living with her elder half sister. So far as I know she has not remarried. Nor do I know whether her situation as a widowed sister is a happier one than that of widowed daughter-in-law would have been. She has achieved her aim of leaving the household and agricultural labor behind her. But her children remain in the village, cared for by Bujai, until her death, by aging Aamaa and by still unmarried Kanchi. They are reaching an age where they can begin to perform some of the labor left behind by Bhauju.

This is about all I know of recent happenings in these women's lives, for letters are stubbornly quiet on daily details. Jethi's marriage, child, and legal troubles were suitable news and gossip, recounted with some relish. But otherwise, letters have a distinctive cast—elaborate assurances of health, enumerating each person, brief recordings of deaths, and in between attempts to sustain, through reminiscences of past mutual activities, relationships now sundered by distance. Coming from a place where health is never a given, death walks too often, and distance separates too many, the form of these letters, as much as their content, conveys the news—that people are going on building the best lives they can with the materials at hand. But I hear about Bhauju only when I ask directly, and then ever so briefly. Thus I fear that the news is not happy. Even at a distance it is best not to give people shocks.

Where initially Bhauju and Jethi seemed to me to be dissimilar, both in personality and in circumstances, I have come also to understand their commonalities. Both looked to alter course from that which their structural positions most easily afforded them. For Bhauju it was the bleak existence of an overworked daughter-in-law and then the bleaker future of a widowed one. For Jethi it was, in the long run, the position of an unmarried woman dependent on her brothers and thus beholden to her sisters-in-law. Even before Jetha's death she had determined to avoid such dependence. Both took genuine risks to resist these futures. Bhauju risked her health and suffered separation from her children. Jethi risked her reputation and, to some extent, that of her father and entire household.

Other women viewed both Bhauju and Jethi as experiencing a descent into misfortune. Where assessments differed was with regard to causes and agents of misfortune, and thus in moral judgments of it. Bhauju was regarded as, if you like, a victim, herself behaving with grace in adverse circumstances. She thus deserved support and protection. Jethi, on the other hand, was seen as the source of her own misfortunes and some of Bhauju's. She was thus perceived as dangerous, to herself and others, a source of disharmony and, potentially, illness. Other women gradually disengaged from her, yet did so cautiously and with some subtlety, for they did not want her wrath directed toward them.

Jethi's vision was, in many respects, the more radical one. Bhauju sought decent life circumstances, a daily life lived out in accord with Gurung standards of sociality and civility. This she sought both before and after her husband's death, though her strategies and goals had to be modified as circumstances changed. Jethi sought something quite different. She sought economic independence and social independence. She opted out of cooperative forms of labor, and though she continued to make deals, these were recognized as an altogether different kind of exchange. She exerted authority in transgression of gender and generational norms within her household. She did these things publicly, thus appearing to be in brazen disregard for local standards of comportment. And she risked exposing herself, through her business and her travels, to whispers of sexual promiscuity.[34]

Before she decided that I was too much in Bhauju's corner to be a confidant, she told me many times that she did not care what others said. She held her head a little higher, spoke more loudly, and redoubled her public, pathside sociality. It seemed that she did care, but her strategy was to challenge others, within and outside her own household, to directly rebuke her, or to overtly reject her. She thus effectively circumvented the usual indirect forms of social control. But in doing so she often created havoc in her wake, not least for Bhauju. It is not easy to say who paid the greatest price or in what coin for the clashes that ensued from these two women's efforts to redefine themselves and to exert some control over how structural arrangements would affect the circumstances in which they lived.

Reading Bhauju's Story

Some might say that the story I have narrated here should not be told at all; that the transportation of this saga from the place of its occurrence to these pages, and my orchestration of its telling are violations of privacy, voyeurism in academic guise. Those who would conceivably express these views might include Jethi and some Nepali intellectuals who object to foreign social science that peers into private lives and takes away stories to relate, for personal advancement, in arenas not available to its subjects.

Others might say that this story should be told; that each of us, whether we stand in a relation close or distant to the particular lives and the cultural milieu described here, may learn from it, and that if we do then Bhauju's trials, while not changed, gain a meaning they did not have before.[35] Among those who might hold these views I know Bhauju to be one, for she expressed the hope, on the eve of her departure to India, that I might one day "write [her] *dukha*" (hardship), so that others might better understand *āimāīko dukha*—what women suffer. Others who might hold with the second view include Nepali intellectuals who find their own society, like any, to be imperfect and think that the road to improvement is not necessarily through more and more five-year plans, but through documenta-tion of particulars that illuminate broader social patterns, and can, cumulatively, render visible aspects of the diversity of "Nepali" lives.[36]

In the end, and it was not an easy decision, I have listened to the second set of voices, and especially to Bhauju's, in choosing to write her story. But I have also tried to attend to the first set of voices in choosing how to write it. I view this paper, first of all, as having been written for Bhauju, and look forward to the day when I tell her what I have written here. But since I have chosen an academic venue for the telling, I seek in what follows to suggest some ways that various readers might find Bhauju's story to inform their own concerns. In particular, I reflect on its place among writings on the lives and circumstances of South Asian women.

Fashioning and Refashioning Female Lives: Structure and Circumstance

Renato Rosaldo has remarked on the frequent disparity between "dense case histories and slender conclusions" (1993:96) in processual analyses like the social dramas narrated by Victor Turner and the thick descriptions of Geertz. He suggests that this is due, in Turner's case, to a final reduction of richly described human dramas to mere illustrations of structural principles and, in Geertz's case, to a stress on "free-floating cultural idioms," insufficiently situated within structures of power. In the following reflections on what social theorists might learn from Bhauju's saga I have tried to avoid both extremes by always returning to what I understand to be the various actors' points of view. Nonetheless, I suspect it may be inevitable that conclusions that seek to make the particularities of life illuminate general principles or cultural phenomena will be found to be thin, for they necessarily strip away detail, idiosyncracies, even cultural specificities.

This account has sometimes taken on the true complexity of a saga but its twists and turns all issue from a few central tensions between structural arrangements and contingent circumstances. There is, first of all, resistance by two women to a prescribed course of life. Since these women were daughter-in-law and eldest daughter within the same household, their struggles brought them, inexorably, into conflict. They were, however, not just members of a household, but of a larger community. The second constant is the tension between community ideals—of household harmony and of female comportment—and the individual desires and wills of these two women who defiantly imagined different futures for themselves.

During most of the events recounted here, Bhauju and her husband's eldest sister, Jethi, occupied, respectively, what are generally agreed to be disadvantageous social positions for South Asian women: widow and spinster. Bhauju was, moreover, the only daughter-in-law of her household, also commonly a disadvantageous position for a woman. The combination of daughter-in-law and widow adds up, by common consent, to tragedy.[37] Jethi, by contrast, while marked as unfortunate by apparent spinsterhood (she was unmarried into her late twenties), held a favored position as eldest daughter within her household. The two women thus had different problems and different material with which to attempt to fashion solutions. But each, for disparate reasons, was working to create a measure of independence for herself in a devotedly relational world.[38]

In narrating this saga, or rather a small portion thereof, I have sought a route between structure and circumstance, one that may better facilitate understanding women's life choices. It is now commonplace to acknowledge a place for both social structure and human innovation in anthropological accounts, yet either structure or circumstance usually remains the subtle hero of the narrative. Where women are the subject, one can argue plausibly for either. The structure-as-hero (or villain) account posits that women's lives are, by and large, more constrained by social structure than are men's; they are less likely to be able to transform the structures within which they must live. Accounts that privilege agency concur, but argue that precisely because of their structural subordination, women must innovate and improvise; women's power is informal, operating in the interstices between formal structures. If both arguments have merit, then the study of women's lives provides a good chance to consider the juxtaposition, the intersection, and sometimes the collision, of structure and circumstance.

I do not use the more familiar dichotomy, structure and agency (Giddens 1979), because I don't find this formulation sufficient for thinking about Bhauju's story.

In my usage "circumstance" would fall within the range usually glossed by "structure." I use it to point to the contingent happenings of daily life, which might be thought of as instantiating, in the experience of individuals, that thing we call social "structure." Agency, with its problematic implication of a voluntarism that is somehow experienced apart from structure seems to me to have no place here. Rather I have tried to narrate points of view, motivations and plans as far as I am able. But I have tried to make evident that such "agency" does not just take place against a backdrop of norms for conduct or sociological attributes (gender, jāt, kin position, and so on). Rather, people think through their position and act from within a host of structured but also contingent circumstances. Thus, for example, the long-standing structural arrangements of patrilineality, patrilocality, and inheritance through males are realized in the contingent circumstances of Bhauju's dilemma over her children. These traditions she was well aware of, but they were not her focal concern. Rather, with knowledge of these structural arrangements, and experiencing their impact on her life, she tried to navigate toward a solution with which she could, quite literally, live.

In thinking about women's lives, anthropologists first tended to focus on points of transition, especially those that are publicly marked, like marriage and childbirth. There are good reasons for this focus. The first is that women's lives, as Rosaldo (1974) argued some time ago, are frequently defined by domestic sphere activities. The second reason is that much writing on women has necessarily been corrective: women too must achieve adult status; women may be exchanged á la Lévi-Strauss, but they may also be brokers in marriage markets, and the nexus of relations among lineages or households.

But to bring into view the structural significance of women in social orders, or to focus on life cycle rituals still leaves in the background the bulk of anyone's life, female or male. How often, after all, do any of us go through puberty or, for that matter, get married? Clearly such events affect the future in important ways; yet they are not the whole story. What of the more mundane aspects of life, daily happenings and concerns? What of extraordinary events that are not planned, not formal, not ritualized? And when we speak of women in "households," or in "the domestic sphere," should we not also mean houses and homes—physical places where people live, and the ways they think and feel about those places—as well as kin units and theoretical constructs? It is in the minute practices of daily living, mundane and extraordinary by turn, that the working out of chance, pattern, and worldview that anthropologists seek to portray is best discerned. I make no claims to have gotten under anyone else's skin, inside another mind, or any other metaphor of penetration. My account of Bhauju's story is but one account by a deeply implicated participant, though I have worked hard to try to understand others' points of view. A story like this one can probably not be learned or told from any but an involved position. And this leads me to reflect that, while such involvement may lend partiality (in both sense) to our accounts, it is precisely what makes them accounts of social life.

Accounts that privileged structure have produced, overall, quite a dismal portrait of South Asian women's lives, caught within the confines of patriarchal systems, permanently displaced (whether in their natal or affinal homes), systematically devalued by ideology and in practice (cf. Raheja and Gold 1994). These portraits were not necessarily wrong, but they were partial. Recently, in an attempt to redress the balance, much attention has been paid to South Asian women's expressive traditions (e.g., Appadurai and Mills 1991; Holland and Skinner 1995; Narayan 1986; Raheja and Gold 1994; Trawick 1990). Collectively these works mark an important turn to the privileging of women's points of view and to women's efforts to shape their own destinies. They teach us that by listening to women's songs one often discovers pungent critiques of patriarchy. Attending to context, it becomes clear that ritual moments, like marriages and public festivals, in which women are sanctioned to speak publicly, may be turned into opportunities for critical social commentary (e.g., Enslin 1992; Skinner, Holland, and Adhikari 1994). These works, together with some earlier ones (e.g., Wadley 1980) provide an important corrective to the stereotype of South Asian women as passive and submissive.

I have tried to continue on the path opened by such work in that pride of place was given to women's own viewpoints and actions, including reactions by other women to the situations and actions of the main characters. Where the story I have told differs is that it is not focused on an expressive tradition—song, poetry, story—nor does it analyze a marked social occasion, like a ritual. There was an occasion when Bhauju sang laments, and several rituals figured in this saga, but the focus here is on a longer span, with equal attention to what happens after the lights go down and everyone goes home.[39] This seems to me critical, for while moments of *"communitas"* can be profoundly important, they are usually brief. Bhauju's life is as much shaped by the days of quiet agony in a dark corner while her hand swelled up beyond recognition as it is by the moments when others gathered around to support her in her grief as a new widow. Even when observing formalized social occasions, we should pay equal attention to what precedes and follows them in order to understand how they matter in people's lives.

Another way in which this account departs from the current emphasis on expressive traditions is that it is often focused on nonverbal or otherwise indirect ways that women make statements of support or disapproval, and thus exert influence on others' ways of being. Our present emphasis on discourse and verbal performances, productive of insight as it has been, should not lead us to overlook the significance of a glance, a carried load, or where the children sleep, for understanding what people are saying to one another. In a Gurung village at least—and I doubt this is unique—a great deal of the commentary on moral conduct is not verbal, but is expressed in action, deed, and gesture. When and if we learn to read that commentary, it strikes me as important that it be rendered, as far as possible, in the idiom in which it is originally "said," not subsumed into a reported set of moral precepts. This is important not only in the interest of attending to cultural form, but because it makes evident the disagreements and the varying viewpoints that people hold of proper and generous conduct and of their opposites.

The tale I have told can be read as one of resistance to social definitions and to familial authority. "Resistance" is a term much in vogue at the present time. Always suspicious of sudden confluences between the preoccupations of those we study and our own theoretical concerns, I use this term with some hesitation (cf. Ortner 1995). The caveat I would introduce is that resistance not be conflated with heroism nor with victorious outcomes. The romanticist note I perceive in some work on resistance would be out of tune in this case. Both women make many compromises; there are no obvious winners and many painful losses. Jethi's resistance to her situation, in particular, ramified in the lives of others in unfortunate ways. And, crucially, each woman's "resistance" stymies that of the other.

Finally, it is important to note that this paper is about the lives of two Gurung women. It is thus not about women whose lives are structured, first and foremost, by Hindu notions of women's place, purity, or value,[40] as in much literature on South Asian women.[41] Gurung women are often described by Hindu Nepalis (men and women) as strong and autonomous. This may be said in criticism (strong-headed, willful) or in admiration (resilient, courageous). Until very recently Gurung women have been clearly identifiable when they travel to town or plain by their blouses of burgundy velvet, their numerous gold hoop earrings, and large turquoise, gold, and coral necklaces.[42] Gurung women are likely to look one in the face, to joke, and to drive a hard bargain. No one, particularly meeting a group of middle-aged Gurung women in a situation in which they are comfortable, would think of them as shy and retiring. Even the British officers who recruited their husbands remarked on their demeanor: "Gurkha women…enjoy a freedom unusual in the East and are well able to stand up for themselves. They smoke and drink only slightly less than their menfolk, and are very outspoken" (Leonard 1965:48).[43]

Whether their "freedom" is "unusual in the East" is not a question I would care to pursue. But between the life of an orthodox Brahman woman and a Gurung woman one could doubtless find many differences. There are few gendered ritual restrictions and the sexual division of labor is, as Gurung women frequently pointed out to me, all in favor of men. That is, Gurung women do almost every kind of work.[44] Yet there are many quiet forms of constraint on the "freedom" of Gurung women woven so finely into the texture of daily life that they can be difficult to discern. In Bhauju's story, both social structural and cultural constraints on women become visible: the structural constraints of the marriage system, inheritance, and domestic authority, and the cultural constraints of public opinion, family honor, and definitions of possible female comportment. Bhauju, like others, crafts a life, in response to contingencies, out of such materials.

I end with a final reminder. In Bhauju's life, as opposed to her story, these structural and cultural constraints are vivid realities with particular shape and, most importantly, particular effects. Bhauju also found general significance in her particular circumstances, but her perspective is different from that of an external observer or reader. As she put it, "We women must try to live."

Notes

A brief version of Bhauju's story was first presented at the meetings of the Association for Asian Studies in 1992. Thanks to Kathryn Hansen, Nancy Levine, Kathryn March, Carla Petievich, and Debra Skinner for comments on that paper. Later versions have profited from discussions with and comments by Ashok Gurung, Ernestine McHugh, Kirin Narayan, Pratyoush Onta, and Debra Skinner. My thanks for the combination of a warm reception and incisive criticism. Special thanks to Pratyoush Onta for many conversations that enabled me to finish this work. Bhauju's story is also incorporated into another essay, " 'We Women Must Try to Live': The Saga of Bhauju," *Studies in Nepali History and Society* 2(1):125–172. The research I was doing while the events recounted here transpired was funded by the Social Science Research Council and the American Council of Learned Societies. None of those mentioned here or in the body of the paper are responsible for the interpretations put forth.

1. We had not met during the first few weeks I had lived in her house, for she had been away. I anticipated the return of the woman whose children had already found their way into my heart; she, of course, had heard of the foreigner now in residence. *Bahinī* means younger sister, and Bhauju always referred to me this way, although I called her *bhāujū* (elder brother's wife) in keeping with my fictive placement within the household. To call me bahinī was to mark the warmth of our relationship and to place me apart from the rest of the household, all related affinally to her. Throughout this paper I use kin terms as names. This is in keeping with Gurung village practice, in which the use of kinship terms is a mark of social inclusion. The terms are, unless otherwise indicated, from my vantage point, placed as a "daughter" within the family described here. They are not, in many cases, precisely the terms I actually used, but are appropriate to the relationship described. The terms I use here are Nepali, which will be familiar to more readers than Gurung ones. Each kin term is defined on first use.

2. Bamboo baskets are used for all and sundry agricultural labor. A *hāsiyā*, a curved knife, like a sickle, is used for everything from peeling potatoes to harvesting grain. They are the ubiquitous companions of women farmers in the hills.

3. Gurungs or Tamus are one of the Tibeto-Burman peoples whose historical homeland is in the west central hills of Nepal. The northern Gurung hill economy combines agriculture and shepherding with significant male migratory labor, most famously as Gurkha soldiers in the British and Indian armies (see Des Chene 1991), but also as laborers in the Middle East, India, and many pursuits within Nepal. In recent years, Hong Kong, Japan, and Korea have also become common labor destinations. Since the 1960s there has been increasing migration to the Nepali Tarai (southern plains) and to urban areas within Nepal. Gurungs may be Buddhist, Hindu, or followers of their own shamanic traditions; many are syncretistic in religious orientation although the appropriate place of Hinduism within their culture is currently a topic of debate. Gurung villages, often situated on ridgetops,

are densely settled in contrast to the dispersed Brahman and Chetri communities that sometimes surround them, providing a visual hint of the intense sociality of daily life. The most comprehensive ethnography of Gurungs is Pignède (1966); see also Gurung (1977), Macfarlane (1976), McHugh (1985), Messerschmidt (1976), Mumford (1989), and Ragsdale (1989). For recent Gurung discussions of Gurung society, see the magazines *Rodhī* and *Tamu Sum̐ Tam̐*. See Des Chene (1996) for an introduction to current Gurung analyses of their own culture and society and their relation to the Nepali state.

4. There is a large literature along these lines in anthropology; here I obviously ignore the fine points of argumentation. See Kondo (1990) for a particularly nuanced account.

5. My point here concerns the relative explanatory weight of the theoretical paradigms and concepts that we bring to bear on our experiences and observations on the one hand, and those concepts and paradigms (more often called "worldviews") that we encounter elsewhere. Clifford (1988) and others have remarked on the manner in which social scientific theory serves as the master narrative within which others' conceptions are subsumed and to which they are made to refer. It can be seen as one of the political tasks of rethinking anthropology's aims to reverse that relationship. I believe it also to be an important epistemological enterprise if our aim is, in fact, to learn about other ways of being and knowing.

6. *Jeṭhī* is a birth-order term for eldest female. This particular jeṭhī is the eldest daughter in her family, but younger than her brother, Bhauju's husband.

7. *Nānī* is an affectionate term for eldest female. *Bābu*, while it can mean father, and be used as a term of respect for elder men, especially Brahmans, is also commonly used as a term of endearment to address young male children.

8. *Kānchī* is a birth-order term for youngest female.

9. As will be seen below, there can be a stronger link, not merely a matter of reputation, but of substance. The kind of talk one hears, the thoughts and deeds that surround one, may have material effect on one's own state, for better or worse. As McHugh says in defining the Gurung concepts *plah* (soul) and *sae* (the site of self-consciousness), "both concepts...articulate ideas about the interactive nature of the self. People are believed to be susceptible to the actions of others, which are thought to influence a person's character and so shape that person's future feelings and behavior" (1989:82).

10. This is not to discount the importance of talk, as will be evident later. The point here is that declarations of intentions, self-reported explanations of motivations, and so on, are so much background noise to the much louder and clearer declarations made in deeds. It is other kinds of talk that encircle actions and thus place them in particular interpretive contexts that is important. What one says about oneself has much less force than what others say about one.

11. Reactions within the household were more difficult to gauge. Kanchi followed her sister's lead in most things, though she was far more compliant. When possible she left all demanding physical labor to Bhauju, but when ordered by mother, father, or grandmother, she did such work. Jethi's two younger brothers looked to her as a catalyst; they hoped she would be able to set them up in the trekking business through the contacts she was developing. The money that Jethi was earning seemed to exempt her from other

household duties, and my presence doubtless lent further weight to her claim to contributing to the household in other ways since I paid her for food on a monthly basis. None of the three senior members of the household ever told her what to do. Only her father, whose prestige with other men was affected by her obvious independence, sometimes seemed upset by her behavior, yet he never challenged her directly.

12. *Bujai* is a Gurung term for grandmother. Bujai was Bhauju's husband's paternal grandmother. The Nepali word for mother is *āmā*. Aamaa is Bhauju's mother-in-law.

13. My own labor was, in theory, an optional addition, for I paid for food and board, was there for other reasons, and was not a family member. Yet it was also a carefully watched commodity, for where I chose to lend a hand made statements about my allegiances.

14. This includes, first of all, those living in the same hamlet and nearby, but also relatives further away, and those with social ties such that they would hear accounts of Bhauju's treatment. Thus the effect of the treatment of Bhauju on the household's reputation was quite widespread.

15. At these times Bhauju was permitted to join in cooperative work groups, but only so that she could be sent to contribute the labor required of the household.

16. *Kānchā* or *kāncho* is the birth-order term for youngest male. Kancha was about twenty. He had finished school but not passed the S.L.C. examination, a common predicament in Nepal. He did no regular work for the household and spent much of his time playing ball games with his friends. Only in the most intense part of the harvest period did he ever do agricultural labor, and then a limited amount.

17. These general consanguineal relations are invoked where a close actual kin tie does not exist. In several cases Bhauju was sufficiently closely related to men of the hamlet that other, more specific terms were used, but this is immaterial to the point being made. She was also related, through other marriages among their natal families, to a woman in an adjacent house, who thus felt special loyalty to her and did much to assist her, while still retaining civil relations with the rest of the household.

18. There could be many motivations for these urgings, and doubtless motives varied. I paid what was locally a significant sum of money for food and lodging, and others might have liked a share of that income. The intimate view of what they considered reprehensible conduct was not what most community members would wish for one who was there to learn about their way of life, and thus they might have hoped to counter what I saw there with a better example. But for some women, I think the primary concern was the deleterious effects on one's well-being of living in the midst of social disharmony. When I fell ill, it was always attributed to this environment.

19. In fact, posing Bhauju for pictures was one of the rare occasions on which she was allowed to hold the children.

20. This word is not readily translated. I follow McHugh whose work has helped me to understand this aspect of readings of Bhauju's condition. The sae is the site of cognition and memory, and the locus of the will. She likens assessments of the sae to American folk notions of personality, but notes that it differs "in the connections that are drawn between internal states and external events…the idea of the *sae* describes an interactive process between an individual's inner condition and the outer events of the world. Misfortune or

humiliation causes the sae to shrink, and a small sae, in turn, leads to bad judgment, incorrect behavior, and unfortunate events" (1989: 82). She goes on to say that the concept of sae "acts as an ideology that enforces the moral order of the Gurung world, offering an image in which social virtues are rewarded by personal well-being, and social failings are punished by a diminishing of self" (1989: 82). Assessments of Bhauju and Jethi show how complex such assessments can be, for Jethi, who remained in robust health, was spoken of in just these terms, whereas Bhauju was held blameless for the series of unfortunate events that befell her. Her sae was said to be growing small out of despair, not because of her own misdeeds. In keeping with McHugh's analysis, the primary concern was with the state of her *plah* (souls), which were thought to be in danger of fleeing the body, bringing death, due both to her weak physical condition and, crucially, to the cumulative effects of small acts of unkindness and enforced asociality.

21. I paraphrase here, as I was not at this moment thinking of tape recording. I heard this and similar laments sung by Bhauju over the following days, though overt criticism of her treatment became much less specific. But the refrain, "What is to become of me now?" sung in both Nepali and Gurung, persisted.

22. We heard this directly only later, but since he died in India it was assumed from the outset.

23. This lama was a man from the hamlet of Bhauju's own natal clan.

24. That the shirt must be inside-out was something about which I never inquired. It stayed that way until she was able to re-plait her hair at the end of the mourning period, and could thus be easily seen as a rather classic marker of liminality. But a question that Baba asked of me warns me not to read too much into others' practices. Baba wanted to know why it was that he, as Jetha's father, could eat no salt or ghee for twelve days. For him, it was just a matter of observing form according to the instruction of ritual specialists. Old clothing worn inside-out may or may not have had any more significance for those involved. Bangles are a relatively new mark of married status, borrowed from Hindu Nepalis, but they have clearly acquired centrality in women's thinking and experience.

25. I should stress that Bhauju always said that her greatest sorrow was that she was allowed little contact with her children. Jethi and Kanchi acted in all respects like their mother, even instructing them at times to call them āmā (mother). If Bhauju picked them up they were quickly taken away from her. After the death, Jethi began to explicitly teach Nani, the daughter, that her mother was "no good."

26. He had written to Jethi during this time, and he had sent money at least once with a man returning from India. One reader suggested that if he was not providing monetary support, this could be one explanation for Bhauju's harsh treatment. I do not know details of Jetha's financial contributions to the household before or after Bhauju returned to live there, but I never heard any complaints about lack of contributions, which leads me to think that he did send regular remittances.

27. I have concentrated here on women's views and talk because they are the central actors in these events insofar as Bhauju is concerned. But my research—which continued on despite all—was primarily with men who had served in British Gurkha regiments. Many of the men involved in these pension debates I thus knew well, and they let me

know their views on the state of my household.

28. *Saila* is a birth-order term for third-born male. Saila shepherded when he was at home, and so was often away from the house for long periods. He had, unwillingly, taken over this work when another brother, Maila (about whom more later), had followed Jetha to India five years before. At the time of Jetha's death, Saila had been away in Kathmandu trying, with some success, to get work in the trekking business, but he returned when the news of Jetha's death arrived.

29. Bhauju's mother was her father's second wife. The rodhī is an association of girls who form a cooperative work group and sleep together in one designated house at night. Boys come in the evening and sing songs and court. Rodhī are less common now, but at the time of Bhauju's birth, they were ubiquitous. Her parentage was public knowledge and in no way a revelation. What was remarkable was the message of her speech, disavowing her own mother whom she often fondly described to me as her greatest supporter.

30. Ernestine McHugh (personal communication) points out that this is an idiosyncratic view of the danger of overheard talk. She points out that while it is common to consider one's own anger or grief as damaging to the sae, as well as anger or blame directed at oneself by others on whom one is dependent or about whom one cares, it is not generally believed that simply witnessing expressions of ill will can cause physical or emotional deterioration. She also rightly points out that such a belief would logically result in avoiding such situations, and I concur that nothing draws a crowd faster than a noisy public argument or fight though, thinking back, it also strikes me that some individuals regularly stay away from such altercations. After mulling over these observations, rereading letters and scattered notes, and thinking about this woman, who was my closest female friend in the village, I am inclined to think that she has developed her own variation on more commonly held beliefs. Indeed, she was one person who always stayed away from unpleasant exchanges of any kind, and did not even want to hear accounts of them afterward. Despite, or perhaps because of these inclinations, she was frequently called upon as a mediator in others' arguments. And it may be that because of this role, she was especially sensitive about the deleterious effects of hearing too much negative talk.

31. *Maīlā* is the birth-order term for second-eldest male. As the son of a different mother he was not, in fact, called maīlā, but I use the term here for the sake of simplicity.

32. More than one reader has remarked on the sexual connotations of feeding choice foods to a woman. It is true that Bhauju and Maila stood in a marriageable relation to one another, and remarriage to the brother of a deceased husband, while not common, is not unknown or taboo among Gurungs. Maila had lived for some years with Bhauju and Jetha in India. My own sense is that he was deeply fond of her for the kindness she had shown him there, and that they shared two added bonds. In relation to this household, both were marginal members and had not been well treated. Both were also the offspring of junior wives and had mixed-jāt parentage which in some situations placed them in an equivocal position. Jethi started rumors about a sexual relationship between Bhauju and Maila, but these died quickly as no one took them up. Whatever the case, then, locally their relationship seemed to be understood as a friendship, two people who "mixed," a common way of

talking about people whose outlooks and sensibilities draw them to one another. I have found the responses of readers to be most informative of the strength of stereotypes about South Asian women, in this case the limited possible range of relationships they may have with men.

33. Saila, after an unsuccessful attempt to get work in the Middle East through an Indian labor broker, had returned to Kathmandu to look for trekking work.

34. I know only the bare fact that Jethi later married and moved to town, but I do not know in what order these events took place. It may be, or it may not, that in the end her route out of the village was the more traditional one of marriage. Nor do I know anything about her own situation as a daughter-in-law.

35. Enslin (1994) and, within her text, Pramila Parajuli, raise questions about the adequacy of any merely textual representation of women's struggles that are not adequately addressed by this position.

36. I place "Nepali" in quotation marks here, because just what counts as Nepali is currently contested in many arenas. Much debate has centered around narratives of the nation, and whether a single encompassing cultural identity is essential to the viability of the Nepali state, or whether pluralism and difference can be genuinely accommodated within a single state structure (e.g., Fisher 1993; Shah 1993; Sharma 1992; Tamang 1992). While these debates are important and illuminating, in the end the choices discussed in them will be made by Bhauju, and by millions of other bhaujus living quite different lives throughout Nepal. Knowing more about the local worlds they inhabit and trying to take account of these in debates about what constitutes "Nepali-ness" seems to me vitally important.

37. Clearly the consequences for different women will vary. Structural arrangements make a great difference here, and the fact that Gurung women may remarry can make an important difference. Personal relationships with affines also matter a great deal. But as lived experience, no one should doubt that women think of this combination as tragic. The number of songs and stories that lament the fate of widowed daughters-in-law in South Asian women's repertoires makes this clear enough.

38. See McHugh (1989) and this volume on the centrality of social relatedness in Gurung society.

39. Margaret Trawick's *Notes on Love in a Tamil Family* (1992) provides both inspiration and exemplar. A narrative of the emotional tenor of daily life, Trawick's work renders visible the creation of "self...in the confrontation between selves" (1992:xix).

40. The question is sometimes posed whether Gurungs are Hindus or Buddhists. As an effort to categorize, this does not strike me as a useful dichotomy. One finds significant regional and individual variation. More importantly, while religious affiliation is now becoming a political issue, at the time of the events recounted here, most Gurungs I knew seemed little vexed by syncretism, calling on Brahmans, lamas, and their own shamanic practitioners for different purposes, and many continue to do so today. What strikes me as most important in this context is that Gurungs do live within a Hindu state in which Hindu female comportment may be considered prestigious, and Gurung women are not unaffected by this. While I did not elaborate on it, knowledgeable readers will have noticed Hindu,

Buddhist, and specifically Gurung practices and ideas in the preceding account.

41. There is, of course, also a considerable literature on Muslim women. Here the focus has often been on purdah, and so on situations in which women's movements and interactions are highly circumscribed. See, for example, Jeffery (1979) and Papanek and Minault (1983).

42. Middle-aged and elderly women often still wear this garb, but younger women tend to wear a *lungi* (long skirt) and T-shirt or store-bought blouse and a Hindu *pote* instead of coral and turquoise. Many Gurung women, of course, now live in towns and in the plains. Whether residing there or visiting, they usually wear saris in public.

43. Using the term "Gurkha," Leonard could have in mind Gurung, Magar, Rai, or Limbu women. But these army handbooks take Gurungs as the cynosure of the Gurkha type; they are thus usually the model for generalized statements of this kind. On this and other aspects of representations of Gurkhas, see Des Chene (1991).

44. Gurung women do not plough and do not weave with bamboo. There are other activities, most importantly shepherding, that are usually men's work, but these are the only forbidden activities, due to their association with fertility and male sexuality.

References

Appadurai, Arjun, Frank F. Korom, and Margaret A. Mills, eds. 1991. Gender, Genre, and Power in South Asian Expressive Traditions. Philadelphia: University of Pennsylvania Press.

Brenneis, Donald. 1984. Straight Talk and Sweet Talk: Political Discourse in an Occasionally Egalitarian Community. *In* Dangerous Words. F. Myers and D. Brenneis, eds. Pp. 69–85. Prospect Heights, IL: Waveland Press.

Clifford, James. 1988. The Predicament of Culture. Cambridge, MA: Harvard University Press.

Des Chene, Mary. 1991. Relics of Empire: A Cultural History of the Gurkhas, 1815–1987. Ph.D. dissertation, Department of Anthropology, Stanford University.

———. 1996. Ethnography in the Janajāti-yug: Lessons from Reading Rodhī and other Tamu Writings. Studies in Nepali History and Society 1(1):97–161.

Enslin, Elizabeth. 1992. Collective Powers in Common Places: The Politics of Gender and Space in a Women's Struggle for a Meeting Center in Chitwan, Nepal. Himalayan Research Bulletin 12(1–2):11–25.

———. 1994. Beyond Writing: Feminist Practice and the Limitations of Ethnography. Cultural Anthropology 9(4):537–568.

Fisher, William F. 1992. Nationalism and the Janajati. Himal 6:11–14.

Giddens, Anthony. 1979. Central Problems in Social Theory: Action, Structure and Contradiction in Social Analysis. Berkeley: University of California Press.

Gurung, Jagman. 1977. Gurung Jāti Tathā Saṁskriti. Yanjakot, Nepal: Author.

Holland, Dorothy, and Debra Skinner. 1995. Contested Ritual, Contested Femininities: (Re)forming Self and Society in a Nepali Women's Festival. American Ethnologist 22(2):279–305.

Jeffery, Patricia. 1979. Frogs in a Well: Indian Women in Purdah. London: Zed Press.

Kondo, Dorinne K. 1990. Crafting Selves: Power, Gender, and Discourses of Identity in a Japanese Workplace. Chicago: University of Chicago Press.

Leonard. R. G. 1965. Nepal and the Gurkhas. London: HMSO.

Macfarlane, Alan. 1976. Resources and Population: A Study of the Gurungs of Nepal. Cambridge: Cambridge University Press.

McHugh, Ernestine L. 1985. The Social, Cultural and Personal Worlds of the Gurungs of Nepal. Ph.D. dissertation, Department of Anthropology, University of California-San Diego.

————. 1989. Concepts of the Person among the Gurungs of Nepal. American Ethnologist 16(1):75–86.

Messerschmidt, Donald. 1976. The Gurungs of Nepal: Conflict and Change in a Village Society. Warminster, England: Aris and Phillips.

Mumford, Stan. 1989. Himalayan Dialogue: Tibetan Lamas and Gurung Shamans in Nepal. Madison: University of Wisconsin Press.

Narayan, Kirin. 1986. Birds on a Branch: Girlfriends and Wedding Songs in Kangra. Ethos 14:47–75.

Ortner, Sherry. 1995. Resistance and the Problem of Ethnographic Refusal. Comparative Studies in Society and History 37(1):173–193.

Papanek, Hannah, and Gail Minault, eds. 1983. Separate Worlds: Studies in Purdah in South Asia. Delhi: Chanakya Publications.

Pignède, Bernard. 1966. Les Gurungs, une population himalayenne du Népal. Paris: Mouton.

Ragsdale, Tod. 1989. Once a Hermit Kingdom: Ethnicity, Education and National Integration in Nepal. New Delhi: Manohar.

Raheja, Gloria, and Ann Grodzins Gold. 1994. Listen to the Heron's Words. Berkeley: University of California Press.

Rosaldo, Michelle Z. 1974. Woman, Culture, and Society, A Theoretical Overview. *In* Woman, Culture, and Society. M. Rosaldo and L. Lamphere, eds. Pp. 17–42. Stanford: Stanford University Press.

Rosaldo, Renato. 1993 [1989]. Culture and Truth: The Remaking of Social Analysis. Boston: Beacon.

Shah, Saubhagya. 1992. Throes of a Fledgling Nation. Himal 6:7–10.

Sharma, Prayag Raj. 1992. How to Tend This Garden? Himal 5:7–9.

Skinner, Debra, Dorothy Holland, and G. B. Adhikari. 1994. The Songs of Tij: A Genre of Critical Commentary for Women in Nepal. Asian Folklore Studies 53(2):259–305.

Tamang, Parshuram. 1992. Tamangs under the Shadow. Himal 5:25–27.

Trawick, Margaret. 1990. Notes on Love in a Tamil Family. Berkeley: University of California Press.

Wadley, Susan. 1980. The Paradoxical Powers of Tamil Women. *In* The Powers of Tamil Women. S. Wadley, ed. Pp. 61–92. Syracuse: Syracuse University Press.

Chapter 3 ⎯⎯⎯⎯⎯⎯⎯⎯⎯⎯⎯⎯

Narrative Subversions of Hierarchy

Steven M. Parish

Narrative consciousness can link self, state, and history in ways that are contradictory but powerfully felt, animating conflicting visions of self and society. Narratives that celebrate the structure of life sustained by society and state may be countered by narratives that dissent, in which actors as selves captured in the structures of society and history tell themselves stories that subvert social hierarchies. Narratives may compose a sense of moral conviction for the self-in-society, portraying the relations of self and society as natural, necessary, moral, and sacred, or melt this away, and propose other visions of self and social life. These later narratives—subversive, dissident, utopian in varying degrees—may disclose something of the way persons-in-history, as selves-in-society, respond to their cultural construction by the dominant order of state and society.

Even in a place where hierarchy has been asserted as the ultimate foundation of social life, where it has been propagated as the key value of the political and cultural order, where it has been legitimated as necessary, natural, moral, and sacred—as in Nepal's Kathmandu Valley until very recently—dissident narratives exist and have social and psychological significance. Alternative cultural possibilities may be continually generated and kept alive in such dissident and utopian narratives, sustained in critical counterpoint to the actuality of caste practices. Telling stories constitutes one way that people relate self to caste hierarchy, respond to their experience of caste hierarchy, and reflect on its ideology and practices. Narratives offer a means of thinking and feeling about the world—as actuality—and for going beyond the actuality of the social world, for reimagining it. Narratives can bring together elements of the actual world of caste life with elements from an imagined world, constituting a compound narrative world that stands at once as critique of the actual world and as a construction of the moral grounds of a possible and better world. Narrative work can generate a dialogue between "what is" and "what should be" that alters a sense of self and identity.

The visions of society, morality, and self constructed in the particular narratives I will discuss reject many of the concepts and values that justify and legitimate the caste hierarchy. They can be seen, therefore, as narrative subversions of the premises of caste hierarchy.

The narrative work of low-caste actors may help them constitute, focus, and sustain a critical consciousness in counterpoint to the consciousness of self and society implied in the ideology and practice of caste life. Telling stories is one of the ways caste can respond to caste ideology and develop a "counter-ideology" (Lynch 1969). In their own narratives, they can subvert some of the stigmatizing constructions of themselves manifest in the ideology, narratives, and practices of others. In narratives, they can create and explore alternative visions of self and society, shelter their hopes and resentments from a world that stigmatizes, subordinates, and threatens them.

Before I turn to the narratives through which some Newars attempt to reimagine the social order of caste society, I will sketch in the background against which these narratives have meaning, to suggest how massive, and yet intimate and person-defining, the caste hierarchy is.

The Caste Hierarchy in Newar Society

Nurtured by Hindu kings over the centuries, caste civilization flourished in the Kathmandu Valley of Nepal. In many ways, traditional Newar society came to embody the *ideal* that people are unequal; the state rendered this an actuality in law, enforced it in practice. After the defeat and conquest of the Malla kings of the Newar city-states, the early Shaha dynasty and the later Rana regime continued to give legal support to caste hierarchy.[1] While the social and political context has changed significantly and continues to change, the caste *system* as a symbolic and moral order survived in the town of Bhaktapur at the time of my study in the mid-1980s.[2]

What is termed a "caste" in English, Newars call a *jāt*. However, although the word jāt denotes those hierarchically organized divisions of society designated by the word "caste" in English, it refers as well to Newar occupational and ethnic groups and to gender—or to any other distinct category. It is used broadly to mean "kind."

No one, not I, and not any of the Newars I know, would deny that the opposition of pure and impure is one basis for the caste system (Dumont 1980), one of the key models of and for social relations, although it is only one among many. States of purity and impurity separate Newar castes, and purity is one idiom of rank: higher castes are relatively more "pure" than lower castes. Among Newars, this is expressed concretely in a number of ways. As in much of South Asia, food is one medium. High-caste Newars will not accept boiled rice or certain other foods from individuals of any caste lower than their own; they will accept nothing, not even water, from members of some still lower castes. There are restrictions on sharing cigarettes or a hookah, the water pipe smoked by some Newars.

Some castes are viewed by others as dangerously impure or untouchable. Persons of such castes cannot enter the upper stories of houses of high-caste Newars (the bottom story being conceived either as outside the house or impure in its own right). They have occupations and symbolic roles that are stigmatizing: for example, to serve as sweepers, play stigmatizing roles in death rites, and so on. My informants still conformed to these practices.

In the past, exclusion was practiced and symbolized in a variety of ways. The higher castes lived in the center of the city, while lower castes lived on the peripheries. Some of the more stigmatized castes lived in separate neighborhoods; the untouchable Sweepers, the Pore, lived outside the traditional boundaries of the city, in an area near the river, across from one of the city's cremation grounds. This location resonates with their symbolic association with filth, decay, and death. Certain occupations were reserved for certain castes; occupational mobility was limited. Education was limited to members of high castes. Members of the lower castes were required to wear distinctive dress. Among other legal disabilities, the untouchable Sweepers could construct only one-story houses with thatch roofs. These untouchables could not use the same water taps as pure castes, at least not when higher-caste people were present. Untouchables could not enter the city after sundown. In the past, many recalled, any wealth untouchables might accumulate would be seized by the kings.

The modern Nepalese state no longer enforces this system of exclusions, but the basic pattern persisted at the time of my field research. In Bhaktapur, untouchable sweepers still lived outside the city. Untouchables might use water taps once reserved exclusively for use by the higher castes, but be met with verbal abuse. Members of higher castes still sometimes objected to untouchables entering tea shops in their neighborhoods. (Traditionally they could be served outside, and would wash their own utensils.) Exclusion may no longer receive the active support of the state, but groups, households, and individuals remained under pressure to conform to traditional practices or else leave Bhaktapur altogether.

Many low-caste people still perform their traditional stigmatizing occupations. They may be refused employment outside of such occupations if they are recognized as belonging to a stigmatized jāt, as they would be in Bhaktapur. Even moving or commuting to Kathmandu, some thirteen kilometers away, they may be barred from such lowly work as office "peon," a position in which a person performs miscellaneous chores and menial tasks, because, informants report, untouchables filling this post would have to serve tea to high-caste office workers.

But change is reflected in educational aspirations for children, in the improved economic circumstances of a few groups, in increased tolerance by some members of other castes, and in the absence of explicit legal sanctions supporting the traditional caste order. Stories are told about individuals who have been successful in the modern sector, and of rare cases of low-caste solidarity that have produced concrete gains.

Much of the social, economic, and religious life of the city rests on the caste system; it constitutes a division of labor, not only for much economic activity, but for citywide ritual activities (Levy 1990). Brahmans and other religious specialists have essential roles in key temples and officiate at some of the domestic rites of families. Several castes have symbolic roles that are stigmatizing, but essential to the traditional social and symbolic life of the city.

The impurity of untouchable sweepers is necessary to the purity of the city; the impurities, misfortunes, and suffering of the city are conceived to flow into the untouchables, especially the Sweepers, who live in a separate area outside the old boundaries of the city. Their impurity defines the purity of the city. Untouchables are seen as dirty, disgusting, impure, as highly sexual and promiscuous, as ignorant and lacking the discipline and mastery of language that would make them truly human. In sum, for high-caste actors, they embody an "otherness" that is devalued and disturbing. This may provoke efforts to achieve and maintain a psychological distance from them, to reassure oneself that one is not ultimately like them. Thus, high-caste actors view low-caste actors, individually and collectively, as deserving their fate. The low castes are polluted, that is, naturally defiled, a notion based on a cultural theory of the flow of person-defining substances.[3] Moreover, they are viewed as realizing the fruits of the sins of previous lifetimes—their fate is justified by karma and ordained by dharma.

How do low-caste actors respond? Low-caste Newars may resent the way they are defined in practice. Let me offer an example of how one person in such a world voices his felt reality in contrast and opposition to the social reality of caste practices. In his monumental study of Newar society and religion, Levy (1990) quotes a Newar untouchable's comments on the practice of accepting polluted leftover food from members of higher castes. Taking such leftover food on ritual occasions embodies in practice the opposition of the pure and the impure, partitioning the social world into categories and ranking them. Those who are ranked lower in the caste system acknowledge their inferior rank every time they accept leftover food from those ranked higher. Such practices undoubtedly have an important role in constituting and substantiating the caste hierarchy (Höfer 1979). Newars refer to the polluted food given to persons of lower status as *cipa*. The untouchable—a Po(n), or Sweeper, a jāt also called Pore—quoted by Levy declares that the cipa he takes from high-caste patrons is "dirtier than feces," and offers an explanation of why he takes it:

> When we hear that the *sāhu* [merchants] have a feast, we Po(n), we poor people
> who have nothing to eat, go to the houses of our own patrons, and take their

cipa, the food that has come out of their mouths, their leftover food....Their thrown away things are our meal, in which we get dust and hair, and everything....We eat dirty food. (Levy 1990:385)

This untouchable makes sense of cultural practices that embody concepts of purity and pollution by appealing to images of necessity that justify the self-violation that he presents as integral to participating in such practices. His words (which echo what many others told me) call us back from the "purely structural universe" of the opposition of purity and impurity (Dumont 1980:43). They return us to a felt world, bring us back into the world of self-experience, where people struggle to live and know themselves. In this world, deprivation and necessity define the basic conditions of existence for many. Clearly, the idea that the caste hierarchy is a nurturing hierarchy, expressed in the notion that accepting the polluted food of high-caste actors means lower-status persons incorporate into themselves substance that will sustain them "like mother's milk" (Levy 1990:385), is not seamlessly shared and universally endorsed by all actors. Rather, actors speak in terms of deprivation and necessity, *recoding* their participation in the cultural practice. People who experience or fear deprivation may want to eat whatever they can get—even if it is "mixed with dirt and hair," "dirtier than feces," even if accepting "the food that comes out of" other mouths stigmatizes and declares one's inferiority.

As the testimony of the untouchable quoted in Levy suggests, individuals and groups ranked lower than others (certainly farmers and below, and perhaps anyone who feels subordinate to anyone else) may resent the way they are stigmatized and excluded in the caste system. In the past, however, and at the time of my study, there was often not much they could do about their discontents, since the state and/or other segments of the population (including those just above them who feared losing relative status) weighed in on the side of keeping them in their place. Despite the formal removal of legal sanctions, overcoming the initial set of life chances determined by their caste standing remains exceedingly difficult, and for most low-caste actors of modest means perhaps virtually impossible. Since the invidious distinctions of caste are linked to issues of subsistence and survival, the historical reality is that low-caste actors could not readily act on whatever analysis or critique of caste society some of them may have developed.

Nor could they easily avoid encountering the meanings and practices that stigmatize them in the eyes of others. I have suggested how for many high-caste Hindus, the lowest castes generally and untouchables in particular embody "the other." No doubt some low-caste actors fall into the trap of embodying "the other" in their own eyes (Sartre 1963). They may take themselves as what the dominant ideology says they are. Doing so, they must doubt or devalue themselves; or more subtly, they may not identify with stigmatizing visions of themselves, but rather identify with those who see them in such terms. They may identify with high-caste practices that are in part constructed in contrast and complementation to the untouchable, and seek to emulate or internalize these. Doing so, I suspect they help reproduce the basic sense of reality that attaches to hierarchy, implicitly recognizing it as self-defining and as an ultimate standard of self-judgment. Untouchables may only slowly reconstruct themselves in terms of a dissenting personal vision or counter-ideology (Lynch 1969)—a process in which narrative work that established a narrative consciousness opposed to ideology may be important.[4]

If so, many untouchables at once identify with yet repudiate cultural meanings they embody for others and even for themselves. They do this as the objects and agents of processes of cultural construction: as cultural subjects who are objects of cultural constructions, they project themselves and are appropriated into ideology, meanings, and practices that construct hierarchy in multiple modes; as cultural agents who interpret themselves and the cultural world they inhabit, they formulate themselves in critiques and counter-ideology that responds in multiple registers and voices to such constructions. The low-caste person finds identity in both these processes, multiplying his or her consciousness of self and society. Moreover, whatever critique of caste ideology low-caste actors make, that critique develops within a (multiple) cultural self-consciousness that (a multivalent) ideology helps constitute. The critique will be a critique from the inside, from within self and about self, and from within a culture in intimate ways. Narratives offer one way of constructing such critiques. They constitute a reflexive tool for revaluing culture and self.

Narrative Subversions of Hierarchy

Like other South Asians, Newars use stories to construct moral arguments (Narayan 1989; Shweder and Much 1987). In general, narratives have special characteristics that lend themselves to making critical judgments. First of all, narratives provide a way of overcoming the transparency of culture, the way culture is "not there" to common sense because it presents itself to experience as natural, as reality, simply the way things are. Narratives can make the premises of cultural practice "visible," presenting them as mental objects that can be thought about, evaluated, and reinterpreted—a story is detached from reality, although it may be about it. A story is a manipulable representation of culture, unlike "common sense," or the unarticulated and largely unconscious sense of reality enculturated subjects develop in every culture. Moreover, a story is told by a person, who can manipulate the materials the narrative works with. The act of narration requires an agent, who is, at least potentially, a reflective agent. Narrative work may inspire or allow the development of critiques and reimaginings in a way that other less reflective modes of "having" culture do not. While stories also lend themselves to affirming a cultural status quo, the narratives I am concerned with here achieve a certain critical distance from cultural life and are used to formulate a critique of hierarchical values and practices.

Many narratives, of course, are not critical; they affirm the legitimacy of the status quo and they may help produce the hegemony of certain cultural concepts of reality, such as those which define low-caste groups as inferior. In the context of caste life, such narratives may disseminate hierarchy-affirming cultural concepts that settle into common sense, and so tend to escape critical scrutiny, forming layers of unconscious meaning that have political significance. In Brahmanical texts and discourse, narratives may sustain a vision of caste life as objective and unalterable, necessary and moral; this can be done, for example, by portraying hierarchy as an expression of sacred and natural law, perhaps showing the consequences of violating this natural order. Other narratives, however, call into question the morality of the caste hierarchy, and attempt to break down the objectification of hierarchy, and resist the sedimentization of hierarchical meanings in embodied knowledge, common sense, and habitus. They attempt to show that the caste hierarchy, constituted in terms of karma, purity, wealth, or birth, is not natural, not necessary, not the only way things could be, and not the way things should be.

Knowing, hearing, and telling *anti-hierarchical* stories is a way for some low-caste Newars to critique hierarchical ideas and values that construct their own place and identities within the caste system. I believe that such stories constitute efforts to "neutralize" the stigmatizing construction of their caste identity perpetuated by the dominant ideology. Telling such stories may help them "recode" their experience, allowing them to find value in themselves and their lives. In such stories, they can mock the pretenses of the high castes, and undermine the moral premises of the dominant ideology. They can point out the incoherence, the capriciousness, of the caste system. These narratives also keep alive the idea that social life might be organized according to other moral principles. They may reject concepts of purity and pollution, or any of the other concepts used to organize and justify the caste system.

Opposing the caste hierarchy does not entail rejecting any possible form of social hierarchy. When Newars use stories to cast doubt on the morality and justice of the caste hierarchy based on purity, pollution, karma, and other constructs, they may propose alternative hierarchies, with different moral foundations, as well as invoke the concept of equality (Parish 1996). For example, they imagine alternative hierarchies that are "open" rather than "closed," so that movement up the hierarchy is possible. In these alternative, "open" hierarchies, the moral worth and achievements of individuals rather than caste status count for something. These alternative hierarchies are not the hierarchy of caste as understood in terms of purity, pollution, or karma.

Like many stories used to make a moral point, the particular stories I am concerned with unfold in a highly simplified version of the world, only loosely anchored in time and place, where persons are reduced to the schematic simplicity of social positions. The encounter of two or three such persons reveals the arbitrary nature of the caste hierarchy. The stories may go on to propose a different set of premises for society. Each of my low-caste informants, and even many high-caste informants, had one or more anti-hierarchical stories to tell me.

The stories are told in the third person. Little, if any, effort is made to make the physical setting or place of the story tangible and concrete. At most, the story may be located "in a forest" or "in a palace." Time and history are also simplified; the stories often do not take place at a definite moment. The events narrated do

not occur "in the nineteenth century," or "when I was young."[5] They are not embedded in social, biographical, or historical time. If framed in terms of temporal
setting at all, most often the events described simply happened "long ago."

The simplified world of the story is inhabited by kings, Brahmans, beggars,
untouchables, and so on; or, in other words, by persons incarnated in roles. No
effort to convey the complex qualities of individuals in their wholeness is made.
The aspect of individual identity that is dealt with is social or political, not psychological—we get to see the social dimensions of individual identities, not the
world of feelings of a self responding with emotion to caste life. However, in the
interviews in which these narratives were recounted, glimpses of the narrators'
feeling were available in their facial expressions. I detected, or thought I could
detect, anger, distress, hesitation. Asked directly about concepts like karma, or
the impurity attributed to them, low-caste Newars often responded with anger or
discomfort. Their reactions in interviews provide some grounds for saying that
they dislike, and find painful, the way they are defined by others. The narratives I
discuss here can thus be seen as motivated; they do not expressly deal with feelings, with emotions, but perhaps they are "good to tell" because they resonate
with the psychological tensions, the emotional costs, the ambivalences, the identity dilemmas, inherent in caste life.

In the more impersonal stories examined here, the actors in the story may
have names, but are often referred to by the narrator, or addressed by other characters in the story, by caste titles. The cast of characters presupposes, or represents, hierarchy. For the purpose of the story, they constitute a hierarchy "on the
ground," within the world of the story. Dumont's paradigm (1980) of hierarchy
works at this level of the story's structure: it takes two, a dyad consisting of a
higher and lower actor, to constitute a hierarchy. The stories generally reduce the
complexities of a caste hierarchy to the interactions of two or three actors: a low-
caste or mendicant figure, a Brahman and/or a king. These figures constitute a
hierarchy, but the plot shows that the hierarchy in which they are constituted as
"persons" is morally defective, or arbitrary.

The typical story seeks to reveal a radical gap between a person's social role
(place in the caste hierarchy) and a person's moral worth as judged in terms of
alternative moral concepts. The narratives distinguish between what the caste hierarchy makes a person, what they are "through and for" the caste system as
Bourdieu (1977) might put it, and what this person is as an individual, "in and of"
himself or herself, or "through and for" an engagement with higher forms of
morality and reality than caste hierarchy represents. This severs the link forged in
the dominant ideology between place in society and the moral nature of the person. As the story progresses, the person constituted within the caste hierarchy (as
proposed by the dominant ideology) and the person seen in the light of the moral
(as proposed in the narrative) become radically incommensurate. I would argue
that such narrative acts are implicitly self-affirming. Such narratives represent
one way of driving a wedge of *difference* between self-identity and social identity. Opening up this distinction may allow actors to generate moral meaning for,

and derive it from, the contrast between a complex and fluctuating personal sense of who they are, and a painful sense of how they are constructed and stigmatized in the caste system.[6] This struggle was evident in the person-centered interviews in which the stories occurred. To establish this difference—to declare to yourself and your interlocutor that you are not what the social system makes you—makes a difference psychologically. I present here stories and discussion by a Brahman, by Kancha, an untouchable Sweeper, and by Krishna Bahadur, from the border-line "impure" Gatha caste.

First Story: The King and the Beggar

Since Brahmans have often been "essentialized," reified as embodiments of hierarchy, treated more as hierarchical tropes than as persons, not only by anthropologists but by untouchables and Brahmans themselves, it may seem paradoxical for a Brahman to tell an anti-hierarchical story—but we should credit Brahmans with a capacity for reflexivity. In any event, this story does not question the preeminence of Brahmans. Rather, it puts a king in his place, challenging the hierarchy of power that focuses on the figure of the king. And yet, in principle, the story makes a point that could be applied to any high-caste person. Without ever mentioning Brahmans, the story places value on the kind of religious knowledge Brahmans may claim; the hierarchy of knowledge (centered on ascetics and Brahmans) is valued over the hierarchy of power (centered on the king).

The story was told in response to the question, "How do you know the dharma?" In South Asia, dharma is a key moral and religious concept. While what dharma means in a concrete, experience-near sense varies in ways that reflect life-experiences and caste standing (Parish 1994), among my Hindu Newar informants the concept was typically invoked to frame discourse in moral terms, to assert that some action is obligatory. It would not be wrong, but would miss many of the subtleties and nuances of the term, to gloss dharma as social and religious duty, prescribed custom, or moral law. Generally, the concept of dharma proposes that an objective and nonarbitrary basis exists for morality and social roles; dharma exists as a standard against which human behavior can be judged. Human beings have dharma that is specific to their social roles; yet dharma may be used to indicate universal obligations or precepts that transcend or encompass the dharma of social roles. In a sense, dharma is the moral order that is the ultimate foundation of the cosmos and human society. People, however, may not know the dharma. They may have to discover it for themselves, or with help from those who do know the dharma.

> Once there was a king. One day he went out to learn the dharma of kings. But a king does not walk as we do. In the past there were no cars, and people were carried [in palanquins]. For this, a minimum of four persons were needed. Four men set out carrying the king, but one man was weak. This man fell on the road, so another was needed. They saw a man over there—a beggar. The king called the beggar over, and said to him, "I must go to the rishi's ashram. You will carry me."

The beggar did not know how to carry a palanquin. Even so the king scolded him, saying "You must carry me, but I'll give you wages." The beggar agreed. Now they again had four men to carry the king, but the beggar did not know how to carry the palanquin. He carried it jerkily, shaking it. The king fell off, and got a cut. The king rebuked the beggar, crying out, "What are you doing? I'm cut and bleeding. Carry me properly."

But it happened again. The king hit the beggar with his scepter. He yelled, "What are you doing?" He beat the beggar. Then the beggar addressed the king, "Maharaja, where are you going?" The king replied, "I am going to learn the dharma." At this, the beggar told him, "Your mouth says that you are going to learn the dharma, but with your acts you inflict suffering (*dukha*) on me. After I have carried you, you beat me. Is this the form dharma takes?"

Given this reply, the king experienced a shock of realization. "I have come to learn the dharma, and what this beggar says to me is a true thing. He thinks truth. I made him carry me. I have sinned." The king achieved understanding (*bibek*). When he did so, he greeted the beggar with respect, saying "Oh ho, although you are a beggar, what you said has brought knowledge (*gyān*) to me. One should not cause others to suffer," so the king said to the beggar.

The king asked the beggar, "Why did you jump around like that while carrying the palanquin?" The beggar replied, "On the ground here are insects, many small bugs. Should we walk straight, we will step on them. If we step on them, they will die. To avoid the insects, I had to walk in that way. Since I stepped like that, the palanquin shook. One ought not kill insects, so I did that." When he heard this, the king got down, and bowed to the feet of the beggar. This is one story. The king learned that you should not give dukha to others.

The story neutralizes the arbitrary power of the king. The king has coercive power, but not knowledge of dharma. He lacks proper understanding, I take it, of his role-specific dharma (his dharma as king) and its proper relationship to the universal dharma (which defines the arbitrary infliction of suffering on another as morally wrong). As superior, he addresses the beggar with familiar pronouns and verb forms, harangues him and commands him to carry the palanquin. I visualize this as done with that blend of commanding and cajoling that high-caste Newars often actually use with low-caste persons who are unwilling to do something. The beggar responds with high-respect terms of address, pronouns, and verb forms, and obeys. The hierarchical dimensions of the relationship, of superiority and inferiority, are sharply marked.

The king is journeying to learn the dharma proper to kings, the *rājdharma*; but he fails to act in accord with a "higher" dharma. This dharma—which we might see as more universal, role-transcendent dharma which "includes" or "trumps" the king's role-specific dharma—mandates justice and nonviolence. The king uses power, but does not give justice. He coerces and later beats the beggar, whose motive is obedience to the broader imperatives of dharma which require reverence for all life. He seeks to avoid taking even the life of insects, at the risk of causing some discomfort and pain to the king. The story urges us to believe that reverence for life is a more worthy motive than the kingly virtues of force and command.

The king punished the beggar by beating him. Force is a prerogative of kings. But the beggar responds by pointing out a contradiction between the king's goal of learning dharma and his actions. As a result, the king experiences a sort of "shock of recognition." He realizes the "truth" of the beggar's words and develops bibek, a term often used in the sense of a kind of moral understanding or judgment, or as the agency in the mind that originates moral insight. The king gains knowledge (gyān) and expresses his gratitude to the beggar. This insight the king achieves has social consequences. This develops further as the king inquires into the reasons the beggar had for shaking the palanquin. Hearing that the beggar did so in order to avoid killing, the king bows to the feet of the beggar. Their relationship is reversed: the king acknowledges the beggar to be his moral superior. The king is put in his place—subordinate to those who embody the dharma, even if they are beggars. Indeed, the beggar figure here is aligned with the figure of the world-renouncer, or ascetic.

This story is anti-hierarchical in the sense that it places limits on one model of hierarchy—the hierarchy of power, of force, of command that is embodied in the figure of the king. The story subordinates power to dharma. Ideally, dharma should direct the action of the king; it should rule the king. In this sense, dharma is the "king of kings"(Khare 1984).

Dharma itself is portrayed as nonviolence; perhaps this identification devalues the royal attribute of force, making the king's specific dharma a lesser dharma. Playing a beggar-renouncer against privileged king may implicitly unite those who possess religious insight or knowledge—renouncer and Brahman—against the power of kings. Getting the Brahman into the picture, by way of reasserting his superiority, takes some "overinterpretation," but seems like a fairly plausible implication of the story.

The story constructs a nonroyal model of hierarchy. It asserts the superiority of those with an active knowledge of dharma—the king bows to the feet of the beggar in homage to his moral superiority. The story supports a hierarchy based on knowledge of dharma. Since the beggar is aligned with the renouncer, and Brahmans may align themselves with the renouncer figure, the story advances a theme that could be used to legitimate the superiority of Brahmans. Note that purity is not an issue here.

The story constructs reality in a way that qualifies the power of kings. The "reality" the story constructs involves the following premises: first, dharma is worth seeking; the story establishes a hierarchy of value, and places the figure of king and beggar within this value system. Second, dharma may not be recognized or properly understood without seeking; it is not an attribute of birth-status, at least not for kings. The intervention of others, as teachers and exemplars, may be crucial for learning the dharma. Third, dharma is a moral imperative which sustains life. Fourth, it also transcends social distinctions, even while defining the duties of particular social stations (so that the dharma of the king may allow the use of force but the misuse of force is not consistent with dharma). Dharma as defined in the story requires that people of all social stations be treated fairly and not harmed. Those who most perfectly embody dharma, however, are superior to others, and the object of hierarchical reverence and respect. .

Second Story: A King's Son Is Made a Butcher

Newars often attribute the origins of caste to the actions of kings. I suspect this view of the origin of caste may help Newars conceive of the caste system as a cultural construction, as something made in history, rather than as an objective reality that cannot be changed. The following minimal story was told by an untouchable Sweeper, Kancha:

> Long ago, it is said, there was a king who had no workers. There were no sweepers. So messengers were sent out to tell people to seize anyone found defecating while facing east, and bring him to the king, and he would be made to kill buffalo [a stigmatizing occupation]. So they got the king's youngest son— or was it the middle son?—and made him a butcher.[7]

The story posits a time before there were castes, but this time is not made part of "history," as is sometimes done, by placing the origins of the caste system in a definite period (such as the reign of a particular king). The story makes the caste order in its inception not totally arbitrary (one should not defecate while facing east, an auspicious direction), but arbitrary in the sense that anyone caught could get assigned to a stigmatizing occupation—even a king's son, even the son of the king creating the caste order. An action, not an innate quality, serves as the basis for recruitment into caste. Assuming a marriage with a woman of the same caste status, the king's son cannot be more impure than the king by birth. As for his action, he might not have gotten caught. Furthermore, the need that prompted the effort to place people into castes was economic or functional—the king needed workers—and not based on some principle of just desert or of natural kind. In this story, the king made caste; castes did not arise out of people's innate nature, did not reflect an original state of relative impurity, or even have much to do with a moral biography. The story thus asserts the arbitrary nature of caste hierarchy, and treats it with a certain distancing irony.

Given the premises of the dominant ideology, the narrative, as brief as it is, also poses a fundamental question about the basis of the caste system. Perhaps kings make castes because it is in their "nature" to do so—that is, their actions in constituting the caste system flow from their "biomoral" substance, their essential being. But how can a father and his son have such profoundly different "natures," so that one is a king, the maker of castes, while the other becomes a lowly butcher? The only similarity one can discern is that kings and butchers alike may resort to bloodletting; they are both creatures of force.

A high-caste person might, of course, respond to this story by attempting to close the gap it has opened between "action" and "nature." Perhaps the king's son was different to begin with; maybe his act of defecating while facing east reflected his moral essence, his personal being. He may have sinned in previous life times; he may have shared "substance" with lower-caste people, making him deviant. But this reconstruction, I think, distorts Kancha's intent. Efforts to revise what low-caste actors mean—to reconstruct what they say to make their positions appear ultimately consistent with the premises of the dominant ideology if "properly" understood, or to make low-caste discourse seem irrational and misguided—are as much a part of the ideological scene as the tendency for the low-caste actors to censor their own views to make them more acceptable to high-caste audiences.

While some of the responses to the problem proposed by stories of this kind attempt to reunite "nature" and "action," and so justify the caste order, this is not the only response possible to the rift this story constructs. Many of the efforts to resolve the rift this story opens up tend to "soften" the caste system, making it seem more subject to human action. This can take several forms. The caste system may be taken as an arbitrary construction, imposed through willful human acts, instead of an immutable natural order, as I think Kancha intended. Alternatively, the caste system may be seen as a social order that responds, in one way or another, to human action. In this view, the caste system may be taken as subject to manipulation and failure (your present place in society was the result of tricks, or mistakes, or conspiracy). Or the system may be viewed as responsive to ethical modes of action, so that you can, or should be able to, "rise" in the hierarchy. In this view, you should be able to "rise up" in this life, by engaging in moral acts, by obtaining "knowledge," or by transforming one's qualities—if not in this life, then in future lives, through the medium of karma and reincarnation. Use of the karma doctrine, of course, ends up reconstituting hierarchy, by bringing fate and action into alignment.

Kancha, by posing the problem, has not resolved it. He is forced to face the rifts that open up between action, nature, and self; his experience flows out of the contradictions of caste life and ideology. He must seek some kind of closure—however brittle and fragile—of the gap between his sense of self (based on "action") and his social personhood (based on cultural representations of his "nature"). Interviews with him suggest that his insight into the arbitrary nature of the caste system exists in tension with a need to live in the caste world. He needs to make a living, and this requires that he participate to some degree in caste practices; he cannot afford to alienate the high-caste actors who employ him. He needs to find ways to fit himself into the caste system as a means of feeding his family, and at moments in our discussions he seems to justify the caste system as a way of justifying his participation in it.

How does he do this? Kancha told this little story during an interview. I had asked him, "Do you think that the matter of caste is unjust? What's your own idea about this?" Kancha responded by saying that the caste system is simply a reality. "It was made long ago." The image of coming from "long ago" is a validating construct for him—the value of a social form is established by placing it within tradition, by having it come from "long ago." Kancha then went on to *neutralize* the implications of being low caste by excluding his caste from comparison with other, higher castes: "Your own caste is important for you. My caste organizes my social life. A Sweeper is one who follows these ways. And so, I think, you have your own caste." While some may speak of caste in terms of impurity, he speaks of it as a way of life, not as an expression of essence. The practice of caste makes social life possible, and constitutes a positive identity he values as well as a stigmatized identity he rejects. "A Sweeper is one who follows these ways." By declaring the value of one's own caste for oneself, Kancha recovers something of value, and neutralizes the implication that he is "low."

The story followed. I am unsure about the significance of telling such a story just at that moment; but, arriving when it did, the story would seem to disconcert the case he was making for accepting the caste system, if that was what he was doing. The story exposes the arbitrary nature of the caste system. How, then, can anyone justify or accept it? Perhaps, however, Kancha saw something else in this story, something that justified, not the caste system itself, but his own stance toward the caste system. He may have felt the story justified his practice of surface accommodation because it shows how powerless everyone, even a king's son, is in the face of the blind political force that establishes caste roles.

Whether meant as a critique of the caste system, as a justification of his relationship to the caste system, or both, the story marks the limits of his commitment to the caste system. Moments like this, when social actors jettison concepts used to objectify the social order, and invoke ideas that are critical and dereifying, when they shift from asserting the value and naturalness of caste to telling stories that make caste appear arbitrary, show that people have more than one way—the dominant ideology's way—of understanding self and society. In this case, the story expresses a different vision of reality, a vision that contradicts the hierarchical construction of reality that this untouchable works hard and long to maintain, at least outwardly, making a show of diffidence and respect.

He cannot sustain the critical insight. He cannot, after all, do much about it, not unless he is willing to risk the ostracism and retaliation that overt acts of resistance might provoke. Telling a story by itself does not transform the conditions of social existence, whatever inner transformations it may reflect or initiate. Insight into the arbitrary nature of the social order itself often has no immediate, practical effect on life, not in the absence of any social movement that might attempt to put critique into action. Kancha's mind is not totally in the grip of caste ideology, but he insists that to live he must practice caste. He insists he must accept his caste occupation; he must get up early in the morning and sweep the streets. To fit himself into this role—to be an untouchable in practice—as he must be to survive, means he must find ways to acquiesce to hierarchy, to permit engagement with it. Justifying hierarchy—on his own terms, not precisely those of the dominant ideology—makes a certain sense. His hierarchy-affirming values overlap with those of higher-caste actors, but also diverge in important ways. He rejects purity and pollution, but believes Brahmans should be respected for their religious knowledge and ritual practice. He wishes to replicate hierarchy among the lower castes. He believes other castes are lower than his own, and that he should not associate with them.[8] He fears any breakdown of the caste division of labor that might threaten his livelihood. On his own terms, then, Kancha often does endorse the caste system: unlike some of the other low-caste people I spoke to, he does not reject it entirely. He seeks ways to make it work and actively participates in the system that oppresses him.

In our discussions, whatever critical comments he makes, he soon reverts to his equivocal defense of the caste system. When he concludes his story, I ask (not really comprehending the implications of the narrative), "But do you think [the caste system] is just?" He responds "It is good. It was made long ago. Although I say I will go up, I cannot go up." This is the effective reality from his point of view. He feels he cannot change his caste status. He cannot act on the insight into the arbitrary construction of the caste hierarchy implied in his narrative (although it may develop in his reflections, making a difference in how he interprets and experiences the world); as a practical matter, he has to live within the political reality of the culturally constituted caste hierarchy. Glimpses of the arbitrary nature of caste relations do not provide him with freedom of action, and do not establish the moral grounds for the making of a different society.

The following story, by a second low-caste informant, more clearly calls the caste order into question. The story not only exposes the arbitrary nature of the caste hierarchy, it proposes alternative grounds for constructing social hierarchy.

Third Story: A Brahman Has an Untouchable Guru

This story is told by Krishna Bahadur, a member of a borderline impure caste, the Gatha, that provides the members of a ritual troupe who dance as gods and goddesses in the streets and courtyards of Bhaktapur. He uses his story to make the argument that earned religious knowledge, not one's caste of birth, should be the basis for hierarchy, and that the right to gain knowledge should be based on moral qualities. The argument links moral qualities, religious knowledge, and power. Krishna begins by saying "We must respect those who know."

The story goes like this: An untouchable—a Cyamakhala, almost the lowest of the low—served a renouncer and respected him as a guru. The renouncer gives him a mantra, a verbal formula that channels spiritual power. (The story thus begins with the violation of a Brahmanical code, since untouchables are not supposed to be given mantras: by doing so, the renouncer and untouchable are implicitly identified with each other in opposition to the Brahmans.) With this mantra, the untouchable can cause fruit to grow magically on trees—sweet, ripe, delicious apples, pomegranates, and oranges. The untouchable uses this power to feed his family.

A Brahman hears of this, and asks the untouchable to teach him the mantra, showing him more respect (in the way he addressed him) than a Brahman would usually show an untouchable. He begs the untouchable to take pity on him because his family is large, and he is poor. Hearing this, the untouchable says, "I will teach you. And then you will have to respect me as a guru." The Brahman hesitates, but accepts, thinking that he has to eat.

This introduces necessity into the picture. Krishna comments on the Brahman's dilemma and decision with these words: "The Brahman's caste is great, but he would have to respect the Cyamakhala as a guru. He was in a quandary. He knew he did not want to, but he was forced to consider that he had to eat. Finally, he said, 'I will respect you,' and bowed to the untouchable in respect."

After the Brahman learns the mantra, the untouchable tells him, "Now you know [how to make plants bear fruit]. You can eat and sell fruit wherever you go. Do not lie." The untouchable tells the Brahman he trusts him to tell whoever asks that he has been taught by "that one," the untouchable. The Brahman promises that he will not lie about his. He goes forth and makes his living by selling fruit. One day he sells fruit to a functionary, a soldier, associated with a king's court. The Brahman is asked to take a post in the king's palace and provide the king with fruit.

There comes a time when the king has to go out from his palace, and he takes the Brahman with him so the Brahman can use his mantra to provide fruit to eat on the journey. During the journey, the king asks the Brahman who taught him the mantra. In Krishna's words, "The Brahman couldn't say this, couldn't say that, since his guru was a Cyamakhala. He was of the Brahman jāt, so he was ashamed to say a Cyamakhala" was his teacher. The Brahman lies—he says a respected person, a great man, taught him. He does not acknowledge that an untouchable sweeper was his guru. The King asks for fruit, and the Brahman goes to a tree to produce it, but when he recites his mantra, nothing happens. He tries again, and yet again, but no fruit grows.

When he returns empty-handed to the king, the king reproaches him, saying "What are you doing, Brahman? I am not prepared to sit here hungry." The Brahman has to admit he was not able to produce any fruit. As a consequence of his lie, the Brahman lost the power to make fruit grow. His *siddhi*, his efficacious power, was ended. The king dismisses him, saying, "You are useless. Go." The Brahman then goes hungry, and not knowing what else to do, returns to the untouchable and begs for forgiveness. Krishna supplies the dialogue.

> "Oh ho, Guru, forgive me, [pleads the Brahman]. Because I have lied. Teach me again." The Guru replies, "Oh ho, it is a sin to teach those you cannot trust. As it is said, once is enough, twice is broken." He refused to teach this Brahman. Straightaway, the Brahman died.

Krishna concludes his narration by saying, "This is what *biswās* means." The word biswās is polysemic, carrying meanings we would link to such English words as trust, faith, belief. What Krishna perhaps means to say is that the story tells us what trust is all about. It shows the importance of keeping faith with others—or that it would matter in a just world, which is not what the real world, the world outside the story, is. Krishna may perceive biswās as supplying the integrity that binds people to their word, so that they will keep faith with others, making them trustworthy. I believe he was also implicitly commenting on what the terms of my relationship with him should be.

In this narrative, the dominant ideas in terms of which caste identities are conceived (e.g., low-caste actors are impure, low-caste actors are repositories of inauspiciousness, low-caste actors sinned in previous lives) are passed over in silence, although they are perhaps presupposed in the idea that the Brahman's caste is "great." The story proposes an alternative way of viewing human relations. The narrative floats a possible world—one in which moral worth is the basis for moral respect and social rank. Purity and karma are not directly considered at all. Instead, the narrative reconstitutes the grounds of hierarchy. Social esteem and rank, the narrative proposes, are to be based on empowering knowledge; access to such knowledge is a matter of trust, and granting access to empowering knowledge should, the narrative suggests, be based on directly perceived moral qualities and moral actions.

This is a moral story, and it functions without reference to the ethno-physical theory of impurity and the flow of shared substance that is one of the main bulwarks of the caste hierarchy. Rather, it links untouchability to the ascetic tradition, undercutting Brahmanical hierarchy through a fusing of identity—the figure of the untouchable guru as a source of wisdom and spiritual power is keyed to the figure of the renouncer. This does not fit easily within the value system of the Brahmanical caste hierarchy. The Brahman, an individual of socially ascribed "high" status is portrayed as morally undeserving of religious knowledge and its powers, while an untouchable has the right to possess such knowledge. The untouchable shows his fitness to possess power by respecting a renouncer, a figure from outside the social world. The terms on which the untouchable agreed to transmit his knowledge of the mantra to the Brahman were in one sense conventionally hierarchical: he asked to be respected as a guru. This elevation of untouchable into teacher subverts the social hierarchy with Brahmans at the apex and untouchables at the bottom as the most degraded group. The Brahman hesitated, in a quandary, but gave in to the untouchable's condition out of fear of starving. Thus, the narrative places him in the state of need that untouchables repeatedly declared was their motive for acquiescing to the caste hierarchy—we have to eat.

The Brahman learns the empowering mantra, but fails to keep his word. He could not bring himself to acknowledge that a lowly untouchable was his teacher. By lying, he showed his lack of moral worth, and so lost the power of the mantra.

Since knowledge is available to anyone of worth—even untouchables—this second hierarchy constituted in terms of possession of sacred knowledge is more permeable than the caste hierarchy constituted in terms of purity and impurity. In the hierarchy based on relative purity, one can only fall; but since knowledge can be learned, one can rise in a hierarchy based on knowledge—if that is the exclusive principle defining hierarchy. (Brahmans in fact fuse the two; they supplement their claim to preeminence based on purity with claims to possess, and to have exclusive access to, sacred knowledge.)

The hierarchy proposed in the narrative is based on knowledge that can be attained regardless of caste status, and on moral virtues—honesty, trust, and reverence for those who hold knowledge—that can be achieved by any moral person, not just by those who are high caste or "pure." Krishna repeatedly attempts to define the difference between the closed hierarchy of purity and impurity and a relatively open hierarchy of knowledge and virtue. The distinction has great significance for him.

It is easy to see why he maintains this. On the one hand, as a member of a low-caste group, on the borderline between pure and impure castes, he feels ambivalent about being excluded and stigmatized. On the other hand, as a member of the Navadurga troupe—the ritual dancers who embody important Hindu gods and goddesses, a group with vitally important symbolic and ritual roles within the city—he wants to claim a higher status for his group and himself. He wants to be acknowledged as priestly, as combining sacred power and knowledge in his person. He wishes sacred knowledge, not purity, to define hierarchy. He wants to preserve hierarchy, but not the hierarchy given by purity and impurity. When he focuses on the way that higher castes exclude and stigmatize his own group, he sometimes asserts equality.

In the following passage from an interview, Krishna reveals his ambivalence about hierarchy and equality. He affirms each, in different contexts, and yet he expresses uneasiness with hierarchy and disappointment with equality. He views equality as useless rhetoric, impotent in the face of the problem of hierarchy. Krishna uses a story to make his point that caste is not a moral order, that people are the same, and that discrimination on the basis of caste lacks moral justification; but the ideal called for in the narrative is unrealizable in the "real world," and he breaks away from the narrative to say, in a rather bitter way, that power, wealth, and knowledge are held by some, and not by others—and that is the way it is. He includes me in this—as part of the actual world that differs so profoundly from the ideal of equality and nondiscrimination evoked in the narrative. Although Krishna is a Hindu, he draws on Buddhist sources for the narrative. Bhaktapur is predominantly Hindu, but there are a few Buddhist enclaves, and Krishna has some Buddhist friends.[9]

We must keep in mind the fact that Krishna Bahadur *practices* hierarchy; he does not show through his behavior that he accepts as equals the men and women of castes lower than his own. To do so would provoke ostracism as well as criticism. Since he can attribute his conformity to local hierarchical practices to social pressure, we cannot be certain whether he in fact rejects caste as a system, or only his own position in the system. We can only be certain that he is aware of the ideal of equality, and of the tensions between this ideal and reality.

(Would you eat boiled rice made by a low-caste person?)
I do not accept boiled rice from untouchables. These are the Pore, Cyamakhala [the two Sweeper groups], the Sa:mi [Oil-pressers]. You should not eat food prepared by these low castes. If you eat with them, the people around you will talk, will rebuke you—what things they will say. If it is known, the high-caste

people, and the people of your own caste, will criticize you. And so you cannot eat with untouchables.

After he has stated that he conforms because of social pressure, however, Krishna goes on to declare that "people are the same." He shifts into narrative to construct a foundation for this idea:

> People are the same. Buddha Bhagavan said they are the same in this world. Once when Buddha Bhagavan was out wandering, he needed water to drink. He was with his friend Ananda the monk. At the time they needed water, they saw an untouchable Sweeper woman drawing water out of the well. They told her they needed water. She said, "I won't give you water because I am not of caste" [meaning she is untouchable or outcast]. Ananda then said, "Woman, I only asked for water, I did not ask for your caste."

Krishna then puts Ananda's action in the context of Buddha's teachings. He assumes "the voice" of Buddha, who says to his followers, "In this world, all men are the same. People are equal. We are all the same. The same God created us all. Do not discriminate by caste."

Here Krishna shifts away from the narrative world to the "real" world. I follow up with some questions (in parentheses).

> And what is the use of saying that? Great people have great knowledge. Those who do not have knowledge, do not have knowledge. Those who do not have knowledge cannot be the same as those who have knowledge. You and I cannot be the same.... You have much money. If I had a lot of money I would be a little proud in my heart. Any man who has knowledge will be proud. He won't be able to give up his pride.
>
> (In your opinion, men are equal?)
> They are equal.
> (But according to caste, they are different.)
> Different. Men are the same.
> (For you?)
> My mind is like that. Society is not ready.
> (If men are equal, why is there caste?)
> It was made to correspond to the degree of understanding that people had.... Knowledge is not equal. Understandings are different. And then consider the king. He is a man, and we are men, but we cannot be his equals. We have to defer to him.
> (If men are equal, why do you have to follow caste?)
> If there was no caste, then our affairs could not be put in order. There would be fights.

Krishna invokes the ideas of equality in the narrative, and then distances himself from it. He seems to see it as a powerful and true idea—he frequently reverts to the position that all men are the same—but also as a fragile, useless ideal that cannot be achieved in the actual world. His words suggest resentment, as did his tone in the interview; in particular, when he says "And what is the use of saying that?" and (bringing it home to me) "You and I cannot be the same." He resents differences in wealth, in knowledge, and in power. He resents the way higher castes treat him in the closed hierarchy of purity and impurity, and would prefer an open hierarchy based on mastery of sacred knowledge in which low-caste people could rise, in which his own mastery of sacred knowledge would count for more.

Krishna Bahadur also sees power as a factor in keeping men unequal; even though people are the same, they are forced to defer to those with power. Finally, perhaps the ultimate rationale of the caste hierarchy is to create order and to prevent violence.

Krishna thinks that it is the actual distribution of "empowering" knowledge in society that makes people unequal; he seeks to affirm the idea that you can rise in the hierarchy by gaining such knowledge. Implied is the idea that knowledge was kept from low castes—that the high castes attempt to keep a monopoly on such knowledge. As a ritual specialist at his own level in the social system, he wishes to claim knowledge to make him high. He asserts a different hierarchy.

Many orthodox Brahmans and members of the other highest castes deny that low castes can rise in this lifetime; they emphasize the impurity, the "essence," of the low castes as an insurmountable obstacle to mobility. Krishna prefers to see "knowledge" and "understanding" as the basis of status. This is ritual or religious knowledge. People do not simply inherit some quantity of purity or impurity; knowledge confers status. Equality and inequality are questions of access and opportunity, not "nature" or "impurity."

Asked if an untouchable could rise, Krishna answers affirmatively.

> If he was educated, he could go up. And if Brahmans don't study and do their own true karma, by honoring their scriptures and following their rules and rites, then they will come down....A low-caste man can rise up. This arrangement is good. It is good because Bhagavan made us and this world. He gave us life. In life, no one wants to be low. They want to be high. To rise up, they have to improve their understanding. They have to gain knowledge, and then they will be high. In the past, because they did not have understanding, they were not educated, they were placed low.

Implicitly, the hierarchy cannot, for him, be unalterable, because Bhagavan made people. He posits an "open," rather than a "closed" hierarchy. Note that the separation of *castes* is constructed—it does not, in his account, arise from some preexisting quanta of purity or impurity. Separation arises rather from a lack of *buddhi*, "understanding," which is something individuals and groups can acquire or lose. Understanding is socially developed. Furthermore, although some were made low, no one wants to be low. Krishna identifies this wish not to be low as an inherent feature of life itself; the desire not to be low flows from "the life" that God gives. In this construction, he ethicizes and sacralizes aspirations.

Brahmans and other high-caste people attribute their high-caste status to the fact they do "karma," which in this context has the sense of "religious acts and rites." This makes them "pure"; but again this is constructed, not an inherent attribute. This claim may be buttressed by invoking karma in the first sense; high-caste people will say one must do good works for many generations before one is worthy of being born in a high caste. This argument would seal off their status in this lifetime. But Krishna, a ritual leader of a caste that stands just above castes that are fully impure and untouchable, emphasizes that it is possible to rise through an improvement of understanding, by gaining religious knowledge. He reinvents hierarchy for himself.

Comparative Discussion: Untouchables and the Figure of the Renouncer

In a study of Indian untouchables, Khare (1984) demonstrates that asceticism as a significant cultural form is shared by untouchable and Brahman alike, but its meaning differs. In untouchable ideology, the ascetic emerges as a contested concept—and as a key symbol they seek to seize for themselves. Within their critical discourse, the untouchable may define the role and meaning of the ascetic in ways that distinguish it from the concept of ascetic in high-caste thought and experience.

Untouchable critics of caste culture may seek to "liberate" the concept of the ascetic. Khare (1984:24) writes that they attempt to distinguish a "culture of the deprived" from the culture of upper-caste Hindus and thus "free the genuine content of Indian asceticism from the caste Hindu's distortion." Delivered from Brahmanical Hinduism, the ascetic embodies untouchable hopes and aspirations— he figures in their minds as a "moving utopia," represents "a forceful moral critique of a caste-ordered society," "subverts unjustified inequality," and launches "alternative symbolizations" of the social world (1984:23). Compare this to Krishna's use of the figure of the untouchable ascetic in narratives that project and support the idea of alternative ways of constituting the social world and hierarchy.

Khare discusses five central features of Indian asceticism (1984:24–25):

1. Identification of the personal self and ultimate-sacred self.
2. The ascetic is beyond the moral categories and controls of society: not immoral, but amoral.
3. Egalitarianism.

These three, he suggests, are not as contested as other characteristics. The stress placed on the last two qualities of the ascetic, he argues, characterizes the untouchable's concept of the ascetic.

4. The ascetic achieves an "ultimate" spiritual state from which he can know

and reveal the "root of morality that upholds the length and breadth of the entire Indic tradition." (1984:25)

The untouchable ideologist, says Khare, stresses this ability to reveal the basis of morality, while he maintains it has variable significance for caste Hindus.

5. The ascetic is a symbol of self, representing an aspect of an ideal self; and as such the ascetic is treated as "a moral image immanent in all humans." Untouchables and Brahmans alike told Khare that "the yogi and bhogi [the ascetic and enjoyer of life] reside in everyone." The self-image the ascetic embodies is supposed to be cultivated over the long term as self-control.

Again, Brahmans and untouchables share the concept but make different uses of it. Evidently, the untouchable uses this idea to sustain arguments for equality and mutual recognition. In his study of the Lucknow Chamars, Khare quotes Jigyasu, an Untouchable intellectual and writer, on the role of ascetics.

Ascetics as gurus have always been very important to the Chamar. We have lived in their company in villages and cities for centuries. For the people whom the Hindus had systematically isolated and excluded, the Untouchable or low-caste ascetic was a guide, a doctor, a teacher, a benevolent companion, and a true friend. We, the Chamars, did not have ambivalence toward the ascetic. He was always more on our side than any Brahman. Even if we did not dislike the Brahman, he did. A Brahman ascetic, on comparison, was congenial only out of his benevolence; if he did not care for us, there was nothing that we could do to change his mind, except try to win him by our genuine devotion to a Hindu deity. The common Chamar is still too much in awe of a Brahman ascetic, though it is unnecessary and out of ignorance. The awakened Chamar should suspect the Brahman ascetic, especially these days. He could do so only if he put distance between himself and all things Brahmanical. The Chamars routinely bring their families in close contact with a sympathetic ascetic. Again, unlike the Hindu, they do not know ambivalence toward him. The Hindu householder fears the ascetic's wrath, but craves his miraculous blessings. He is caught forever in his own doubts about the nature of the sacred. Actually, this is a trap Brahmanic thought has produced and maintained. Spared of this, the Untouchable ideally approaches the ascetic with full, unwavering faith. The householder interiorizes the ascetic. The Untouchable has little difficulty in doing so, for both the Untouchable and the ascetic receive little from society, the first under denial and the second under self-denial. But both the Chamar householder and the Untouchable ascetic impart critical lessons to each other: The Chamar reminds the ascetic of worldly reform and of restoring will within the oppressed; the ascetic reminds the Chamar of his true spiritual heritage and individual worth. (1984:26, diacritics omitted)

Jigyasu goes on to say that the ascetic who does not uphold Brahmanical premises but rather truly embodies the sacred order "symbolizes hope in despair and reminds us of social justice based on spiritual equality." He distinguishes this kind of ascetic from those who affirm Brahmanical (or caste Hindu) ideology:

Those [ascetics] still dominated by the Brahmanic rites and viewpoints are counterproductive; those unwilling to see a fundamental difference between the social justice of the caste system and of the spiritual order [*atmavadi dharma*] are of limited value. The ascetic of the spiritual order clearly sees how the Hindu weaves a cobweb along castes, gods, Brahmanic rites, karma, *maya* [illusion], and *samasara* [rebirth] that he begins to view social exclusion and justice as a form of dharma.

The ascetic tradition of true persuasion, however, needs to be carefully rescued from the surrounding Brahmanic forms and images. The mentality of this ascetic, who is most often not a Brahman, is best tested when he fights for the social justice denied to others. He does not believe in Hindu gods and their discriminatory rites....He is a true wanderer and a true renouncer. He is free himself and makes others free. (1984:34, diacritics omitted)

The caste Hindu is "Other" here—portrayed as ensnared by the illusions he has woven to oppress others, while the untouchable and ascetic engage in a dialogue in which each "imparts critical lessons" to the other and seek emancipation. Khare (1984:26) argues that the untouchable thinker seeks to formulate an alternative cultural ideology for untouchables. "He strives to make the ascetic *the* independent variable within the Indian spiritual and social order, for the ascetic reveals to him the roots of all his caste-engendered deprivations" (1984:26). To achieve this state of revelation, Jigyasu portrays the ascetic as a key symbol in a liberation ideology, but maintains this key symbol must be rescued from the mystifying distortions of Hindu culture—the "cobweb" of castes, gods, rites—that have obscured the potential for emancipation and transformation embodied by the ascetic. This requires a critical stance. Not all ascetics have equal value. The untouchable and the "true" ascetic (who is unmystified and demystifying) exist in a mutual dialogue, each "reminding" the other of critical values: Jigyasu says, "the Chamar reminds the ascetic of worldly reform of restoring will within the oppressed; the ascetic reminds the Chamar of his true spiritual heritage and individual worth."

Like Jigyasu, some Newars align ascetics and untouchables. In Krishna's story, the untouchable ascetic guru is true and generous, while the Brahman is deceptive and unfaithful. The Brahman desires the untouchable's teaching, and accepts the provision that he will acknowledge having an untouchable guru, but betrays this trust. In his acceptance of caste distinctions by denying his teacher was an untouchable, he loses the power he has gained. He loses his power—and falls.

We should interpret this in light of Krishna's general theory of hierarchy. As the Brahman can fall, so can the untouchable "rise up." The key is knowledge, not birth status. Knowledge is learned, and can be held and wielded by ascetics, and by ritual leaders such as himself. His denial of status as birthright aligns Krishna with the critique of the Chamars—arguably, this idea is as "good to think" for low-caste people as purity and impurity are for high-caste people.

The untouchable internalizes the ascetic, Jigyasu says. This sheds an important light on Krishna's stories. In Krishna's story the Brahman did not—and could not, because of his caste standing—truly internalize the ascetic who was an untouchable, while the untouchable had internalized moral and spiritual values derived from *his* ascetic teacher. Krishna's story converges with Jigyasu's critique: the untouchable and the ascetic are united in a way the Brahman and renouncer cannot be. They portray the ascetic tradition as belonging to the untouchable. This depiction carries with it a forceful argument that knowledge and moral action, not birth status, should be the basis of social life. Jigyasu also repatriates the moral concepts embodied in this tradition, bringing the idea of spiritual equality to bear on social injustice. He does not treat the ascetic pursuit as sealed off in socially transcendent "otherworldliness," but as a position from which concerns of the social world can be addressed. Not directly part of the caste world, the ascetic tradition provides a cultural basis for political engagement and moral critique of that world.[10]

Of course, the high castes also align themselves with the ascetic and draw him into their construction of the world. The renouncer is a resource in an ideological struggle, a tug of war between opposing viewpoints. High-caste concepts have hegemony—are diffused throughout society, seem natural, shape common sense, and generally have a strong grip on millions of minds—but alternate views make inroads; reformist thinkers like Jigyasu subject dominant views to critique and suggest alternative ideologies, which over time are picked up by others, who extend or apply them.[11]

Thus, as a key cultural symbol, a fluid symbol that can be "thought" and "read" in various ways, the ascetic renouncer is enlisted on both sides. Let us look at the ascetic-Brahman alignment. Fuller (1992), in his effort to summarize popular Hinduism—which is Hinduism as it is in caste society, that is, for the most part, Hinduism in which the ideology of hierarchy has achieved some degree of cultural hegemony, forming an integral basis for religious thought and practice—discusses the way Brahman and renouncer are assimilated to each other. We can compare his remarks with Jigyasu's:

> A vital aspect of the relationship between Brahmans and renouncers is that the former, although they are mostly householders living in the world, have come to be partially assimilated with the latter, so that the "ideal Brahman" is or is like an ascetic renouncer....the ideological significance of the Brahman-renouncer assimilation is indisputable. In particular, it means that the social and religious supremacy of Brahmans partly depends on their likeness to renouncers. Hence Brahmans can represent themselves as independent of inferiors, just like renouncers who ideally avoid all entangling ties with members of the society they have left, even though the Brahmans' purity is still partly preserved by the lower castes who carry out polluting tasks for them. Paradoxically, therefore, Brahman supremacy is a function of both their asymmetrical, complementary relationships with inferior castes, and their ideal detachment from such relationships. (1992:18)

This helps us see what is at stake in Jigyasu's and Krishna's re-visioning of culture. By assimilating the renouncer to the untouchable while rescuing the renouncer from the Brahman, a key basis of the social and religious supremacy of Brahmans is called into question. Jigyasu and Krishna might argue that Fuller has merely stated the Brahman's ideology, since they want to assert that the actual role of renouncer is to neutralize and subvert the Brahmanical synthesis of a world in which the Brahman has supremacy.

Indeed, a critique of academic studies of South Asian society and religion by untouchables might be very interesting. They might accuse us of doing little more than transcribing cobwebs. They might detect, and criticize, a tendency to leave them out of the picture.

Fuller (1992) in his discussion, for example, does not mention the assimilation of untouchable and ascetic—the untouchable is seen in relation to the Brahman in terms of the purity complex and the caste society (1992:17), but not in relation to the ascetic renouncer. In fact, Fuller's remarks on the linking of Brahman and renouncer are found under the subtitle "Brahmans, Renouncers, and Kings." These three figures are presented, in Fuller and other academic discussions, as crucial figures in Hindu culture, and they certainly are; but so is the untouchable, about which much less is said. Hinduism is virtually defined in terms of the figure of Brahman, Renouncer, King—but not in terms of the untouchable, who defines the Brahman's purity, but is otherwise often represented, if at all, as a marginal figure. Even the single cultural dimension of untouchability that is analyzed—symbolic impurity—is often treated rather one-dimensionally, when in fact this is a multifaceted reality.[12]

Arguably—as Dumont's work first forced us to acknowledge, but left hanging in abstraction—the untouchable as "Other" is the invisible fourth that completes this trinity, an essential figure against which all the other figures define themselves. Without the untouchable, would the "three hierarchical models" (Burghart 1978; cited in Fuller 1992:16) represented by the other figures, each of which can claim superiority to the others in some contexts, coalesce into any kind of unity? Or, at least, the unity they do have? Brahman, Renouncer, King—they share an identity as non-untouchable: the king's power against the untouchable's powerlessness; the Brahman's purity against the untouchable's impurity (or: knowledge against ignorance); the renouncer's freedom against the untouchable's subjugation to a social world of suffering. Nonetheless, the untouchable is often relatively neglected in studies of Hindu society and culture.

No doubt this is because the untouchable is not celebrated, but stigmatized. Yet if untouchables have an essential role in defining the high-caste Hindu self, we must explore this; to neglect the untouchable is to attempt to understand Hindu caste culture without analyzing the way that culture has produced the images of self and other by which identity is ultimately defined. Actual untouchables embody stigmatized otherness—which is more than impurity. Thus, our unit of analysis should be at least fourfold, as in figure 1. The untouchable is opposed conceptually to the other three—perhaps we should say the other three are opposed to the untouchable. The untouchable embodies filth, impurity, and inauspiciousness, embodies suffering, embodies moral degradation and desert, and actualizes in tangible ways everything the high-caste householder, Brahman, or king is not,

and do not want to be or suffer. In Hindu Newar culture, I believe, from the perspective of the higher castes, one may coherently desire to become a renouncer,
although this is typically discouraged, but the desire to be an untouchable would
be deviant and irrational, an incoherent wish. If the renouncer can be assimilated
to self, the untouchable cannot. The renouncer is a potential self, but the untouchable is what one rejects in, and for, self.

Figure 1. The symbolic value of the untouchable for high-caste actors

---

Social centrality and power   Set apart (transcendent vs. stigmatized)

Brahman   Renouncer   *Sacred knowledge and power*
King   **Untouchable**   *Secular functions*
                         \
                          \
Protected self   **Symbolizes what is rejected in self and for self:**
                          filth, impurity, ignorance
                          servitude, suffering, powerlessness
                          unrestrained sexuality
                          inauspiciousness and misfortune

The untouchable becomes cultural symbol for many high-caste actors—meanings
are imposed on actual untouchables, whatever their own sense of self. The
untouchable is a tangible symbol of the contents of the political unconscious, an
embodiment of much that is rejected in the high-caste Hindu self: impurity and
inauspiciousness but also powerlessness. Their political and economic oppression
is legitimized in concepts and sentiments that are animated by a fear and loathing
that derives from the cultural psychology of caste life.

If the householder-renouncer opposition pits "this-worldliness" against
"otherworldliness," the opposition of Brahman/untouchable (and with it all high
castes against all impure castes) is not merely a matter of abstract quanta of purity
and impurity: the untouchable exposes the underside of this world to the eyes of
the high castes, revealing the full potential horror of thisworldly existence. One
Newar Brahman said the Pore live a hell on earth, representing the ultimate in
filth and impurity and suffering. One Newar Sweeper echoed this, with no apparent irony, when he defined "hell" for me as "our feces." Thus, the opposition of
Brahman and king with untouchable contrasts the protected moral world of the
high-caste householder with a kind of existential horror-in-the-world: the
untouchable's living hell. The renouncer announces an exit and holds out the
promise of salvation; renunciation for the high-caste Hindu may assuage guilt or
guarantee continued transcendence of the untouchable's world, but for untouchables the concept of salvation may be infused with meaning deriving from their
interest in emancipation from the caste system.

The untouchable may reject Hinduism, and a reformed Hinduism without the untouchable as a symbolic social category is no doubt possible. In a future Hindu fundamentalism, perhaps, a radically different choice of Other will be made, an outer Other rather than an inner Other—perhaps embodied by the Moslem, the Christian, or the West—but historical Hinduism has made extensive use of the untouchable, and we will not achieve a full understanding of Hinduism (in popular, state, or textual forms) if this is left unexplored.

Conclusion

Note that all three of the Newars' stories deal with problems of recognition. In all three, a hierarchically dominant figure—king or Brahman—fails to recognize another person in a way that provides the complication of the story. In the first story, recounted by a Brahman, a king seeking knowledge of dharma fails to recognize the way the beggar embodies the dharma. In the third story, recognition is withheld from the untouchable when he is not acknowledged by the Brahman as the Brahman's guru—an injustice and a lie that rebound on the Brahman. The second narrative, Kancha's, is the most resistant to analysis in these terms—or perhaps the most subtle and sweeping. The problem of recognition in this story is cast as a problem of misrecognition. The king did not intend to make his son a low-caste butcher. The king's son was not recognized as a king's son: it was not who he was, but what he was doing, that made a difference. The king's son was at the wrong place at the wrong time, just happened to be doing something that was declared the basis for making a person a butcher. Caste status, the story intimates—in ways, to be sure, that can be neutralized by others who will be able to find ways of making it mean something else—is not based on recognition of who a person is, but on being caught up in a net of power (the king's men hunt for someone who fits the criteria the king has given them). What you become in the caste system is determined by power extrinsic to self, not by any quality having to do with "who you are."

I think many low-caste Newars seek to declare—to themselves and others— that their caste status does not reflect their moral essence, express their sense of self, or constitute them. They argue that caste practice is not definitive of who they are, is not something that arises out of the very ground of their being, as the predominant ideology of caste maintains. They experience caste as a constructed order imposed on their lives and identities.

In response, they manipulate, reconstruct, and resist their social identities in complex ways, in moral rhetoric, narratives, and fantasies. By showing that there are other ways to view themselves and society, they melt away some of the powerful sense of reality that caste hierarchy has, make it seem less solid, less natural and moral, less self-defining. People propose other moral worlds, alternative hierarchies, in which they might stand higher. The conditions of life, practices, and ideology that create and sustain caste hierarchy are locked in perpetual conflict with the impulse to escape and alter that hierarchy.

This has fundamental consequences for self-awareness and moral consciousness of self and society. In the case of the Newars, hierarchy embodied in practice is something that people must know and engage, since it is central to their lives. The Newar experience reflects something of the way that human awareness adapts itself to the exigencies of inequality. Let me suggest that most Newars, much of the time, must find ways to make themselves not be fully aware of what, in some important sense, they know—that the caste system is an arbitrary human construction. To get on with their lives in caste society, they must often suppress the kinds of insight and analysis that they display in critical discourse and in anti-hierarchical narratives.

They develop what I would call, borrowing the term from Fredric Jameson (1981), a "political unconscious." I doubt that Jameson and I would ultimately agree as to what the term should mean. I use it in this sense: the "political unconscious" designates mental and social states in which some key understandings about social reality are kept out of intentional awareness or behavior, because they are socially unacceptable, place the actor at risk, cause painful dissonance, or threaten the coherence of the actor's self or worldview. When social understandings are relegated to the "political unconscious," they can be acted on in certain ways—for example, an individual may pursue his or her self-interest—without engaging the person as a full, conscious agent. If actors were always fully cognizant of the nature of their social actions—if, to use a term of Bourdieu's (1977:171–183), they did not "misrecognize" the organization and implications of their conduct—they would often not be able to act in the way they do, because the actor would have to engage the world in other terms, those demanded by the socially "repressed" understandings. This would threaten the actor, putting him or her at psychological or political risk. It is this danger that drives these understandings out of immediate awareness and off the stage of social action. The political unconscious is as fluid and permeable as awareness. What is suppressed and what enters into awareness, what is denied and what is animated, shift in context-sensitive ways, along with the experience, goals, and needs of actors. In caste life, actors invoke hierarchical modes of knowing self and society to make it possible for them to interact with members of other castes, reduce the otherwise painful dissonance, and avoid exposing themselves to the risks that overt opposition would entail.[13]

And yet—although the insights may have to be suppressed and hidden, even from self—I have shown how in narratives some Newars do see caste as arbitrary, as alien to their essence or nature. They reject their construction by others, by caste ideology. This *is* expressed in critical discourse and anti-hierarchical narratives, which should be seen in part as constituting processes of self-construction. A critical consciousness can coexist with the political unconscious; this critical consciousness, which interprets self and society in ways not simply given in the dominant ideology, can be developed through and made manifest in narrative work.[14] If at times critical consciousness is driven from awareness and dissipates as hierarchical models and modes are triggered, then at other moments, hierarchical models and the awareness of self and society that goes along with them will be suppressed, as critical models are activated as salient interpretive schema. The suppression of moral and political awareness thus cuts two ways; the political unconscious of actors has revolving faces, or alternating phases, as actors embrace and animate conflicting models of self and society. The activation of any one model of self and society may require the suppression of others. Yet the conflicting perspectives of incompatible models both are part of the total mental world of low-caste men and women in Newar society, and will be asserted as values in relevant contexts.

Inconstant selves in an equivocal world, actors in caste society may shift from resistance to acquiescence, and back again. Moral fantasies and narratives tell us something about how actors experience such shifts in their mode of relationship to society, suggesting what is at stake for them: moral conceptions of self are asserted against stigmatized identities, alternative visions of the world shouted in the face of harsh, hierarchical social realities. If actors need at once to adjust themselves to hierarchical realities and rebel against them, then an "inner" politics of self parallels the politics and exigencies of caste life.[15]

The worldview of resistance is as real as the worldview of submission. I suspect the self-consciousness presupposed in hierarchical models, narratives, and practices is not any more real or any more false than the consciousness implied in non-hierarchical models, anti-hierarchical narratives, and resistance to caste practices. The structure and objective situation of both of these modes need to be recognized, without privileging one as somehow culturally more real than the other, whatever the theories or values of the researcher may be. Actors' narratives disclose both.

What do we make of the morality asserted in the narratives we have considered here? Perhaps like Nietzsche in *The Genealogy of Morals* we should say that these narratives represent "uprisings in ethics" that begin "when *ressentiment* becomes creative and brings forth its own values." We have seen evidence that low-caste actors resent the way they are constructed and incorporated in caste practices, and such resentment is part of what moves them to reimagine the world. Moreover, the historical reality has been that they could not act, not easily or without putting themselves at great risk; so like Nietzsche, we could say these narratives reflect "the *ressentiment* of those to whom the only authentic way of reaction—that of deeds—is unavailable, and who preserve themselves from harm through the exercise of imaginary vengeance."[16] And yet, I think we hear more in these stories than resentment. Low-caste actors may wreak an imaginary vengeance in narrative (the bad Brahman in Krishna's story dies, after all), but they also imagine a better world. These narratives express as much hope as resentment; as much resignation as hope. If we view these narratives as constituting moral fantasies, the strongest desire they disclose is not the desire for vengeance, but the desire for mutual recognition.

Thus, I would modify Nietzsche's formulae to read: these narrative uprisings in moral thought begin when resentment and hope become creative and bring forth stories that explore the problems of identity and meaning, of powerlessness and practice, posed by caste life. These narratives rise up against the constructions of self expressed in the dominant Brahmanical ideology and implied in caste practice—they are uprisings in ethics and in self-concept.

What the narratives work with are constructions and counter-constructions of the morality of social life, which necessarily stand as constructions and counter-constructions of the social actor, who experiences and interprets these constructions in terms of self. What is contested is the moral ground on which actors have value, and for low-caste actors and untouchables this is very much a question of self-identity, of who they are and what meaning they have, for others and for themselves. The narratives here are thus subversions of constructions of morality that imply and legitimate stigmatizing constructions of the low-caste actor. The revolt against stigmatizing constructions of self leads to affirmations of self. In their stories Krishna and Kancha establish a voice for themselves, and a point of view, that rejects the constructions of the dominant ideology. I believe they constitute a sense of self in this rejection, applying alternative standards of worth to themselves.

This affirmation may embrace others and affirm solidarity with them, as when untouchables voice a collective sense of suffering. In such moments, the individual self identifies with others, speaking not just of personal suffering or struggles, but of the experience of a community. We poor people suffer, they say; we untouchables do what is necessary to survive. At such moments, they constitute a self-identity by constituting an implied community of suffering and solidarity.

Such narrative work draws on, and helps create, a narrative tradition that has the potential for helping constitute a moral and political tradition. In the absence of the power to act, such narratives keep alive alternative possibilities; they stand as moral fantasies and utopian thought to social reality, and offer one way low-caste actors can construct themselves in contrast and opposition to their ideological construction in the caste system. That the consciousness of self and society they imply may be only part of the consciousness of low-caste actors—who may at times be drawn into and encompassed by the consciousness proposed in caste ideology and practice—does not detract from its psychological and cultural significance. At the very least, aside from the way narratives may help actors adjust themselves to difficult social realities, we need to consider the ways that critical and utopian narratives might keep actors flexible, preparing them to seek and accept, to promote and impel change should conditions allow it.

By listening carefully, we can come to understand something of the way that people experience themselves and society, something of the dynamic tensions of the lives they live. We can get at some of the flux and politics of identity. The dominant ideology is not all that people know. People have moral fantasies, construct critiques, imagine utopias for themselves. By listening to people's moral fantasies we can know something of how they might wish to know themselves, in addition to what they must know of themselves to live in caste society.

Notes

This chapter presents material from my book, *Hierarchy and Its Discontents: Culture and the Politics of Consciousness in Caste Society* (Philadelphia: University of Pennsylvania Press, 1996. Reprinted with permission). I am grateful to Roy D'Andrade, Robert Levy, and Ernestine McHugh for comments on some of the material and issues discussed here. Portions of this chapter were also given as a paper at the 1988 American Anthropology Association meetings, Phoenix, Arizona. I wish to thank Nicholas Dirks and Vincent Crapanzano for comments on that paper. Al Pach and Debra Skinner also have my gratitude for their comments on this version.

1. The Newar castes were incorporated by the state into a national caste hierarchy that incorporated Indo-Nepalese and Tibeto-Nepalese (Bhotya) peoples as well. This was codified in a fascinating document, the Muluki Ain of 1854 (and subsequent versions until the post-Rana era) (Höfer 1979). The document juxtaposed tribes, castes, and ex-nations, people of different religions and communities with fundamentally different social organizations, in a kind of Alice-in-Wonderland way for political and administrative convenience. In constructing this code for society, the state also constructs itself as a state that embodies and applies a Brahmanical ideology. See also Sharma (1977) and Holmberg (1989).

2. Of these castes, a few may recently have disappeared as families left Bhaktapur, and a few may be present only in a symbolic sense—they are there in thought, not as actual groups (Levy 1990; Parish 1996). Castes also vanished or abandoned their identifying symbolic roles in the past, if the manuscripts of the nineteenth-century British Resident in Kathmandu, Brian Hodgson, held at the India Office Library, are any guide. Indeed, for whatever reasons, as K. P. Malla once pointed out to me (personal communication), scholars have failed to come up with a wholly consistent list of Newar castes. Chattopadhyaya (1980/1924) collates early 19th and 20th century lists of Newar castes; Levy (1990), Rosser (1978), and Toffin (1978) also discuss and attempt to enumerate Newar castes. See Levy (1990) for a more detailed discussion of the caste ranking and segmentation among Bhaktapur's Hindu Newars, and of the criteria for such ranking and segmentation.

3. Marriott (1976, 1989) interprets South Asian concepts of the person as assuming porous boundaries through which moral substances can be emitted or received.

4. On the kind of "psychoexistential complex" and identity work that may develop in encounters between dominant and subordinate groups, see Fanon (1967), who explores the consequences of the encounter of blacks and whites in a colonial context. In South Asia, the process of emulation of higher castes known as Sanskritization is well known, but the cultural self-psychology of the process has not, I think, been fully explored.

5. Of course the internal unfolding of events and responses is necessarily ordered by time, by the temporal quality of the acts that take place within the story. This is one of the essential qualities of a narrative—it possesses time. Such stories may be historicized, that is, referred to a particular time and place, such as the reign of a historical king, but this seems to be optional.

6. The particular implicit distinction between self and person I make here (a blurred one in any event) is inspired in part by reflections on a discussion of Ameile Rorty's

typology of ways of construing "persons" in Bruner (1986:39–41). In my view, selves possess the power to interpret themselves, but must draw on cultural meanings to do so. That selves are self-interpreting and society-interpreting means they transform, in a Vygotskian sense, external cultural material, including information about and constructions of themselves. The process of self-definition may begin with internalization of external constructs, but does not end there.

In many ways, the concept of person stresses external definitions and constraints, social not self-constructions, where these are derived from the way the actor has roles and a place in social systems. My concept of you as a person—which exists within a zone of action and interpretation in which actors engage in social practices—does not necessarily correspond to your concept of yourself, although you may have to take account of it. Personhood in this sense is the product of processes of social construction, and can be distinguished from the self as an interpreting agent and locus of self-experience. An individual may repudiate his or her own social construction. Thus the untouchable as dramatis personae in the symbolic drama of the caste order is not the untouchable as self who may experience this as repugnant or oppressive and claim an identity as a poor person who must engage in caste practices to live.

Personhood in this sense is a kind of objecthood, perhaps for some lower-caste actors even the kind of "crushing objecthood" that Frantz Fanon (1967) found himself "sealed into" as a black man in a colonial world. Although the distinction between a socially constructed, imposed "personhood" and a self-interpreting self is easily overdrawn, and fails to suggest the ambiguity and ambivalences inherent in the process of being at once a socially constructed person and a self-interpreting self, I find it analytically useful because it suggests how some actors/selves evaluate and re-value the value that society places on them—and seek to identify themselves with the revaluation. They see themselves at once in terms of how others in the caste system construct and "valorize" them, and in terms of their revaluation or transvaluation of this. On self, see Ewing (1990) and Parish (1994).

7. This story may be a transformation of an episode from the story of how King Harisimhadeva brought the Goddess Taleju to Nepal. In this story, as Levy (1990:236) records it, the king sees a man defecating while facing east, indicating that he is not of twice-born status, and assigns this man the role of killing buffalo. The killing of water buffalo during sacrifices to Taleju are done by the Nae, the Butcher caste, and this episode accounts for this.

8. None of these castes would accept his claims, however, and most rankings by other groups agree in placing his caste below these groups; Kancha's claim reveals resistance to accepting the consensus about his caste's status.

9. Ironically, Newar Buddhists practice caste, despite the more universalistic and egalitarian traditions of Buddhism.

10. It is instructive to compare and contrast Jigyasu's and Krishna's views with Dumont's (1980, Appendix B, "World Renunciation in Indian Religion").

11. This is a critical enterprise, but one that takes place within culture. We do not need to posit a mind entirely separate from culture to account for this. People rework cultural symbols and schema, work out their implications, cross symbols with other symbols to generate new meanings, transpose symbols, shift them into new contexts, activate schema

in new contexts, unite separate schemas to create new schema, and so on. See Ortner (1989).

12. Levy (1990) stands out as a richer study of some of the symbolic roles of the untouchable in Hindu Newar society, even though (since his study had other goals) he does not explore their lives, selves, communities, or their critiques of the dominant culture that constitutes them as symbolic figures.

13. Perhaps the amnesia that replaces insight into the arbitrary nature of the caste hierarchy serves as a psychological defense for some, for whom the problem, the impasse created by the fact that alternative social relations cannot be enacted, is too painful and disorienting to be confronted for long.

14. If telling stories is one way of doing this, singing songs may be another. Holland and Skinner (1995) show how songs sung by some Nepalese women during the festival of Tij constitute critical voices and embody a critical consciousness of social practices.

15. In terms of the psychology of self, the shifting mode of actors' relationships to society, the qualitative variation in their identification with and opposition to social practices, and the successive triggering of alternative cultural models in response to such shifts and variation, may shape the development of self-identity and the organization of psychological processes. The displacement of self-consciousness and world-perception from one mode to another, from submission to resistance, may provoke or redirect processes of identification and rejection, defining what is perceived as ego-alien or as having relational value, and influence psychological defenses and processes of self-identity differentiation. Shifts in the basic premises of one's relationship to social practice, in the way one envisions one's relationship to society, may sway felt evaluations of self, perhaps reordering the way persons feel about themselves and their lives, reconstituting their expressive behavior and "personality" styles (Riesman 1983), or restructuring their goals and motives as they activate schema to help them flesh out their stance toward society (cf. D'Andrade 1992; Strauss 1992). The context-sensitive activation and suppression of conflicting modes of relationship and models of self and society may affect the unity and inconsistency of the self (Ewing 1990).

16. The passage from Nietzsche is quoted in Jameson (1981:201); comparing several translations of Nietzsche's *Genealogy of Morals*, I, 10, I have decided I like the rendering in Jameson best, perhaps because "uprising" suggests to me a rising up into consciousness and a raising of consciousness, which I think are appropriate secondary images not conveyed by the standard "revolt in morality."

References

Bourdieu, Pierre. 1977. Outline of a Theory of Practice. Cambridge: Cambridge University Press.

Bruner, Jerome. 1986. Actual Minds, Possible Worlds. Cambridge, MA: Harvard University Press.

Burghart, Richard. 1978. Hierarchical Models of the Hindu Social System. Man, n.s., 13:519–526.

Chattopadhyay, K. P. 1980 [1924]. An Essay on the History of Newar Culture. Kathmandu, Nepal: Educational Enterprise Pvt. Ltd.

D'Andrade. Roy G. 1992. Schemas and Motivation. *In* Human Motives and Cultural Models. R. D'Andrade and C. Strauss, eds. Pp. 23–44. Cambridge: Cambridge University Press.

Dumont, Louis. 1980. Homo Hierarchicus: The Caste System and Its Implications. Complete Revised English Edition. Chicago: University of Chicago Press.

Ewing, Katherine. 1990. The Illusion of Wholeness: Culture, Self, and the Experience of Inconsistency. Ethos 18(3):251–278.

Fanon, Frantz. 1967. Black Skin, White Masks. New York: Grove Weidenfeld.

Fuller, C. J. 1992. The Camphor Flame. Popular Hinduism and Society in India. Princeton: Princeton University Press.

Hodgson, Brian. The Hodgson Collection. India Office Library, London. Manuscripts written by Hodgson while British Resident in Nepal, 1822–1844.

Höfer, András. 1979. The Caste Hierarchy and the State in Nepal: A Study of the Muluki Ain of 1854. Innsbruck: Universitätsverlag Wagner.

Holland, Dorothy, and Debra Skinner. 1995. Contested Ritual, Contested Femininities: (Re)forming Self and Society in a Nepali Women's Festival. American Ethnologist 22(2):279–305.

Holmberg, David H. 1989. Order in Paradox: Myth, Ritual, and Exchange among Nepal's Tamang. Ithaca, NY: Cornell University Press.

Jameson, Fredric. 1981. The Political Unconscious. Ithaca, NY: Cornell University Press.

Khare, R. S. 1984. The Untouchable as Himself: Ideology, Identity and Pragmatism among the Lucknow Chamars. Cambridge: Cambridge University Press.

Levy, Robert I. 1990. Mesocosm. Berkeley: University of California Press.

Lynch, Owen. 1969. The Politics of Untouchability: Social Mobility and Social Change in a City of India. New York: Columbia University Press.

Marriott, McKim. 1976. Hindu Transactions: Diversity without Dualism. *In* Transaction and Meaning. B. Kapferer, ed. Pp. 109–142. Philadelphia: Institute for the Study of Human Issues.

———. 1989. Constructing an Indian Ethnosociology. Contributions to Indian Sociology (n.s.) 23(1):1–39.

Narayan, Kirin. 1989. Storytellers, Saints, and Scoundrels. Philadelphia: University of Pennsylvania Press.

Ortner, Sherry. 1989. High Religion: A Cultural and Political History of Sherpa Buddhism. Princeton: Princeton University Press.

Parish, Steven. 1994. Moral Knowing in a Hindu Sacred City. New York: Columbia University Press.

———. 1996. Hierarchy and Its Discontents: Culture and the Politics of Consciousness in Caste Society. Philadelphia: University of Pennsylvania Press.

Riesman, Paul. 1983. On the Irrelevance of Child Rearing Practices for the Formation of Personality: An Analysis of Childhood, Personality, and Values in Two African Communities. Culture, Medicine, and Psychiatry 7(2):103–29.

Rosser, Colin. 1978. Social Mobility in the Newar Caste System. *In* Caste and Kin in Nepal, India, and Ceylon. C. von Fürer-Haimendorf, ed. New Delhi: Sterling.

Sartre, Jean-Paul. 1963 [1952]. Saint Genet: Actor and Martyr. New York: Pantheon Books.

Sharma, Prayag Raj. 1977. Caste, Social Mobility and Sanskritization: A Study of Nepal's Old Legal Code. Kailash 5(4):277–279.

Shweder, Richard, and Nancy Much. 1987. Determinations of Meaning: Discourse and Moral Socialization. *In* Moral Development Through Social Interaction. W. M. Kurtines and J. L. Gewirtz, eds. Pp. 19–39. New York: Wiley.

Strauss, Claudia. 1992. What Makes Tony Run? Schemas as Motives Reconsidered. *In* Human Motives and Cultural Models. Roy D'Andrade and Claudia Strauss, eds. Pp. 197–224. Cambridge: Cambridge University Press.

Toffin, Gérard. 1978. Intercaste Relations in a Newar Community. *In* Himalayan Anthropology. J. Fisher, ed. Pp. 461–481. The Hague: Mouton Publishers.

Chapter 4 _____

Contested Selves, Contested Femininities: Selves and Society in Process

Debra Skinner and Dorothy Holland

I n Naudada, a mixed-caste hill community in central Nepal, Kamala,[1] a thirteen-year-old girl, composed a song entitled "Tyranny Over Women" for the 1992 Tij festival. Her verses demanded that women be given equal access to education and jobs, and the recognition that they were as capable as men of performing significant feats. Kamala sang with her female friends and relatives:

> Listen sisters, listen society,
> Today I am going to speak about tyranny over women.
> The male and female born from the same womb,
> Do not have equal rights.
> The son gets the ancestral property at the age of fourteen,
> Whereas the daughter has to get married when she is only twelve.
> Parents engage in great trickery,
> Sending their daughter weeping to her husband's house.
> Parents send the son to school,
> Whereas they are afraid to provide education to the daughter.
> Father bought books and pens for my younger brother,
> Whereas he wove a basket [for carrying loads] for me, the daughter.

My name is Kamala, who has studied only to the eighth grade,
But who has a great desire for further education.
Parents, don't take me out of school,
See if I can study well or not.
Parents, if you provide me an education, I won't fail,
And after study, I can live by myself.
Parents, provide me an education at any cost,
And later when I hold a job, I will repay you.
We women are also energetic and want justice,
We also have the right to hold a job.
A red ribbon tied around black hair,
We women are always deprived in Nepal.
Women have even climbed Mt. Everest and reached the moon,
Women have done so many things in this world.
Women of other countries are pilots,
We Nepalese women will be happy if we get the chance to be great women.
Therefore, women of Nepal, this is not the time to be silent,
Let's fight to obtain our rights.

Kamala expressed in interviews and in this Tij song anger and resentment over the differential treatment of sons and daughters in her social world, and criticized the patriarchal system of inheritance and gender relations that fashioned inequalities between males and females. Moreover, she went beyond the lived world of her primary experience to envision another world in which education would help her circumvent the gender restrictions she faced in Naudada, a world in which women would be allowed to accomplish great deeds and be the equals of men. In her verses, she imagined not only an alternative social world, but identified herself in this world. As we came to learn during our fieldwork in Naudada, Kamala envisioned herself and was fashioning herself, both in song and in daily life, as an educated woman and a politically aware person.

Our aim in this chapter is to examine the co-developmental process whereby Kamala and other girls in Naudada (re)produced gendered identities, and in so doing, made and remade the cultural worlds in which these identities had meaning. Over the last thirteen years, Skinner has followed a group of thirty Naudadan girls and boys who, in 1985, ranged in age from eight to eighteen. In 1985–86, she met almost daily with these children, talking with them about events in their lives (and hers). She recorded their narratives, songs, poems, and life stories, and participated in their activities in home, school, community, and ritual contexts. Since that time, she has periodically visited these children (now older adolescents and young adults) as they have moved beyond Naudada for marriage, employment, and/or further education. Holland joined Skinner in Naudada specifically to study the Tij festival as an important site where girls and women produced understandings of gendered identities and cultural worlds. Through our past dialogues and in more recent encounters with these individuals, we have gained some idea of the processes whereby and the contexts or sites in which they have constructed self-understandings and come to inhabit creative cultural worlds that position and define them in various ways.

Children have often been portrayed in studies of socialization as passive recipients of a cultural code handed down from older generations. Our longitudinal research with the children and adolescents of Naudada indicates, in contrast, that they were actively engaged in the task of making sense of themselves in a changing social and political world and in heteroglossic or multi-voiced sites and activities. Their identities, which we define here as self-understandings to which they were emotionally attached, emerged through their engagement with cultural genres (such as songs), local relations, sociohistorical events, political discourses, and other discursive practices around them.[2] Children's understandings of themselves were certainly shaped and constrained by these discourses and practices, yet they were not determined by them. Because of the multi-voiced and open-ended nature of situations and practices, because meanings are contested, and because of people's agency,[3] the outcomes of any activity are often improvised and not entirely predictable.[4] Children in Naudada—as recreators of cultural knowledge and practices through the course of their development—worked to produce understandings of themselves and others in specific sites, and co-produced with others the worlds in which these identities were relevant. Their recreations in changing sociohistorical contexts are one way in which subjectivities change and altered cultural worlds can come into being. This focus on children's development in time and place directs our attention to persons-in-history and history-in-persons. From this perspective, a child becomes "a historical point for union of ideas with material conditions" (Toulmin 1978:56), that is, they are formed in, yet makers of history. We now turn to Naudada to explore Naudadan girls' constructions of gendered identities and cultural worlds.

Growing Up Female in Naudada of the 1980s and 1990s

Naudada is our pseudonym for a subdistrict unit in central Nepal, which lies some 120 kilometers west of Kathmandu. In the ethnographic terminology used for Nepal, Naudada is a mixed-caste, predominantly Hindu area. "Mixed caste" distinguishes it in the literature from those areas where one of Nepal's many ethnic groups (e.g., Sherpa, Tamang, Gurung, Magar) predominates. "Hindu" signals the importance of caste and Hinduism in the everyday lives of the people of the area.

In local talk and practice, the people of Naudada divided themselves into a number of caste/ethnic groups (*jāt*): Bahun and Chetri—the two highest or "big" (*ṭhulo*) castes, which together constituted a slight majority of the population; Newar and Magar—ethnic groups fitted into the middle of the caste hierarchy; and the lower or "small" caste (*sāno jāt*) groups including Damai, Sunar, Kami, and Sarki. This latter group was also labeled "untouchable." The groupings varied in significance and in their implications for the day-to-day lives of

Naudadans from one context to the next (e.g., from home to tea shop to school). They were variously reflected upon in some situations and seemingly taken for granted in others.

The daily activities of Naudadans, especially the women, revolved around agricultural work. Most families were subsisting by farming and raising livestock. A few people held salaried or wage jobs located in or near Naudada, and some worked outside the area, coming home weekly or even less often. At the time of our research, women could legally inherit land, but only under rare circumstances. In Naudada, women who had lost the support of their husband and his family seldom had property of their own. They had difficulty surviving.[5]

Because of the practices of exogamy and patrilocality, women expected upon marriage to leave their natal homes to live with a husband who lived several hours or even days away. Marriage, as girls and women described it in songs and in talk, meant being sent to a household where one was a stranger and being placed in a lowly social position, vulnerable to the whims of many, possibly without emotional support, expected to work from predawn to late at night, and threatened by the potential of having an abusive husband or one who would bring in a co-wife.

In the interval between the 1990 pro-democracy movement (the People's Movement) in Nepal that overthrew the one-party Panchayat government and the 1991 elections that brought about the current multi-party system, a remarkable incident took place in Naudada. Before the elections, girls and women from one of the eastern hamlets (*gaon*) began a procession toward Tarara Gaon, the administrative and social center of the community and a place renown for its teashops where some of the Naudadan men gathered to drink and gamble. Along the way, females from other gaons joined them and together they marched, shouting their demands: "Men, stop your drinking and gambling. Let women inherit property. Give women equal rights. Don't marry your daughters so young."

This case was remarkable for Naudadan females', both young and old, banding together to voice demands at odds with patriarchal principles and power. At that time, it was an unusual, if not unprecedented, event for this area of Nepal.[6] The literature to that date on Hindu high-caste women in Nepal (e.g., Bennett 1983; Gray 1982; Kondos 1982, 1991) had not led us to understand how a group of women could be rapidly transformed into angry active protesters, openly questioning their treatment as women. Until quite recently, most of the anthropological literature on women in Nepal and India emphasized the Brahmanical[7] view of "the Hindu woman," or described them as subjects of patriarchal practices that relegated them to relatively powerless positions vis-à-vis men.[8] Although this literature provides a crucial cultural view, portraits of females and female lives that are derived from religious texts or other dominant discourses can lead to a conceptual dilemma that traps persons permanently, either in an unchanging, ahistorical "culture" or in "subject positions" or some combination thereof.[9] Without accounts of daily lives, with all their ambiguities, struggles, and improvised responses, we lose sight of people's agency—the ways in which individuals and collectives, however constrained by material and social conditions and however cast in discursive and practical genres, nonetheless remake themselves, these conditions, and genres (Holland et al. in press). By taking into account how girls recreate gendered identities in their daily lives, we can see one way in which rapid transformations, such as the women's march on Tarara Gaon, can arise.

Good Selves and the Expected Life Path

In word and action, the Naudadan girls in our study often tried to approximate the ideal Hindu woman, one who follows the ideal life path as set out in Brahmanical writings and teachings. In their self-descriptions, the girls frequently talked about themselves as good workers, good girls, and obedient, honorable daughters. When asked to describe or to tell about themselves, most girls recited the good habits they had and the bad ones they avoided. Parbati, a Damai girl, described herself in this way:

> I am a very good girl. I don't fool around with others...I am very good...I don't speak that much also. I will say, *"Namaskār, didi"* ("Greetings, older sister") on the spot when I meet you. I am like that. I am very good. I don't even like to fool around much. In my being, I am very good. I do my own work by myself.

These self-descriptions did not vary much by caste or socioeconomic status. Maiya, an eleven-year-old Chetri girl, described herself, saying: "I am a good, nice girl. I don't get mad at anyone. I don't fight. I don't steal...I don't deceive anyone and don't lie."

The girls' responses had a certain rehearsed quality. They were recitations that varied little in content or format. These self-descriptions suggest that the girls were learning to speak of themselves in relation to the culturally constructed world of women's lives, a world figured by the Brahmanical cultural model of the life path of the "good woman." This dominant ideology of gender identities, roles, and relationships has been described extensively (e.g., Bennett 1976, 1983; Caplan 1985; Das 1979; Stone 1978; Skinner 1989, 1990). In Naudada, as in other areas of Hindu Nepal and India, the model presumes that, except in cases where bad luck befalls or the woman has bad morals, a woman's life will follow a particular trajectory. In the culturally constructed world organized around this life path, the woman's roles are family-centered and the favored characteristics are those that support the patriarchal family. During the first stage of life, a girl is a daughter and sister. She grows up, surrounded by relatives who urge her to cultivate the habits that will mark her as a good daughter, wife, and daughter-in-law. Through their teachings and scoldings, she learns to work hard in the fields and home; behave obediently and respectfully to elders; and comport herself as shy, gentle, and virtuous. The prototypical female is married soon after she reaches puberty. With marriage, she becomes a daughter-in-law and wife, and eventually a mother. She is hard-working, faithful, and devoted to her husband; obedient and helpful to her mother-in-law; and a respectable and honorable woman about the community. With the birth of children, especially sons, she acquires what some have described as the central or prototypical identity of Hindu women: that of childbearer or mother (Stone 1978). A woman who has sons has proven herself to be a good woman with a good fate. Finally as a mother-in-law—a position that is accorded higher status than other female roles in the family—she can direct and control the lives of her daughters-in-law. Ideally a woman never becomes a widow. A good and virtuous woman, through ritual observance and daily practice, ensures the health and long life of her husband and will die before him (Bennett 1983; Caplan 1985).

In daily life and in rituals experienced in childhood and beyond, Naudadan girls encountered a variety of messages about this cultural construction of women's lives, and they were evaluated against this ideal female and her life course. In the taken-for-granted world presumed by the model, women who deviated from the life path of the "good woman" were aberrant and problematic. Those who withheld their labor from domestic and agricultural chores, who talked about their husbands' shortcomings, who committed adultery, who contradicted their mothers-in-law, who did not give birth to sons, and who were widowed, were suspect. Good women labored for the benefit of their households. Good women never talked unnecessarily or wandered about to malinger or flirt.

Women who deviated from the life path did so because they were intrinsically immoral or the victims of bad luck. A woman who did not have children, for example, was presumed to be barren, and her condition was attributed to her sins in a past life. Her supposed inability to bear children was seen as a punishment for these misdeeds. Widows, too, had fallen off the expected life path. They had the bad fate to outlive their husbands. Widows were to be pitied, but they were sometimes feared as witches.

Talk about "bad" or "sinful" women was part of daily conversation, a great deal of which included evaluations of self and others in relation to these dominant cultural constructions. For example, Devi, a Chetri woman in her late twenties, often talked with Skinner about different women they both knew. Devi explained that one woman was a *nāthi* (a flirt or a woman who goes with men other than her husband). Another woman was a *pāpini* (female sinner) because she did not feed her grandchildren while her daughter-in-law was working long days in the fields. Devi thought one of her neighbors was a bad woman (*narāmro āimāi*) because she was very jealous of others and mistreated her father who lived in her household. The negative types that commonly figured in such conversations—the *boksi* (witch), *rādi* (widow), *aputri* (barren woman), *alacchini* (a female who brings bad luck to her household), *sāṛhe āimāi* (a woman who acts masculine, like a "bull")—were all characters who had gone awry in this culturally constructed world of good women's lives.

These evaluative terms for females indexed a moral universe and acted as a mediating device or cultural tool for identity formation (see Holland and Valsiner 1988; Skinner 1989, 1990). Naudadan girls developed understandings of these gender-related terms and the discourse of evaluation in specific sites and activities such as everyday events of gossiping and scolding; and they used these terms as a means of evaluating and identifying themselves and others as particular kinds of actors in the social life of Naudada. They scrutinized their own and other females' behavior through the lens of this moral discourse. They came to describe themselves in ways that defined them as good daughters or good women, and they attempted to avoid or dispute the negative labels.

Use of these terms began very early, especially in the cases where the words were hurled as insults. Even children of four or five knew that rādi (widow, with connotations of "loose woman," "prostitute") was not a good word, yet it was one of the most common insults used for any female regardless of her age (and *rādiko chorā*, or widow's son, was often used as a term of abuse for males). It was employed frequently in scolding and cursing. However, while the younger girls knew only that a rādi was a bad thing to be called, the older girls of eight or so knew why a rādi was bad. They knew that a rādi was a woman who deviated from the life path of a good woman. Likewise, from scoldings the younger girls knew only the behaviors they were supposed to avoid, whereas the older girls had acquired a broader understanding of the proper comportment of daughters in relation to the life path. The older girls also talked frequently about their future lives as daughters-in-law and wives and knew the restrictions they would be expected to observe and the characteristics that they would be expected to exhibit as they carried out these roles.

This moral discourse censured and divided females. Aruna, a Damai adolescent of fourteen, related that anyone, even a close girlfriend, would say a girl is bad if she went to a boy's house. Kapila, a fourteen-year-old Chetri, complained that she could not show her anger because others would say, "How angry that daughter seems to be." Tika, a Damai of fifteen, offered a description of herself as being of a "straight line."[10] She talked about a woman who had run away with her husband's brother, saying, "It is better to take a straight line than to do such a scandalous thing. A good wife stays with her husband; a bad one leaves and goes with another." Kapila, discussing the same event, said that others in Naudada were saying that this woman was a *kukurni* (female dog) and had spoiled the *ijjat* (prestige/honor) of her family. In contrast to this woman, Kapila described what a good wife and daughter-in-law should be like:

> a good wife never criticizes her husband and she never complains about her husband to other people. A good daughter-in-law always gets up early in the morning and she does all the work she has to and obeys her mother-in-law. She obeys her husband. She does not run away to her natal home. She never steals to eat, and she does not steal corn which grows in another's field. Daughters-in-law are not good if they do not obey their mothers-in-law or if they move about here and there. They do whatever they like. They steal and they spend their time at others' houses. They go to festivals sometimes.

From these evaluations and the "identity claims" made by Parbati and Maiya, it appears that these girls not only knew the expected life path and the behaviors that counted as those of a good daughter, but also embraced these concepts and behaviors as ways to define themselves. They, as well as the others, presented themselves in terms of the culturally constructed world of women's lives and, indeed, seemed to pride themselves on being good girls and daughters, and future good wives and daughters-in-law. They cared about what other people thought of them, and they did not wish to dishonor their families. They hoped to avoid negative evaluations, and so tried to avoid behaviors that would categorize them as a bad type. By striving to enact good behavior, they embraced the locally valued identities; by self-censoring bad behavior, they "backed into" these same identities.

Angry Selves and Contested Views

As we have portrayed them so far and as they often portrayed themselves to us, Naudada girls appear simply to be absorbing the dominant gender ideology. The reproduction in Naudada of the dominant model of gender relations seems assured. From the censuring comments of the girls, one might assume they accepted the "ideal" life path and the roles it held for them as daughters-in-law and wives, or if not accepting, at least acquiescing to their fate and complying with the dominant ideology.[11] This picture of the girls' self-understanding becomes more complex and nuanced, however, when we consider other things that the girls said and did. Although the girls laid claim, in interviews, discussions, and arguments with others, to being good girls and good daughters, and said that if they married they would try to be good daughters-in-law and wives, they also questioned the expected life path, were critical of the unequal treatment of males and females, expressed anger and sadness about the way they were treated because they were female, and schemed to avoid marriage. Consider the following:

Maiya, like many of the other girls, compared her life to that of her brothers. In response to the question, "Are you happy to be a girl?" Maiya replied that she would rather be a boy because "sons don't have to work hard. Girls have to carry water and cut grass, while the sons can just sit and eat." Sunita, a ten-year-old Bahun, described to Skinner how she had argued with her parents against the idea that boys, but not girls, should go to school. She told her parents, "You are sending boys [to school], why not send girls?" Tika also complained: "If I were a son, I would have been allowed to study. Since I am a daughter, I did not get to study."

In another conversation, Skinner asked Maiya what she thought about the future. She replied:

> In the future, now when I see others get married and have fights in their new home, um...why do we give daughters to other's house? These thoughts play in my mind. I think about it...If I am not able to study and unable to work, if I am not treated well after I am married in my new house—when I think that this may happen to me in the future, I fear it and am very worried.

What emerged from Naudadan girls' narrative accounts and actions were images, understandings, and feelings about themselves that varied within and across contexts. The ways girls talked about themselves and their lives, and the ways they presented and represented themselves were not consistent.[12] Sometimes girls and adult women identified with culturally dominant notions of what the proper Hindu woman should be. They portrayed themselves in terms of this ideal woman who accepts her submissive and relatively powerless role vis-à-vis men. But they also expressed a sense of sadness, anger, and resentment about their expected roles as females. They gave extensive reflective and critical commentaries, both in discourse and in song, concerning their status. They denounced the treatment females received at the hands of some males (and sometimes other females such as mothers-in-law) and lamented their unequal positions in society. Girls were at times critical of the dominant gender ideology; they sometimes rejected it, or tried to find acceptable alternatives to the expected life path. All but two of the girls Skinner interviewed stated emphatically that they did not want to get married, and a number of them had plans—usually involving going to school and becoming a teacher or office worker—for avoiding, or at least postponing, marriage (Skinner 1990).

The girls had been encouraged more or less daily by their parents and others to develop a sense of themselves as engaged with the taken-for-granted life path and to see themselves as accountable in that culturally constructed world. They had clearly developed such an identification, but they also retained a definite sense of injustice and unfairness. They voiced their discontent with the treatment they received because of the social position afforded females, and they recounted situations in which they were shamed, hurt, or angered. While developing an understanding of the meanings underlying the Brahmanical cultural model of women's lives, the Naudadan girls were also developing a sense of the hardships (*dukha*) associated with carrying out the actions required of them in this cultural world. If we look closely at the girls' reactions to specific contexts where productions of knowledge and practices related to gender were taking place, we can better understand how they arrived at the point where they both embraced and rejected the expected life path for females.

Contexts of Learning

Practice and production theories in anthropology focus attention on the processes and sites in which knowledge, identities, power relations, and so forth are (re)created by individuals or groups. They turn our attention to agency and action, to the constitution of social formations in historical circumstances, and to the making and remaking of cultural conventions in contestations of power and privilege.[13] Unlike earlier cultural accounts, these theories do not view persons as passive receptors or transmitters of cultural meanings and relationships, nor unlike some more recent accounts do they view persons as subjects positioned and trapped within webs of discourse. They are viewed instead as partially constrained by, but actively (re)producing cultural meanings and social structures with others in the context of specific activities.

In Naudada, there were a number of activities in which gender-marked terms and gender-specific rules were expressed: scoldings that children heard, received, or gave; gossip sessions that they overheard and sometimes contributed to; exchanges of complaints and worries about one's life, often in the form of dukha stories (stories of hardship and suffering); domestic scenes in which girls observed and heard women's problems; the telling of their worries for the future; the singing of songs about women's lives; and the conduct of rituals that marked girls' transition from one status to another. Most of these activities—scolding, gossiping, telling dukha stories, sharing worries with friends, and singing (both alone and with friends)— were fairly common, if not daily activities. These activities, more than the less frequent rituals, were what the girls talked about in our conversations.[14] We have already alluded to some of these activities—scolding and domestic scenes. Here we will emphasize girls' reactions to these activities and relate them to a third site of the production of gendered identities, the Tij festival.

Scolding Activities and Domestic Scenes

Scolding and cursing others were ubiquitous, everyday activities in Naudada. Children were the frequent targets of scoldings for transgressions and problems that they caused their parents, other adults, and one another. The general form of such scolding was to begin with an insult. "Rādi"—one term for "widow," as mentioned above, was a common insult to hurl at any female, even a toddler. "Nāthi"—"loose woman," was another. "Rādi," the scolder would scream. Then the girl would be told the rules that she had violated. Aruna said her mother always scolded her, saying "rādi" when she did not do her work. Kapila related that mothers sometimes called their daughters "nāthi," scolding them, saying, "Don't walk with boys this way." Maiya explained how she felt when she was scolded: "I feel very sad...when my father and mother scold me when I am not doing any work, and get angry with me, when they say something and scold, I feel very sad and unhappy. I feel sad when they scold my friends."[15]

Girls heard mothers-in-law and husbands call the daughters-in-law and wives rādi for a variety of perceived offenses. Often the girls themselves were the targets of scoldings in which rādi was hurled at them as an insult and epithet. As already mentioned, over time they learned the meaning of the term and came to know that a rādi was a deviant type, one who had left the proper life path and failed to be a good woman, but beyond the semantics of the term and a grasp of the cultural world in which the term made sense, the girls also retained embodied, personal senses of the word that were more contextualized. The term *rādi* also, at times, evoked memories of situations in which they had been scolded unjustly by parents, humiliated by boys, or saddened and angered by the taunts and insults of strangers.

In addition to scolding activities, girls witnessed scenes from everyday life that involved gender and kin relations. They were admonished as they worked and went about their household and agricultural chores to be good, obedient, hardworking, and honorable. But, at the same time, as daughters in the natal home, they were noticing differences in treatment. They were given fewer rights and privileges than their brothers; they saw their brothers getting more and better food and clothes, and they often had to work in the fields while their brothers went to school. They were teased by their parents and others about being married off "beyond nine mountains" while the sons, they knew, had the opportunity to stay at home. They observed cases in which parents were in such a rush to marry off their daughter that they chose a bad match for her with a man who would cause her many problems. In Naudada, they saw that the incoming daughter-in-law was expected to work long days without complaint at arduous tasks while the mother-in-law sat by idle or went out of the way to scold her.

They heard daily the expectations for wives: be respectful, virtuous, and diligent in household and agricultural tasks. The reward for all this servitude and hard work was supposed to be the husband's affection and support for the wife and her children and increasing status in the household as she herself gave birth to sons and became a mother-in-law. But girls observed and heard of numerous cases in the community in which women were abused or forsaken by their husbands. Marriage was an uncertain fate. A woman's husband might turn out to be a drunkard who would beat her and lose the family property through drinking and gambling. If the wife scolded him, there was the threat that he might bring in a co-wife who would not only take away his affection, but also scarce resources.

Devi often told her life story to many of the Naudadan girls. Devi's husband once had a good job with a local development agency. He owned quite a bit of land, a house, and other wealth. But he drank the locally brewed liquor to excess and gambled away all of the money and property. He not only sold his wife's gold jewelry, but her kitchen pots and pans as well. He would drink until late at night, then come home and beat Devi. Finally he deserted her and their five children and has not been seen or heard from in years. Even with his long absence, Devi continued to tell her story, recounting to listening girls the times she would hide with a baby at her breast in the terraces until her husband fell asleep.

Certainly abusive treatment to this degree was not the norm in Naudada; there were many married couples whose interactions were congenial, who provided happier models of marriage and kin relations. Still girls heard about and witnessed enough problematic scenes to make them worry that their own future might include similar hardships.

In the activities of scolding and the performance of daily domestic scenes, we see not only a potential source of the semantic meanings that the girls were appropriating to talk about their own and other women's behaviors in Naudada, but also a potential source of their embodied *sense* of the treatment they received as women. On the one hand, they were developing an understanding of themselves as participants in a culturally constructed world organized around the life trajectory of a "good woman." They were developing the disciplines and characteristics that could earn them praise for being good daughters—disciplines and characteristics that seemed to stand outside of history, outside of time, and in isolation from caste or other local social groupings in Naudada. On the other hand, they recounted to themselves and others vivid memories of abrupt encounters with these expectations—memories of the particular people who scolded them, of their feelings of shame and anger, of bodily sensations associated with their sense of having been unjustly accused. Where their parents were involved, they retained the question their parents' treatment had evoked at the time: "Why am I expected to do all of this work and my brother is not?" Thus, subsequent reminders could evoke, for them, both the conventional cultural meanings as well as a sense of personal injustice, anger, and other emotions that are not accounted for in the culturally constructed world of the good woman.

In the domestic scenes in which they were participants and observers, the girls were directed by everyday exhortations and evaluations of women to accept their roles and to strive to obtain the favor of kin in both the natal and husband's home, but their experiences and observations provided them with images of the difficulties and pain possibly awaiting them as they embarked on this life path. The culturally expected life path gave females one means of envisioning their lives, but it did not address all the ways that they thought and felt about their positions as female.

These contextualized senses of being female, we argue below, were cultivated by and fueled a form of critical commentary that was produced and passed on by groups of females, mostly adolescent girls. This commentary, in turn, suggested alternative femininities and alternate worlds to the hegemonic one of the ideal life path. It is to this third site, the annual Tij festival, that we now turn.

Songs and Activities of the Tij Festival

Tij is part of a larger ritual complex called Tij-Rishi Pancami during which women fast, do *pūjā* (worship), and ritually bathe to protect their husbands' health and life and to purify themselves from sins connected with menstruation. Bennett (1983) has described in detail the rituals and symbolism of this festival, but what interests us here is not the ritual complex so much as the content and contexts of the songs that the girls and young women compose and perform for the Tij festival.[16]

Tij songs are a genre of song that gives voice to girls' and women's critical commentary, extending their thoughts and experiences of hardships from intimate conversations to a public setting where hundreds of people gather to listen to their singing. In Naudada, females identify and perform two main types of Tij songs: the dukha song and the *rājnīti* (political) song. An example of a dukha Tij song composed and performed by Naudadan girls in 1991 follows:

> Daughter: I rose in the morning to pick flowers,
> But did not pick them because they were covered with dew.
> Parents just keep the daughters to do work at home,
> But even a small piece of the courtyard [i.e., land] is not given [to daughters].

Parents: The small piece of courtyard is needed to dry the paddy,
          Go, daughter, to your husband's house to get your property.

Daughter: We have to go empty-handed [to our husband's home],
          The brothers fence in their property.
          Brothers' clothes are so many that they rot away in a box,
          But when they have to give us a single cloth, tears come in their
          eyes.[17]

These verses express a daughter's resentment that she has no rights to inherit property. She complains that she labors diligently each day, but sees her brothers receive good clothes and property while she gets nothing. She questions the patriarchal system of inheritance and legal codes that relegate her to an unequal position vis-à-vis men.

We have collected and analyzed literally hundreds of Tij songs: their lyrics, the nature of their production, and the contexts of their performance (Holland and Skinner 1995a; Holland and Skinner 1995b; Skinner et al. 1994). We found that Tij lyrics provided an interpretation of females' hardships and problems. Dukha songs express girls' fears of marriage and the treatment they may receive at the hands of their future husband and in-laws, their criticism of their parents for marrying them far away or into a poor or bad family, and their feelings toward the mother-in-law or husband who mistreats them. Peopled by unkind and sometimes abusive, (unnamed) husbands, mothers-in-law, fathers, and co-wives, the dukha songs portrayed—poignantly, if we may judge by the tears of listeners on the day of Tij—the unhappy situations of their female protagonists. But the songs went beyond affecting portrayals of the suffering of individual women. They usually implied that the protagonists deserved a better lot in life; and they often included a more general social and political analysis to the effect that women were unfairly underprivileged. The songs stated and criticized differences in the treatment and rights afforded sons versus daughters and husbands versus wives. They opposed the gender privilege instituted in Nepal's legal code, carried out in social practice, and interpreted through religious texts and teachings. They criticized women's limited rights to inherit land, women's lesser access to education, and their constant vulnerability to the division of their husband's resources and affections with a co-wife.

We found that these dukha songs were usually jointly composed by the *didi/ bahini* (those girls and young women who were related as sisters or cousins) of the gaon or hamlet where they lived. To compose these songs, they drew upon their sense of anger, sadness, and resentment engendered in contexts in which they were held accountable by the dominant cultural model of the "good woman." They told us these feelings were stored in and came forth from their *man* (heart/ mind, seat of emotions). Renu, a young woman who had experienced a bad marriage and was now living in her natal home, often composed and performed dukha songs with her didi/bahinīs. She told us she "placed" and "stored up" thoughts and feelings in her *man* where they "churned about" and "poured forth" in the verses of Tij songs. She also told us that once she composed these songs, she kept them in her *man* and often sang them to herself, even after the time of Tij had passed.

In producing Tij songs, these Naudadan girls were envisioning a femininity counter to the Brahmanical one. Their dukha songs were oriented to the world of household relations, of local social relations with husbands, mothers-in-law, and co-wives.[18] They provided a critical commentary on these family relations and a protest against the system that relegated them to the least powerful positions. As girls were producing this alternative view of women, externalizing their more privately spoken thoughts and feelings in a cultural medium available to a broader audience, they were also producing alternative ways of envisioning themselves in the lived world of family and domestic relations. As for Renu, Tij songs were an important means used by girls and young women to organize and express their thoughts and feelings about their lives, not just at Tij, but the year round (Skinner 1989, 1990).

These songs were also important forms whereby girls developed agency. Through these songs, girls developed a particular consciousness of themselves in the world of domestic relations as construed in Naudada. They became, through the medium of Tij songs, critical commentators on their lives in families and their various roles as daughters, sisters, daughters-in-law, and wives. For many of those who became engaged with the women's Tij groups and with composing and singing the songs, the role of commentator was salient. Over the course of our research (Skinner first watched Tij sessions in Naudada in 1986), we watched young girls in households that participated in Tij hover on the periphery of the practice sessions and gradually start to take on a larger role. Over the years they became proficient in producing critical commentaries, and they, inferring from their descriptions of their concerns and choices in life, developed identities or self-understandings informed by this critical stance on women's positions within the family (see Holland and Skinner 1995a; Skinner 1990). As the cycle of song production continued, these girls not only developed expertise and cultural knowledge about the domestic worlds in which they participated as daughters, sisters, and, eventually, young wives, but also developed a critical sense of themselves as participants symbolized through Tij songs.

The 1990 People's Movement

The picture of gender production becomes more complex than this, however. As we observed Tij in 1990 and 1991, we began to see another counter-hegemonic femininity being produced in the site of Tij and in other arenas as well,[19] one that was in contest with not only the Brahmanical view, but also the view expressed by dukha songs.

The 1990 People's Movement affected many arenas of life in Nepal. After the movement's success, King Birendra relinquished some of his powers under the new constitution. Nepal's government was transformed from an absolute monarchy to a constitutional monarchy, and political parties became legal and gained strength. This new era ushered in a feeling of freedom and a call for human rights. Beginning in 1990 after the revolution, and especially in 1991 after the establishment of the multi-party system and general elections, political Tij songs became much more widely sung by women in Naudada and throughout Nepal.

These political, or rājnīti, songs were significant in producing, on the individual level, a different kind of identity and agency than that associated with dukha songs, and, on the collective level, an orientation to the world of party politics. Dukha songs provided commentary on domestic relations; rājnīti songs provided commentary on the government's treatment of women. What we saw in the Tij festival of 1991, the year after the uprising, was a burgeoning of songs that criticized the former Panchayat government as well as the Nepali Congress Party (the party that was victorious in winning a majority of positions in the new government) for their treatment of women.[20]

Although the groups of girls and young women who sang together during Tij were the same in 1991 as in years before, we found a different set of participants stepping forward to write the rājnīti songs. Kamala, the girl who composed the song at the beginning of this chapter, provides an example. At the time of our in-depth study of Tij in 1991, Kamala was a student in the eighth grade. In her statements and actions, she revealed a strong sense of herself as a student, and was clearly developing, as were many of her sister students, a view of herself as a politically active person. She was recognized as an expert at song composition, but her songs were oriented to a different field of action than were the dukha songs, largely composed by the less educated girls of Naudada's gaons. Kamala composed political Tij songs that were critical of regional and national politics and that called for equal rights before the law and in government policy for women and the poor.[21] In a rājnīti song produced and performed by Kamala and her Tij song group, we find verses that condemn the old political system for exploiting women and call for a new political party that will give women equal rights under the law[22]:

Oh, dominated sisters of Nepal,
We have so much tyranny.
The *pancha*s (officials of the former one-party panchayat system) ate the flesh
    and also the blood [of the people],
At last we have the multi-party system.
The thirty year Panchayat reign gave so much trouble to women,
They [the panchas] drank liquor by selling unmarried girls.
They sold our innocent sisters,
And filled their bellies with liquor and chicken.
For even a small thing, they call a meeting [to get money],
Panchas took bribes, their reign is like this.
The administration [panchas] was like this,
The panchas dominated women.
Now this type of rule cannot be tolerated.

Women will no longer tolerate what they did in the past.
 Understanding these things, we moved forward,
We fought in the people's movement.
Rise up, women, now we don't have to fear,
Clapping cannot be done by a single hand.
On the day of Baishak 29, 2048,
There will be a general election.
There are so many parties in the multi-party system,
At last we need the party which benefits us.
A party called the Democratic Party was established,
It deleted the name Panchayat and deceived the people.
If this party wins, it will be the same as before,
Women will not have rights and they will have to weep all of their life.
There is a party called Congress,
If this party wins, women will have to suffer more.
There is another party called Communist,
If this party wins, women will get rights.
The symbol of communists is the sickle and hammer,
Women, let's publicize the communist symbol.
Though I want to stop my pen, it doesn't stop,
Goodbye to my respected listeners.

In this song, Kamala's group accused officials of the former Panchayat system of selling women as prostitutes to India, taking bribes, and exploiting the people. The singers assailed two political parties as abusers of women's rights, and promoted the Communist Party as the only one that would bring justice to women.

These rājnīti songs, we argue, were important in the formation of individual identity and agency, as postulated for dukha songs, but they, as had the dukha songs, also affected the Tij groups as a whole. The songs described women as actors in the world of politics who were creating a new role for women in that world. In place of the criticism of mothers-in-law and husbands found in dukha songs, these songs had to do with the political world of voting, elections, and processions. The singers were constructing ways of understanding themselves and other women as figures in a world of party politics. Young girls and women produced and incorporated political song texts as a way of conceptualizing themselves as politically aware actors and activists in a political world.[23]

Although somewhat muted in Naudada as compared with several regional centers, there was some contest over the value of the different forms of femininity presented in Tij songs and in other discourses: there were tensions and contradictions between being females in the world of domestic and gaon relations and being females in the world of school and politics, that is, between being uneducated versus educated women. Girls expressed their sense that educated women were more valued than uneducated women, and that, perhaps, the valuations were justified.

These distinctions between educated and uneducated females were emerging in Naudada and elsewhere in Nepal (Enslin, this volume; Holland and Skinner 1995a; Skinner and Holland 1996), and were being constructed in part through Tij songs. One such song, written by an uneducated young wife, included the following verses:

I gather the fodder in the early morning sun.
I educated my husband, thinking this would bring happiness.
After completing his education, the husband found a job.
He came home to take his wife with him.
[Husband to wife]: I have come here to take you with me.
How much did you study in order to go with me?
[Wife says]: I should not tell him I did not even study.
I have not studied at all.
At my *māita* since my childhood, I herded the livestock.
If I tried to write *ka*, I could just draw a stick.
[Husband to wife]: Then you stay at home which is the whole world to you.
What is the use of an uneducated wife?
[I have got] seven thousand rupees,
I'll marry another and take her with me.
[Wife to husband]: Finish my life by killing me with a knife.

Despite the uneducated girls' considerable talent in composing dukha songs, they sometimes disparaged themselves because they lacked an education. Especially for the less educated girls, the worlds of the *māita/ghar* (woman's parents' home/ woman's husband's home) and the context of school were juxtaposed in their personal histories and identities. If we may credit what they said and expressed in their songs, they strongly felt the contradictions and tensions between the two.

Uneducated girls could and did sing rājnīti songs—all the groups sang rājnīti songs at the 1991 Tij festival, but the uneducated girls and women viewed themselves as peripheral to the wider world of which those songs were emblematic. The political songs largely composed by the educated girls were oriented to a different field of action, no longer the world of local social relations with husbands, mothers-in-law, and co-wives. Their identities and the ways they talked about themselves and their plans derived more from their lives as politically conscious citizens of the country than from their lives as daughters and sisters in the gaon. For these female students, the activity of producing Tij songs was situated differently than for the other women.

Dukha songs were emblematic of growing up as a sister and daughter of the gaon. They were associated with learning the limitations of the social position ascribed to women, adjusting to the lived results of gaon exogamy, and often trying to survive—with practically no material or social support—a husband and/ or in-laws they considered abusive. For educated girls, rājnīti songs provided the more powerful associations. The songs depicted and were emblematic of the fast-moving, exciting political arena opened by recent events and of their own access to this arena through schooling.

These educated girls and young women provided the main impetus for turning the 1991 Tij festival more squarely to the venues of government and party politics. Although the uneducated girls' participation in the festival encompassed the possibility of rājnīti songs, their identities did not lie so much within the world depicted in such songs. For the schoolgirls, they did. The students were developing a different gendered identity, a different construction of being female. The Tij festival not only constituted a space for the development of alternative views of women's lives, it also constituted a place for the contest of the alternative critical voices and subjectivities developing there.

Summary and Conclusions

We have traced how Naudadan girls' participation in particular sites and activities gave rise to emotionally charged visions of and rehearsed dialogs about themselves as women. These selves were contradictory and contested, selves that Bakhtin might have called "heteroglossic" (see Bakhtin 1981, 1984).[24] Led by cultural production and practice theories to examine specific sites and activities, we noted both the meanings to which the girls were being exposed in these sites as well as the reactions that girls expressed to us and friends about incidents that they experienced in the course of these activities. Analysis of the interviews and observations suggests that the girls were developing a nuanced and varied understanding of the culturally constructed world of Hindu women's lives and an emotional attachment to identities in that world. Our analysis also suggests that the girls were, at the same time, developing an embodied personal sense of themselves as females and as recipients of unfair treatment because of their female status. Unaccounted for by the public meanings associated with the conventional life path of Hindu women, these senses of injustice and dread were of ongoing concern to the girls.

In addition to the sites of scolding and domestic scenes, we paid attention to a third site, that of the Tij festival. In this annual festival women expressed through song a critical commentary on the position of women in the domestic relations of Naudada, and, in 1991, after the country's first multi-party election for many years, on the bad treatment of women by the government. These Tij songs, especially the ones addressed to family relations, resonated with the reactions that girls were having to the scoldings that they were receiving and the domestic scenes they were witnessing. Not surprisingly, some of the girls in our study used these songs as a mediating device to express their sense of their lives.

In Naudada, in short, we see the ways in which females appropriated not just one dominant voice or perspective, but formed personal senses and different perspectives, some of which were in conflict both within a heteroglossic self and in a society that was multi-voiced. Girls' selves in this formulation were a part of a dialogic process emerging in social interactions and sites where different voices existed, and a part of dynamic, changing social formations tied to competing interests in the sociohistorical context of their emergence. In the site of Tij, we see an example where females were authoring new worlds, and in turn, new selves. Different constructions of being female and newer senses of agency were evolving along with visions of different worlds.

Notes

Portions of the material in this chapter on Tij were originally published in an article by Dorothy Holland and Debra Skinner, "The Co-development of Identity, Agency, and Lived Worlds," in *Comparisons in Human Development*, edited by Jonathan Tudge, Michael Shanahan, and Jaan Valsiner (New York: Cambridge University Press, 1996) and in a 1995 article by the same authors, "Contested Ritual, Contested Femininities," in *American Ethnologist* 22(2):279–305. These segments are reprinted with permission of the publisher. Skinner's research in 1985–86 was supported by a Fulbright grant; Holland's research in 1990 by a University Research Council grant from the University of North Carolina at Chapel Hill. Our 1991 research was supported by the National Science Foundation (BNS-9110010). We want to acknowledge our research associates in Nepal, especially G. B. Adhikari, Renu Lama, Sapana Sharma, and Maheswor Pahari, for their assistance and dialogues with us over the years. We continue to remember the people of Naudada who have been very generous and helpful to us in our different quests. Although we have tried to contribute to community projects and reciprocate their kindness to us in other ways, their gifts to us have been by far the greater.

1. Names of people and places are pseudonyms.

2. Holland et al. (in press) describe in detail their theoretical approach to the ways in which identity, agency, and cultural worlds co-develop.

3. Our view of agency is one envisioned by the cultural-historical school of psychology (see Holland et al. in press), that is, agency that is constrained and enabled by cultural forms and social interaction. This view is far afield from that underlying Western debates about the possibility of free will.

4. For a good example, see Dirks (1992).

5. See Bennett (1979) and Gilbert (1992) for accounts of women's legal rights and family law in Nepal.

6. Other incidents also occurred about this time. In another case, a group of Naudadan women brandishing sticks entered some local teashops to break the drinking glasses, bottles of *raksī* (locally brewed liquor), and equipment used to make the raksī. The third case involved a woman who was beaten by her drunken husband. A group of about fifteen women descended on him, armed with sticks, and threatened to beat him if he ever again abused his wife.

7. We use the term "Brahmanical" to refer to ideologies and practices promoted by Vedic literature and by most Bahun priests, many of which place women in less powerful and less esteemed positions vis-à-vis men. The texts and practices of the "Brahmanical" are also multi-voiced and complex, but refer to a narrower field than the more encompassing term, "Hindu."

8. For recent works which provide alternative views of South Asian women, see N. Kumar (1994); R. Kumar (1993), O'Hanlon (1992), Oldenburg (1992), and Raheja and Gold (1994).

9. A "subject position" is a view of the person that discourses and practices create, determine, and offer for the individual. Subject positions are given by the social structure, and are exhibited or inhabited by individuals (Smith 1988). In the conceptualization of "subject position," the individual's creation and understanding of his or her own position, identity, and subjectivity and how these develop in history are *not* the focus. Rather, a subject position is understood as one's "subjection" and placement within particular forms of control and discourse.

10. For an example of Tika's representation of herself in song, see Skinner et al. (1991).

11. Although most informed readers would not now assume such a view, much of the past work on child socialization or women in South Asia presented the dominant patriarchal ideology as a very powerful one, perhaps the only one. For example, in one book on Hindu women, the author (Dhruvarajan 1989) asks how in India it comes to be that "everyone develops a conviction of the legitimacy of the subordinate position accorded to women" (1989:vii). She concluded that the socialization process throughout the life cycle works well to ensure that women "silently comply" with the dominant patriarchal ideology and that women have "implicit faith in male superiority and female inferiority" (1989:98).

12. Many, of course, have noted seemingly inconsistent stances in what people say and do. See Strauss (1990) for a review of this problem in the literature and a contribution to its resolution. Our interpretations, to follow, are compatible with her position; however, we take an explicitly developmental, or as Vygotsky called it, a genetic or longitudinal, historical approach. For a psychoanalytic perspective on this problem, see Ewing (1990) and Obeyesekere (1981).

13. See, for example, Bourdieu (1977, 1990), Connell (1987), Dirks (1992), Dirks et al. (1994), Ortner (1984), the historical anthropology of Comaroff (1985) and Comaroff and Comaroff (1991), and the work of Willis (1977, 1981) and other members of the Center for Contemporary Studies. Cultural production, as Willis defines it "designates, at least in part, the creative use of discourses, meanings, materials, practices, and group processes to explore, understand, and creatively occupy particular positions in sets of general material possibilities" (1981:59).

14. There were folktales, epics, and rituals that conveyed Brahmanical concepts of women and there were ceremonies that marked girls' transitions from one status to another along the life path (see Bennett 1983; Skinner 1989, 1990). Nonetheless, as judged by the commentary they gave, the girls were more impressed by the everyday activities we have listed. In their interviews, they seldom referred to rituals per se. One important exception to the pattern of not talking much about rituals concerned Tij, a ritual event for women, that we discuss below.

15. Some Nepalis from other areas of Nepal were appalled when they heard of this scolding, saying they had never been scolded in such a way when they were children and had never even heard it in their village. They associated such scolding with poorer and lower-caste and lower-class families, and considered someone who did such scolding as

low class or less educated or as someone who had fallen away from the religious path. In Naudada, not all parents scolded their children in such a manner, but parents from all castes would employ these terms to scold their own and others' children. Some parents said they did not know how to scold, distinguishing themselves from those who did such things, but even they could be heard scolding their children in such a way when they were angry.

16. We have done extensive research both individually and jointly since 1985 on Tij songs as a form of women's critical commentary (see Holland and Skinner 1995a; Holland and Skinner 1995b; Skinner 1990; Skinner et al. 1994). Other accounts of the importance of Tij and other arenas as spaces for the production of critical commentary on South Asian women's lives are also emerging (see Enslin 1992, this volume; Raheja and Gold 1994).

17. We collected verses from and/or information about more than 1,000 songs. A sample of twenty-six songs, including this one, are both translated and transliterated in romanized Nepali in Skinner et al. (1994). The different subtypes are discussed as well.

18. The production of critical songs has existed and continues to exist within a ritual complex that by and large celebrates a compliant femininity. Two days after singing critical songs on Tij Day, the same women engaged in ritual bathing said to absolve them of sins they may have inadvertently committed while menstruating, for example, the sin of polluting men with their touch. The earlier anthropological analyses of Tij, as of many other rituals, explained contrary moments such as we find here as superficial paradoxes which, through deeper intellectual or psychological analyses, could be shown to have a fundamentally consistent rationale. Structuralist accounts, for instance, interpreted such "oppositions" as a necessary feature, the underlying intellectual logic of communicative systems (e.g., the ascetic/householder and austere/sensuous contrasts of Bennett's analysis). In this case we argue another and not "resolved" possibility: the inconsistencies represent positions and counterpositions emotionally invested in and urged by groups in conflict and struggle. Structural-functional accounts posited underlying mechanisms of social systems that would ensure the amelioration or, at least, indefinite deferral of tensions and contradictions. We embrace the possibility that the conflicts were not successfully resolved, even temporarily, but merely suppressed for the time being (see Holland and Skinner 1995a).

19. A similar accounting was being developed in sites and activities other than Tij. Schools, literacy classes, and the activities of political workers were important in this regard (see Skinner and Holland 1996; Enslin 1990, this volume). We give precedence to Tij in this article because the development of this critical commentary in Tij predates its development in these other sites in Naudada.

20. There were also pro-Congress Tij songs and ones that criticized the various communist parties in Nepal and practices of communist governments abroad, although these were fewer in number. See Holland and Skinner (1995a) and Skinner et al. (1994) for more details on the types of political songs and the composition of the groups that performed them.

21. Rājnīti songs were in the repertoire of Tij song groups before the 1990 pro-democracy movement. After the movement, it was less dangerous to sing them, and they proliferated in great number (see Holland and Skinner 1995a).

22. Many of these lines were taken from published Tij songbooks that greatly increased in number after 1991. However, the ways Kamala altered the lines and combined them with her own verses was novel (see Holland and Skinner 1995b and Skinner et al. 1994, for notes on the cultural construction of authorship of songs).

23. For the importance attached to a gendered "awareness" or "consciousness" in relation to Nepal's political and social history, see Holland and Skinner (1995a) and Skinner and Holland (1996).

24. For more on our reliance on Bakhtin's concepts of voices, heteroglossic sites, and the authoring of selves, see Holland et al. (in press).

References

Bakhtin, Mikhail M. 1981. The Dialogic Imagination. M. Holquist, ed. Austin: University of Texas Press.
———. 1984. Problems of Dostoevsky's Poetics. C. Emerson, ed. and trans. Minneapolis: University of Minnesota Press.
Bennett, Lynn. 1976. Sex and Motherhood among Brahmins and Chhetris of East-Central Nepal. Contributions to Nepalese Studies 3:1–52.
———. 1979. Tradition and Change in the Legal Status of Nepalese Women: The Status of Women in Nepal, volume I, part 2. Centre for Economic Development and Administration. Kathmandu: Tribhuvan University Press.
———. 1983. Dangerous Wives and Sacred Sisters: Social and Symbolic Roles of High-Caste Women in Nepal. New York: Columbia University Press.
Bourdieu, Pierre. 1977. Outline of a Theory of Practice. Cambridge: Cambridge University Press.
———. 1990. The Logic of Practice. Stanford: Stanford University Press.
Caplan, Patricia. 1985. Class and Gender in India: Women and Their Organizations in a South India City. London and New York: Tavistock Publications.
Comaroff, Jean. 1985. Body of Power, Spirit of Resistance. Chicago: University of Chicago Press.
Comaroff, Jean, and John Comaroff. 1991. Of Revelation and Revolution: Christianity, Colonialism, and Consciousness in South Africa. Chicago: University of Chicago Press.
Connell, Robert W. 1987. Gender and Power: Society, the Person and Sexual Politics. Stanford: Stanford University Press.
Das, Veena. 1979. Reflections on the Social Construction of Adulthood. In Identity and Adulthood. S. Kakar, ed. Pp. 89–104. Oxford: Oxford University Press.
Dhruvarajan, Vanaja. 1989. Hindu Women and the Power of Ideology. Granby, MA: Bergin & Garvey Publishers.
Dirks, Nicholas B. 1992. Ritual and Resistance: Subversion as a Social Fact. In Contesting Power: Resistance and Everyday Social Relations in South Asia. D. Haynes and G. Prakash, eds. Pp. 213–238. Berkeley: University of California Press.
Dirks, Nicholas B., Geoff Eley, and Sherry B. Ortner. 1994. Introduction. In Culture/Power/History: A Reader in Contemporary Social Theory. Nicholas B. Dirks, Geoff Eley, and Sherry B. Ortner, eds. Pp. 3–45. Princeton: Princeton University Press.
Enslin, Elizabeth. 1990. The Dynamics of Gender, Class, and Caste in a Women's

Movement in Rural Nepal. Ph.D. dissertation, Department of Anthropology, Stanford University.

———. 1992 . Collective Powers in Common Places: The Politics of Gender and Space in a Woman's Struggle for a Meeting Center in Chitwan, Nepal. Himalayan Research Bulletin 12(1-2):11–25.

Ewing, Katherine P. 1990. The Illusion of Wholeness: Culture, Self, and the Experience of Inconsistency. Ethos 18(3):251–278.

Gilbert, Kay. 1992. Women and Family Law in Modern Nepal: Statutory Rights and Social Implications. New York University Journal of International Law and Politics 24(2):729–758.

Gray, John. 1982. Chetri Women in Domestic Groups and Rituals. *In* Women in India and Nepal. M. Allen and S. N. Mukherjee, eds. Pp. 211–241. Canberra: Australian National University Printing.

Holland, Dorothy, William Lachicotte, Debra Skinner, and Carole Cain. In press. Identity and Agency in Cultural Worlds. Cambridge, MA: Harvard University Press.

Holland, Dorothy, and Debra Skinner. 1995a. Contested Ritual, Contested Femininities: (Re)forming Self and Society in a Nepali Women's Festival. American Ethnologist 22(2):279–305.

———. 1995b. Not Written by the Fate-Writer: The Agency in Women's Critical Commentary in Nepal. Folk: The Journal of the Danish Ethnographic Society 37:103–133.

———. 1996. The Co-development of Identity, Agency, and Lived Worlds. *In* Comparisons in Human Development: Understanding Time and Context. J. Tudge, M. Shanahan, and J. Valsiner, eds. Pp. 193–221. Cambridge: Cambridge University Press.

Holland, Dorothy, and Jaan Valsiner. 1988. Cognition, Symbols and Vygotsky's Developmental Psychology. Ethos 16(3):247–272.

Kondos, Vivienne. 1982. The Triple Goddess and the Processual Approach to the World: The Parbatya Case. *In* Women in India and Nepal. M. Allen and S. N. Mukherjee, eds. Pp. 242–286. Canberra: Australian National University Printing.

———. 1991. Subjection and the Ethics of Anguish: The Nepalese Parbatya Parent-Daughter Relationship. Contributions to Indian Sociology 25:113–133.

Kumar, Nita, ed. 1994. Women as Subjects: South Asian Histories. Charlottesville: University Press of Virginia.

Kumar, Radha. 1993. The History of Doing: An Illustrated Account of Movements for Women's Rights and Feminism in India 1800–1990. London: Verso.

Obeyesekere, Gananath. 1981. Medusa's Hair: An Essay on Personal Symbols and Religious Experience. Chicago: University of Chicago Press.

O'Hanlon, Rosalind. 1992. Issues of Widowhood: Gender and Resistance in Colonial Western India. *In* Contesting Power: Resistance and Everyday Social Relations in South Asia. D. Haynes and G. Prakash, eds. Pp. 62–108. Berkeley: University of California Press.

Oldenburg, Veena T. 1992. Lifestyle as Resistance: The Case of the Courtesans of Lucknow. *In* Contesting Power: Resistance and Everyday Social Relations in South Asia. D. Haynes and G. Prakash, eds. Pp. 23–61. Berkeley: University of California Press.

Ortner, Sherry. 1984. Theory in Anthropology Since the Sixties. Comparative Studies in Society and History 26(1):126–166.

Raheja, Gloria Goodwin, and Ann Grodzins Gold. 1994. Listen to the Heron's Words: Reimagining Gender and Kinship in North India. Berkeley: University of California Press.

Skinner, Debra. 1989. The Socialization of Gender Identity: Observations from Nepal. *In* Child Development in Cultural Context. J. Valsiner, ed. Pp. 181–192. Toronto: Hogrefe and Huber Publishers.

———. 1990. Nepalese Children's Understanding of Themselves and Their Social World. Ph.D. dissertation. Department of Anthropology, The University of North Carolina at Chapel Hill.

Skinner, Debra, and Dorothy Holland. 1996. Schools and the Cultural Production of the Educated Person in a Nepalese Hill Community. *In* The Cultural Production of the Educated Person: Critical Ethnographies of Schooling and Local Practice. B. Levinson, D. Foley, and D. Holland, eds. Pp. 273–299. Albany: SUNY Press.

Skinner, Debra, Dorothy Holland, and G. B. Adhikari.1994. The Songs of Tij: A Genre of Critical Commentary for Women in Nepal. Asian Folklore Studies 53(2):257–303.

Skinner, Debra, Jaan Valsiner, and Bidur Basnet. 1991. Singing One's Life: An Orchestration of Personal Experiences and Cultural Forms. Journal of South Asian Literature 26(1/2):15–43.

Smith, Paul. 1988. Discerning the Subject. Minneapolis: University of Minnesota Press.

Stone, Linda. 1978. Cultural Repercussions of Childlessness and Low Fertility in Nepal. Contributions to Nepalese Studies 5(2):7–36.

Strauss, Claudia. 1990. Who Gets Ahead?: Cognitive Responses to Heteroglossia in American Political Culture. American Ethnologist 17(2):312–328.

Toulmin, Stephen. 1978. The Mozart of Psychology. The New York Times Book Review. Pp. 51–57, September 28, 1978.

Willis, Paul. 1977. Learning to Labor: How Working Class Kids Get Working Class Jobs. New York: Columbia University Press.

———. 1981. Cultural Production is Different from Cultural Reproduction is Different from Social Reproduction is Different from Reproduction. Interchange 12(2/3): 48–67.

Chapter 5 _____

Narrative Constructions of Madness in a Hindu Village in Nepal

Alfred Pach III

M eanings of madness are created and situated within social relations and local forms of knowledge and practice. In Nepal, constructions of madness have been traced out in various communities. For example, Desjarlais (1993) has described how the cultural ideology of the Yolomo Sherpa defined the bounds of socially acceptable actions and shaped perceptions of incoherent behavior. In a case of madness among Brahmans in Central Nepal, competition over scarce resources created conflicts that challenged hierarchical relations and informed perceptions of disruptive behavior (Stone 1988). This chapter continues this exploration of how persons are constructed as "mad" and how particular social relations shape the accounts and identities of sufferers.

In the early 1980s, I collected descriptions and explanations of a number of cases of "madness" in Degalgaon, a Jaisi Brahman village in the Kathmandu Valley. The purpose of this study was to examine how people there responded to individuals with severe behavioral disorders—individuals whom villagers described as being *baulāhā* (mad). As a means of explaining unusual behaviors, family members and other villagers produced various accounts that drew upon local explanatory models of causation and treatment, and situated the experiences of sufferers within household and kin relations and histories.

Here I explore how various accounts of two cases of madness depict contradictions and ambiguities in the social positions of sufferers and narrators, especially in relation to the indeterminate and unresolved nature of the sufferers' predicaments. Such accounts are not simple descriptions of madness; they are forms of social action that work to construct meanings out of the strategies and struggles of individuals in ongoing relationships (Mattingly 1994).

The approach I take in the analysis of these cases follows that of recent research in psychiatric anthropology (e.g., Estroff et al. 1991, 1993; Good 1994; Lovell 1997; Saris 1995). This research focuses on sufferers' experiences of symptoms and treatments, and on the difficulties they face in their interpersonal and institutional worlds. In these formulations, the impact and meaning of disorders are viewed as emerging from "interactive processes" (Jenkins 1991:388). This work contrasts with the monolithic discourse and practice of professional psychiatry (Foucault 1965), which responds to disturbed behavior in terms of formal criteria purported to be objective, atheoretical, and neutral (Young 1991). This approach eliminates attention to the diversity and context of experiences among sufferers in various times and places.

Unquestionably psychiatric practices have been crucial in treating mental disorders in different societies. However, the transference of these practices across cultures has not been without problems, and critiques of these practices are many (Higgenbotham and Connor 1989).[1] For example, poststructuralist critiques have provided important challenges to the assumptions and categories of psychiatric practice, expanding our understanding of the ways in which institutionally constituted realities and relations of power impact subjective experience (e.g., Barrett 1988; Foucault 1980).

Although I am informed by these critiques, I seek to develop a more "multidimensional understanding" (Estroff et al. 1991) of the experiences of afflicted individuals. To do so, I draw upon surveys, ethnographic interviews, and observations to depict the multiple voices, actions, and social spaces of sufferers and other actors, including myself, that located and defined sufferers. These diverse sources of data provide multiple vantage points from which to view the predicaments of sufferers. Though partial and open-ended, they move beyond the confines of personal illness stories to provide a number of perspectives on the ways in which meanings surrounding madness and its sufferers are constructed in temporal and social spaces (Lovell 1997; Mattingly 1994).

In the case studies described below, we see sufferers and others in the midst of creating stories and envisioning possible endings to problematic behavior and situations. These stories situate social actions and conflicts within a temporal succession of events that are part of larger social configurations (see Ricoeur 1981). Differences in the social positions of narrators and sufferers lead to disparate accounts of disorders and reflect the aim of narrators to establish and legitimize their relation to material and symbolic resources (see Bourdieu 1989). Relations of power are realized in authoritative assertions about sufferers' conditions and in the responses of others to these conditions. In Degalgaon, authorized viewpoints, although sometimes challenged, created and legitimated the support or dispossession of sufferers. Struggles over narrative may therefore be understood as "struggles over identity" (Somers 1994:631). As Saris notes, "power inheres in the production and promulgation of specific interpretations of a socially-situated story" (1995:61).

I now turn to an examination of social and productive relations in household formations, the inherent contradictions in these relations, and the degree to which these contradictions served to organize meanings of madness and responses to sufferers. Following this section, I describe the forms and meanings of madness in Degalgaon. Finally, I present a number of perspectives on two sufferers, describing how accounts of their behavior positioned narrators and sufferers in various ways, and entailed claims for sufferers' inclusion or exclusion from Degalgaon life.

Degalgaon

This research took place in Degalgaon, a village of 1,202 people, nineteen kilometers east of Kathmandu within the Kathmandu Valley. Degalgaon was largely made up of Jaisi Brahmans and Khatri Chetri *jāt* or castes. Jaisi Brahmans are high-caste Hindus who cannot perform priestly functions, although they maintain other Brahmanical practices. Khatri Chetris in this village were the offspring of Jaisi Brahmans and Chetris (Chetris, along with Brahmans, are the two "highest" or "twice-born" castes in Nepal). There were 164 Jaisi Brahman, thirty-one Khatri Chetri, nine Dhami (tailor), and five Newar households in the village.

In Degalgaon, as in other parts of Nepal, households were the key units of production and consumption. At the time of my research in 1982–1984, and during a visit in 1992, subsistence consisted of a mixed economy of agricultural production, and less extensively, animal husbandry. Almost all households sold grain and milk and more than 60 percent had at least one member involved in salaried employment. In the last decade, salaried employment outside of Degalgaon has become increasingly crucial for household economies, reconfiguring the meanings of status, productivity, and prosperity (see also Pigg 1996). Households here, as elsewhere in Nepal, provided the key social context for the everyday experiences and identities of its members, and mediated individual and group relations within wider historical and cultural processes (Gray 1995).

Households in Degalgaon exhibited asymmetries of power along lines of age and gender, with elder male agnates and their sons dominating most activities. Forms of power and authority were realized in privileged rights to property, ritual knowledge, and opportunities for education and salaried employment. Although household relations were asymmetrical, there were also equivalences among agnatic kin.[2] For example, senior brothers deserved respect and obedience from younger brothers, although on another level they were equals as coparceners in the joint ownership of property, in pooling income, and in the distribution of goods. These moral and practical equivalences among relations were inherently unstable and contradicted by imbalances in individual efforts to generate resources (e.g., through salaried income, education, and contacts) and in individuals' competitive strategies and self-interests. Women played a central role in the distribution of household goods and in the division of domestic and agricultural tasks. Senior women dominated these decisions. Affinal women reproduced the relations of asymmetry and equality found among brothers, as well as certain tensions and conflicts.

Household relations in Degalgaon thus reflected contradictory processes of aggregation (e.g., pooling resources, virilocal extended households) and individuation (e.g., inevitable partitionings of household property). This created inter- and intra-generational conflicts over distributions of valued familial resources and contributions of labor and income. As noted in the two case histories that follow, the partitioning of household property, especially before the apical father's death, often produced anxiety and exacerbated antagonisms among household members.

Tensions related to the dialectics of cooperative and competitive processes were central concerns in everyday life in Degalgaon, and created a constant instability and suspiciousness in interpersonal relations (see also Stone 1977). The strains of everyday life and inevitable household partitionings placed individuals who were less productive, and therefore dependent upon other household members for their support, in vulnerable positions. When sufferers exhibited disturbed behavior, household and kin conflicts surfaced and provided the social and referential context for interpretations of the behavior, its cause, and cure. Social tensions, personal histories, and cultural idioms of illness causation (e.g., witchcraft, spirit attack) and healing shaped narrative accounts of troubled individuals. The meanings of problematic behavior and the inherent instabilities of household and kin relations provided the social and temporal context—the points of reference (Ortner 1989)—for individual and group responses to sufferers.

Madness in Degalgaon

Our initial research consisted of observations of sufferers in everyday life and in healing sessions, and of interviews with sufferers and other villagers on the meaning of madness and attitudes towards those labeled baulāhā.Villagers informed us of fifteen current and former cases of individuals considered to be baulāhā. We were able to gather substantial information on nine of these cases, including retrospective reports of disordered behaviors that had subsided, transformed into more withdrawn and passive behavior, or resulted in a sufferer's disappearance.

We also distributed a survey designed to inform us of Degalgaon villagers' attitudes about madness (Pach 1990). Their responses indicated that they found madness to be a particularly distressful and demanding disorder. They commonly described those who were baulāhā as exhibiting disruptive behavior, including shouting or arguing with others, showing extreme restlessness and agitation, wandering about, and refusing to work. Some persons with this condition were also considered to exhibit, though to a lesser degree, bizarre behavior such as walking around naked or being extremely disheveled. Other common characteristics of baulāhā were destructive behaviors, such as destroying crops or foodstuffs, or hitting others. Other prominent characteristics involved speaking incoherently and talking to oneself.

Villagers described the main causes of madness as witchcraft and spirit attack. These causes were believed to stem from ritual aggression related to interpersonal conflicts, or from a happenstance encounter with a dangerous spirit. Villagers also described emotional shocks and frustration from conflicts or personal losses (e.g., abandonment by or death of a spouse) as possible causes. Divine punishment, astrological disjunctions, heredity, and karma were mentioned less often, and were typically portrayed not as direct causes, but as conditions that made one more vulnerable to ritual attacks or shocks.[3] These causation beliefs reflected local idioms of illness and healing where illnesses and their treatments took shape in transactions between individuals and between individuals and the physical and extramundane world, governed by notions of balance, propriety, and forms of ritual power.[4]

Responses to disturbed individuals largely occurred in relation to these local schemes of knowledge and practice. Villagers commonly consulted deity and spirit mediums, and occasionally ayurvedic healers. Although most families cared for sufferers within the village context, some enlisted modes of assistance, such as psychiatric services, that were beyond the village. At the time of this research, state intervention and psychiatric treatment existed only on a small scale, although they were expanding within Nepal's public and private health care system. As described in the cases below, some families brought sufferers to clinics in Kathmandu,[5] and a few of the more disruptive cases were confined in jails or the state institution for the mentally ill (*pāgal khānā*).

The following cases of madness show similarities in forms of behavior and in the social tensions and struggles they evoked. The first case involves a sufferer who received extensive treatment and support from his family. The second case presents a sufferer who received no treatment or support, and who became increasingly dispossessed from household and kin relations. Differences in the sufferers' positions within the social alignments of their household relations affected whether they received supportive responses, particularly from those with the power to manage their care and social integration.

Madev

In the beginning of our research, I was informed by one of our field assistants that a man who lived on the eastern edge of the village was considered baulāhā. His name was Madev. He was twenty-six years of age and the youngest son of a wealthy family. During our initial meetings, he was very reticent. He smiled shyly and would barely speak when I asked him about his problems. Since he was not forthcoming, I talked with his wife, brothers' wives, father, and a local healer.

Their varied accounts of Madev's behavior provided partial descriptions of his problems. Though incomplete, they drew into relief many of the cultural meanings and social factors that influenced how people in Degalgaon responded to his disturbed behavior.

Villagers recalled that Madev's troubles began fifteen years earlier. Bimala, one of Madev's older brother's wives, described his unusual behaviors in detail. She first noted his problems when he suddenly quit going to school and stopped working in the fields. He also refused to see his friends. His family noticed that he began to bathe excessively, especially if he happened to touch a woman.[6] Madev's unusual behaviors had begun when he was eleven, two months after his sacred thread ceremony (*bratabandha*). One day, instead of going to school, he wandered off to the city of Bhaktapur and did not come home for several days. He then started to wander off periodically for days at a time. Bimala mentioned that he began to speak incoherently or "in waves" (*tarangi kurā*). Family members thought that his "brain was not good" (*magaj ṭhik chaina*), and they allowed him to drop out of school. They never described him as being baulāhā.

At the time of this research, Madev continued to exhibit unusual behavior. Syanumaya, another of Madev's brothers' wives, described him as being restless and agitated (*man urdne*).[7] He could not sit still for long. He ran, jumped or sang, and some nights did not sleep at all. He was unruly, throwing his plate on the floor, breaking pots, and yelling at family members. On one occasion he even hit his mother. Kamala, his wife of two years, described his problem as *aūsi purni lāgne* (being agitated or quiet and withdrawn).[8] Depending on his mood, Kamala said, he might talk to others and work on the family's land, or he might not. The only people he would regularly speak to after the beginning of his problems were his brothers' wives.

His sisters-in-law detailed the numerous healing specialists the family had employed for him over the duration of his illness. Most of the treatments were standard practices in the village. They were aimed at removing the effects of hostile spirit attacks, such as excising by blowing and sweeping (*jhār phukne*) the dangerous objects (*bigār*) which Madev supposedly had been fed or which had been buried (*ched*) in his house. Treatments also involved exorcistic offerings (*manchaune*) to remove spirits of the cremation ground (*masān*) and other evil spirits that had been sent to attack him, and offerings (*pūjā*) to appease the powerful "sky" deities (*ākās devī*).

After contact with our project and a lack of success with other remedies, Keshav, Madev's father, decided to try other treatments. He brought Madev to the inpatient psychiatric ward of Bir Hospital in Kathmandu, where they both stayed for fifteen days. After this, Keshav invested the time and money to take him to the large psychiatric hospital in Ranchi, India. Madev returned from this treatment quiet, withdrawn, and subdued in behavior. He continued to take antipsychotic medication which suppressed his disruptive behavior. Keshav also attempted to normalize Madev's life by finding him a wife. He managed to negotiate a marriage with the uncle of a young woman who did not inform the prospective bride's family of Madev's problems. These efforts of Madev's family were notable for their committed effort and investment of resources. Also notable was the lack of discussion among family members about social conflicts or malevolent forces that may have caused Madev's problems, causes that figured prominently in most explanatory accounts of serious illness in Degalgaon.

The Social Positioning of Narratives

Perhaps the least contentious, though most consequential, perspective on Madev's problems was offered by his father, Keshav. Keshav was reticent to talk with us about Madev's behavior or the many ritual treatments he had received. When he did, he talked about taking Madev to the hospitals in Kathmandu and Ranchi, but he did not mention that they went to treat Madev's "mental disease" (*mānasik rog*). Keshav was also reluctant to talk about what he thought might have caused Madev's aberrant behavior. He seemed uncertain about how I (the Western educated scholar) or the Nepali doctor on our team would judge "village" (*gāũi*) perspectives on illness and healing. Because he was an educated person, his reticence was perhaps a sign of his ambivalence toward "village" beliefs about illness causation and treatment and his own identity along a "traditional"–"modern" continuum (see Pigg 1995).

Keshav repeatedly told us he wanted Madev to have a salaried job like his other sons, although he mentioned that Madev's brothers thought he was not capable of such work because he lacked the necessary intelligence. Keshav, too, expressed some concern that Madev might be retarded. Madev's father was continually interested in expanding his son's productive capacity and often asked us if we knew of any medication that could improve his intelligence.[9] Although he recognized Madev's cognitive limitations, Keshav also noted his strengths, describing him as being very strong, capable of carrying two loads at once, and, depending on his mood, able to work "seven days a week." The ability to "work well" (*rāmro kām garne*) was highly valued in Degalgaon society. This positive attribution countered other perceptions of Madev's lack of intelligence and occasional disruptive behavior, and worked to place him in a more favorable light.

There were other accounts of Madev's disordered behavior and the many treatments he received. His wife and brothers' wives described his disorder in terms of a series of symptoms and behaviors (e.g., restlessness, agitation, and mood swings). His father focused more on the cognitive attributes of his problems, especially his slow-wittedness. Their accounts thus avoided the stigmatized attribution of madness. Madev's relatives, with the exception of his brothers, sought to improve his social functioning and integration in village life. Madev's closeness to his brothers' wives, his family's adequate resources, his ability to be productive, and his subdued behavior while on psychiatric medication were likely reasons for his household's support. Critical to his social integration and favorable responses toward him was his support of his father after his brothers had taken their share of the family property. His being an asset to his father aligned him on the side of power and authority in the family.

Although family members, through their accounts of Madev's behavior and their responses toward him, cast him in a positive light, other accounts of Madev's problems expressed social conflicts and moral critiques that were both related to his problems and to the social positions of the narrators.

Other Readings and Narrative Positions

Madev's immediate family at first did not admit to having a history of conflicts. A number of villagers, however, talked about the troubles Madev's family had faced for many years. Their accounts placed the origin of deep-seated conflicts at the time when Keshav and his brothers partitioned the land and household goods. Neighbors claimed that these tensions led Madev's uncle to commit suicide, although the family claimed he died in a landslide.

After I had worked a number of months in Degalgaon, Madev's father and other family members told me that they were considering hosting an elaborate ceremony (*bāyu utārne*) to transform the suffering, dangerous spirit of this uncle, who had died inauspiciously.[10] Madev's relatives considered this expensive and elaborate ceremony to be a solution to Madev's problems because it would appease the suffering spirit that might be causing his madness. The ceremony was also aimed at ameliorating the disturbances of a number of other family members, including Madev's mother and an elder brother's wife who suffered severe fainting spells (*chopuwā*).

Over time I was able to collect several perspectives on Madev's problems. These perspectives folded Madev's problems into a larger narrative of his family's history. One of the more conflictual portrayals of Madev's family and his problems came from Vishnu, a healer who was the clan deity medium (*dāṅgre*) of Madev's local descent group. His structuring of the events leading to Madev's problems expressed a history of conflicts in terms of gender and power relations. Vishnu's account also represented a moral critique of Madev's family and a strategic claim by which he argued against his exclusion from performing duties as the family's ritual healer.

In his role as clan deity medium, Vishnu was called upon to divine the causes of maladies and other misfortunes for this descent group. He was also a *dhami jhankri* (shaman), capable of possessing other deities and spirits for divination and for exorcism of harmful spiritual influences. Since he was a powerful healer, related to the family's descent group, and lived near Madev's house, I asked Vishnu his view about what had happened to him. He stated matter-of-factly that Madev's mother, Rita, and her mother-in-law were both witches (*boksi*).[11] He claimed that Rita wanted to destroy her mother-in-law because she had caused Rita many problems. Vishnu related that her mother-in-law and one of her sisters-in-law suppressed and dominated her and other affinal women in the household. Their actions led to rivalries over distributions of food and clothes and over assignments of domestic and agricultural tasks. Not long after Rita arrived in the household, she began to suffer chopuwā, fits of unconsciousness and possession, which lasted the rest of her life. Rita once mentioned to me that she believed that someone in the household was "sending" (*pesuwā*) something to her, that is, attacking her and causing her to suffer daily symptoms of chopuwā.

Vishnu believed that Rita played a key role in Madev's and her own problems. He claimed that she precipitated their problems by seeking instruction in witchcraft (*kubidyā*) from a powerful healer in a nearby village. Because she had been unsuccessful in learning witchcraft properly, she and her son became overwhelmed by the dangerous powers she had invoked, but failed to control. Vishnu maintained that this was the cause of both her chopuwā and Madev's disturbed behavior.

In further discussions of the sources of Madev's problems, Vishnu also maintained that the household's clan deity was angry because the family had persisted in eating chicken.[12] This was especially serious because the deity's shrine was close to Madev's house, and eating meat in the home made the shrine ritually impure. Vishnu added that the clan deity was further angered because it had not been consulted for Madev's problems as was typical in times of serious illness and crisis in the village. Rather, Madev's family had brought healers in from "outside" (i.e., both outside the local descent group and outside the village). Although the family employed many healers, Vishnu's criticisms centered on one local healer whom Keshav was considering as a replacement for Vishnu in the divination and transformation ceremony for Madev's uncle's ghost. Vishnu asserted that this healer lacked knowledge, had harmed others, and was not strong enough to subdue the powerful spirits of the cremation ground. Members of Keshav's local descent group, however, also viewed Vishnu as dangerous and as someone who had ritually extorted money from others.

By replacing Vishnu in the divination and healing ceremonies, Madev's family denied him the recognition and remuneration he expected. Vishnu perceived this as an insult. It placed him in an antagonistic position vis-à-vis the family and very likely fueled his more negative account of Madev's problems. While his view of Madev's and Rita's problems drew on some of the same relational conflicts that Rita had alluded to, his account was in stark contrast to the supportive constructions of Madev's father and sisters-in-law. Vishnu's interpretations of Madev's problems may also be seen as a strategy to enhance his own social position because he argued for interventions that would benefit not only Madev, but also himself as clan deity medium and shaman. In this instance, as Mattingly observes, narrativity becomes a form of social action for it is created out of "direct concern to the actor in the midst of action" (1994:812). Vishnu, however, did not have the symbolic or material power to assert his version of Madev's situation.

A Final Note on Madev

In a discussion with Madev before I left the field, he attributed his problems to his worry that his brothers would take his share of the land when his father died. This worry was not unfounded since they had already aggressively obtained their share of the property and expected much of their father's portion after his death. Madev's father had always been supportive of him. His brothers, on the other hand, did not seem supportive of him at all. They did not think that treatment was necessary for his condition and generally regarded him as retarded and incapable of employment outside of the village.

His brothers' accounts of Madev's problems as intractable, in contrast to his father's optimism, had critical implications for his rights to the family property. Nepali law allows family members to withhold portions of land from a member considered "mad" or incompetent. Thus, Madev potentially faces a crisis of representation when his father dies for accounts, rumors, and extended narratives of his being "crazy" or retarded could diminish his rights to property and other claims to material support if his incompetence became legally established. In his brothers' accounts, we can see how narratives not only construct the nature of an individual's problems, but also assert claims to positions within the social space of resources and status.

Part of Madev's problem with his brothers and the source of his anxieties were that he could not take advantage of the wider economic opportunities available and increasingly necessary in Nepal's changing economy. This limitation denied him access to the sources of status and material advantage that his brothers had realized. It seemed that his uneducated, village-oriented, and retiring image made his problematic behavior and incompetence more pronounced in the views of some. Nevertheless, with his father's support, he was able to benefit from cosmopolitan psychiatric treatment that improved his social functioning within the family. This allowed him to assume an acceptable, if tenous, position within the household and village, and freed him from being engulfed by an identity of a person considered baulāhā.

In the next case history, a sufferer named Nani Ram encountered some of the same hostile responses that Madev did. Yet he never experienced favorable relationships nor the same social support and integration that were accorded Madev.

Nani Ram

When I first encountered Nani Ram, he was yelling at a group of boys. He seemed agitated and distracted. I soon learned that people in the village considered him to be baulāhā. I tried to talk to him at first, but it was difficult because he was so agitated. He soon left the village and I was never able to get in touch with him again. Accounts of his madness derive from interviews with his father, stepmother, brother, and neighbors, and from a number of interactions with Nani Ram before he departed.

As recounted by his neighbors, Nani Ram had been troubled from his youth. He spent much time alone as a young boy and often argued with other children without provocation. As he grew older, he began to smoke marijuana and would rarely work in his family's fields. He became increasingly disruptive and isolated from his family and others in the village. Eventually he left for India. Yet it was not until he returned from a India after many years that he was viewed as acting like a *baulāhā manche* (mad person).

Villagers described Nani Ram's most serious troubles as beginning when his father married a second wife, who brought her own small children to live in the household. Soon after her arrival, Nani Ram's father, Hari, moved Nani Ram, his brother, and mother to a house near the main house. He gave them only a small share of crops to support them. Nani Ram and his brother, Shiva Ram, complained that the new wife dominated their father's household and denied them for the sake of her own children. They found it difficult to get along with her and often argued with her. This conflict was particularly deep-seated because it pitted Nani Ram and his brother against their stepmother, an older affinal woman, who had benefited from their loss. Their share of the land was so inadequate that their livelihood had to be supplemented by Shiva Ram's modest salary from outside employment.

Villagers in Degalgaon claimed that Nani Ram, his mother, and brother had "barely enough to eat" (*khāne napugne*), and noted that these circumstances led Nani Ram to look for work in India at the age of seventeen. Even later, when they had further knowledge of Nani Ram's aggressive behavior and purported lack of morality with women, villagers continued to depict his plight as a result of his having been treated unfairly by his father and stepmother. They maintained that Nani Ram's dispossession from his portion of the family's resources led to his problematic behavior.

When he returned to Degalgaon some years later, Nani Ram boasted of his experiences in India. He claimed that he had worked at a movie hall for four years and had made a good salary. He openly stated that at the end of this time, he raped the daughter of the movie hall owner and lost his job. When he was twenty-one, he received a letter informing him that his mother had died. Rather than return home, he roamed throughout India for six years, and never obtained adequate employment again. Nani Ram claimed that he had lived with little food or money during this time. His father had felt no obligation to send anything to him because Nani Ram had never sent any money or goods home when he was working, as was expected of a son in a salaried position.

My encounter with Nani Ram occurred not long after he had returned from India. People told me that he was much worse than before. He would laugh for no reason, speak incoherently, rarely bathe, and sometimes would not sleep at night. At times he would sit and stare into space. Whenever I saw him and tried to talk to him, he was wary. He complained that people were taking advantage of him. His behavior varied between being incoherent and passive to being defiant and angry. Many of his actions were viewed as being those of a baulāhā.

Nani Ram's stepmother's account included descriptions of his behavior, its etiology, criticisms of others' behavior towards him, and notions about proper treatment. She described his behavior as subject to mood swings and fits of anger (*aūsi purni lagne*). She attributed Nani Ram's incoherent speech and behavior to

his brain not being right (*magaj ṭhik chaina*). She thought that his problems were
due to someone putting a destructive "love spell" (*tunā munā*) on him when he
was in India. In her moral evaluations of the other characters in this domestic
drama, she thought that his father and brother had not taken adequate care of him.
She held the opinion that Nani Ram's brother should now take care of him since
he was managing a portion of the family's property. But she also thought it would
be better if he lived somewhere else with strangers whom he could not abuse. She
was afraid of him, claiming that both Nani Ram and Shiva Ram yelled at her and
treated her badly.

Nani Ram's father had a different version of what caused his problematic
behavior. He attributed it to Nani Ram's lack of money. He thought that Nani
Ram's problems might be alleviated if he had a wife and a share of his property.
He quickly added, however, that the crops were bad that year, so he could not
afford to provide him with either a wife or property. Like his wife, he thought it
would be better if Nani Ram returned to India for treatment, especially since the
destructive spell had been placed on him there. He and his wife reasoned that
spells in India were different from those in Nepal, so that the appropriate cure for
him could only be found in India.

Unlike Madev's family, Nani Ram's relatives did not attend to him when the
project psychiatrist sent him to receive treatment at the psychiatric ward at Bir
Hospital.[13] Neither did his family employ local healers to treat him even though
there were healers in the village who had learned cures in India and in all likelihood
knew the ritual antidotes for the putative spell he had received. His father never
adequately supported him in the household nor provided resources for his treatment
or independent livelihood. Rather, Nani Ram's father and stepmother encouraged
him to leave the village. If he stayed, his father would have been obliged to give
him an additional share of the property since the portion of land his brother cultivated was inadequate for both him and Nani Ram. After his treatment at Bir Hospital and feeling somewhat better, Nani Ram decided to go back to India. His father
gave him enough money to pay for the trip and for treatment there.

Accounts of Nani Ram, especially in contrast to those of Madev, point us to
the sociocultural and economic factors that may possibly explain why little support was forthcoming for him. He often acted disruptive and unruly, mistreated
his stepmother, and made claims to have acted inappropriately with women in
India. For his irregular performance of household work, he was considered defiant rather than disabled. These behaviors were often not described as symptomatic of an illness, but were spoken of as inappropriate and devoid of moral responsibility. His disruptive behavior, his lack of productivity, his brother's borderline
economic conditions, and his father's expanded family responsibilities challenged
the capacity and interest of his brother and father to support him.[14]

Nani Ram's behavior created additional tensions between members of his
father's household for it led to his stepmother's criticism of her husband for not
taking better care of him and having him removed from the extended household.
His brother also found Nani Ram to be demanding and argumentative; he fought

with Nani Ram, and at one point hit him forcefully on the head. Although Nani Ram's problems represent a configuration of many factors, his father's unusual actions of prematurely dividing the household's property and denying his sons their expected share of it, in effect, dispossessed Nani Ram of his expected livelihood. It also placed Nani Ram and his brother at odds over the small portion of land they could cultivate, and positioned his stepmother in a competitive position with him, which he further exacerbated.

These various perspectives on Nani Ram's behavior suggest why his father and stepmother opted not to support him. In a patrikin-dominated society such as Degalgaon, providing only minimal support for a son is tantamount to rejection—an unusual situation. Nani Ram's argumentative and antisocial behavior and the structural shift that occurred in household relations when his father brought home a second wife and her children, set the groundwork for the subsequent loss of support for Nani Ram. His father's new wife and children increased the number of supportive progeny and heightened economic pressures on the overall patrimony, pressures that would only increase as the children became older. Moreover, Nani Ram's threatening behavior strained his father's relationship with his second wife. In general, Nani Ram did not adhere to social expectations of reciprocity and respect with those in either hierarchical or equivalent relationships with him. It seems that because of his lack of cooperation, his disruptiveness, and his perceived responsibility for his condition, he was not supported in assuming a "sick role." Due to the household's structural and productive realignments and the ways in which his behavior was narrated, his kin saw him as deviant and troublesome. Providing support for treatment in India seemed to be a means to get him to leave the village. On the other hand, as Abu-Lughod (1990) suggests, violations of moral codes of behavior, such as Nani Ram's defiant and angry outbursts, may be understood as forms of resistance to perceived injustices.

As a result of his own behavior and the responses of others, Nani Ram was isolated and rejected from his family. He received little support from his family members for treatment, and no efforts had been made to find him a wife or secure his rights to his household property. Villagers believed that this situation was unjustified and a major cause of his distress. Nani Ram's lifelong dislocation from household and village relations suggests that his suffering and poor social adjustment were not the result of a linear trajectory of cause and effect, but more a "spiral of suffering" (Pandolffi 1991) in which he actively produced, along with others, a "nonrecognition" of his legitimate place in household and village life. In his incoherent behavior and breaks with family members, Nani Ram may be seen as articulating his own form of agency and critique (Ortner 1995). I am not suggesting that Nani Ram did not have psychological problems, but rather that his symptomatic behavior, though perhaps not always in his control, had the resonance of anger and resistance, signifying reproach as well as distress. Among other things, it could be viewed as a "cry for recognition" (Estroff 1989, as cited in Hopper 1991:312) of a person trying to survive in the face of personal and social difficulties. Unfortunately, the expected source of his material and social support in Degalgaon was unavailable to him. His departure to India may be seen as both a concession to his father's silencing of his claims to property and recognition, as well as a way for him to find a means to construct an identity in a less confined and conflicted situation.

Conclusion

Nani Ram's defiant behavior and Madev's fears and uncertainties indicated struggles within relations of power and dependence that involved contested resources and inequalities in status. Contradictions in structural and historical relations, with their internal alliances and antagonisms, created an unstable and tenuous context for the care and social integration of sufferers in Degalgaon. These relations mediated sufferers' access to immediate and wider sources of support. Although interpretations of sufferers' problems—such as viewing them as retarded, immoral, threatening, or mad—affected social responses toward them, the impact and emergence of these notions were tied to family politics and socioeconomic relations.

The plights of Nani Ram and Madev suggest that the sources of distress most troubling to them were not the pain and experience of their symptoms so much as their fragile social positions. As noted for cases of madness in other places, their "psychotic symptoms were among the least mentioned and least observable sources of distress and dysfunction" (Estroff 1993:274). Although it was their problematic behavior that propelled the sufferers into their debilitated situations, it was their key relations as sites of both struggle and support that narrators recounted as influencing their functioning as well as their survival and identity over the long term.

The social positioning of narrative accounts reveals how the disturbed episodes and conditions of sufferers were embedded within larger temporal and social configurations of events and relationships. Situated within the life histories of sufferers and within the politics of households, these narrative accounts revealed the impact of disorders and surrounding social conflicts on the lives of sufferers. Although the sufferers responded in various ways, it was those in positions of power—the elder male heads of households—who defined and legitimized the social spaces and possibilities for the afflicted individuals (see Bourdieu 1989). Contrasting narrative accounts, such as Vishnu's desire for recognition as a clan deity medium, or Nani Ram's protests over his loss of property, lacked the power and authority to impose their views and affect conditions for themselves or others. However, these alternative narrative accounts critiqued the moral position of dominant accounts and provided important perspectives on sufferers' problematic behavior and social identities.

Notes

While the interpretations in this paper are finally my own, I am indebted to Adam Sigerson for his perceptive conceptual and editorial insights. I am grateful to Dr. Dhruba Man

Shrestha who provided valuable information on psychiatric issues, and to Krishna Prasad Rimal, a colleague and source of support throughout the period of fieldwork. I am also grateful to Heidi Larson for her support while at UNICEF/Nepal. This research was supported by a Fulbright Hayes Doctoral Dissertation Research Award, a National Institute of Mental Health Predoctoral Fellowship, and funds from UNICEF/Nepal.

1. Currently within cross-cultural psychiatry there is much effort to define disorders, particularly schizophrenia, in more descriptive detail and over a longer span of time, as well as to identify social and cultural variables that affect their course and outcome (Craig et al. 1997; Edgerton and Cohen 1994). This is an area of much potential for collaborative research. However, the complexities of integrating the distinctly different levels of analysis in epidemiological and anthropological research, and the continuing ethnographic issues of comparing personal realities across cultural contexts are yet unresolved (Hopper 1991). Jenkins' (1991) contribution to an anthropology of expressed emotions within families with a member diagnosed as suffering schizophrenia and Estroff's (1993) identification of sociocultural and economic factors that affect the chronicity of disorders are two innovative approaches that may be applied in collaborative cross-cultural psychiatric and anthropological research focusing on the outcome and course of severe mental disorders. See Hopper (1991) for further discussion of these issues.

2. Gray (1995) provides another account of household relations that are typical of those found in Degalgaon.

3. These categories of causes were similar to the broad causal domains of ghost possession, sorcery, and "malfunctioning of the head," or shocks and other ayurvedic notions, that were described by clients and specialists in a study on madness in West Bengal (see Bhattacharyya 1986).

4. Ritual power took the form of spiritual (*śakti*) or physical (*tāgat*) force. There were also claims to spiritual and moral authority expressed in seances, for example, in which shamans and mediums claimed to possess the god Brahma, one of the three deities at the pinnacle of the Hindu pantheon.

5. In 1980, there were 3,000 visits for outpatient mental health services recorded at Bir Hospital in Kathmandu. This patient load was a strain on the resources available in this clinic. Sufferers came from as far as 150 miles away. Although this was an enormous growth in the use of psychiatric services in Nepal, which was less than 20 years old at the time (Kirsch n.d.), it still represented only a fraction of the many cases of mental disorders estimated to exist in the country.

6. Madev's excessive displays of Hindu cultural practices continued beyond his youth, though in the less extreme form of a preoccupation with Hindu festivals (e.g., Tihar, Janai Purnima) and devotional music (e.g., *bhajan*).

7. Literally his "heart-mind," or feelings and thoughts, were in flight.

8. This is directly translated as "affected by the waning and waxing moon." This is a common expression used for people who are sometimes angry and sometimes taciturn; that is, they display mood swings.

9. Influential Sanskrit medical texts in ayurvedic medicine (Weiss 1977:85–102) describe forms of mental disorders and mental functioning as related to balances and

imbalances in the body's natural elements or humors (*tridosa*) arising from an interaction of foods, climate, behavior, and body type. Keshav seemed to be conflating ayurvedic practice and concepts with the conceptual orientation and treatment of the physical body in cosmopolitan medicine.

10. An *agati* is an inauspicious death caused by accident, murder, or suicide. *Bāyu utārne* refers to the divination of "raising the suffering spirit of a deceased relative" to establish and legitimate its cause of death and presence as the source of problems. If the spirit identifies itself, then the *khali khelne,* the fire-walking ceremonies for transforming a suffering deceased relative's spirit (*kancho bāyu*) into an ancestral, deified spirit (*pako bāyu*) would be necessary (see Gaborieau 1974; Stone 1977).

11. People in the village described seeing witches at night dancing naked around a tree, with their hair unfastened and making an offering of a baby to gain power. This was not an uncommon image of aggression and danger in the village. Calling any woman a "witch" had extremely negative connotations and served to slander those with whom one had an antagonistic relationship.

12. Chicken is considered an impure food for high-caste Hindus, especially if they are orthodox Brahmans. For further discussion of the social identity and practices of Jaisi Brahmans, see Pach (1990).

13. Typically when a member of a Nepali family was in the hospital, other family members cooked their meals for them and one or more persons stayed with them at all times. Receiving no visitors was a strong statement of disinterest, if not rejection, of Nani Ram, which again contrasts with the attention received by Madev.

14. See Estroff (1993) for an overview of how such conditions can lead to chronic disorders.

References

Abu-Lughod, Lila. 1990. The Romance of Resistance: Tracing Transformation of Power through Bedouin Women. American Ethnologist 17(1):41–55.

Barrett, Robert J. 1988. Clinical Writing and Documentary Construction of Schizophrenia. Culture, Medicine and Psychiatry 12(3):265–299.

Bhattacharyya, Deborah P. 1986. Pāgalāmi: Ethnopsychiatric Knowledge in Bengal. Syracuse: Maxwell School of Citizenship and Public Affairs, Syracuse University.

Bourdieu, Pierre. 1989. Social Space and Symbolic Power. Sociological Theory 7(1):14–24.

Craig, Thomas J., Carole Siegel, Kim Hopper, Shang Lin, and Norman Sartorius. 1997. Outcome in Schizophrenia and Related Disorders Compared between Developing and Developed Countries. British Journal of Psychiatry 170:229–223.

Desjarlais, Robert R. 1993. Body and Emotion: The Aesthetics of Illness and Healing in the Nepal Himalayas. Berkeley: University of California Press.

Edgerton, Robert B., and Alex Cohen. 1994. Culture and Schizophrenia: The DOSMD Challenge. British Journal of Psychiatry 164: 222–231.

Estroff, Sue E. 1993. Identity, Disability and Schizophrenia: The Problem of Chronicity. *In* Knowledge, Power and Practice: The Anthropology of Medicine and Everyday Life. Shirley Lindenbaum and Margaret Lock, eds. Pp. 247–286. Berkeley: University of California Press.

Estroff, Sue, William Lachicotte, Linda Illingworth, Anna Johnson, and Bob Ruth. 1991. Everybody's Got a Little Mental Illness: Accounts of Illness and Self among People with Severe, Persistent Mental Illness. Medical Anthropology Quarterly 5(4):331–369.

Foucault, Michel. 1965. Madness and Civilization: A History of Insanity in the Age of Reason. New York: Random House.

———. 1980. Power/Knowledge: Selected Interviews and Other Writings 1972–1977. C. Gordon, ed. New York: Pantheon Books.

Gaborieau, Marc. 1974. Les Bāyu du Nepal Central. Parusartha (Paris): 67–90.

Good, Bryon. 1994. Medicine, Rationality and Experience: An Anthropological Experience. Cambridge: Cambridge University Press.

Gray, John N. 1995. The Householders' World: Purity, Power and Dominance in a Nepali Village. Delhi: Oxford University Press.

Higgenbotham, Nick, and Linda Connor. 1989. Professional Ideology and the Construction of Western Psychiatry in South East Asia. International Journal of Health Services 19(1):63–78.

Hopper, Kim. 1991. Some Old Questions for the New Cross-Cultural Psychiatry. Medical Anthropology Quarterly 5(4):299–329.

Jenkins, Janis H. 1991. Anthropology, Expressed Emotion and Schizophrenia. Ethos 19(4):387–431.

Kirsch, Cindy. n.d. The Status of Modern Psychiatric Care in Nepal. Kathmandu: University of Wisconsin Year in Nepal Project.

Lovell, Ann M. 1997. "The City is My Mother": Narratives of Schizophrenia and Homelessness. American Anthropologist 99(2):355–368.

Mattingly, Cheryl. 1994. The Concept of Therapeutic Emplotment. Social Science and Medicine 38(6):811–822.

Ortner, Sherry B. 1989. High Religion: A Cultural and Political History of Sherpa Buddhism. Princeton: Princeton University Press.

———. 1995. Resistance and the Problem of Ethnographic Refusal. Comparative Studies in Society and History 37(1):173–191.

Pach, Alfred. 1990. Disordered Experience in Nepal. Ph. D. dissertation. Department of Anthropology, University of Wisconsin—Madison.

Pandolffi, Mariella. 1991. Memory within the Body: Women's Narrative and Identity in a Southern Italian Village. In Anthropologies and Medicine: A Colloquium on Western and North American Perspectives. Beatrix Pfleiderer and Gilles Bibeau, eds. Pp. 59–65. Braunschschwieg: Fiedr. Vieweg and Sohn.

Pigg, Stacy L. 1995. The Social Symbolism of Healing in Nepal. Ethnology 34(1):17–36.

———. 1996. The Credible and the Credulous: The Question of "Villagers' Beliefs" in Nepal. Cultural Anthropology 11(2):160–201.

Ricoeur, Paul. 1981. Narrative Time. In On Narrative. W. J. T. Mitchell, ed. Pp. 165–186. Chicago: University of Chicago Press.

Saris, A. Jamie. 1995. Telling Stories: Life Histories, Illness Narratives and Institutional Landscapes. Culture, Medicine and Psychiatry 19(1):38–72.

Shrestha, Dhruba Man, Alfred Pach, and Krishna Prasad Rimal. 1983. A Social and Psychiatric Study of Mental Disorders in Nepal. Kathmandu, Nepal: UNICEF.

Somers, Margaret R. 1994. The Narrative Constitution of Identity: A Relational and Network Approach. Theory and Society 23(5):605–649.

Stone, Linda S. 1977. Illness, Hierarchy and Food Symbolism in Hindu Nepal. Ph.D. dissertation. Department of Anthropology, Brown University.

————. 1988. Illness Beliefs and Feeding the Dead in Hindu Nepal: An Ethnographic Analysis. Lewiston, NY: E. Mellen Publisher.

Young, Allan. 1991. Emil Kraeplin and the Origins of the American Psychiatric Diagnosis. *In* Anthropologies and Medicine: A Colloquium on Western and North American Perspectives. Beatrix Pfleiderer and Gilles Bibeau, eds. Pp. 175–181. Braunschschwieg: Fiedr. Vieweg and Sohn.

Weiss, Mitchell G. 1977. Critical Study of "Unmada" in the Early Sanskrit Medical Literature: An Analysis of Ayurvedic Psychiatry with Reference to Present-Day Diagnostic Concepts. Ph.D. dissertation. South Asian Regional Studies, University of Pennsylvania.

Part Two

Cultural Productions of Identity

Chapter 6 _____

Consumer Culture and Identities in Kathmandu: "Playing with Your Brain"

Mark Liechty

New things we have seen, now we have to have them.

(42-year-old Kathmandu resident)

Mounted on the wall in the courtyard of one of Patan's[1] most magnificent multi-tiered "pagoda-style" temples is a peculiar inscription. Probably the most recent addition to a series of inscriptions that record pious donations to the temple by generations of wealthy benefactors, what is unusual about this inscription is not its content, but the fact that it is in English, not the formal Nepali, or Sanskritized Newari most often used for temple records. Although undated the inscription records a donation probably made sometime in the first half of the twentieth century. Because it was in English, and since its location on the wall seemed to indicate that it was among the last donations memorialized in this manner, this inscription struck me as being a particularly interesting historical artifact. The gifts of the proud patrons harkened to a tradition of public giving rooted in centuries of local practice, but the language employed seemed to signal an uneasy recognition that new modes of public discourse and prestige were on the horizon. Now more or less dilapidated, and maintained precariously through donations from UNESCO and the German government, the temple stands surrounded by carpet factories and multi-storied concrete homes, the new monuments of local prestige.

In this paper I begin by sketching out the rough contours of this transformation in community values (toward what I describe as a new consumer materialism) before turning to a more detailed discussion of the broader social and economic factors that underlie this particular local history. After focusing on the experiences and comments of two middle-class Kathmandu residents, I examine various aspects of local commercial and prestige economies in order to show how in the 1990s members of the city's middle class are forced to negotiate their places in new cultural economies and systems of value. Although often highly ambivalent about their participation in the new consumer culture, those who would maintain claims to membership in Kathmandu's middle class find themselves drawn ever deeper into consumer values as social reference groups transform their identity standards.

Before proceeding let me stress that this article deals with a particular social formation—a middle class—in a particular place in Nepal—Kathmandu. As is clear when contrasting this article with others in this volume, members of Kathmandu's middle class lead lives that are not representative of Nepali lives generally, nor even of the growing numbers of urban poor in the Kathmandu Valley. Although rural and/or poor Nepalis are by no means shielded from the material and discursive inroads of capitalist modernity (often in the guise of development rhetoric and practice [Pigg 1992, 1993, 1996]), members of Nepal's urban middle class have both the ways and means to experience modern cultural processes in more direct and sustained ways. Indeed one of the central themes of this article, as well as the larger project of which it is a part (Liechty in preparation), is that Kathmandu's middle class actively (often critically) engages these forces of global modernity as it constructs its own class culture between the mass of poor Nepalis and Kathmandu's small but powerful transnational elite.

Public Patronage in the Religious Idiom

Writing in the ethnographic present of a timeless, unchanging past, the Indologist Jan Pieper noted that in Kathmandu:

> The Newar[2] consume communally whatever wealth they have been able to accumulate....Newar cities are so rich in temples and public resting places (*pāṭi*) and votive structures, for the construction and maintenance cost was raised from [public] contributions. (1975:68)

Although these practices were likely no longer in place when Pieper wrote of them, there is indeed a wealth of inscriptional and other historical material to support Todd Lewis's contention that "Formerly the characteristic way to spend excess wealth was through the conspicuous patronage traditions" (1984:588). The wealth of medieval and early-modern religious architecture documented so meticulously by scholars[3] bears witness to centuries of public patronage.

What this built environment points to is a mode of social existence in which religion was the primary idiom or arena for public life. This is not to suggest that social process was propelled by some set of benevolent, pure religious motives, but rather that religion formed the conceptual frame in which other domains of life were articulated. For example Kathmandu businessmen today speak of a time when their grandfathers pursued business objectives similar to their own, but through different means. At that time entrepreneurs were expected to take active roles in community ceremonial events as sponsors, hosts, and participants. Similarly, the community expected businessmen to register both their merit and social standing through public gifts ranging from gold butter lamps, to temple repairs, to gifts for priests. Businessmen speak of how in earlier days anyone who chose *not* to participate in this religious arena was likely to become more or less invisible in the community, have little opportunity to forge or maintain business contacts, and have few avenues available for social or political advancement. In this nineteenth- and early twentieth-century social setting, religious values and practice formed the medium within which practically all forms of social transaction—including economics—transpired. As the temple inscriptions illustrate, religious piety (in the form of donations) was a mode of public display and a means of converting economic into cultural capital.

My point is that while the modes and means of public life in Kathmandu at an earlier time were enacted in a religious idiom, the basic logic of that practice was not so different from that of today. One way to illustrate this point is to dig deeper into the details of Rana-era[4] public practice. As I have discussed elsewhere (Liechty 1997), early-modern Nepal's political isolation by no means implied total cultural isolation. This suggests that when considering Kathmandu in the nineteenth century, neither public consumption patterns nor local business practices should be seen as "pure" or autochthonous expressions of "local culture." For example long before Nepal's "opening" to the world in 1951, people in Kathmandu were well aware of a range of modern mass-produced commodities. By the mid-1800s European and Indian textiles had been imported into Nepal for centuries,[5] and European goods such as needles and teapots were for sale in Kathmandu shops (Egerton 1852:217). In the early twentieth century commercial interests were actively promoting tea consumption throughout the hill region, and soldiers returning from two world wars brought with them tea-drinking habits, as well as a hankering for such basic consumer commodities as soap, shoes, umbrellas, and tooth powder (Stiller 1993:159–160). But far in excess of their own firsthand experience as consumers of modern commodities, Kathmandu residents also had centuries of experience as observers of the objects of Rana and Royal family consumer desire. From luxury autos to Paris fashions, people in Kathmandu were fully aware of a universe of consumer goods that existed beyond their reach.

For the most part these consumer goods were kept in the hands of the ruling elite. Through a combination of travel and import restrictions, as well as sweeping sumptuary laws, the elite ensured that public and private consumer behaviors were tightly regulated. Many living Kathmandu residents remember when the few commoners who could afford to acquire Western-style clothing were forbidden to do so. Others recall that few would have been foolish enough to wear such clothing even if allowed for fear of attracting the "evil eye" (as one acquaintance sarcastically put it) of the Ranas. Because the Rana elite recognized no distinction between state and private resources (Rana 1995:46; Stiller 1993:164), members of ruling families were free to confiscate property, and even female family members, from townspeople (Lewis 1984:42). Through the course of the nineteenth and early twentieth centuries a number of Kathmandu families amassed fortunes transporting commodities between Calcutta and Lhasa via Kathmandu, but lived in constant fear of having their resources levied, impounded, or simply appropriated.[6] Wealthy merchants appeared before the Ranas in simple clothing and lived in relatively simple homes even though they often controlled valuable properties in Calcutta and Lhasa.

My point is that even while on the surface Kathmandu appeared to be a proto-, even pre-capitalist society with a noncommercial consumer culture, in fact this state of affairs was anything but "natural." The feudal state's extractive authority helped to minimize the potential for unimpeded capital accumulation and transformations in consumer practices even though some in Kathmandu were able to amass capital outside of Nepal.[7] The religious ethos that pervaded Kathmandu's local economy into the early twentieth century, and its relatively simple commodity culture were "real" to the extent that they reflected a certain mode of sociality and a certain set of community-oriented values. But by the end of the Rana regime in 1951, the sociocultural context of Kathmandu was already deeply influenced by competing logics of prestige and consumer values. While the ruling elite pursued social strategies based on an almost hyper-display of distinctive consumer goods (Liechty 1997), the mass of Kathmandu's commoners were restricted by decree and necessity to a prestige economy that maintained earlier patterns of public charity. The early twentieth century votive inscription rendered in English seems to capture some of this tension by both continuing a community and state sanctioned mode of public consumption, and hinting at new but forbidden modes of distinction.

The New Materialism

One evening during the summer of 1991, Nepal Television aired a drama about an old man whose children were disrespectful and negligent because the old man had no property to pass on at his death. Then, at the suggestion of friends, the old man started wearing a large key on a string around his neck and before long his offspring were attending to the old man's every wish.[8] The TV drama highlighted the commonly held perception that values once holding society and family together are breaking down as the role of money increases. For weeks after the program the somewhat uneasy joke that floated around town was that the number of savings accounts had suddenly shot up in area banks! Whether or not viewers actually rushed to the bank, the drama seemed to prod middle-class, middle-aged city residents into thinking about saving money, not to pass on to future generations, but for their own security in old age. While a certain kind of materialism—built around practices of accumulation and property transfer—is surely age-old, people in Kathmandu recognize a new kind of materialism associated with the new highly monetized economy and changing modes of cultural capital.

I was frequently reminded of the difference between earlier and contemporary modes of materialism. Middle-class adults often spoke of the consumer values practiced by their parents' or grandparents' generation in which people worked to accumulate land and gold. While earlier generations also wished to live comfortably, they viewed various forms of wealth primarily as something to accumulate in order to propel future generations into more desirable social circumstances. Now, however, patterns of accumulation and forms of patrimony have shifted to better fit the realities of a new social and material logic.

Some spoke of this change in terms of new understandings of parents' obligations to their children as well as their own rights to personal pleasure. One middle-aged Brahman woman, a mother of two, explained that nowadays people believe that parental investment comes in the form of providing education for sons (and increasingly daughters) after which children are expected to more or less take responsibility for themselves. In other words, the woman explained, the transfer of resources occurs in a different manner (in the form of education, not in traditional forms of wealth like land or gold) and at an earlier time (in the child's youth, not at the death of the parent). She said that now parents feel enormous pressure to provide the best possible education for their children, and often will deplete the family's fixed assets to do so, but once this is done they feel somewhat less compelled to scrimp and save for their children's sake. Instead they are more inclined to evaluate their own living standards and pursue the comforts and pleasures they feel are their rights. Yet this woman recognized that the standards of comfort her grandparents would have felt to be suitable were to her totally unacceptable. She noted that "comfort" was a completely relative notion that hinged on an awareness of options and the means to pursue them.

Another man in his early forties, a Newar who had grown up in a small town outside of the Kathmandu Valley, voiced a similar realization when he said, almost as a complaint, "You know now there are so many things to enjoy!" He explained the changing nature of materialism in terms of choices. As a child in a rural town, "fun" (*majā*) had been singing, dancing, and eating good food at festival times. He contrasted this with his present life, but even more so with the lives of his two children. Now opportunities for enjoyment and entertainment cluttered his daily existence to the point of distraction, and he willingly blamed his son's poor school performance on an excess of majā. People typically characterized the shift from old to new forms of materialism in terms of generations, but more particularly in terms of values; the new materialism represented a trend away from the accumulation of wealth, toward the pursuit of enjoyment, even though both forms involve elements of display (whether of gold ornaments or color televisions).

By describing materialism in terms of "old" and "new" I do not mean to imply that one has replaced the other. Many people shared the opinion of one young woman who explained why she saves her money to buy land. "Other things, if you eat it, it's finished; if you turn it on, it breaks; if you wear it, it tears; but land can't be exhausted in this way." People frequently contrasted the permanence of land and gold with the ephemerality of the new goods and pleasures that surrounded them. Rather than replacing an earlier consumer ethic of accumulation and permanence with the new materialism of consumer goods and enjoyment, the two coexist in an uneasy combination of logics.

This uneasy coexistence struck me one day while quizzing a friend on what constituted the ideal Kathmandu middle-class sitting room. I asked if this was the room where people would put their most valuable possessions on display. At this he laughed and said, "Of course not. People would never display their gold ornaments in this way!" Instead, he explained, this is where people put their television and often their refrigerator, suitcases (to display their ability to travel), and other modern goods. His remarks pointed to two contrasting though intermingled modes of consumer logic. One is built around a logic of conservation and protection against possible future hardships, while the other communicates participation in a rapidly expanding commoditized regime of value in which personal status and identity are tied to the control and display of possessions.

The tension between these two consumer logics runs like an undercurrent through popular middle-class consciousness in Kathmandu. One illustration is in the form of a story I was told so many times[9] that I came to recognize it as a kind of morality tale. Conveyed with a mixture of disgust and reprobation, the story tells of a man who (usually hounded by wife and/or children, depending on who tells the story) sells either gold or land in order to purchase a television, motorbike, or some other high-status consumer item. A variant of this tale recounts the drug-addicted son who, in the ultimate act of filial depravity, exchanges his mother's gold ornaments for a fix. Aside from indicating an awareness of two coexisting, even competing, modes of consumption, the moral tone of these stories points to a kind of ethical ranking of goods. Gold and land are somehow stabilizing and nurturing, tied to notions of permanence and family, while televisions and motorbikes are portrayed as almost hostile intruders into the domestic sphere, extracting resources and, not insignificantly, often associated with addiction.[10]

As I have suggested already, what is "new" about the new materialism is not some sudden appearance of commodities, much less the association of identity with possessions. Commodities have been at the heart of local economies since the city's founding as a trading center in the first millennium, and even imported capitalist mass-produced consumer commodities (from textiles to kitchen utensils) had been widely consumed in the city at least since the late eighteenth century (Liechty 1997). Rather, what is "new" is the abrupt lifting of import bans, sumptuary laws, and other consumer restrictions in place during the Rana era, the new predominantly cash-based economy, and the subsequent sudden explosion of goods and services in local commodity markets. The transformation is not a matter of essence but of scale; it is tied to an enormous increase in the quantity of commoditized forms and their sudden ubiquity in daily life.

It is this recent surge in material consumer abundance that provides members of the middle class—people with a combination of economic resources and social ambitions—with an extremely useful communicative medium or currency for constructing new modes of class distinction. Even while recognizing the intrinsic ephemerality of distinction based on consumer goods (objects which "break," "tear," or are "finished"), as I show in the next section most people in Kathmandu's middle class feel they have no choice but to transact in the new currency of consumer distinction.

Consumer Anxiety: "Playing With Your Brain"

If middle-class people in Kathmandu often speak disparagingly of the new materialism—if they sometimes characterize modern commodities as almost predatory agents—why is there such enormous pressure to consume? What drives people into a consumer economy that they themselves regard as threatening and even immoral? To begin to understand people's behaviors and motivations we have to keep in mind the almost overwhelming sociocultural flux that many people experience. Over the past decades Kathmandu residents have faced a situation of fixed (or declining) resources (e.g., income but also social capital such as privileges once tied to caste membership), combined with a huge increase in mobility (social as well as in terms of migration and suburbanization), and also an enormous increase in the quantity of consumer goods that become vehicles of marking and claiming distinction for families and groups.

To introduce something of what it means for middle-class urban Nepalis to confront a vastly transformed social and cultural order, I will recount at some length conversations with two Kathmandu residents. Both of these statements capture the sense of anxiety and the experience of moral dilemma that accompany people as they move increasingly within the domain of a new system of commodities and values. Both statements effectively convey what Jameson calls "the misery of happiness" (1989:518), or what Appadurai has referred to as "the agonized drama of leisure" (1991:207). In other words, these people describe the trauma of living the middle-class "good life."

When I spoke with him in 1991 Kedar was already well into middle age, had two teenaged children, and held down two jobs: as businessman and English teacher. A Chetri[11] originally from Nepal's Tarai region, Kedar was proud of his academic achievements (he held a master's degree) but felt financially insecure.

In the course of a long conversation, talk turned to the subject of household economics. Expounding in his characteristically dramatic manner, Kedar explained:

> Here the pressure is affecting the housewife especially. Because, well, they need...I mean we are not in *need* of a refrigerator, but now it is a *prestige* issue. Like me, my own TV purchasing. On my street everyone else had a TV antenna sticking out. Even I pretended about that. [I said to my family] "Why do you need that? You're only looking at third-class Nepali programs!"

> But my wife and kids, they started to go to the neighbor's house. Every time a good program was coming, they were going and spoiling their education! So I started to wonder, what should I do?

> Then I sold my gold, I mean my wife's gold and everything, and then I bought it. That's right! It was just like a trap. I was in a *trap*! I mean this is the kind of thing that is happening here! And I, an educated man, was in this trap. Just imagine the others. They can't afford to buy a TV, but now everyone needs a very *good* TV, not some low-class model. They look down on you if you have a black-and-white, or even a Gold Star.[12] They say [in a swaggering voice] "Oh, *I* have a *Sony!*"

At this I asked where such influences were coming from.

> Like the *new-rich* people here bought it, everything, right? New-rich people, I mean the Manangi people, with their illegal money,[13] and with that they bought *anything*. And everybody started to see that and they started thinking, "Why not in my home? Why only them?" [They said to themselves] "You are educated and you can't buy this. Look at him. He's only 10th class. And he did like this, and he doesn't have *this* [pointing to his head]." Use this *brain*!

> Look, I'm a good person, but what's the use of your image if you can't earn money? Yeah, it happened to *me*! That's why I sold off that gold. That's why.... I'm thinking, "Hey, I'm an educated person in Nepal. It's affecting *me*, then, what for others?" Well, you can imagine! They will have an inferiority complex and from that complex you can't survive for long. [They have to say to their families] "Oh, I can't give you good food. I can't give you a fridge. I can't even give you a *fan!*" Even if you have something, you are always lacking something. You can't fulfill everything, you know.

When I asked if it was really the Manangis who were causing people to feel these anxieties, Kedar admitted that it was not so easy as that.

> All around are things that make you think, "Oh, I wish that I could have that one also!" I mean it's always playing with your brain. And whenever you get the chance, any chance—like for taking bribe money—you leave your values and that's not a good thing. But the whole thing is coming there. [Everybody says] "Oh, my wife was pressing me on this thing, on that thing. Oh, if I only had that money."

Like my relatives, one is a customs officer,[14] and right now he has everything. My wife and my children are saying [to me] now, "See there, he's a less experienced, less famous man than you but he has a carpet, he has a refrigerator, he has a TV. He has *everything*! He has ornaments, he has gold, and whatever he likes, he can do that."

But I told my wife, well, he's only arranging for the family. But he, look at the very cheap-class watch he's wearing. And the cheap-class clothes he's wearing. Because, the government will suspect him. Got what I mean? He can't expose what he's earning [bribes]. And *I know* what is his mental state. You don't know that. I know that. Always suspicion, suspicion....In this way he will die. Always having boozing and this and that.

Me? I'm doing my body building.[15] I don't have any pressure. I'm free to do anything. Which life do you like?

From his earlier statements about feeling "trapped," it would seem that Kedar was not in fact "free" and without pressure to conform. Yet by drawing a sharp line of distinction between himself and his corrupted relative, Kedar clearly tied the life of consumer abundance to a life of moral compromise. There is almost a Faustian contract in Kedar's account of the customs officer driven to corruption in order to provide consumer goods for his family, and destined to die a paranoiac and "boozing" death. For Kedar consumer goods are "all around," always "playing with your brain," and challenging your sense of self-worth. "I'm a good person," "I'm an educated person," but why are these other people better off than me? One question seemed to sum up the dilemmas Kedar faced: "What's the use of your image if you can't earn money?" Part of Kedar's "trap" is the fact that the forms of cultural and social capital he holds (especially family background and education) are losing value, or at least being outpaced by a new index of value that resides in an economy of possessions. Kedar's comments clearly illustrate the enormous seductive powers of a new domain of consumer goods, and the moral and economic dilemmas that this domain throws up. But his words also contain a powerful critical dimension. This love-hate ambivalence toward consumer goods is a central theme in middle-class discourse in Kathmandu.

If Kedar's represents a male's point of view, how do women experience and deal with the pressures of the new middle-class consumer economy? While Kedar (and other men) frequently blamed wives and children for the pressures to succumb to consumer demands, what are the factors that compel women to enter the new domain of consumer goods?

I found some answers to these questions in the remarks of a young Brahman woman interviewed by a female Nepali co-worker. In 1991 Gita was in her early thirties, identified herself as a "*housewife*"[16] (though she was still officially a student working on incomplete exams), and was the mother of two sons, ages three and seven. Gita's comments capture very effectively the precariousness of daily existence for many people struggling to maintain their position in Kathmandu's middle class. By local standards Gita's extended family—which includes members in high positions in the civil service, and others living abroad—would be seen as relatively well-to-do. Yet what the family could claim in social capital and prestige always seemed threatened by the limited economic resources it could muster. Gita's anxiety focused precisely on how, as wife and mother, to maintain what she called a "*standard of living*" in the face of severe economic shortages.

After talking about problems that parents have disciplining their children, the conversation took an interesting reflective turn. According to Gita:

> A decade ago the situation of children was different. Today there's less control. I feel that now the *standard of living* is increasing. Maybe that's because people are earning more. But for us, we still have problems, troubles, hardships for living, not enough money for food. Well, we are a family, and everybody brings in a little but still we feel hardships.

> What I see now is that even lower-level people are wearing clothes the same as people in the middle class (*madhyam barga*). Or, the high-class families are wearing expensive, high-quality clothes, and the middle-class people are wearing the same things.

> How are they doing this? *That's what I want to know*! It's very surprising. *How are they coming up with the money*? You see some soldier on the street wearing pants that cost three or four hundred rupees. That's the same as his officer is wearing!

> Interviewer: So, how does this happen?

> It's hard to say how they can *maintain* this. Maybe they have some *part-time job*, or *business*, or wear such nice clothes only once a year.

> But there's one thing that people from *our* level do. For instance, if I buy clothes for the children, they wear those only when they go out [of the house]. And then when they come back I wash them if they are dirty, otherwise I just put them back on the hanger, and then I have them put on other clothes that are only used when they're around the house. This is what we must do these days.

Clearly for Gita increases in the society's "*standard of living*" are intimately tied to changes in consumer patterns as they relate to class. When soldiers are appearing on the streets wearing the same clothing as their officers, "people from *our* level" resort to new strategies to improve living standards, or at least put forward the appearance. Gita elaborated on the theme of maintaining public appearances by suggesting that things nowadays are different than before:

> I don't think the previous generation had it like this. They just didn't care so much about clothes. They could go out [of the house] wearing any kind of clothes. At that time *fashion* wasn't so common, but now, now the mothers are educated, they like *cleanliness*, they want their children to be clean, they put them in special schools....Because of all this, the changes have come. This is the reason for the changes in the *standard of living*. People are now willing to eat less, in order to show themselves to be of a high *standard*.

For Gita education and a concern for "*fashion*" and "*cleanliness*" are all inseparable parts of being a modern woman and being a modern mother. Because of these things, "the changes have come," even to the point where people are willing to sacrifice food for public prestige.

> Interviewer: How can it be that people think that wearing is more important than eating?
>
> Well, wearing *isn't* more important than eating, we all need *nutritious* food. I mean I'm not one of those who thinks spending more money on food is not good. One should eat properly, with a balanced diet, as long as it is within the budget, not going over the expenditure limit, and if possible having some savings.
>
> I usually don't spend extra money. My husband does a little. I don't go outside much and that way I can save some money, like what would have been spent on a taxi or something. For example, if I go outside, and see a restaurant, I feel like eating! So I just try not to go out that much. That way I can save money which later can be spent on constructive things.
>
> Like I don't buy the cheap cotton bed sheets, because they are not colorfast. Yet, these are the cheapest ones, only Rs. 100. So if my husband gives me Rs. 200 for buying sheets, I wait for one more month and add another Rs. 100, and buy the *terri-cotton*, the better quality ones, and then just do the sewing myself. I like the *terri-cotton* sheets, it gives you a better *standard of living*. When it is seen, it looks nice, and also it lasts longer, at least eight years. I feel that if I invest my money like this, I get a long time *duration*. In this way we can maintain a good *standard of living*.

In these sentences Gita suddenly launches into the language of classic economic rationalism. With budgets, limits, and savings; with investments, calculations of duration, and delayed purchasing, Gita is a housewife who has very consciously embraced economic maximization strategies in order to "maintain a good *standard of living*."

> Interviewer: Why do you think people want to show off this *standard of living*?
>
> It's because....Now European society has come here. Everywhere there is talk about high thinking, clean environment, high *standard of living*. Everybody wants a comfortable life. The older generation used to just light a fire, but now [we use] gas stoves or *heaters* [electric cooking elements]. The main reason of wanting a *modern* life is so that you can have a comfortable life.
>
> And now people are sending their children off to school. There's competition in this too. Here people are sending their children.... They don't want their children to have some *inferiority complex*. So people are trying to send [their children to school] even if they don't have the [financial] capacity to do it.
>
> So now in the boarding school you'll find children from all levels of the society—high, middle and low are all there. I was thinking that my children won't have any problems if their friends are from wealthy families, but they [my children] feel poor. So for this reason, they are always suffering from this *inferiority complex*, they are afraid to talk to other children! So I just don't want my

children to have this *inferiority complex* and if we can increase our *standard of living* little by little, they won't have it.

Like suppose if we don't have a *cassette player* and our children don't know anything about this. And then they see some other person's *cassette player* and we say to them, "Hey, don't touch that! You shouldn't play with that." [If we say that] Then they're going to fear these things and they may never learn how to use something like that.

But as for my son, *he knows* how to turn on the *television*, and the *deck* [VCR], even though I fear that he might break something in the process.

In these comments Gita begins by equating "*modern* life" with the comforts of modern consumer goods as well as disciplines like cleanliness. Yet these ideas are closely tied to her own class consciousness and she soon returns to her feelings of anxiety, especially as they relate to her children who have been thrown into the "competition" of an expensive private school. Here she admits that whereas she had thought it would be good to have her children in school with children from "wealthy families," in fact they were now suffering from an "*inferiority complex*" and have trouble talking with the other children. In order to save her children from feeling inferior she wants desperately to raise the family's living standards so that the children will not grow up feeling underprivileged. For Gita it is her parental duty not just to *own* modern consumer goods, but to make sure her children know how to *use* them. She can be proud that *her* seven-year-old knows how to use a TV and VCR.

For both Kedar and Gita the problem is how to construct and maintain a middle-class material existence in the face of constantly upward-spiraling standards on the one hand, and extremely limited resources on the other. Like a card game where the stakes are constantly being raised, it takes more and more cash outlay for people in Kathmandu to stay at, as Gita put it, "our level." For Kedar this had meant selling off some of his wife's gold in order to buy a TV and thereby avoid the humiliation of having his family members troop off to the neighbor's sitting room every evening. Compared with Gita, Kedar was more willing to portray the forces of consumerism as immoral. In his opinion some people may appear to be living high, but they do so only by lowering themselves to a state of moral baseness. For Gita however, moralizing does little to change the (perceived) reality of children stigmatized for not consuming at certain material standards. As a wife (in charge of a household) and mother (in charge of children), Gita can ask "How are [other people] coming up with the money?" But ultimately much of the burden of projecting an appropriate living standard falls on her, whether in making sure the children change into good clothing whenever they leave the house, resisting frivolous purchases and maximizing her returns when she does "invest" in things like bed sheets, or doing whatever she can to save a rupee here and there. As a modern woman it is her duty to "increase [her family's] *standard of living* little by little," whether she likes it or not.

Prestige Inflation

A popular rhyme often recited by Newars in Kathmandu goes like this: "While Brahmans are ruined by greed, and Chetris are ruined by pleasure, Newars are ruined by feasting!"[17] As many accounts of Newar social life have documented in great detail, patterns of sociality in Kathmandu have historically revolved around the festivals and feast days that fill the community's ritual calendar.[18] At many of these events families or individuals take turns bearing the responsibility for feeding others in their neighborhood and/or caste group and/or *guthi*[19] association. Because these are extremely important occasions at which social status is claimed or maintained, sponsors will go to great lengths to ensure that their obligations are carried out in an acceptable manner. Indeed for many people failure to meet these obligations is tantamount to abandoning any claims to respectability in the eyes of the community.

While these ritual events remain important points in the annual cycle for many people in Kathmandu, my aim was less to study or describe their dynamics than to inquire as to how these events have changed in the context of the new economic patterns, social dynamics, and material culture of contemporary Kathmandu. While it is clear that Kathmandu's prestige economy is nothing new, what *is* new is a kind of rapid inflationary effect brought about by increased cash flow and the influx of new material goods (and commercial services). In this new economy even once unquestioned forms of prestige (such as caste status) have to be backed up with the display of goods, as those able to adopt new consumer lifestyles threaten to subvert traditional systems of prestige altogether.

I met Sano Raj Shrestha while hanging out in central Kathmandu's Ratna Park one sunny spring afternoon in 1991. A Newar from an old Kathmandu family, Sano Raj had been born within a stone's throw of where we sat and, at age forty, was still living nearby, married, and the father of three children. Sano Raj and a friend were smoking marijuana and passing time in the park while they waited to meet two Italian tourists who had agreed to purchase airplane tickets from them. Sano Raj worked as a "*broker*" for a local travel agency and was paid on a commission basis for bringing in business. From this job his monthly earnings were about Rs. 1,200 (about US $22.00 in 1991) which he supplemented with occasional income from acting as a guide for foreign tourists, and from the illegal sale of ganja and hashish. He confided that life was tough and that drinking alcohol or smoking pot "brings bliss" (*ānanda lāgyo*) when he is "feeling down" (*bor lāgyo*). From his somewhat ragged clothing, generally disheveled demeanor, and public use of hallucinogens, it was fairly clear that Sano Raj was among those in Kathmandu in danger of falling out of the social system and being left behind in modernity's wake.

When I asked how he could support his family on such a small income, Sano Raj shook his head and explained, "Before things were cheap and money was valuable but now goods are expensive and money is worthless." For example, he complained, now a Western-style suit costs Rs. 2,000 and a person can no longer wear simple shoes, but instead must buy leather shoes. Before long the conversation turned to the subject of Newar festivals. Sano Raj complained that community ceremonies were getting out of hand, dragging common people into poverty, and poor people into deeper poverty. He explained that things are not just bad, but are in fact getting worse.

For example, whereas previously one was obliged only to invite one's relatives in the general vicinity for most feast occasions, now one was expected to send invitations to relatives scattered out across the Kathmandu Valley and even beyond. With public transportation and communications devices like telephones, the number of relatives that might show up had become almost limitless! Even worse, Sano Raj explained, was the fact that a host could no longer provide "simple food" like beaten rice and meat dishes prepared by women in the family and served on leaf plates to guests sitting outside. Now a "respectable" or "prestigious" (*ijjatdāri*) host must serve his guests "*buffet-style*," that is, catered by some local restaurant which serves fancy restaurant fare and charges high rental fees for crockery, cutlery, folding chairs, tents, etc. In other words, the respectable host can no longer stage a feast by mobilizing family labor and acquiring ordinary foodstuffs either from his own land or in the local markets where commodity transactions might be made in kind. Instead he must mobilize *cash*, and large amounts of it.

In the same vein, a wealthy Tibetan businessman complained to me of how one of his Newar subcontractors had come to him pleading for a Rs. 40,000 cash advance—an amount equivalent to a full year's salary for a well-paid government civil servant—because it was his turn to feed the people in his local guthi association. When the businessman asked "Can you afford it?" the man blurted out, "It is not a matter of affording!" In other words, like Sano Raj, this man was in a position where the continuation of his very social existence depended on his ability to generate cash and thereby keep his stake in his community's prestige economy.[20] While Sano Raj had already essentially bowed out of this economy and lived a life of substance abuse and shame, this Newar man was still fighting to maintain his family's place in a local prestige system that threatened to destroy him. As local prestige economies become not only increasingly cash-based, but more and more lavish in their demands, Kathmandu residents experience extraordinary pressures to enter the wage/market economy (and the social logic of class), or risk sinking into social oblivion.

Consumer Buying Schemes

Part of the ensemble of forces feeding into these experiences of consumer anxiety and desire are a number of new systems of resource mobilization and consumer promotion. More than simply a matter of seeing new goods in shop windows or in other people's homes, there are now more and more organized channels that make it "easy" for people to buy consumer goods. One of the most common schemes is known as the *"ḍhukuṭi* (treasury, storehouse, or cashbox) system"—a kind of rotating credit club in which groups of acquaintances agree to each contribute a certain amount of money to a kitty every week or month and then either wait their turn or bid to receive the pooled capital. Although ḍhukuṭi credit schemes in Kathmandu are likely as old as cash itself, in the early 1990s their numbers and popularity were rising to the extent that the commercial banking sector in Nepal began to complain of lost business (Uprety 1991). From housewives contributing a few rupees to business people laying out hundreds of thousands a month,[21] ḍhukuṭi participation was extremely widespread across a range of ethnic and caste groups in the middle class. With the funds mobilized through these credit systems, Kathmandu consumers were buying everything from gold and real estate to motorcycles and furniture.

Smaller-scale investors in particular often directed ḍhukuṭi funds into another popular consumer promotion scheme known as an *upahār kāryakram* or "gift program." The "gift program" is a kind of consumer buying scheme that combines advance installment payments with a lottery. For example someone interested in buying a steel cabinet or sofa set might join a "gift" scheme through which after twelve fixed monthly payments she or he is guaranteed delivery of the furniture. "Players" pay their monthly installments and every month the scheme operators hold a lottery. A certain number of winners then receive their furniture for fewer than twelve payments while the rest must pay in full. Everyone gets his or her desired commodity at the going market rate, but a few lucky ones get it for some fraction of the price. "Gift program" schemes help entice hesitant consumers into making purchases by throwing in the element of chance and possible good fortune; at worst one only pays market price. But for "gift program" organizers, such schemes bring in huge amounts of cash to be invested or loaned at high rates of interest.[22]

Finally, even more common than "gift program" schemes are Kathmandu's ubiquitous consumer lotteries. Rather than offering cash, these schemes play directly off people's desires for prestige goods by offering payoffs in the form of popular consumer items ranging from new homes to cars and motorcycles, to televisions and refrigerators, to furniture and bicycles. Motorcycles were particularly popular lottery items. For a few rupees a lottery player might join the film heroes and urban elites riding about on the city's streets. On street corners and in magazines and newspapers, these schemes seemed to be advertised everywhere. Stories abounded of people being ripped off by scam artists who were entirely unregulated (Upadyaya 1991).

Whether plastered across banners or shouted in megaphones on the streets, blaring from television or radio, or jumping out in eye-catching ads in local newspapers, consumer buying schemes seemed to be everywhere in Kathmandu in the early 1990s. Even if many people would have nothing to do with these schemes and scams, the sheer cacophony of images and promotions that assault Kathmandu residents as they move about the city can only contribute to an environment that privileges a material realm of consumer commodities as the domain of *real* value and fulfillment. In the words of Kedar quoted earlier, "All around are things that make you think, 'Oh, I wish I could have that one also!' I mean, it's always playing with your brain."

Class and the Hierarchy of Goods

Yet like all forms of advertising, Kathmandu's consumer promotions are effective less in their ability to "brainwash" consumers, than in their proficiency in feeding off of, or capitalizing on, the social imperatives that people face in daily lives. Consumer goods become necessary to the extent that they become part of the social currency, discursive resources, and cultural modes at play in projects of class formation in Kathmandu. Not everyone participates with the same intensity, and even those heavily invested in the local middle-class consumer economy often articulate a sense of moral compromise as they embrace a new form of materialism. But regardless of the ambiguity in their relationships with the new material culture, all Kathmandu residents share in an experience in which personal or corporate (usually family) prestige (*ijjat*) is increasingly tied to the acquisition and display of consumer goods. Like the Newar man who flatly asserted that "It is not a matter of affording," other people in Kathmandu struggle to maintain parity with those in their communities.

For example, when I returned to Kathmandu in 1991, I was astonished both by the ubiquity of video rental shops throughout the city and at the number of VCRs in private homes. When I asked one man (the owner of a small tourist cafe in Kathmandu's "Freak Street") how so many people could afford to buy VCRs, he said bluntly:

> People can afford it. It doesn't matter what it costs. New things people buy just like that. When they want something it doesn't matter. It doesn't matter if you've got enough money to eat or not, it just doesn't matter.

Because the consumer domain is so intimately tied to the representation and negotiation of status, for people in Kathmandu with any claims to middle-class membership, consuming modern goods is essentially not a matter of choice.

When people in Kathmandu described the difference between their lives and those of earlier generations, one of the most common contrasts made was in terms of increased needs for cash and consumer commodities. One man I interviewed, a social worker in his mid-thirties, commented that:

> Now there are many areas where you can spend money. Before, even if you had money, there was no place where you could spend it. Before there was money saving. Nowadays generally you cannot really save money.

Another man echoed this same frustration. A journalist of about forty, he described how his father had saved all his resources for investment in land. When I asked if he did the same thing, he sighed and said "No" even though he would like to buy land. He went on to explain:

> It's just that now we want so many *other* things: like TV, video, car, motorcycle, mountain bike, nice clothes, nice shoes....I mean a pair of shoes now costs Rs. 1,600 and I get paid maybe Rs. 2,400 a month. If I buy one pair for my son, two-thirds of my pay is gone. So what do you do? It is stressful! That's why we're in the habit of working two or three jobs.

As heads of households these two men characterized the changing consumer economy in terms of the inability to save money or invest in nonperishable resources.

Younger people also recognize changing material conditions, though, because they have fewer financial responsibilities, their experiences in the consumer society are somewhat different. For example one young woman, a masters level student in chemistry, explained how previously everyone in a family would have been busily preoccupied with matters of basic subsistence.

> But look at us now. In our time how to have fun, to enjoy, how to pass time, these are our main concerns. So there is a big *difference*. Their life, from a mental point of view, was very peaceful, but physically, it was tough. But look at our life, physically it's easy, but not mentally.
>
> Interviewer: Why is it that there's no mental peace today?
>
> There is so much competition now. We have to eat *equal to* others. We have to wear [clothing] *equal to* others. Otherwise the society looks down at us. So all this competition has to do with raising one's level and this is why there is no possibility of having mental peace.

Even if it is unlikely that household subsistence was always a mentally "peaceful" endeavor in earlier times, this young woman echoes the sentiments of many others in pointing to social "competition" and the need for "raising one's level" as the main source of mental stress in their generation.

From all of these voices emerges an array of related ideas concerning competition, change, consumer goods, social class, and progress. For many people in Kathmandu the story of the city's past few decades is the story of changing consumer demands. One longtime Kathmandu resident, a mid-level civil servant, described Kathmandu's past fifteen years in terms of changing needs.

> Previously, like fifteen years ago, they didn't have anything. Only cassette players. That was enough for Kathmandu people. Even for me that was enough! But when television came [in 1985], then people afforded, or I mean, they *tried* to afford a television set. Yes, then their necessity went up! And after that they thought, "I have a television set, why not a VCP[23] to see movies?"

Other people spoke of the same changes but from the slightly different perspective of goods necessary for maintaining social status. For example, one acquaintance, a young man from a wealthy Newar family, explained how through most of the 1980s owning a VCR had been one of the key symbols of an upper middle-class lifestyle (even before the advent of local television broadcasting). Now however, he explained, for people of his social standing electronic goods were more expected than distinctive. Now his group had moved on to a higher (more costly) level of distinctive technology, namely, private vehicles like motorcycles and even automobiles.

This consumer hierarchy of goods and social groups was a commonly recognized feature of urban life for almost everyone in Kathmandu, from "low" to "high" social standing. From clothing styles and various degrees and types of education through a range of consumer electronics to the ultimate status symbols like foreign travel, imported luxury four-wheel-drive vehicles, and sprawling suburban homes, Kathmandu residents took it for granted that consumer goods indexed social standing. For example, one young woman from an untouchable caste group who had recently arrived in Kathmandu and worked in a tailor's shop explained why she wanted to buy a TV. When my co-worker asked what she would do if she won a lottery prize, the woman explained:

> Well I'd buy whatever I'm most interested in. But I should buy a *television* because every house has that now. Now everyone watches. My son is always going off to some place to watch this. Rather than going to knock on someone's door, having a *television* here would be better, no?

Indeed, television ownership was among the main requirements for anyone with even vague aspirations to membership in the broad middle class. Few people could choose to ignore the common association of success and progress with television ownership. One acquaintance, the daughter of highly educated parents working in local development agencies, told me that her family had recently bought a television not for immediate family members, who were busy with other things, but to silence relatives who gossiped that her parents must be in financial difficulty. Another friend—well educated, and supporting a family of four through a respectable but low-paying job—admitted that he felt terribly ashamed when relatives or friends visited because he had no television in his rented flat. Yet he confided that he had a plan to set things right. He was working multiple jobs and saving money in order to buy a motorbike. He planned to leapfrog right through the standard consumer sequence to a motorcycle that would be good for his business, but even better for his ijjat in the eyes of his extended family. The sight of him and his wife on a motorbike would guarantee them—he hoped—a respectable place in their community.

In all of these stories and statements we see a link between a variety of consumer goods on the one hand, and popular understandings of success or accomplishment on the other. People interpret new standards of living and the new material culture not simply in terms of change, but in terms of progress. For many people the state-promoted ideology of development, or *bikās*, has become the interpretive lens through which they perceive change and with which they judge its value and directionality. Thus a certain hierarchy of goods comes to index both historical progress and social progress at the level of the nation and the individual.

These associations came through with exceptional clarity in the comments of one 23-year-old high-caste Newar woman who spoke about the meaning of change in Nepal:

> If there's no change, there's no development (bikās) in the country. Now many peoples' life standards have improved. And once this has happened others want to do it too, right? It's because people have desires (*icchā*) and these are unlimited. While comparing one person with another, people decide they need more money and so they go looking for all kinds of work. The more money people make the more people will get jobs and the country will develop. If everyone finds work then there is development and there is change.

What is interesting about this statement is that it combines more or less timeless understandings of human motivation with a number of thoroughly "modern" notions of means for attainment. Thus on the one hand she proposes that when one person's living standard improves, others naturally desire to reach that standard (assuming that they also regard the change as improvement). Surely this is human nature. Yet on the other hand she proposes that the natural impulse that arises when comparing one's condition with the desired state of some other, is to "need more money and so...go looking for all kinds of work." For this woman "standard of living" is a thoroughly material phenomenon that is indexed by cash and predicated on wage labor. As I have suggested throughout this article, in Kathmandu the language of class ("standard of living") is a language that naturalizes money and market economies.

Regardless of whether the ideological link between labor and resources has much solid grounding in practice in Nepal,[24] it is a link that in the West, and arguably in a place like Kathmandu, signals an ideological paradigm that corresponds to a whole range of "modern" and/or "bourgeois" assumptions concerning the role of the individual, status achievement, the value of labor, and so on.[25] Important also is this woman's assumption that desires are "unlimited" and, since it is this unlimited desire that drives people to labor which in turn propels "development," progress itself is unlimited. What emerges in this statement is an explicit link between limitless consumer desire and the need for labor in the cash economy, which are then ultimately tied to national development, and to limitless growth in the capitalist economy. For this woman consumption becomes not only a key communicative domain for negotiation of middle-class membership in Kathmandu, but a moral and patriotic duty that the middle class can claim and take pride in.

Conclusion: Consumption and Communication

In the statements I have recorded above, one of the most common themes has to do with the anxiety that arises from if not a new, then a heightened sense of social "competition"—a competition often played out in the commodity realm, thereby driving more and more people deeper and deeper into the cash economy. What I have called a kind of "prestige inflation" in Kathmandu is related to a large and rapidly growing consumer field. Even if we cannot say that "culture" is on the increase, we can certainly say that material culture is now far more varied and ubiquitous, as is a kind of "culture of the material" embedded in a host of new ideologies ranging from "development" to "education" and embodied practices such as "*fashion*." As one man quoted above put it, "Now we want so many *other* things." Yet as another lamented, "Even if you have something, you are always lacking something." With every new consumer delight comes another consumer anguish—a tension reflected in the deeply ambivalent attitudes toward goods in the middle-class language and practice of consumption.

Along with the increased availability and variety of material goods in the local economy come increased opportunities for consumption aimed at producing or claiming distinction. From televisions, to bed sheets, to "buffet-style" banquets, as more and more distinctive commodities enter a social setting there are ever greater opportunities for persons to harness these goods to their own projects of individual or group advancement. A rapid influx of distinctive commodities has severely disrupted established codes or modes of display, thereby opening up avenues for persons or groups either to stake claims in higher social categories, or more often, raise the stakes for maintaining membership in groups to which they already belong.

This is especially true when these new cultural goods enter an already volatile social setting characterized by an influx of new people, a huge increase in local cash flow, and new permeable and shifting social formations emerging out of once relatively stable and closed (endogamous) caste hierarchies. For example, in Kathmandu successful immigrant groups (or portions of them) that have arrived in the city over the past few decades—such as the Tibetans, Manangis, Darjeeling Nepalis, and Sherpas—have adopted modern material lifestyles converting newfound cash resources into the cultural capital of modern consumer materialism. These groups pursue a relatively unadulterated strain of class/consumer politics. Yet on the other hand the stories of Kedar, Gita, and Sano Raj illustrate how for the majority of people in Kathmandu more long-standing social identities linked to caste and kin remain highly relevant (to the extent that they can be used to legitimize claims to social superiority) even as these groups increasingly confront the modern pressures of class differentiation. While never purely homogenous in terms of resource distribution, in previous generations a variety of leveling devices and a broad sense of corporate caste/kin identity (often based on a shared mode of labor) tended to keep these groupings relatively united. But now most caste/kin groups in Kathmandu are beginning to show signs of cracking along class lines. While Kedar and Gita have been more or less successful in maintaining ties with their caste fellows within a broad middle class, it has been only with considerable difficulty. Sano Raj on the other hand has fallen victim to the increased costs of maintaining cultural parity with his onetime social equals.

Middle-class competition is real; it is about making and defending claims to power. But while the competition may produce "losers" (like Sano Raj), it does not really produce "winners." In other words, the middle class is a kind of discursive space (where goods play active communicative roles) characterized by constant alignment and realignment with class others. Because different persons and groups claim status based on different configurations of cultural capital (combinations of education, job status, political power, cash wealth, business assets, caste), ranking is almost impossible. A person's rank within the middle class shifts with context (depending on where one's own form of cultural capital is most valuable), and is subject to never-ending debate. Ultimately middle-class membership is not about fixing rank, but about *claiming* and *maintaining* a place in the ongoing debate.

Herein lies an important point: For the most part the inflationary consumer "competition" that people speak of is *not* competition intended to set "winners" *apart* from their social reference group and into some "higher" social category. Instead the anxiety of consumer demands is about the necessity of keeping open the channels of communication that link members of a social group. Here I am in agreement with Mary Douglas and Baron Isherwood who argue that consumption is at least as much a matter of intragroup reciprocity as of intergroup competition. By "keeping up with the Joneses," people are not necessarily trying to *outdo* each other, but are simply "trying not to be excluded" (Douglas and Isherwood 1979:126). The consumer anxiety that people speak of in Kathmandu is typically less a matter of competition aimed at surpassing others, and more about discursively synchronizing the categories of value within groups who share similar social and material conditions. To "win" in this competition is to maintain social parity within the space of the middle class. To "lose"—as Sano Raj and thousands of others in Kathmandu have experienced—is to be left behind, unable to meet the changing demands for membership as one's social reference group transforms its identity standards.

Notes

Research for this paper was conducted during sixteen months between 1988 and 1991 with the help of the Departments of Anthropology and South Asia Regional Studies of the University of Pennsylvania, and a Fulbright-Hays Doctoral Dissertation Research Abroad grant. Special thanks go to Som Raj Ghimire, Krishna and Ganu Pradhan, Ang Tshering Sherpa, and Surendra Bajracharya. Thanks also to Laura Hostetler, Debra Skinner, and Rachel Tolen for helpful comments on various drafts of this paper.

1. Kathmandu's adjacent sister city.

2. The Newars are the original inhabitants of the Kathmandu Valley (see Nepali 1965).

3. See for example Slusser (1982) and Levy (1991).

4. The Ranas were a line of hereditary prime ministers who—having subjugated the royal family and reduced the king to a figurehead—ruled Nepal from 1846 to 1951. Rana rule was characterized by extreme political isolationism, rapacious domestic policies, and the lavish consumption of imported consumer luxuries, a policy that I have described as "selective exclusion" (Liechty 1997).

5. The Armenian merchant Hovhannes Joughayetsi brought English woollen broadcloth to Kathmandu already in the 1680s and, seeing as he followed routes established by previous Armenian merchants, there is likely to have been European fabric in Kathmandu even earlier than this (Khachikian 1966).

6. One of my acquaintances, a Newar businessman from a long-established trading family, maintained that Jung Bahadur's visit to England in 1850 was funded by a special tax extracted from Kathmandu Newar merchants, as was the construction of Chandra Shumsher's magnificent Singha Durbar Palace (completed in 1904). I have been unable to directly confirm this in published accounts though P. S. Rana describes the palace as having been built largely of appropriated materials using pressed labor (1995:162).

7. It is worth noting that when the Lhasa-Calcutta trade collapsed after the Chinese invasion of Tibet, a number of Kathmandu trading families were able to transfer capital resources in Calcutta in the direction of new business opportunities. For example, in the nineteenth and early twentieth centuries Calcutta was the heart of the South Asian tourist industry and several Kathmandu families were able to segue into the tourist trade in Kathmandu via already established Calcutta holdings and business contacts.

8. The key implied that the old man had a cashbox or safe hidden among his possessions.

9. Including twice in the first person.

10. For more on the popular critical discourse in Kathmandu that metaphorically links modern consumerism with drug addiction see Liechty (1995).

11. Chetris (Sanskrit: *kṣatriya*) are members of a high (and traditionally dominant) caste group that includes much of Nepal's social and political elite, including the royal family.

12. Gold Star televisions are assembled in Nepal from Korean components and are slightly less expensive than most imported models.

13. Manangi refers to a group of people from West-Central Nepal who have for centuries been involved in long-distance trans-Himalayan trade. In the decades following Nepal's opening, they were able to use their trading networks and expertise to capitalize on a number of legal, quasi-legal, and illegal business opportunities. In the process members of the community were able to amass enormous personal fortunes (see van Spengen 1987; Watkins 1996). The combination of their Tibetan ethnic background and their great wealth makes the Manangi community a "natural" whipping boy for Kathmandu's middle class (usually upper caste) which views them as a threat to their traditional forms of cultural capital.

14. In Nepal customs officers are widely believed to be corrupt and able to make big money through bribes, smuggling, and kickbacks. Stories abound of families "investing"

large sums in order to acquire a job in the customs service for a son or nephew.

15. Kedar followed a daily regimen of calisthenics.

16. Asterisks in quoted material designate English words used in spoken Nepali.

17. In Nepali, *"bāhun bigryo lobhle, chetri bigryo mojle, newar bigryo bhojle!"* See also Lewis (1984:337).

18. See, for example, Levy (1991), Nepali (1965), Lewis (1984).

19. "A Newari word which means approximately a social structure or organization or establishment which is in charge of certain religious property or charitable funds. The Guthi system divides the Newars into various social groups based on religion, kin, and caste" (Hedrick and Hedrick 1972:57).

20. Writing of the Kathmandu Newar community, Declan Quigley notes:

> To be excluded from [one's *guthi*] association is tantamount to being casteless, which is an option that few Newars are prepared to consider. To be casteless means to be without potential marriage partners ....This is the ultimate force in the obligation to conform to the demands of ...*guthis*. Not to do so is to jeopardize the future of one's offspring (1993:108).

21. Some wealthy investors join up to ten ḍhukuṭi schemes at a time. By borrowing from one fund at relatively low rates and lending to another at higher rates, savvy investors can make good money playing on the margins—not unlike in a stock or currency trading market.

22. For more on ḍhukuṭi and upahār kāryakram schemes in the Kathmandu Valley, see Rankin and Shrestha (1995).

23. Video Cassette Players (VCPs), produced in India, are like VCRs but capable only of playback.

24. In fact the reality of Nepal's political economy historically, and for the most part today, is that labor is *not* associated with wealth or resources, but with poverty. In Nepal wealth and/or property is more often linked with inheritance, conquest, or religious-ethical rights. Stacy Pigg (1992) describes how in rural Nepal "development" or *bikās* is associated not with labor, but with freedom from labor.

25. For discussions of this ideological and class-based shift in Western history, see Arendt's *The Human Condition* (1958), especially her discussion of labor and property/wealth (pp. 109–118) in her broader discussion of labor (pp. 79–135); and volume two of Elias's *The Civilizing Process* (1982), entitled *State Formation and Civilization* on bourgeois rationalization and class distinction.

References

Appadurai, Arjun. 1991. Global Ethnoscapes: Notes and Queries for a Transnational Anthropology. *In* Recapturing Anthropology: Working in the Present. Richard G. Fox, ed. Pp. 191–210. Santa Fe, NM: School of American Research Press.
Arendt, Hannah. 1958. The Human Condition. Chicago: University of Chicago Press.
Douglas, Mary, and Baron Isherwood. 1979. The World of Goods. New York: Basic Books.

Egerton, Francis. 1852. Journal of Winter Tours in India with a Visit to the Court of Nepal. Two Volumes. London: John Murray.

Elias, Norbert. 1982 [1939]. The Civilizing Process, Vol. II: State Formation and Civilization. Oxford: Basil Blackwell.

Hedrick, Basil C., and Anne K. Hedrick. 1972. Historical and Cultural Dictionary of Nepal. Metuchen, NJ: Scarecrow Press.

Jameson, Fredric. 1989. Nostalgia for the Present. South Atlantic Quarterly 88(2):517–537.

Khachikian, Levon. 1966. The Ledger of the Merchant Hovhanes Joughayetsi. Journal of the Asiatic Society 8(3):153–186.

Levy, Robert I. (with Kedar Rajopadhyaya). 1991. Mesocosm: Hinduism and the Organization of a Traditional Newar City in Nepal. Berkeley: University of California Press.

Lewis, Todd T. 1984. The Tuladhars of Kathmandu: A Study of Buddhist Tradition in a Newar Merchant Community. Ph.D. dissertation, Columbia University.

Liechty, Mark. 1995. Modernization, Media and Markets: Youth Identities and the Experience of Modernity in Kathmandu, Nepal. *In* Youth Cultures: A Cross-Cultural Perspective. Vered Amit-Talai and Helena Wulff, eds. Pp. 166–201. London: Routledge.

———. 1997. Selective Exclusion: Foreigners, Foreign Goods, and Foreignness in Modern Nepali History. Studies in Nepali History and Society 2(1): 5–68.

———. in preparation. Fashioning Modernity in Kathmandu: Mass Media, Consumer Culture, and the Middle Class in Nepal. Book manuscript.

Nepali, Gopal Singh. 1965. The Newars: An Ethno-Sociological Study of a Himalayan Community. Bombay: United Asia Publications.

Pieper, Jan. 1975. Three Cities of Nepal. *In* Shelter, Sign and Symbol. Paul Oliver, ed. Pp. 52–69. London: Barrie and Jenkins.

Pigg, Stacy. 1992. Inventing Social Categories Through Place: Social Representations and Development in Nepal. Comparative Studies in Society and History 34(3):491–513.

———. 1993. Unintended Consequences: The Ideological Impact of Development in Nepal. South Asia Bulletin 13(1, 2):45–58.

———. 1996. The Credible and the Credulous: The Question of "Villagers' Beliefs" in Nepal. Cultural Anthropology 11(2):160–201.

Quigley, Declan. 1993. The Interpretation of Caste. Oxford: Clarendon Press.

Rana, Pramode Shamshere. 1995. Rana Intrigues. Kathmandu: R. Rana.

Rankin, Katharine N., and Madan Gopal Shrestha. 1995. The Implications of Local Credit Markets for Financial Policy. ECONews (Kathmandu) 6(2), May 1995.

Slusser, Mary Shepherd. 1982. Nepal Mandala: A Cultural Study of the Kathmandu Valley. Princeton: Princeton University Press.

Stiller, Ludwig F. S. J. 1993. Nepal: Growth of a Nation. Kathmandu: Human Resources Development Research Center.

Uprety, Hari. 1991. Banking Reform: Dhukutis are Doing It. The Rising Nepal Nov. 14, 1991, p. 4.

van Spengen, Wim. 1987. The Nyishangba of Manang: Geographical Perspectives on the Rise of a Nepalese Trading Community. Kailash 13(3-4):131–277.

Watkins, Joanne C. 1996. Spirited Women: Gender, Religion, and Cultural Identity in the Nepal Himalaya. New York: Columbia University Press.

Chapter 7 _____

Situating Persons: Honor
and Identity in Nepal

Ernestine McHugh

Honor as a Cultural Model

Honor, for Gurungs, provides an organizing principle according to which people are situated in social space and accorded deference, and in terms of which individuals apprehend their own significance.[1] Here, I shall examine honor as a cultural model, a set of linked ideas affording a reference for understanding experience and behavior. To discuss honor among Gurungs is to discuss practice, as people in Gurung society devote much attention and effort to defending and enhancing their honor, as well as evaluating the honor of others. To address honor in modern Gurung society is to draw on many domains, to look at what we might call "multiple slippages." One slippage involves the differential interpretation of cultural models, that is, the understanding that individuals will internalize at least slightly different versions of any given cultural model, depending on their life experience (see D'Andrade 1984; McHugh 1985; Strauss and Quinn n.d.). Another slippage involves the fact that as many villagers have migrated to towns, where social, political, and economic circumstances differ greatly from those in the villages, there is no discrete and monolithic, or even nicely homogeneous cultural base, rather the intermingling of contrasting and overlapping value systems according to which honor is defined, and in reference to which people act. Here we will investigate ways in which people negotiate the areas of ambiguity these slippages create, and consider the possibility of an overarching concept of honor in Nepal.

For the past forty years, Nepal has been in a period of rapid change. The political system has shifted, first from Rana autocracy to a multi-party system, then to a Panchayat system advisory to the monarchy (where real power rested), and most recently to a multi-party democracy. During this period of political flux, tourism and other industries, like carpet making, have grown and a wide variety of imported goods have become available in the cities and towns. The availability of luxury goods, dwellings with electricity and running water, education, health care, and nonagricultural employment has attracted many families to the towns from rural areas. Relatives in towns draw villagers to visit more frequently so that people remaining in rural areas are also exposed to ways of life beyond the village. Having conducted research among Gurungs periodically since 1973, I have found it interesting to see how people organize their lives in the face of the changes they have encountered. One concept that has remained a guiding principle for the people with whom I worked is that of honor. As one man, the plaintiff in a case before the village council, noted "The Himalayas are great, but greater still is honor."

Honor arose as a point of attention in many contexts: in the public arena in the evaluation of political action and marriage alliances, in more private contexts in which lineages were assessed and compared, in discussion of appropriate and inappropriate behavior and its consequences, and, most importantly for our purposes here, in people's discussions of their own motivation and speculations about the motives of others. It is this link between honor as a normative concept and as a model coming to bear on a sense of self that makes it so relevant a point of consideration in the examination of identities, experience, and history.

Our focus in this section is on the active production of selves. This can be investigated in everyday life (see Bourdieu 1977, 1990) and in more delineated political and ritual situations (see Dirks 1992; Holland and Skinner 1995). Whether examining more general or more particular situations, it is helpful to remember that action is complexly motivated, not entirely determined by ideology or circumstance. People act in reference to goals they have formulated or feelings that impel them. Whether reaching for goals or responding to feelings, the individual draws on a framework of ideas, or schema, in determining a course of action. These frameworks of ideas, or cultural models, provide bases for understanding the significance of acts or feelings, for evaluating the rewards of achieving various goals, and for formulating causality and so reasoning out the steps by which a given goal might be reached (see Quinn 1993; Quinn and Holland 1987; Strauss 1992; Strauss and Quinn n.d.).

While the idea of a model, framework, schema, set of linked propositions, prototype, or template implies a fixed, ahistorical structure, I would assert that these models are, in fact, more inchoate than the descriptive language would imply, that they are negotiated and operationally defined in specific situations.[2] Roy

D'Andrade usefully differentiates schema and prototype, as follows:

> Note that a prototype is not the same as a schema; a schema is an organized framework of objects and relations which has yet to be filled in with concrete detail, while a prototype consists of a specified set of expectations. The filling in of the slots of a schema with the individual's standard default values creates a *prototype*. A prototype is a highly typical *instantiation* (i.e., an instance) of a schema. [Langacker 1987] (D'Andrade 1995:124)

His definitions, while precise, underline the idea of the schema as somewhat ambiguous in nature, with the prototype seen as a more well-defined instantiation of the schema. We might remember, too, for the purposes of discussion here that prototypes may change over time as the experiences of an individual or group of individuals within a given domain alter. Insofar as individuals wish to promote their prototype as the legitimate instantiation of a shared schema, the discussion of cultural models not only does not preclude, but also may necessitate a discussion of practice.

Honor is an evocative word. While it carries a certain romance of past times and faraway places for the Western reader, it has powerful significance also for those who use it in reference to their own lives. For the Westerner, honor may have an aura of exoticism, suggesting perhaps a coherent set of values and a profound commitment to them, for which those in the West feel nostalgia (honor in the modern West being generally more attenuated and less salient than in many other places [cf. Stewart 1994]). For the Gurungs of Nepal, honor has a practical dimension that might amend the romantic view. Honor in Gurung society has a powerful moral valence, strong implications for social personhood, and great influence on self-worth. Insofar as it is related to social regard and therefore to one's status in social networks, honor also has profound pragmatic consequences in the everyday lives of Gurung people.

The Gurungs of Nepal

Ethnographic Setting

The material that I shall present here is derived from over four years of fieldwork among the Gurungs of Nepal, conducted intermittently between 1973 and 1987. The Gurungs are believed to have migrated some millennia ago from Tibet. They practice Tibetan Buddhism, but also participate in some major Hindu festivals. Their language use also draws on Tibetan and Indic strands: in the villages where I conducted research both Gurung, a language derived from Tibetan, and Nepali, a Sanskrit-based language, were used by local people, most children being bilingual by the age of about seven.

Gurung villages are located mainly in the foothills of the Himalayas in north-central Nepal. The area in which I worked is north of the town of Pokhara, toward the Annapurna Himals, where there are wide gorges with tall scraggy ridges rising above them. These are dotted with villages, set high on the mountainsides. Most villages in that area have jungle above them, and below a cascade of terraced fields. As in most regions of Nepal, agriculture is the main occupation. On the rocky terraces maize, millet, potatoes, wheat, and barley are grown. The fields near the river, much smaller in number, produce rice. Only a few of the wealthiest families whose land is abundant are able to sell a portion of their crops. Most families farm for subsistence. Above the jungle, one or two days' walk from the village, is high pasture where buffaloes, cows, and sheep are taken to graze for long periods of time. Within the last fifty years, though, the herds have dwindled and there is much less activity in the high shepherds' huts. Besides subsistence agriculture, Gurungs engage in service in Gurkha regiments of the British and Indian armies. This provides an essential source of cash income.[3]

From far away one can recognize Gurung villages. They are built high on the ridges, a closely clustered group of whitewashed stone houses with slate roofs. Gurungs reported to me that they preferred the high-density arrangement of the villages because they like to spend time together and also because this makes it more convenient for them to fulfill social and ritual obligations at each other's houses. This rationale reflects the ethos of cooperation and solidarity of Gurung communities.[4] People work and chat together in the courtyards; those who pass by on the path to the fields or the water tap will call out a greeting, or linger a while in conversation.

Gurung society is one in which there is a strong egalitarian ethos. Though it could not be said to be an egalitarian society since status differences occur along the lines of gender, age, wealth, clan, and caste (*jāt* in Nepali), and high status is noted and valued, the muting of status differences is itself said to be a mark of high status. Gurungs remarked that it was rude and unbecoming to call attention to one's own prestige or accomplishments or to the lack of those in others. It was said by many that even though persons might be inferior for reasons of caste, office, or income, they should be included in interactions and treated with consideration and graciousness. Though a high-status visitor would be offered more lavish hospitality, even an untouchable who happened by at mealtime would be given some portion of food on the doorstep. In keeping with such egalitarian values, deference to those with honor should be volunteered rather than demanded.

Honor in Gurung Society

Honor (*ijjat* in Nepali; *nami* in Gurung) and status (*thulo hunu* in Nepali; *theba ba* in Gurung) are interrelated but not identical for Gurungs. While status has to do with social rank, moral behavior is integral to honor. In the village in which I lived while conducting research, the man who in most contexts had the highest status was the village headman or *jimwal mukiya*. His status was contingent on his inherited office and on the fact that he concurrently held high elected office.

His wife took great care to differentiate honor from status or wealth, saying:

> We used to be one of the richest families around, one of the few that had money. Now we have many children and are not so wealthy but we are still among the most honorable. Lesser people have become [Gurkha] officers and wealthier than we are. They like to pretend to be big and make us small. But they cannot touch us. We have our honor.

She went on to discuss the obligations attendant on those with honor, pointing out the fact that though wealth may not be the basis of honor, it is useful in maintaining it.[5] She underlined how this is all the more so in the urban center, in speaking of her son, who was studying there: "Saila spends a lot of our money studying in Pokhara. What to do? And he has to dress well and rent bicycles to go off with his friends, because he is the headman's son."

The headman's office contributed greatly to his honor, as did his lineage and his wealth. Critical to his honor, however, but not to his status, was his behavior and that of his family. Sexual restraint (especially on the part of women), generosity, and evenness of temper were all important to maintaining the family honor.

Among Gurungs, reasoning about honor, lineage, and behavior has a circular quality. A pure lineage, one in which marriages outside appropriate ethnic and clan boundaries have not taken place, is critical to the honor of members of that lineage. It is believed, however, that people from pure lineages are more likely to have good characters[6] and so to behave in ways that are judged honorable. Should they fail to behave in the appropriate ways, the honor of the lineage, especially that of their own household, will suffer. While status greatly enhances honor, even those of low status speak of being motivated to behave in accordance with social rules in order to protect their honor.

Here we have a sketch of the model of honor as it operates within a Gurung village. This can be considered a specific instantiation of a more general schema since models of honor are held among most ethnic groups in Nepal. Constituent features of the model vary somewhat across groups, but the basic schema is very similar. The schema would involve status, wealth, lineage, and appropriate moral behavior. Concern for honor or ijjat was often used in explaining motivation for behavior across ethnic groups, and members of other ethnic groups (Thakalis, Newars, Magars, Brahmans, Chetris, and Kamis) all reported attending to the question of honor when weighing various options for action. Definitions of status and appropriate moral behavior are the features that tend to vary according to context and are sometimes the topic of debate about the moral worth of other ways of life. In order to understand the larger social context in which Gurung discussions of honor are located, it is helpful to examine their relationship to the caste system.

Gurungs in the Multi-ethnic State

Gurungs and Caste

The Gurungs have their own stratification system, which includes two tiers of clans, the high-ranking *chār jāt* (four clans) and the lower *sora jāt* (sixteen clans) (see also Messerschmidt 1976; Pignède 1966), but it is not elaborated to the same degree as are caste rankings in the Hindu system. Though they have their own system of social rank, the Gurungs also exist within the nation-state of Nepal, a Hindu kingdom whose government in 1854 assigned caste rankings to the various ethnic groups of Nepal. Under the legal code of 1854, Gurungs were classed as a superior (i.e., unenslavable) midcaste group (Höfer 1979).[7] The legal caste rankings were abolished in Nepal in 1962, but they continue to influence understandings of relative status.

While orthodox Hindus prohibit the touching of water or water vessels and physical contact between high and very low castes, and forbid hypogamy, as well as commensality between twice-born (the high-ranking castes who wear the sacred thread) and other castes, the only prohibition that holds between chār jāt and sora jāt Gurungs is that of intermarriage. Gurungs observe the Hindu taboos in relation to untouchable castes (not to do so would jeopardize their own caste status and was for some time illegal), but they are relatively relaxed about those, performing minimal purification rituals and showing little distress or anger when minor taboos are violated. They are aware of the idiom of purity, but it plays only a small part in their culture. The Gurung model of status is organized more in terms of centrality than hierarchy (I will address this in more detail below). Whereas the twice-born castes accentuate social distinctions in interaction, the Gurungs minimize them, considering friendliness toward all and self-effacement to be virtues and to indicate that one is a good and honorable person.

While the Gurungs do not see eye to eye with orthodox Hindus in relation to the caste hierarchy (expressing skepticism about the superiority of the Brahmans and Chetris) neither do they see themselves as at odds with the Hindu religion as such. Though they mainly practice Tibetan Buddhism, Gurungs call on Brahman priests for divination and horoscopes, and they celebrate important Hindu festivals like Dasai.

Frames of Reference

For the Gurungs, caste or jāt is a loose framework that classifies a number of groups. Their wealthier rural neighbors tend to be midcaste groups (Thakalis and Magars), equal in ranking to themselves, which suits their egalitarian orientation very well. Discussing Nepal as a whole, Bista writes:

> Very few groups have lived in complete isolation, independent of each other, although the degree of group interaction and interdependence does vary according

to geographical proximity, cultural similarity, and other such factors. In varying degrees most Nepali people have been influenced by several groups other than their own. (Bista 1972:195)

Even in the rural context, Gurungs interact with members of other ethnic groups and are aware of differing perspectives, rising to challenge claims to higher status or greater honor. The ritual superiority of the twice-born castes in the area which is the traditional home of the Gurungs is mitigated by the fact that they are inferior in terms of wealth and power; and their way of ordering the world, both ritually and socially, overlaps little with that of the Gurungs and so holds little moral force.

A knowledge of alternative worldviews of neighboring ethnic groups provides frames of reference in terms of which the Gurungs orient and judge themselves. The neighboring groups provide a social context within which the Gurungs construct their own ethnic identity. Thus, in looking at alternatives we can come to understand the contrasts against which the Gurungs see themselves, the likenesses they perceive, and the evaluations they make of others and, explicitly or by implication, of themselves.[8] As contexts shift, different standards of judgment become operative.

Although high-caste Hindus who followed Brahmanical practices for many years controlled both wealth and political power in Nepal, the Gurungs made little attempt to imitate their way of life or adopt their values, seeing their own way of life as desirable and sufficient. Now traditional values in Gurung society are changing rapidly.[9] Many families are moving to urban areas, and individual advancement is becoming more important than community solidarity, as more and more these two are incompatible.[10] Honor in traditional Gurung terms requires displays of generosity, which tend to interfere with the amassing of wealth. In recent times and especially in urban contexts, it has become as important to own and to show as to share.

The cooperative ethos which suits the economic conditions of village life, in which much farm labor is performed collectively, is less suited to the competitive atmosphere of the town. In the village, too, the cooperative ethos is changing. There has long been a recognition of the tension between individual desire and social demand among Gurungs (see McHugh 1989), but now even in the villages, the muting of individual interests in favor of the social good is harder to achieve. After an incident in which an important man in the village was accused of cutting new bamboo before the time collectively designated, one member of the council deplored the social trend he saw indicated by this sort of action:

> If matters go along like this then animals will only be allowed to graze on their owner's fields, and only the rich will be able to get to their land, because people will not be allowed to walk on each other's fields. They'll have to come in helicopters. That's the way it is going, each person looking only to himself. In a society, it is not a matter of "This is mine" and "That is yours."

As population pressure on the land increases (see Macfarlane 1976), village life becomes more difficult. People—especially women, whose work is heaviest—

who are aware of the comforts of town living wish to escape the physical demands of the village. People also hope that education will secure access to modern goods and a comfortable "developed" (*bikāsi*)[11] lifestyle for their children. In the past twenty years many families with sufficient cash have migrated to Pokhara, an urban center about two days walking distance from the area in which I worked. Changes in the economy and migration to the town have had a strong impact on definitions of honor and on the terms according to which identities are forged. We can see how some of these changes have developed by looking at marriage arrangement as a activity in which honor is defined.

Honor Enacted

Some More and Less Honorable Marriages and Their Consequences

Marriage is central to honor both as a cause and an effect. One attains honor partly by being born into a lineage unadulterated by irregular marriages. The reward for maintaining and furthering one's honor and that of the family is the ability to marry into a family of equal or greater honor. This is thought to enhance one's honor still more and may provide access to wealth, especially for women, who enter the households of their husbands, but also for men, whose interpersonal connections may be furthered. While it is important to note that honor is centrally related to self-image and a sense of worth (to be discussed below), the pragmatic concomitants of honor should not be overlooked. In examining four marriages, we can see the criteria for evaluating the matches and map them against ideas of honor in more traditional village contexts and more modern urban contexts.

1. A Good Marriage in Traditional Terms

This marriage illustrates the degree of economic change in the village. It was a replication of an exchange between lineages that had been a great success one generation earlier. A bride was brought from the natal village of the mother in a landowning family to marry the eldest son of that family. The groom was closely related to the headman of the village and the family was one of the village's largest landowners. The mother in the family had told me of her life, reporting that she "came from honor and married into honor," and talking of how she had benefited from the prosperity of her husband's family. The new bride also came from and married into an honorable home. However, her husband had no cash income and many brothers, and when the landholdings were divided among the brothers within a few years of the marriage, they had barely enough to feed and clothe their children. The bride's parents had arranged the marriage calculating on the benefits of honor and land. For them the features of the model of honor were purity of lineage, wealth in terms of land, inherited office, and appropriate moral behavior. Here, however, the wealth that accompanies the honor of a landed family had diminished to such a degree that their daughter suffered a life of great hardship.

2. The Modern and Traditional Intertwined

The headman's daughter married the son of the headman of another village. Here, too, the marriage was one that brought honor on both households, in terms of the conventional, village-based model. Both families were prominent, and the features of purity of lineage, inherited office, and proper moral behavior were all present. One additional element proved to be extremely important: renewable wealth. The groom was a soldier in the British army and therefore added a good salary to the family's resources. The bride occupied a respected position in the village for several years, then moved to the town, building a house with the capital her husband had saved. Much of their wealth was invested in educating their sons at a prestigious boarding school in Kathmandu.

3. An Untoward Marriage With a Good Result

The beautiful daughter of the village's most prominent family eloped with a village boy from a modest household, to the horror of her family. While the marriage did not violate prohibitions in terms of the acceptability of his clan affiliation, her mother cried when she told me of it, and said that the daughter had dishonored the family. Besides being a decent and reliable person, the groom was a soldier in the British army. Later the bride was able to make amends with her family by using her husband's salary to provide assistance with her youngest sister's education, and to carry out the role of a gracious and generous hostess to various relatives who came to visit her in the town, where she and her husband had settled. They also invested money in sending their children to good private schools.

4. An Honorable Marriage with an Untoward Result

The middle sister of the bride who eloped was observed conversing alone with a young man of the village, again a Gurkha soldier in the British army. This provoked gossip among villagers and alarmed her family, who reported to me that they feared the family would be still more thoroughly dishonored if there were another elopement. They forbade her to see the boy and refused his proposal of marriage. Then they arranged her marriage to a young man from a village about a day's walk away, saying that his was a respectable landed family and reporting proudly that the groom-to-be was educated, with a bachelor's degree and a job in Kathmandu. While his education enhanced the honor of the match, he showed little interest in his village wife, and she stayed alone for many years in the village looking after the agricultural work, with occasional visits from her husband and little income from his modest job.

Marriage and Value

When we look at these marriages (cases 1, 2, and 3 having taken place within a few years of each other, in the early 1970s, and case 4 having occurred about eight years later), we can see a pattern emerging. Cash income has become extremely important, migration to the town has become desirable, and education has become a mark of honor that may (or may not) provide connections that will enhance one's status. Marrying into a family with a source of renewable wealth has become more important than continuing the ties of reciprocal exchange between lineages that traditionally enhanced the honor of a match. Thus, the more recent, urban model of honor for Gurungs would place less stress on lineal purity, traditional office, and land and would place more stress on renewable wealth and education. The criteria for moral behavior also come to differ somewhat, but as Des Chene (1992) also points out, Gurungs appreciate the ethos of their society and wish to preserve it. Though demands for generosity may decrease, Gurungs are likely to continue to judge honorable behavior in terms of generosity, graciousness, and evenness of temper.

Honor and Identity

The Personal Dimensions of Honor

Among Gurungs, beliefs about honor are important in the organization of the relationship of self to society, and the fact that honor is highly valued lends it strong motivational force. People describe their reasons for adhering to social rules most often in terms of honor. Here I shall show how honor is conceived and negotiated in social life, then I shall examine fundamental ideas about the nature of self and person, with particular attention to the ways in which honor links personal and social identity. Finally I shall examine the inscription of honor and identity in space, and the importance of the spatial metaphor in constructions of Himalayan identity. By identity I mean a provisionally coherent, more or less continuous image of the self. Personal identity is that image as constructed by the subject, and social identity is that image as constructed by one's social world.

Let us turn back, as we delve more deeply into honor, to an examination of the concept, since what I am looking at here is the Himalayan variant of a much discussed idea. Honor is a term strongly associated in the anthropological literature with Mediterranean and Middle Eastern societies. Appadurai points out that "ideas that claim to represent the 'essences' of particular places reflect the temporary *localization* of ideas from *many* places" (1988:46). The Nepali word ijjat has its roots in the Middle East, as it is a transformation of the Hindi *izzat* which derives from Persian and Arabic (Turner 1965). The concept of status with a moral valence, which is basic to the idea of honor, should not, however, be thought to be limited to Middle Eastern societies. Such concepts can be seen to exist in many places,[12] though perhaps not in the well-articulated, developed, and salient way in which they operate in the Middle East and South Asia. Pitt-Rivers's (1966) definition of honor, with reference to the Mediterranean area, as the right to value in the eyes of self and society (see also Peristiany 1992; Stewart 1994) holds true in the Himalayan region and makes the complex of beliefs surrounding the idea of honor of special interest when examining the relationship of self to society.

In thinking about honor and its relation to self-image, I have found the delineation of problems and questions in Unni Wikan's work to be very helpful. As she has pointed out in her discussion of honor and shame in the Sultanate of Oman (Wikan 1984), it is necessary to move beyond the paired opposition of honor and shame to a more complex model, examining the processes by which honor is recognized, and examining how and by whom it is defined. To define honor and shame in dichotomous terms is to blur important distinctions between the experience-distant (the overarching normative concept of honor) and the experience-near (the particular evaluation of individual acts, which may, when performed in a sensitive context, erode honor) (Wikan 1984:636). In Nepali, *laj*, the term most often translated as shame, extends beyond the idea of shame to indicate modesty and a sense of propriety, so for men or women to have shame (*laj lagnu*) is for them to behave in such a way as to enhance their honor: that is, to restrain their passions, defer to others when appropriate, and, for women, to maintain proper feminine decorum. Thus, the terms *honor* and *shame* are related, but not in a simple dichotomy or continuum. The idea of honor reflects a larger configuration: through this concept one's place in a given social world is defined and one's character as a moral person is assessed. While Wikan has elegantly examined the ways in which one's social world (the relevant public) defines honor, I shall look at how the negotiation of honor delineates a social world and comes to bear on a sense of self.

At this point some clarifying examples may be in order. In the case mentioned at the beginning of my paper, the plaintiff had sought judgment against a young man from a neighboring village who had publicly suggested that the plaintiff's sister-in-law was a member of the untouchable Blacksmith Kami caste, rather than a Gurung. Continuing his speech, he said, "If the honor of the sister-in-law is lost, the honor of the household is also lost. If the honor of the household is lost, the honor of the lineage is also lost." In his statement we see the linkages through which the honor of the group is enhanced or diminished. Honor can accrue through association and dishonor can contaminate. Thus, even though most lineages consist of three or more separate households, an untoward marriage (as one with a low-caste partner) in one household does not simply reflect badly on the others; it infects them with dishonor (*bijjat*). The most concrete consequence of dishonor is a difficulty in forming marriage alliances within Gurung lineages of equal status to one's own. Thus integration in the larger social group is at stake. If improprieties are known to have taken place in one household, lineage members, whose pressures to prevent the behavior have not succeeded, may distance themselves

from this household, refusing to go there to ritual events and speaking disapprov-
ingly of the party or parties involved. This practice is only partially successful in
protecting the honor of the lineage or individuals within it, since solidarity and
harmony are honorable and divisiveness is not. Honor is shared most strongly in
the household and lineage but is shared in the village as a whole, as well, so that
villages are considered "good" or "bad" to the degree to which their inhabitants
exhibit honorable behavior.[13] In the case mentioned here, the young man was
required to retract his statement and fined five rupees, thus preserving the honor
of the woman, the plaintiff's lineage, and the village.

For Gurungs honor is tightly bound to social integration. The Gurung kinship
system is very elaborate, and to command the precise calculus of relationship and
greet each person with the correct term is an admired social grace and enhances
honor. Embeddedness in social relationships is highly valued in Gurung society:
happiness was often defined by villagers as the condition of being surrounded by
people. An honorable household is by that definition very happy. It is one which
visitors frequent and whose ceremonial events—mortuary rituals, weddings, and
the yearly blessings during the festival of the goddess Durga—command large
crowds. High social esteem facilitates social immersion. Those who are respected
will be surrounded by guests, people seeking advice, and neighbors stopping by
to greet them. When the household of the headman suffered a serious loss of
honor due to a confluence of political and personal circumstances, a nephew in
another village described the decline in the family fortunes and said in summa-
tion, "Everyone used to stop in and chat; now no one goes there anymore."

Social integration and personal wholeness are believed by Gurungs to be powerfully interconnected. The American cultural model of integrity, as honesty in
behavior that implies soundness of character, has some parallels with Gurung
belief, but the Gurung sense of the interpenetration of social and personal realms
is deeper and more precisely articulated than the American view.[14] In the Gurung
model of the self, integrity is more than just metaphorical. People are believed to
have multiple souls or *plah* that can fly out in the face of adversity, including
dishonor, or even as a result of being startled. To prevent plah loss or enable
recovery, the attention of others is required. They pat the shoulders of the afflicted, saying "*shah, shah*" (caught, caught), and in more serious cases, tie a
sacred thread (*rupa*) around the person's neck or offer gifts of cloth. Plah loss can
result in illness and possibly death, so loss of honor (which can cause plah loss)
quite literally constitutes a serious threat to the integrity of the self for Gurungs.
Honor, referred to also in Gurung as the state of being big (*theb*), is believed to
correlate with an inner expansiveness at the site of consciousness and morality,
the *sae*. Thus, people who through good family have honor (and are socially "big")
are believed to have a bigger sae. This large sae confers many benefits. It results
in one feeling peaceful and cheerful and behaving with generosity, self-restraint,
and a gracious demeanor, so enhancing one's social bigness, or honor.[15] The association of honor with integrity of the self and with an inner sense of well-being

lends it powerful motivational force. People explained their motivation for spending large amounts of money to sponsor elaborate rituals (see also Ortner 1989) or offer lavish hospitality in terms of honor. Women reported staying in miserable marriages to protect their honor, former soldiers reported (sometimes in tears) that honor compelled them to carry out orders that they abhorred, and people in general attributed avoidance of confrontation and restraint of legitimate anger to a concern with honor.

Social and Personal Worlds Inscribed

In Gurung society, honor is inscribed in space. Locale is central to personal identity: people were said to be more vulnerable both to evil spirits and to criminals away from their own regions. Gurungs from Tebas reported experiencing feelings of relief and security on crossing the river that bounded the mountainside on which the village rested, thus returning to what was designated as "our own country." Within the village, lineage houses were built adjacent to one another, so that kinship, too, was spatially marked. In a Gurung village people move within nested identities: the household, the neighborhood, the village all define the individual,[16] who refers to those who share these spaces as "our own people." As well as mapping space in terms of boundaries of belonging, Gurungs also give significance to the use of space. There is a choreography to who passes through a door first, who stands in the presence of someone who is seated, who walks ahead on the village path. Most often these arrangements are determined by kinship and relative age, but at formal gatherings honor dictates precedence, with the person who is most honored sitting near the altar of the house and others seated in a descending line of precedence, with the untouchables outside on the porch (see Ortner 1978 for a similar pattern among Sherpas).

What we have in the spatial mapping of identity in both the public and the private spheres is a powerfully integrated model of the world. Beliefs about the plah and sae also employ spatial metaphors, and this metaphoric consistency renders beliefs about the integral connection between social regard and personal well-being all the more compelling. This model is, however, a cultural construction and the world that it represents is not as seamlessly bounded and elegantly integrated as the model implies. Even in a village setting, tensions and contradictions arise and pose challenges to the supposed order. The world within which honor was clearly defined, offering the individual centrality and regard, was one in which the village itself was conceived as central and worthy, and in a moral sense sufficient.

Urban Shifts

Honor in a Changing World

For many Gurungs, however, the political and economic changes of the past twenty years have caused the center to shift from the village to the town. Several wealthier families have set up households in town, leaving poorer relatives or servants to sharecrop the land. Spatial and social orientations no longer coincide in the town. There are several clusters of Gurung households, but neighborhoods appear not to be organized according to kinship or status. Altars are not kept in the public rooms of urban houses, so there is not as clear a point of orientation for precedence in seating. Honor is still of great concern, but the bases of honor are no longer clear. In more traditional terms, the fulfilling of obligation to one's "own people" by offering hospitality and assistance to one's kin and neighbors brings honor. In more modern terms, sending one's child to an elite private school and owning a television also bring honor. As prominent families leave for town, the village becomes the periphery rather than the center and its values lose force.[17]

Nonetheless one should not imagine a dichotomous split between modern urban and traditional rural ways of life, with fixed and divergent models of honor. Gurungs share a tolerance for contradiction and ambiguity that has been celebrated as a South Asian characteristic (cf. Kakar 1978; Obeyesekere 1981; O'Flaherty 1973). This allows them to negotiate the world with models that are flexible, and only provisionally coherent.[18] In general, cultural models tend to become firmly defined in the specific situations in which they are employed (see D'Andrade 1984; Nelson 1981; Quinn and Holland 1987). In a real rather than an ideal world, each situation is somewhat novel, and appropriate behavior requires a certain inventiveness and agility.[19] Cultural models are to a large degree vague and tentative, and they come into focus in specific situations, where people reach a consensus about what should be going on, and compare it to what is actually happening.

Honor and Ideals

Thus, we have the schema of the model of honor, including the features of status, wealth, lineage, and appropriate moral behavior. However, as we can see in examining the marriages that were constructed with these criteria for honor in mind (or in violation of them), they are somewhat ambiguous and so allow for flexibility of interpretation. Thus the constituent features of honor are situationally defined. In the village setting, status rested mainly on inherited office. Wealth derived from land and livestock, and wealth and status were usually linked. An honorable lineage was one belonging to the upper tier of Gurung clans, in which no untoward marriages had taken place. Appropriate moral behavior involved graciousness, generosity, and evenness of temper. Honorable families were expected on occasion to sponsor feasts and give gifts, as well as be generally hospitable. As cash income from sources outside the villages became available, people were able to gain wealth and to claim status (as army officers, or simply as men who commanded wealth) without being from traditionally prominent families. They were able to exploit the usual linkage between wealth and status and make claims to honor by displaying wealth, giving gifts, and offering hospitality, as well as behaving with proper decorum. Like the hereditary leaders of the village, they were addressed by title instead of kinship term—as "captain" or "laptan" (lieutenant). These were the people who competed with those from the historically prominent families for elected office, when the Panchayat system of electoral local government was instituted in 1962.

With the dwindling of land and livestock, and the stripping of power from those who held hereditary office, the traditional bases of status and wealth have waned. Those who are from landed families and traditionally held hereditary office receive deference in the village, but they do not necessarily occupy positions of honor in the urban center. There, status has become determined by wealth, power (gained through elected office), and access to a modern, "developed" (*bikāsi*) lifestyle (see Pigg 1992), which importantly includes consumer goods and education, preferably in an English-medium school. In the urban center, the fine points of the Gurung clan system are little known outside the Gurung community and lineal purity is less important in general than caste endogamy. Among Gurungs, it remains a concern, but is a smaller one than in the village. The Gurungs resist high-caste Hindu domination by stressing the fact that they are a Buddhist people with different values, not a lesser group in the Hindu hierarchy. Gurung ideas of proper decorum assist them in resisting Brahmanical hegemony. Ideals of generosity, hospitality, and gracious self-effacement are common to the ethnic groups that speak Tibeto-Burman languages (Gurungs, Magars, Tamangs, Thakalis, Newars) but are not particularly valued in high-caste Hindu society (cf. Stone 1988). Thus, Gurungs place themselves outside the Hindu framework in reference to which high-caste Hindus have ritual superiority. They value and attempt to preserve the integrity of their own ethnic group by prohibiting intermarriage, protecting the purity of descent as they did in the village setting, but in different terms. These terms are defined in such a way that they challenge claims to Brahmanical dominance implicit in the ideology of caste. The moral vision involved in Gurung ideas of appropriate behavior also gives them a preeminent place in the multi-ethnic urban setting, since as a group they most strongly exemplify the values they espouse.

Conclusion: Situating Honor

We can see here that the constituent features of the model of honor are redefined in the urban setting in order to accommodate the demands of the new situation and also to challenge competing visions of the world that would cast Gurungs in an inferior role. The schema, however, remains consistent, providing continuity in a fundamental aspect of the Gurung worldview, one central to self-image and regard, despite a potentially jarring change in context.

In the urban setting, honor and identity are constructed on different terms. One draws from cross-cutting value systems to accrue honor: wealth and political office become more important than lineage, and education confers esteem. Identity is less strongly determined by one's social origins in the new system because there are multiple frames: the perspective from the village in which embeddedness is celebrated; the more entrepreneurial view of life in the town; political affiliations that define one as a participant in the nation-state or a global movement. There is no fiction of a coherent system in which the individual is enmeshed, and individuals can and must position and define themselves within a looser framework of relations and in terms of a less certain and more diverse set of values.

Does this mean a shift to atomized social relations and an alienated sense of identity in the town? This would be easy to imagine under the circumstances, but it is most often not the case. For Gurungs, the concept of honor acts as an important organizing principle in the construction of social relationships and personal identity. The Gurung model is a local variant of a construct of honor that is widely shared among Nepalis. While interpretations of honor vary, they also converge at essential points, transcending caste, ethnicity, and religion. Tibeto-Burman speaking groups and high-caste Hindu groups differ greatly, yet they share a concern with ijjat, or honor, and they see among its central features generosity and decorous behavior, though these may be variously interpreted.[20] Thus, though the construct of honor is altered when transposed, it remains recognizable in the urban setting and continues to provide a model in reference to which the self can be situated and defined.

Notes

I would like to thank Naomi Quinn and Debra Skinner for thoughtful comments that helped clarify and strengthen this discussion. I am also grateful to Roy D'Andrade for making it possible for me to read *The Development of Cognitive Anthropology* before its publication. Colleagues at the University of Rochester in the departments of Humanities (Eastman School of Music) and of Anthropology have provided indispensable intellectual support.

1. The importance of honor was stressed not only by informants in Tebas, the village in which I primarily conducted research, but also by informants from Ghandruk, Tanchok, Jhilibrang, and Siklis, leading me to believe that the configuration of ideas about honor addressed here is likely to represent, at least loosely, ideas held in common by Gurungs in the Annapurna region of Nepal.

2. See McHugh (1985) for a more detailed discussion. I remind my readers that although I often use the present tense in discussing generalized beliefs that seemed to hold true throughout the fourteen years in which I intermittently worked in Nepal, my reports are, in fact, situated in a specific time period and are historically constrained, not

timeless.

3. See Des Chene (1991) for a thorough treatment of the history of Gurkha service and its impact on Gurung life.

4. See McHugh (1985, 1989) for further elaboration of the ethos of Gurung society and the tensions that exist within it.

5. See Ortner (1989) for a discussion of how wealth is used to achieve social regard among the Sherpas.

6. Literally, *theba sae*, a large heart-mind. This involves qualities of dignity, friendliness, generosity, and evenness of temper. See McHugh (1989:81) for more on this subject. Jeffery (1976) discusses similar beliefs about the relation of lineage to character among Muslim women in northern India.

7. According to Höfer (1979), the Gurungs were considered a *matawāli* (liquor-drinking) group, not entitled to wear the sacred thread, lower than Brahmans and Chetris, but higher than the untouchables, similar to the other prosperous peoples: Magars, Newars, Limbus, Rais.

8. See Mumford (1989) for a thorough analysis of the definition of ethnic identity through dialogue.

9. As the term "traditional" can be problematic, let me define it for my purposes here. In using the term traditional, I am attempting a rough translation of the Nepali term *pahileko calan*, literally "custom from the beginning." This term was used to describe practices (like cooperation and sharing) that derived from the social and economic organization of village life and the values (like generosity and egalitarianism) influenced by local Buddhist beliefs. For those who subscribed to the traditional values, the idea of their being pahileko calan offered legitimation; for those alienated from those values, it had connotations of backwardness.

10. See Des Chene, this volume, for an insightful discussion of the differing perspectives of members of a Gurung household on ambition versus solidarity.

11. See Pigg (1992) for a cogent and insightful discussion of perceptions of the village and concepts of development in Nepal.

12. I am indebted to Ayala Emmett for interesting discussions on this point. Stewart (1994) provides an incisive and comprehensive discussion of honor, and questions the validity of its more exclusive associations with the Mediterranean region.

13. One village several hours walk from where I worked was said to be bad because the inhabitants were "stingy and quarrelsome." Another, across the gorge, was characterized as good because even though poor, the villagers were gracious and kind.

14. See Marriott (1976) for another perspective on South Asian personhood and the permeability of the self. See McHugh (1989) for a critique of that perspective.

15. See McHugh (1989) for further discussion of the plah and sae and their relation to social life.

16. See McHugh (1981) for more on these topics. See Des Chene (1992) for a similar set of beliefs in another Gurung village.

17. See McHugh (1985) for elaboration of this point.

18. I would assert that all but the most technical cultural models are flexible and only

provisionally coherent. The tolerance for contradiction in Gurung society allows them to be more comfortable than many with the ambiguities of their world.

19. Holland (1992) also attends to this issue and uses it as a point of departure for an interesting critique of schema theory.

20. High-caste Hindus, for instance, value ritual generosity in the form of gifts to Brahman priests more than the kind of generalized hospitality shown by Gurungs.

References

Appadurai, Arjun. 1988. Putting Hierarchy in Its Place. Cultural Anthropology 3(1):136–149.

Bista, Dor Bahadur. 1972. People of Nepal. Kathmandu: Ratna Pustak Bandar.

Bourdieu, Pierre. 1977. Outline of a Theory of Practice. Cambridge: Cambridge University Press.

———. 1990. Distinction: A Social Critique of the Judgement of Taste. Cambridge, MA: Harvard University Press.

D'Andrade, Roy. 1984. Cultural Meaning Systems. *In* Culture Theory: Essays on Mind, Self and Emotion. R. A. Shweder and R. A. Levine, eds. Pp. 88–119. Cambridge: Cambridge University Press.

———. 1995. The Development of Cognitive Anthropology. Cambridge: Cambridge University Press.

Des Chene, Mary. 1991. Relics of the Empire: A Cultural History of the Gurkhas, 1815–1987. Ph.D. Dissertation, Department of Anthropology, Stanford University.

———. 1992. Traversing Social Space: Gurung Journeys. Himalayan Research Bulletin 12(1–2):1–10.

Dirks, Nicholas. 1992. Ritual and Resistance: Subversion as a Social Fact. *In* Contesting Power: Resistance and Everyday Social Relations in South Asia. D. Haynes and G. Prakash, eds. Pp. 213–238. Berkeley: University of California Press.

Höfer, András. 1979. The Caste Hierarchy and the State in Nepal: A Study of the Muluki Ain of 1854. Khumbu Himal. Innsbruck: Universitätverlag Wagner.

Holland, Dorothy. 1992. The Woman Who Climbed up the House: Some Limitations of Schema Theory. *In* New Directions in Psychological Anthropology. T. Schwartz, G. M. White, and C. A. Lutz, eds. Pp. 68–79. Cambridge: Cambridge University Press.

Holland, Dorothy, and Debra Skinner. 1995. Contested Ritual, Contested Femininities: (Re)Forming Self and Society in a Nepali Women's Festival. American Ethnologist 22(2):279–305.

Jeffery, Patricia. 1976. Frogs in a Well: Indian Women in Purdah. London: Zed Books.

Kakar, Sudhir. 1978. The Inner World: A Psychoanalytic Study of Childhood and Society in India. Delhi: Oxford University Press.

Macfarlane, Alan. 1976. Resources and Population: A Study of the Gurungs of Nepal. Cambridge: Cambridge University Press.

Marriott, McKim. 1976. Hindu Transactions: Diversity without Dualism. *In* Transaction and Meaning: Directions in the Anthropology of Exchange and Symbolic Behavior. B. Kapferer, ed. Pp. 109–142. Philadelphia: Institute for the Study of Human Issues.

McHugh, Ernestine. 1981. The Women of Tebas: Feminine Perspectives in Gurung Culture. Kailash: A Journal of Himalayan Studies 8(1–2):45–69.

————. 1985. The Social, Cultural, and Personal Worlds of the Gurungs of Nepal. Ph.D. Dissertation, Department of Anthropology, University of California, San Diego.

————. 1989. Concepts of the Person among the Gurungs of Nepal. American Ethnologist 16(1):75–86.

Messerschmidt, Donald A. 1976. The Gurungs of Nepal. Warminster: Aris and Phillips.

Mumford, Stan Royal. 1989. Himalayan Dialogue: Tibetan Lamas and Gurung Shamans in Nepal. Madison: University of Wisconsin Press.

Nelson, Katharine. 1981. Social Cognition in a Script Framework. *In* Social Cognitive Development. J. H. Flavell and L. Ross, eds. Pp. 97–118. Cambridge: Cambridge University Press.

Obeyesekere, Gananath. 1981. Medusa's Hair: An Essay on Personal Symbols and Religious Experience. Chicago: University of Chicago Press.

O'Flaherty, Wendy Doniger. 1973. Asceticism and Eroticism in the Mythology of Siva. Oxford: Oxford University Press.

Ortner, Sherry. 1978. Sherpas Through Their Rituals. Cambridge: Cambridge University Press.

————. 1989. High Religion: A Cultural and Political History of Sherpa Buddhism. Princeton: Princeton University Press.

Perisitiany, J. G., and Julian Pitt-Rivers. 1992. Honor and Grace in Anthropology. Cambridge: Cambridge University Press.

Pigg, Stacy Leigh. 1992. Inventing Social Categories through Place: Social Representations and Development in Nepal. Comparative Studies in Society and History 34(3):491–513.

Pignède, Bernard. 1966. Les Gurungs: une population Himalayenne du Népal. The Hague: Mouton.

Pitt-Rivers, Julian. 1966. Honor and Social Status. *In* Honor and Shame: The Values of Mediterranean Society. J. G. Peristiany, ed. Pp. 19–77. Chicago: University of Chicago Press.

Quinn, Naomi. 1993. Culture in Action: The Case of Americans Reasoning About Marriage. Paper presented at the 92nd Annual Meeting of the American Anthropological Association, Washington, DC.

Quinn, Naomi, and Dorothy Holland. 1987. Culture and Cognition. *In* Cultural Models in Language and Thought. D. Holland and N. Quinn, eds. Pp. 1–40. Cambridge: Cambridge University Press.

Stewart, Frank Henderson. 1994. Honor. Chicago: University of Chicago Press.

Strauss, Claudia. 1992. What Makes Tony Run? *In* Human Motives and Cultural Models. R. D'Andrade and C. Strauss, eds. Pp. 197–224. Cambridge: Cambridge University Press.

Strauss, Claudia, and Naomi Quinn. n.d. A Cognitive Theory of Cultural Meaning.

Stone, Linda. 1988. Illness Beliefs and Feeding the Dead in Hindu Nepal. Lewiston, NY: Edwin Mellen Press.

Turner, Ralph Lilley. 1965. A Comparative and Etymological Dictionary of the Nepali Language. London: Routledge and Kegan Paul.

Wikan, Unni. 1984. Shame and Honor: A Contestable Pair. Man (N.S.) 19(4):635–652.

Chapter 8 _____

Tibetan Identity Layers in the Nepal Himalayas

Stan Mumford

Within two neighboring and historically related Tibetan and Gurung villages in Nepal, Tibetan Buddhist culture has evolved in historical encounters with local non-Buddhist traditions. Rituals—existing as meaningful practices within the cultural and social contexts of the lives of laity and practitioners—are examined on a number of practical and conceptual levels to explore how these vital traditions have incorporated the ideas and imagery of the "other." The following analysis is framed within the reflexive practices of Tibetan lamas who evaluate the ritual images and actions of Buddhist and shamanic ritual discourses in terms of key Buddhist doctrines. Here I focus on the ritual enactments and commentaries of Tibetan lamas as they transmute the images and practices of key ritual sequences within hierarchical layers of meaning and assess them as increasingly superior ethical motivations and orientations within the ideals of Mahayana Buddhism. Since the two villages had economic and cultural relations for many years, it was possible to examine the interpenetration and transformation of elements of each tradition within their shifting social and ideological dialogic interactions.

The research on which this chapter is based was done from 1981–1983 in the Gyasumdo region along the Marsyandi River in the eastern part of Manang District. Fieldwork largely took place in the Tibetan village of Tshap, which had a population of 200 individuals. Tshap was an ideal location for study because it was the regional center of the Nyngma sect of Tibetan Lamaism. It had an active monastery with learned lamas who performed all of the household rites for the villagers and maintained strict ritual and textual training and initiations.

With the Tibetan lamas, I collected information through numerous interviews, textual commentaries, observations of festivals and rites, and lamas' and laity's commentaries on these rites. I also translated relevant textual materials and commentaries on them. An important part of my fieldwork and relationship with the Tibetan lamaist community involved my participation in and completion of the Nyungne fast and initiation.

To explore the encounter of Tibetan Buddhism with active non-Buddhist shamanic practices, I also did fieldwork in a Gurung village on a hillside to the north of Tshap, known as Tapje. Although the Gurungs claim to have come from Tibet a number of centuries ago, and had been clients of the Tibetan lamas, they were deeply committed to their shamanic traditions. Tapje had both Ghyabre shamans who specialized in guiding deceased souls to the land of the dead in the tradition of classic shamanism, and Paju specialists who performed exorcisms and recalled souls who had become lost or stolen. Until at least the 1960s, Tibetans in Tshap had readily employed Gurung practitioners for many of their pragmatic or "worldly" needs (e.g., fertility and healing rites). My research here included a number of in-depth interviews with Gurung Ghyabre and Paju shamans; observations of first fruits, propitiation and death rites; and lengthy explanations of these rites from the various specialists involved in them.

Since the communities of Tshap and Tapje had historical and cultural links with one another, it was possible to explore similar rituals performed by both lamaist and shamanic practitioners to draw out reciprocal transformations in their ritual discourses and practices. Although there has been a growing competition between the practitioners of each ritual complex, the textual prestige of the lamas has been balanced by the superior economic power of Gurung noblemen who supported the shamanic traditions. With changes in the political economy of the region and a decline in Gurung power during the 1960s, there has been an increased rivalry between practitioners in these communities, motivating dialogic comment and interpretation between Buddhist and shamanic practitioners.

Models, Matrixes, and Their Transformation

In the Gyasumdo region of the Nepal Himalayas, there are Tibetan villagers who have migrated from the north over the past hundred years. Their Tibetan identity is highly influenced by their Nyingma lamas, and can be analyzed in terms of three layers, each interwoven with the others. The layers may be defined as the (1) matrix identity, (2) karmic identity, and (3) global identity. Each represents different periods in the life cycle of the individual, the passing of the seasons, and different times in the local history of these villages.

Tibetan lamas promote the Buddhist path by transmuting the images and experiences of the matrix layer—the most natural and pragmatic—into the two higher, more reflexive layers. The transmutations are achieved through ritual discourse performed during household and temple rites. Each layer is important, but the lamas make clear that the matrix model—which focuses on kinship, fertility and health rituals that tie individuals to their conditions of existence (*samsāra*)—is the inferior layer. After being tapped for its power, it must be transmuted into the second level—the individual religious path of merit, faith, and knowledge. For my purpose I am simply naming this karmic identity. After this karmic level is realized, the third global level can be understood, in which the condition of all beings is viewed as interconnected. In Buddhist terms, the third layer is the way of the bodhisattva.

The three-layered model was formulated by Atisa (982–1055), whose coming to Tibet inaugurated the second spread of Buddhism in the eleventh century. The following quotations are selected from Atisa's work: *A Lamp for the Enlightenment Path and Commentary:*

> In that they are Inferior, Mediocre or Superior, persons should be understood as three:
>
> 1. One who by every means seeks out the pleasure of Samsara and cares but for himself alone, that one is known as the Inferior Person.
>
> 2. One who puts life's pleasures behind and turns himself from deeds of sin yet cares only about his own peace, that person should be called Mediocre.
>
> 3. One who wholly seeks a complete end to the entire suffering of others because their suffering belongs to his own consciousness stream, that person is a Superior. (Atisa 1983:5)

The lamas of Gyasumdo view these three types of persons as representing stages of individual maturity as well as modes of ritual orientation. In their view, the local Gurung shamans in Gyasumdo remain at the inferior or matrix level because their rites focus mainly on fertility and health, that is, matters of samsāra that are limited to the matrix model. The second type of persons are "solitary realizers," who have been launched into the Buddhist path of good deeds, faith, and knowledge (the karmic model), which leads only to their own liberation. The third, superior type is based on the Mahayana bodhisattva ideal, with ritual discourse focusing on the "liberation of all sentient beings who are indebted to one another," as well as "offering one's wealth to the entire world"—a global model.

The lamas' ritual sequence becomes a means by which Tibetans may be brought from the inferior matrix identity into the second and third levels. It is a process of transmutation in that matrix-type motivations are acknowledged as valid worldly concerns, addressed ritually, and incorporated into higher levels. Tibetan rites can thus serve functions of abundance, protection, and healing as they do in the shamanistic system, but for the lamas these mundane needs are not the final ends served. Their rites are reflexive in that they incorporate new layers of meaning and commentary on older layers. The Gyasumdo lamas are quite explicit in defining their rites as having these higher teaching functions, and even classify demon exorcism and the death rite as being particularly useful for this end.

The Primal Matrix and the Red Offering

Rituals that remain only at the level of samsāra are acknowledged and then transcended. This is seen by the lamas' repudiation of the "red offering," the animal sacrifices that are performed by the Gurung shamans every spring and fall. During this time Tibetans hold fasts on behalf of the animals killed by the Gurungs since the animals are sacrificed to the "area gods" by the most "sinful deed"—the blood offering. At the same time the lamas teach the laity how to give proper, Buddhist offerings to these same area gods since these gods give benefits related to the natural matrix upon which everyone depends.

This reform program did not always exist. When the forefathers of these Tibetans migrated more than a hundred years ago from Tibet, they at first compromised with the powerful Ghale landlords of the region. These landlords appointed the Tibetan village lay leaders of each village to perform a blood sacrifice each spring. The lamas could not stop this rite. Pasang, the present aging leader of Tshap village, recalls:

> When we first settled here, the Ghale had power over everyone—the fields, trade, everything. We had to sacrifice a sheep or a chicken in our village too. My grandfather's father was the first to do it. When I was young, I also had to sacrifice two chickens: one up to the gods and one down to the serpent deities.

Such compromise with the non-Buddhist form of offerings was challenged in the early 1960s by a great incarnate lama from Tibet, Chog Lingpa Rinpoche. He preached a powerful condemnation of Tibetan complicity in local animal sacrifice. His proclamation sent shock and dismay through the laity, warning that all who participated in the blood sacrifice would be "destined for the Hell Realm (*dmyal-ba*)." Pasang, the village leader, remembers his self-transformation that occurred at that time:

> With great anxiety I went to Rinpoche and asked, "How could we dare to give up the blood offering. Would the area gods harm us or not?" Rinpoche replied, "You must indeed give offerings to the area gods, but these must be 'white' (vegetarian) offerings, not red." Then the lama bound the area gods to the oath. He told us how to do the white offering. Then he wrote a text for our own lama to use in the rite.

The reform text written by the great lama blends the three different orientations—one being the primal matrix—to bring harmony to the conditions of existence, then the karmic model leading to personal liberation, and finally the global model promoting the well-being and liberation of the entire world. The continued importance of giving offerings to the primal matrix is addressed to the serpent deities as follows: "We beg forgiveness for anything we have done against your wishes such as killing wild animals, bringing pollution, digging up the earth, breaking rocks, and stirring up waters."

Then the karmic model is made to overlap with this matrix, using the metaphor of fruition: "May all lands have good harvest and increase of grains...may the truth of the dharma increase...and may all sentient beings practice religion." Then, having set up the first two, the text pronounces on a third model so as to bring both harmony and personal liberation into a global project: "I prostrate before the Buddha, the dharma, and the sangha and to all sentient beings of the six realms who are my parents and whom I would lift up to the Buddha field."

The repudiation of the blood offering in favor of the nonviolent Buddhist version of fertility rites had deep repercussions in the personal identity of the Tibetans of Gyasumdo. While the leader Pasang and the local lamas led the way over, many of the laity continued to fear the wrath of the "area gods" (*yul lha*), particularly since during the 1960s landslides continued to destroy parts of the village of Tshap.

The victory of the Tibetan reform can be seen every spring on the two sides of the Marsyandi River. On their side of the river the Gurung shamans offer the heart of a deer to their underworld gods, while the Tibetans on their side give only Buddhist vegetarian offerings to their underworld gods, the serpent deities. The Tibetan rite culminates when the Tibetan Scriptures are tied to the backs of lay women and children, who then circulate through the agricultural fields (*yum 'khor*). The serpent deities residing beneath are said to hear the text and enter the karmic path toward Buddhist realization, while at the same time they bring the needed rains for that season.

The Gurung shamans still argue that the Tibetans have made a mistake, and that they will be punished by the local area gods for refusing to give them a blood offering. The Tibetan lamas argue the opposite in terms of the karmic doctrine, that the laity would be punished in their afterlife if they return to the red offering. The Tibetan laity are caught in the middle, obedient to their lamas yet half persuaded by the shamanic argument. Some admit to holding both views.

The two models thus collide. The older shamanic layer, as Walter Burkert (1983) has outlined in his study of ancient Greece, is a system of reciprocal exchanges of "life for life" based on the ancient matrix of natural cycles. Retributional punishment results from the failure to achieve harmony. The Tibetan lamas establish a retribution model with a very different project: the individual is to embark on a karmic career, accumulating merit, faith, and insight. The Tibetan lamas' struggle for the identification of the laity with this career amplifies this contest between the two layers.

The Karmic Model and the Nyungne Fast

Each spring the Tibetan repudiation of the red offering is finalized by a fast, called Nyungne, in the temple. In Gyasumdo, the lamas use the Nyungne to gather their laity together to teach the karmic doctrine. The teaching requires a jolt out of the matrix of ordinary life. It is viewed as a kind of initiation: each layperson is expected for a few days to forsake family and the compromises of living in the world (e.g., plowing the fields whereby creatures living in the soil are killed), and huddle in the temple with the monks and nuns without food so as to imitate the life of "religious ones" (*chos-pa*). Scores of sermons and legends are told and thousands of prostrations are done, while the merit accumulated as individuals is dedicated to all beings. In the canonical texts of Tibetan Buddhism, bad deeds (*las gnen*) are causes (*rgyu*) that bring eventual results (*'bras*) in the transmigrational career of each individual. Good deeds (*dge-ba*), accompanied by "one-pointed faith" (*dad-pa tse gcig*) and knowledge (*yon-dan*), are also required in the upward religious path included in the karmic model. Inside the temple where Nyungne was practiced, the consequences were laid out on the wall in a huge wheel of life (*srid-pa'i khor-lo*). Six kinds of rebirth destiny on the wheel are determined, one is reminded, by harmful motivations, particularly those of anger, greed, and ignorance (represented respectively by the snake, the cock, and the pig shown in the middle of the wheel). The rich images of reward and punishment are "warnings" for teaching the karmic doctrine. Such warnings are not sufficient to motivate the Tibetan laity into the upward path, however, and the lamas must in addition illustrate the images during the Nyungne fast with stories.

Certain stories are about serpent deities who do not want to remain in the primal matrix, but desire to be liberated from it by embarking on the Buddhist path. One such story told during one of my Nyungne fasts was about a king who had a beautiful lake. Beneath the middle of the lake lived a serpent deity, who appeared to the king's gardener in a dream, saying:

> I am the serpent deity of this lake. My birth as a serpent deity is punishment for my having broken a Nyungne vow when I was a human in my previous life. Your king and I had been ritual friends, and we attended a Nyungne fast given by a lama. We had to take a vow that we would not sleep with our wives. My friend kept his vow, but I broke mine when my wife made me sleep with her. As a result my friend was rewarded by being reborn a king, while I was punished, being reborn as a serpent deity.

At the conclusion of this story, a solution is found: the king sponsors another Nyungne fast. While the ritual texts were being read, the merit accumulated by the fast was transferred down to the serpent deity in the lake. This enabled the serpent deity to "ascend up to a Buddha field" to gain liberation.

The tale transmutes the serpent deity underworld, usually portrayed as a beautiful natural habitat, into a place of Buddhist retribution, that is, a karmic model. Serpent deities are redefined as "Buddhists" as they join the cultural revolution against the blood offerings that used to be given to them, taking instead only Buddhist offerings that lead up the karmic ladder. It also justifies the repudiation of the natural matrix of ordinary lay life, embedded in family ties, in favor of the extraordinary Nyungne fast, which launches the religious path of liberation.

In a second Nyungne story, which I remember as the most striking, a group of merchants leave their homes and sail far out on the ocean. The ship sinks to the bottom where the merchants find a community of women who invite them to marry them. They do so, forgetting their previous homes.

> One day they came across a prison which was holding previous merchant husbands, caught forever by the demon wives. The prisoners warned them, "You have only one chance to escape. There is a flying horse that comes to the bottom of the ocean on rare occasions. Those who grab onto its mane and tail escape from their demon wives and are taken up to a Buddha field." When the day came the merchants ran to the horse, but only a select few having purity of faith were able to hang on to the horse and ride up to the Buddha field. Others fell back down. Because of their impurity of faith they were tempted to return to their demon wives and children, who cried out to them from below.

It is easy to imagine the impact this story has on the identity of Tibetan Nyungne participants who have come, leaving other members of their families behind and who, perhaps, were tempted not to leave home to undergo these rituals. The merchants, like the serpent deity in the previous story, represent those who, embedded in the world, are caught in the samsaric matrix. Their purity of faith then catches hold of the karmic-religious path and they hurtle upwards.

We must keep in mind that even during Nyungne, the ritual discourse continues to acknowledge the practical importance of samsaric issues. But the lamas use the fast as a particular moment to graft onto this lower matrix the karmic layer of merit accumulation that grows into faith and knowledge on the path toward liberation. The Tibetan laity feel caught between these two layers, particularly after hearing the stories above, which totalize the separation of the two models. Nyungne thus aggravates the Tibetan lay dilemma. For instance, the Tibetan lay-persons who participate in Nyungne are temporarily removed from the samsaric round of work. I myself attended a number of the fasts. Like the select group in the story who did not fall from the horse, we took the vow (*sdom-pa*) to set ourselves apart to live a "faultless day" (*sdig-pa med-par*), to "wipe out" (*sbyang*) past demerits through a rigorous series of prostrations and to accumulate merit for the future through turning prayer wheels and circumambulating the temple. During the second day the fast becomes total: no food or drink, no speaking to anyone, no impure thoughts are allowed.

During the recesses we would sit silently on the rooftop of the temple compound and look down the hill upon the village below, as if peering down from a Buddha field upon a distant world we had left behind. We could see the rest of the Tibetan laity who had refused to come, going about their daily rounds. The farmers who were plowing were, it was assumed, killing innumerable invisible creatures in the soil, dragging the farmer himself farther down into the samsaric cycle, while we imagined that by not eating his produce during the fast we were not implicated in his deeds. To make sure of our virtue we kept our eyes to the ground while circu-mambulating the temple to catch sight of small insects that might be trampled.

The emphasis was on "pure intent" (*bsam-pa bzang-po*), crucial for merit-making. For that reason, admission of feeling hungry by the Nyungne participant was taboo for that would indicate regret for having fasted, a sign of impure intent. As a joke, after the fast was over, those who had attended for the first time were often tricked into admitting "regret." One is asked, "Did you feel hungry?" A simple "yes" brings the immediate retort: "Then you got no merit because you regretted doing it!" I soon learned how to deny any impure intent I might have.

The above discourse is "doubled voiced," that is, partly denying and under-mining that which is asserted (Bakhtin 1981). It illustrates how Nyungne aggra-vates the dilemma of the Tibetan laity, who know they have not really left the world and that motives are not really pure. It also reveals the dilemma of the karmic model, which alone can only arrive at what Atisa called the "mediocre" stage of the "solitary realizer."

Ultimately, the Nyungne fast seems to recognize this dilemma. Although its main theme is to foreground the karmic layer as an initiation, it also gives recog-nition to the global model, the third layer of Tibetan identity, as background. On the altar is Bodhisattva Chenresig, symbol of the compassion that is clearly part of the world system. The wheel-turning king (the sponsor of the ritual) and sym-bols of his sovereignty are displayed below the altar, stuck into the tiers of grain, which represent Mt. Meru and the four continents. It is the wealth of the entire world, constructed in miniature out of the grain of the primal matrix, as if to build the most social and universal from the most basic. The laity, gathered on the temple floor, are given grain and wait for the right moment. Suddenly each per-son holds up two hands and crosses the fourth fingers together as an image of Mt. Meru. The other fingers cross to become the four continents. Then everyone throws grain towards the altar.

This is done on behalf of the Universal Monarch, identified with Bodhisattva Chenresig. As "renunciates," the laity give their small bits of wealth to build up the entire world, the universal kingdom, then wait for return benefits. They could not have gone from the matrix to the global, however, if they had not been initi-ated into the middle, karmic path, making it possible for that which was pre-reflexive to turn reflexively back to the world.

From Matrix to Global: Tibetan Demon Exorcism

One of the most popular Tibetan Buddhist rites of demon exorcism in Gyasumdo is expelling a demon known as "the black three-headed one" (*Nag-po mgo gsum*). This rite employs a "scapegoat effigy" (*glud*), which is viewed as a ransom substitute for the householder who sponsors the rite. The effigy is a three-foot image of the demon himself, made out of dough. The actual demon is, in the course of the ritual, trapped in his own image and then cast out of the village. The demon effigy also represents the entire wealth of the world, pictured as Mt. Meru with the Tree of Abundance rising through the middle, its branches being the thread crosses on top. The demon effigy is exiled from the village, but as "wealth" it is also shared as a ransom to all demons who may be attacking the householder and the village.

The effigy is constructed by the lama in the sponsor's house, with various laity watching and being instructed regarding the meaning of its components. The lamas of Gyasumdo thus use demon exorcism as an occasion to teach. Next I describe how all three layers of Tibetan identity are built into the exorcism, and what they mean to the Tibetan laity being instructed.

Matrix Identity: The Tibetan Horoscope

Tibetan horoscope symbols are block printed onto the dough effigy of the demon. These symbols are fundamental to the Tibetan view that personality is embedded in a matrix of pre-reflexive natural forces. Different components of the self become susceptible to demonic attack according to the waxing and waning of these forces. Each household member knows when his or her "rough" periods are due. These inauspicious times, as wrong configurations, are expelled from the family and the village when the effigy is carried out.

First, the demon effigy is surrounded by twelve small *tormas* (flour cakes), representing the twelve-year cycle of the householder. Each person's birth year, recurring every twelve years, poses a threatening configuration (*lo-skag*) that weakens the self so that demonic harms can penetrate. Block-printed onto the effigy are two other cycles: the nine numerical squares (*sme-ba*), with each square associated with a type of harming demon that will turn up each year, and the eight trigrams (*spar-kha*), as influences of the natural elements, directions, and planetary conjunctions. Horoscope images are thus signs of how conflict and harmony in the matrix of the natural world are interlinked with relationships in society and within personality, with horoscope categories corresponding to emotional states in the psyche.

In the final summarizing statement of the text (*Nag-po mgo gsum*) all types of "disharmonies" (*ma-mthun-pa*) are expelled in the matrix, including those of both nature and the human world: "the clashing of elements, deer fighting in the forest, fish fighting in the rivers, birds fighting in the air, social conflicts such as fist fighting, marriage incompatibilities, sorcerer's competitions, envious talk, hidden anger and blasphemy." All disharmonies are exorcised from the community.

Karmic Identity

Installing the Tibetan horoscope into demon exorcism as a teaching device, the lama draws from the matrix model, implying that the demon is produced by the natural conditions of existence. This model is instantly understood by the laity as a starting point for his transmutations. The lama then seeks to move to the lesson that the demon is produced by bad motives, hence by bad karma. The link is achieved by expelling bad "motives" along with bad "times," even though these are fundamentally different principles.

The lama artistically achieves this by constructing the three heads of the demon to represent bad psychological motives: the middle head is the red ox of greed (*'dod-chags*), the yellow tiger head on the right is anger (*zhe-sdang*), and the blue pig head on the left is ignorance (*gti-mug*). The lama uses the three heads to teach that it is karmic fruition, and not just disharmonies of the horoscope, that caused the demon manifestation. The lamas fully understand that they are using a transmutational device. The essential value of exorcisms, they point out, is to seize on the confidence that the laity have in the cycles of demonic affliction and transmute it into karmic awareness. The exorcism becomes an opportunity, a "means" (*thabs*) to teach the law of karma. The horoscope cycles organize "primary events," which have first impact on awareness and predict the times of suffering for each person. The lamas' exorcism links these crises points to an ethical causal sequence. Critical events of suffering that recur in cycles are turned into visible signs of the sequence of karmic fruitions.

Lay discourse on this matter when the lama is not present indicates that indeed the lesson takes. When there is a series of deaths of children in one family, people assume they are caused by demonic attack. Often people will speculate that it may be karmic retribution (*lan chags*) coming into fruition. The affliction becomes the return of a "creditor," a being whom one has harmed in the past, "cycling back" to demand payment to redress the balance. Demonic attack from the matrix cycle is thus reinterpreted. It becomes reflexive and ethical.

Global Identity

A good part of the ritual text carefully details the sharing out of the demon effigy to all afflicting demons in existence. It is this "distributional" emphasis that requires the transformation of the effigy into a "real" offering that is global. Chanting mantras, the performing lama changes the offering into the wealth of the entire world, making it an attractive ransom. The property of the sponsor is represented on the demon effigy as a part of the offering, magnified into "all desirables of visible existence." Effigies of the sponsor (the "wheel-turning king") and his wife, are put into the construction under the demon as part of the offering.

The five colored threads of the crosses that form the upper branches on the Tree of Abundance take on the significance of a garden paradise of a world king— an illusion meant to attract the demon into the effigy. The green threads are the trees of the garden, blue and black represent sky and lake, yellow is the fertile earth, red is the cliff sides, white the clouds in the sky. Rounding out this utopia are small, block-printed effigies of wild and domestic animals. In the midst is the kingly "palace" of the sponsor, drawn on a wooden tablet.

The lama "beguiles" (*bslus*) the demon into seeing this global vision as if it were real. The demon then enters the effigy as if to be world king himself, rather than seizing the life of the sponsor. Then the text carefully details the "sharing out" of the entire effigy as food given to all demons. Each part and each demon type are named to make sure it is universal.

There is much concern during the exorcism to "expel envious talk in the degenerate era." The central term is *mi-kha* (people mouth; Mumford 1989:153–155), which is the manifestation of demonic attack from envious talk. The Tibetan term mi-kha is highly reflexive. It takes on the meaning of being a sign of post-religious decline, after Buddhism has already been established, and hence is also a sign of what Tibetans view as the evil age (*dus gnan-pa*).

Mi-kha is the opposite global reality to that of the world king. As the demonic symptom of the degenerate era, mi-kha conveys that envious talk is worldwide, and that exorcism must deal with it to expel its harms from the village. The sponsor, because of his leadership, knowledge, or wealth, is assumed to have attracted the attention of envy far and wide. The clothing or rags that are put on the back of the demon effigy when sending it into exile is a worldwide distribution to satisfy this envy.

Also called mi-kha are food leftovers and impurities such as used tea leaves, garlic, onions, black radishes—all dumped into a small bag along with a few coins. The lama's power of visualization turns this mi-kha into "tasty traveling provisions" that are distributed among all envious demonic agents, who will take them away. Epitomizing the envy of the less fortunate in the world, these demons are satisfied and "turn their mouths away" (*kha sgyur*). The lama's solution to the decay of the "evil era" is thus a distribution of equal shares to every source of envy.

The events that impact on each person are thus built into the demon image, layer by layer, and are articulated in the lama's text and oral commentary. When the ritual is over, a carnival atmosphere erupts. Laymen from every household come and parade the three-headed demon through the village in the darkness of night, beating drums and howling to terrify the demons trapped in the effigy. After the demon is expelled at the edge of the village, they throw white flour over each other. All become "purified" (*dag-po*). The lama states, "If the exorcism were totally successful, the evil era itself would be expelled."

From Matrix to Global: The Tibetan Death Rite

The Tibetan death rite involves all three layers of identity, with all three again in the order we have seen. This again allows the lama to use the rite as a teaching device to move from one layer to the other in a transmutational sequence. I base my analysis here on a death rite of a woman named Samden (name fictitious), a member of the village who died during my research period. Much of my data on Samden's death rite are taken from carefully taped recordings of oral performances of the lamas. They are the lamas' own commentaries in front of a lay audience attending the funeral. I have thoroughly detailed the Tibetan death rite elsewhere (Mumford 1989:195–224), but here focus on the "folk heart" of the rite that most clearly dramatizes the three-layered model.

Karmic Interpretation of the Horoscope Matrix

In the Tibetan villages of Gyasumdo, the lama's guiding of consciousness in the death rite may be interpreted as a practice that seeks to realize in death the transmutation process already begun in demon exorcism. This was particularly appropriate in Samden's case since it was widely believed that her death had been caused by demon attack.

Underlying the funeral rite, we find the Tibetan death-horoscope matrix as the starting model used for making interpretations. The response to a death by Tibetans is thus to view the deceased as caught in the web of forces as defined by the horoscope, and then with the help of the lama's calculations, to distinguish this cyclical matrix from "karmic fruition" (*rgyu-'bre*), which is directional. The death horoscope text (*gshin rtsis*) focuses on five components of personality: life force (*srog*), soul (*bla*), body (*lus*), power (*dbang-tang*), and luck (*rlung-rta*). The health of these components wax and wane separately in predictable cycles, depending upon the twelve-year cycle and five elements, the eight trigrams and the nine numerical squares. Each component has periods of deterioration (*nyams*) during inauspicious years, and it is these which are calculated by the lama immediately after a death.

The death horoscope of Samden was a dramatic event. The lama gathered on the roof of the home along with a group of laymen, where he laid out his pictograph and put down white and black pebbles on each of the five components of personality, while reading the textual interpretations and making commentaries.

Portions of the lama's commentary had to do with whether the death was "timely," the direction of demon attack that may have caused the death with warnings of further attack, the compatibility of the horoscopes of those who may carry the corpse, and the direction and time of the procession. All of these calculations were purely cyclical, showing intercausal influences surrounding the death. But the final portion of the commentary was highly directional and karmically significant, showing once again how the lama could use the horoscope matrix for teaching laity the karma doctrine.

The textual commentary eventually showed that Samden's death was the result of karmic fruition, and that the demon that had killed her represented a manifestation of karmic justice from past evil deeds of her previous life. The lama's commentary went on to say that these deeds would require punishment for ten days in one of the Buddhist hells, then she would be reborn a bird or a horse, after which she could gain a good human birth as a doctor. The text then went on to state how meritorious acts by family members during the funeral (e.g., commissioning a thanka painting) could erase the bad parts of the prognosis. But the karmic lesson had been skillfully dramatized, and its message of Samden's prospects immediately spread from the rooftop to the entire village.

The Bardo Guidance: Individual Guilt

In contrast with the horoscope section, the emphasis at the beginning of the Bardo guidance is first to strip away all prior relationships in which the individual had been embedded, forcing the consciousness to focus only on the sequence of "karmic traces" (*bag-chags*) inherited by the individual from past lives. These traces are eventually standardized into the six karmic categories called "poisons," with each assigned to one of the six realms of existence into which the deceased may be inclined to be reborn. Hence, anger (*zhe-sdang*) leads to the realm of hell, greed (*'dod-chags*) leads to a human rebirth, and so forth. They are thus viewed as six destinies of individual karmic tendencies.

I was able to tape record oral performances of the Bardo guidance by the village lamas in a number of funerals. In the earlier parts of the guidance, these psychic tendencies are not yet categorized into standard categories. Instead, of primary concern are the ways in which consciousness is surrounded by uncontrolled psychic influences, which the lama interprets as "karmic."

In the Bardo guidance for Samden, the lama said to her wandering consciousness.

> Samden! You will not at first recognize that you have died because you will continue to have the tendencies of your former life. It is like a person waking up from a dream and continuing to have the thoughts of the dream. Walking on a cliff, enjoying wealth and food, whatever. Then later you realize there is nothing there. You have only this mental body of past inclinations! Your mind goes everywhere. The deeds of the past hurl you about. Like a frightening wind they carry you to the top of a mountain, then back and forth across the river. You experience these former inclinations, not knowing where they will take you.

Samden must learn to equate the past inclinations that hurl her about with karmic fruition. The lama's discourse shifts to the family matrix, recognizing her embeddedness in relationships and possessions. He asks the deceased to forsake her attachments and then transmutes them into the karmic model: "Samden! You have many clothes in the house. Forsake these. Put them out of your mind! Realize you have died or you will harm your family and destroy their wealth. These inclinations arise from your former evil deeds that you have not purified."

We note here how karmic discourse ("evil deeds") overlaps with the shamanic belief in the hovering of the dead around the living. The lama is fully aware of this folk matrix among the Tibetan laity and utilizes the overlap as a teaching device to work his Buddhist transmutation. Samden had at first tried to deny the memory of her karmic past by the illusion that she was still alive, a member of her community. Stripping away family and possessions, the lama leads the deceased to the point of guilt awareness. Further, the influences that she first experienced as a wandering consciousness were fluid, decentered, unbounded. In the Bardo sequence these diffuse relationships are removed, leaving only karmic memories. These are pulled out by the lama and brought into sharp focus: "Now you will remember all your deeds. You will think, 'I did much sin (*sdig-pa*). I killed, I chopped, I said bad things, I thought bad things. It seems I must experience it now!'"

The deeds which Samden must remember include all of her former existences. They are now bottled up inside a boundary of individual guilt, as if it were a measurable record of private deeds that could be counted and weighed. This final transmutation from matrix to karmic identity is completed by the great drama that is well known in the Tibetan Bardo. The Lord of Death (*gShin-rje Chos-rgyal*) now appears along with scales and a mirror.

> Your mental body shakes as you go to gShin-rje Chos-rgyal. You may try to lie, saying, "There is no pile of sin." But you are then shown everything in the mirror of your deeds....Now it will appear to your consciousness that gShin-rje Chos-rgyal is coming with a hammer, an axe, a knife in his hands to pound you, to chop you, to tie you up and beat you...

From here on, throughout the lama's Bardo guidance, demonic imagery is called up in order to further refine the psychic path that has been launched by the karmic layer. After the deceased is forced to look in the mirror, the demons which "come with a hammer" are defined as purely mental, rather than as objective.

As the Bardo guidance proceeds, the horrifying demonic images are used in a variety of ways as a means of psychic shock to initiate the consciousness along the path of ever higher awareness. As guide, the lama can count on the fact that Samden is a member of the local community and has already experienced the "reality" of demons in afflictions and exorcism rites. These memory traces are present as the lama continues to employ them. First the demons extract guilt admission, then the demons rush forward as disguised forms of the Buddhist deities. Then demonic images are presented as metaphors of mental projections, and finally unmasked so that one's psychic inclinations can be "renounced" (*spang*). The lama finally asserts: "These terrifying ones have come from nowhere! They have been produced from your own mental propensities. They will not actually kill you or chop you. It is your own consciousness that strikes you."

The above process emerges as part of the karmic path; thus, it is consciousness still examining only itself, with the danger of remaining at what Atisa called the "mediocre" level of the solitary realizer. It does not yet have the "bodhisattva mind" that is globally aware.

From Karmic to Global: The Sharing of Merit

The threatening appearance of the Lord of Death had at first isolated Samden's individual "pile of deeds." But a dramatic shift of emphasis occurs, which breaks open the karmic path into a global one. The destiny of the deceased is now viewed as interdependent with a vast gathering of aides, starting with the family and reaching out to the whole cosmos. The family is the first circle of help, so the Lord of Death grants a period of "leave," the forty-nine-day period of the funeral sequence, to gather the help needed:

> The Lord of Death says that he grants you leave of forty-nine days before he will judge you. During that period, go to your father, your mother, your brothers and your sisters. You didn't do enough virtue during your life so now your family will have to do it for you. They will send you the merit they make, saying, "Come, take this *dge-ba*!"

Only after the model of personal karmic punishment had been dramatized could this model of shared merit be introduced. The lama continues his guidance:

> You will go to your home now and see your family weeping. "Why are you crying, I am here," you will say, but they cannot hear you. You sit on their laps and hug and kiss them, but they do not see you. Then you cry out to them, "I have died and have committed much sin (*sdig-pa*). Please make merit for me so that I won't have to go to hell (*dmyal-ba*)!"

Samden has been driven to this point by passing through the "karmic" part of the guidance, but the family was prepared by listening to the lama read the horoscope, which warned of a bad destiny if a grand funeral were not held. By "sending merit" (*dge-ba btang*) to the deceased, the worst prognosis of the horoscope would be overturned.

The central merit-sending rite which the family performs is a grand distribution of rice cakes (*tshogs*), carried in baskets to all the other villages of Gyasumdo. This is to "feed all the living and all the dead without partiality," paying all debts and accumulating merit on Samden's behalf. The merit comes from feeding globally, that is, no one in existence is to be left out. This lesson is conveyed to both the consciousness of the deceased and the participating guests, who explain it readily to the anthropologist.

From Karmic to Global: The Severance Rite

There is a grand ritual performed as background to this tshogs rice cake distribution. It is the "severance" rite (*gcod*), which invisibly distributes Samden's body to the world while the rice cakes are actually given out. It achieves what the lamas call the union of two truth levels: the severance rite "cuts away" Samden's ignorance, while at the same time the cut pieces of her corpse are viewed as the rice cakes that are fed to the villagers in Gyasumdo, and hence to all the world.

As a transmutation device, the severance rite turns merit-making into global awareness. It begins by imagining that the goddess Ma-cig lab dron cuts off the top of the skull of the corpse, skins the body, and lays the skin out on the ground. She cuts the body into small bits and places them on the skin. This becomes a mandala pattern of Mt. Meru and the four continents, as a total offering of wealth.

This totality is put into the skullcap. It becomes a huge cauldron in which meat is cooked. "Countless Dakinis" come to distribute the food throughout the three worlds of the cosmos, while their chanted mantras multiply the amount of flesh, blood, and bones so that it "never ends." As the corpse is distributed, it takes on different forms to meet every need in an ideal kingdom. The lama's exposition of the text proceeds as follows:

> Imagine that your corpse has been turned into healing medicines, fine clothes, precious jewels, all kinds of grains and domestic animals: horse, cattle, elephants. Then it is transformed into forests, flowers, and wealth of all kinds. Nothing is lacking. Indeed, your corpse has been turned into the Wish-Granting Tree itself, along with mansions, gardens, gems, and all desirables to satisfy the five senses.

All regions of the cosmos and the beings of each realm are named so they may receive their share, particularly the upper world, the human world, and the underworld. The wealth of the natural world and that of all beings within it is renewed. The image then shifts to the guests, both invited and uninvited, who come to feed on the flesh, visualized as a huge banquet. The lama quotes the deceased: "Since I must die anyway, I give my body to all the guests. All come, I'll feed you! Those who like meat, take my flesh. Those who like blood, take my blood. Those who like bones, take my bones. Those who like skin to wear, take my skin. Take it all, I don't need it!"

The theme that "no one may be excluded" is the central focus that emerges in the rite. No elite in the cosmos is selected to receive more than the rest. This is expressed systematically, using the metaphor of "guests" (*mgron-po*) who are both invited and uninvited, to dramatize that even those ordinarily excluded must obtain their share. The worst demons are uncontrollable, scrambling to pick up anything that falls on the floor.

The total share-out is called the compassion of the bodhisattva mind. In an ultimate sense, the distribution is deserved by those who receive it. It is repayment of a debt owed to them:

> I dedicate this offering to all sentient beings because they are my mother and father and so I repay them for their kindness: the clothes that have been provided for me by my mother, like the first fruit that is always given to children. Therefore, I offer this to all my parents who have been so kind to me. I am in debt (*bul-on*) to them all.

Turning the guests at the feast into one's "mother" is crucial. The mother represents every sentient being that has been one's parent in one's transmigrational career. Every relation of obligation created during the whole of the past returns as a vision in the consciousness of the deceased. No one may be excluded. Psychic liberation is thus fused with global inter-debtedness.

The Tibetan severance rite emerges as the global identity layer after the karmic layer has individuated self-awareness. As a method of transmutation, it begins with a meritorious act of giving one's body to the world, but ends with confession that one is already indebted to the world. The shift from karmic to global identity is made by drawing on ancient elements of the matrix layer to achieve the transmutation. It is initiation into an encompassing identity in which all consciousnesses interact, moving all beings forward into the future together rather than individually.

The Bodhisattva Mind

The global mind portrayed in the severance rite above is the bodhisattva mind, one with compassion for every sentient being. The lamas of Gyasumdo agree that one who is enlightened must also have such compassion, just as Atisa defined the bodhisattva mind as the superior, third identity.

In the Bardo guidance of Samden, reference to the bodhisattva was highly prominent, both as the ideal state of mind of the deceased, and as the ideal image of the Buddhist deities that were supplicated. Even "wrathful" demonic images turn out to be "bodhisattvas in disguise," letting down light rays as "hooks" that would draw the deceased up into a Buddha field. For this portrayal the lama draws on local imagery in Gyasumdo:

> Imagine a village down the trail that appears to contain enemies hostile to the people of Tshap village. As you walk toward that village you see people coming toward you and you think, "They are enemies coming to kill me." But they are not enemies! They are coming to welcome you! You had mistaken welcoming Buddhas for enemies! These terrifying deities are coming to welcome you. There is no need to fear them or to flee.

The bodhisattva mind thus operates horizontally in the world. The deceased is asked to renounce everything that is familiar, while embracing that which is alien, even "enemies," by recognizing the welcoming bodhisattva in the alien.

Toward the end of Samden's Bardo guidance, the bodhisattva's universal compassion is dramatically presented as a narrative. It centers on Bodhisattva Amitabha (*T. 'Od-dpag-med*), whose Buddha field is said to lie in the West. Amitabha's compassion is the last chance of deliverance from samsaric rebirth after everything else in the Bardo guidance has failed. In the narrative, Amitabha as a human bodhisattva is offered Buddhahood by the already enlightened Buddhas. But they make the offer in "karmic terms," that is, in terms of his individual merit and "one-pointed faith." The Buddhas proclaim: "Each one alone must renounce his (her) karmic deeds! Since you have no further deeds to renounce, you are ready." But Amitabha makes a counterargument. He refuses to remove his individual psyche from the relational field to which it is indebted. He replies: "All sentient beings of the six realms are my mother and father. If I were to be liberated by myself, it would be unpleasant as long as they are suffering. If they are not ready to be born in a Buddha field, how can I be ready?"

On the one hand the bodhisattva is qualified for extrication from the global field, but on the other hand he cannot forsake it. Liberation is reformulated into an ironic paradox: the psyche that is ready for enlightenment knows that it cannot be liberated as long as there is suffering anywhere, for a wound would remain within the psyche.

The bodhisattva's refusal is a confession of complicity and indebtedness, appearing on the other side of inner awareness. The definition of enlightenment itself is transformed, recollecting the entire sequence of mother-child links through time. It is a temporal enlightenment that does not empty out the history of sentient beings, but rather incorporates historical links into an ironic awareness from which there is no escape.

The ideal of not forgetting his mother and father clearly draws on the kinship matrix, but now becomes a highly reflexive, post-enlightenment model. Further in the narrative, the rejection of "karmic readiness" (Atisa's "mediocre solitary realizer") in favor of the superior bodhisattva mind, shows clearly how the lama uses this contrast to teach the laity to move from the karmic to the global layer.

Conclusion

My discussion here has focused on a series of important Buddhist rituals as they compared with related shamanic practices within an intercultural setting of Tibetan and Gurung villages in north central Nepal. In an effort to understand how Tibetan Buddhist culture has evolved in historical encounters with local non-Buddhist traditions, this study has explored how Tibetan lamaists have encompassed and reflexively portrayed the ideology and practices of local "other" practices within the ideals of key Buddhist doctrines.

To summarize, the rites and stories outlined above exist in ritual time. The lamas' struggles for the transformations of laity from the matrix layer of identity to the higher karmic and global layers are circumscribed within a complex series of practices aimed toward this goal. Lamas consciously manipulate rich images and elaborate rites as teaching devices and mediators of identity. The villager who participates in these practices is transported from a world of material concerns to a more spiritual plane. Other identities and possible worlds are brought into existence by these rites and commentaries, and the laity move among them. Although they re-enter the material world after the rites are completed, they return as selves reconfigured by these visions of other worlds and levels of existence.

Note

Stan Mumford worked on this chapter until his death in December 1993. The editors added the first five and the final paragraphs to provide some orientation and closure. See Mumford (1989) for more ethnographic details and analyses from a Bakhtinian perspective.

References

Atisa. 1983. A Lamp for the Path and Commentary of Atisa. Richard Sherburne, trans. Winchester: Allen and Unwin.

Bakhtin, Mikhail. 1981. The Dialogic Imagination. Austin: University of Texas Press.

Burkert, Walter. 1983. Homo Necans: The Anthropology of Ancient Greek Sacrificial Ritual and Myth. Berkeley: University of California Press.

Mumford, Stan Royal. 1989. Himalayan Dialogue: Tibetan Lamas and Gurung Shamans in Nepal. Madison: University of Wisconsin Press.

Chapter 9 _____

Crossing Boundaries: Ethnicity and Marriage in a Hod Village

Premalata Ghimire

In a multi-ethnic community like Nepal, identities are constantly in a state of flux. Individuals are engaged in creating, maintaining, switching, or changing their personal and cul tural identities to meet their various needs and life-strategies.[1] In this process, as I have shown elsewhere (Ghimire 1989, 1990) for the Hod[2] of Nepal, individuals often claim a distinct ritual identity different from other members of their larger ethnic group and create diversity and hierarchical categories within what is supposedly a homogeneous and egalitarian group. In this chapter, I aim to demonstrate that even in situations of flux, at a given point among most cultural groups ethnic divisions do become somewhat fixed and recognized among and within these groups. No matter how diverse individuals are within their ethnic group and how much social distance they maintain from each other, they do display a certain degree of homogeneity in their sharing of certain cultural traits and meanings. The Hod of southern Nepal exemplify this sharing in their marriage practices. Here I describe the Hod's various marriage rituals and examine two in detail, the *ghardi jawae* and the *jawae kirinok*. Through an analysis of these marriages, we can see how, even when the Hod violate certain crucial norms of incest, group endogamy, and virilocality, their social system allows them to reconstruct and reassert their ethnicity through different channels.

The Ethnographic Setting

The Hod of this study are from Sunauli, a village about six miles east of the industrial town of Biratnagar, bordering on Bihar, a northern state of India. Sunauli's total population of 346 includes 170 Hod and 176 people belonging to various Hindu caste groups. Hod and caste groups are ethnically and culturally different. The Sunauli caste people[3] have a patrilineal, virilocal organization, and they practice dowry and arranged marriages. They speak Maithili, an Indo-Aryan language. Furthermore, they have a hierarchical ideology based on ritual criteria of purity and pollution (Dumont 1980), and believe that no two castes are equal. Although these Maithil people, with the exception of the Halwai caste, are defined as untouchable by Bahun and Chetri (the two highest castes), they do not accept this label for themselves. They do, however, extend the same logic of purity/ pollution to define the Hod as untouchable, and conceive their own ritual status as higher than that of the Hod.

The Hod have an egalitarian ideology. Their language, *hod rod*, belongs to the Austro-Asiatic language group. They have a patrilineal, virilocal organization, and they practice clan exogamy and brideprice. In addition, they are monogamous, allow marriages by choice, remarriages, and divorce for both sexes.

Hod-Caste Interaction

In spite of cultural differences, Hod and caste groups have been living together, sharing a long history of interaction. In India, the Hod had many unpleasant encounters with caste groups. Many studies show that members of Hindu caste groups exploited the Hod as servants and wage laborers, and forced them into "free" (slave) labor. This caused great resentment and anger among the Hod who had lived and pursued an independent life. In order to regain their autonomy, they organized various revolutionary activities (see Datta 1940; Derne 1991; Fuchs 1965; Jay 1964; Sinha 1961) around the late nineteenth century against the Hindus who, by then, were called *diku* (outlaws) by the Hod. The aim of these unrests was to make the Hindus aware of their exploitation of the Hod, in addition to making the Hod cognizant of their distinct cultural heritage.

In 1874, this unrest pressured the British government to classify the Hod as "aboriginal," "tribal," and a "scheduled tribe,"[4] and to designate an area—Santal Pargana, which is in the Bihar state of India—for them (Dube 1977; Fuchs 1973; Ghurye 1963). Previously one of a series of unrests—the Kharwar movement— had led some Hod, like the Sapha, to combine both Hod and caste rituals in their daily behavior (Bodding 1921), and to use these rituals to define themselves strategically within and between groups (Ghimire 1990; Orans 1965). They were influenced by missionaries as well who encouraged many Hod to convert to Christianity (Basu 1944; Bodding 1935, 1942; Culshaw 1949; Prasad 1971; Skrefsrud 1873; Stock 1899).

Following this period, some Hod migrated from India to Nepal and settled along the southeastern border of Nepal, near Biratnagar and farther east. The scarcity of land and food in India during this period and their love for hunting in the jungles of Nepal were some of the reasons for their migration. This migration was also encouraged by the people who had moved from the northern part of the country to the southern low-lying jungle belt known as the Tarai to expand their fortunes through farming. A few of these individuals were employed by the Nepali government as *jamindār* (landowner) to cultivate that land (Regmi 1976:109–110). These jamindār, most of whom were Bahun and Chetri, hired the newly migrant Hod to clear the forests for farming. In this process, a few ambitious Hod and a few Maithil caste people, who had also moved to the area around that time, were also able to own fifteen to twenty *bighā* (about five-eighths of an acre) of land per person. In Sunauli, a few Hod (especially the Sapha Hod) and the local caste people became landlords in this way. Although this was not much land compared to how much some jamindār owned—1,600 to 2,000 bighā per household—it was nonetheless sufficient to help a Hod emerge as a *mālik* (master) within his small village.

Although still economically deprived compared to the jamindār, the Hod developed a patron/client relationship with the jamindār, whom they called *mundo*. They also continued sharing their physical space with the Maithil people, most of whom were untouchable, and were referred to by the Hod as diku.[5] Their constant interaction with the local caste people has enabled the Hod to grasp each other's differences, and their interaction with Nepalis in the wider region has enabled them to understand the power and politics of the Bahun and Chetri. Since the Hod have encountered many Bahuns consuming alcohol and meat (especially chicken), accepting bribes, and exploiting others, they do not believe in the ritual superiority of today's Bahun.[6] They share the belief that a Bahun's claim of ritual superiority is based on power and wealth, not on purity.

Despite such views, the Hod do share some beliefs with upper-caste individuals. They both divide people into two major categories: Hindu and Muslim. The Muslim category includes all non-Hindus, including Christians, and is ranked lower than the Hindu. In spite of such sharing, however, the Hod differ from caste groups in their definition of Hindu. For members of castes, the criterion of being Hindu is through birth; for the Hod, it is behavior—a particular set of manners and rituals—which distinguishes them from the Muslims. Any alteration in behavior brings a change in Hod identity from Hindu to non-Hindu and is, therefore, highly disapproved of. For the Hod, then, it is possible to be Hindu without being a member of caste society.

Such understanding of "others" and distinction from "others" have compelled the Hod to think about their own ethnic status within and between nations. They see themselves as Nepali, but take an interest in the Indian government's quota system that aims to uplift the socioeconomic and political status of the *ādivāsi* (aborigines), including the Hod in India. Their concern with their ethnicity and culture was clearly expressed in three meetings held in 1985, during my second period of fieldwork. These meetings were attended by Hod from twelve villages, and they addressed issues such as brideprice, arranged marriages, and ethnic law. The need for these meetings arose because of the actions of a particular headman. This headman accepted an excessive amount of brideprice in arranging his daughter's marriage, he acted like a diku and a mundo by not allowing his daughter to choose her own spouse, and he called in the local police to solve ethnic problems. For example, suspecting his servant of having knowledge of his daughter's affair with another man, he beat the servant and asked the local police to imprison him. Also, since his daughter eloped with her lover and married him in a Biratnagar court, the headman was not able to return the brideprice—now doubled—to the intended groom's family as was required of him by ethnic law.

The issues discussed in these meetings clearly indicated the extent of the Hod's understanding of others and themselves. Hod villagers requested that brideprice be viewed as a ritual and not a way to make money or "sell" one's daughter. They also discussed the need to curtail excessive alcohol consumption, continue Hod cultural practices, and educate their children so that they could succeed like mundos.

It is this political, economic, and social background and the multi-ethnic interactive context (Bennett 1975; R. Cohen 1978; Kilbride, Goodale, and Ameisen 1990) that have made the Sunauli Hod more conscious of traditions and their ethnicity. The sharing of fundamental cultural values—such as a common mythical ancestor, language, religion, and dress (A. Cohen 1981; R. Cohen 1978; Keyes 1976; Narroll 1964)[7]—provides a basis for Hod ethnic identity. And it is through interaction with other groups (Barth 1969)—in this case the numerically and socially dominant caste groups—that the Hod have become more aware of the "we/they" distinction.

My research indicates that the more interactions Hod have with caste people, the more engaged they are in maintaining their ethnicity and ethnic boundaries. One of the ways they do so is by inhibiting sexual relationships and intermarriages with caste people. These sexual and marriage prohibitions along with their flexibility and diversity in other marriage practices and the cultural rules of *bitlaha* (social and ritual impurity) work to maintain their ethnic identity.

Over the years, the long-term interaction with the Hindus and the missionaries has divided the Hod into three ritual categories: the Bidin (Hindu) Hod who follow their traditional rituals, the Sapha (clean/pure) Hod who practice both the Hod and caste rituals, and the Christian Hod, who are Pentecostal, Catholic, and Lutheran (Ghimire 1992).

These are not endogamous groups. However, since both the Sapha and the Bidin Hod define themselves as Hindu and distinguish themselves from the Christian Hod, there are more intermarriages between these two groups than between either of these groups and the Christian Hod. Although the Hod, including the Sapha, deny any caste influence on the Hod social structure, the Hod view each other as having higher or lower ritual status. This categorization challenges their egalitarian ideology, although it has not brought about much change in their marriage practices. Except for the Christian Hod, all Hod practice the marriages described below.

Marriage Forms

Marriage is one of the most important rites of passage for the Hod. They perceive married life as the normal and happy life. As a result, it is rare to see an unmarried Hod. To encourage each and every Hod to enjoy the happiness of married life, the Hod social system provides various avenues of marrying within their group. The ten different forms of Hod marriages (*bapla*)—each with a different set of rituals[8]— enable the Hod to choose the form of marriage—with minimum or maximum rituals—according to their economic, social, and ritual statuses. Such diversity and flexibility in marriage practices act both to distinguish the Hod as a group and to separate them from their caste neighbors. Furthermore, I argue, these various forms of marriage function to persuade the Hod to marry within their ethnic group and maintain their ethnicity.

The various forms of Hod marriages have different requirements and implications. Some marriages demand that the bride's status be either *donguo* (maiden) or *chadwi* (divorced woman), whereas other forms do not mandate her status. Some forms are more relevant to one's economic and/or social status. Furthermore, these marriage forms require distinct types of payments which differently define jural, sexual, and reproductive rights. Most marriages are negotiated with brideprice. One—the *ghardi jawae*—demands uxorilocality and bride-service. And yet another one—the *jawae kirinok*—is related to the concept of social paternity, requiring groom-price.

Marriage with Brideprice

The *daudo* (basket) marriage involves brideprice (*pon*). Brideprice includes cash, goods, and feasts that are paid before and after the wedding. This type of marriage requires the groom to rub three handfuls of vermilion powder on the bride's head as she sits in a bamboo basket carried by her male kinsmen.

Two crucial features of this marriage are the use of vermilion powder and the status of the bride, who must be donguo. Among the Hod, a donguo is a woman who has not yet put vermilion powder on her head, but who may have eloped with a man once or twice, and/or has had sexual intercourse with this man.[9] However, if the man with whom she eloped puts vermilion powder on her head, she is no longer a donguo, but becomes a *baplai* (a married woman). If she decides not to live with this man, she becomes a *chadwi* (a divorced woman). The powder, therefore, is the key factor in changing a woman's status from maiden to married woman.

Gender plays a significant role in daudo marriage. Although both men and women regard this marriage as highly prestigious, a man can have as many daudo marriages as he can afford to, but a woman can have this type of marriage only once—when she is a donguo. Figures 1 and 2 demonstrate that no Hod women had daudo rituals in their second marriages, but two men had second marriages of this type because their second wives were donguo. One of these men, a Sapha Hod, also had these rituals in his third marriage when he married another donguo.

Figure 1. Marriages Practiced by Hod Women

Types of Marriages	Number of Marriages			
	1st (n=52)	2nd (n=23)	3rd (n=6)	4th (n=1)
Daudo	29%			
Tharia		13%	17%	
Or Ader Apangir	7%			
Itut				
Baha Sohan	56%	83%	83%	100%
Ghardi Jawae	4%			
Jawae Kirinok				
Church	2%	4%		
No answer	2%			

Figure 2. Marriages Practiced by Hod Men

Types of Marriages	Number of Marriages					
	1st (n=36)	2nd (n=15)	3rd (n=4)	4th (n=2)	5th (n=2)	6th (n=1)
Daudo	30%	13%	25%			
Tharia	6%	13%			50%	100%
Or Ader Apangir						
Itut		7%				
Baha Sohan	50%	67%	75%	100%	50%	
Ghardi Jawae	6%					
Jawae Kirinok						
Church	5%					
No answer	3%					

The daudo marriage is the most prestigious form of marriage among the Hod for several reasons: the girl must be a donguo, the couple's parental consent is necessary, the rituals are more elaborate and traditional, and kin and community participate. This marriage also reinforces one's social class. It provides a context to display one's wealth and demonstrate one's status quo. As a result, it demands more brideprice than any other type of marriage. Therefore, only wealthy Hod can afford the daudo marriage for their children. The *tunki dipil* marriage—yet another form—also requires the donguo status of a woman, but it is only practiced by Hod parents who are poor and cannot afford to bear the expenses of their daughter's wedding.

The third category, *tharia* (plate) marriage, is for the chadwi women. This marriage is completed when the groom applies vermilion powder to the bride's head while she sits in a squatting position on a brass plate. The tharia marriage is the most prestigious marriage for a chadwi; however, only those women who have been divorced once or twice are eligible for this ritual. Since the Hod patrilineal system devalues women for their chadwi status, this marriage is less prestigious than daudo because the bride is always a chadwi. And as a marriage of lesser prestige, it requires less brideprice. However, as with the daudo marriage, gender is significant in tharia marriage. A man can have as many tharia marriages as he can afford, but a woman can participate in this ritual only two or three times (Figures 1 and 2).

Other Hod marriages are for donguo and chadwi. In the *nir bolok* marriage, either member of the couple forcefully enters the household of the other and starts living and working there in order to please the members of the household, including the intended spouse. When the individual finally pleases the concerned party, he or she marries, employing any of the rituals mentioned above—i.e., daudo, tharia, or a simple payment of brideprice—depending on the donguo/chadwi status of the female spouse or the economic status of the concerned parties.

The *or ader* is a marriage by capture, and the *apangir* is one by elopement. In these forms, a man pays a moderate amount of brideprice to a woman's parents if she agrees to marry him. If she does not, he pays a penalty to her parents and to the Hod village council for his "deviant" act.

In *itut* marriage, a man forcefully applies vermilion powder to a woman's head with the intention of marrying her, but without first getting her consent. In many cases, the woman may not even have prior knowledge about the possible occurrence of such an action. It is one of the reasons why among all marriages, Hod regard itut marriage as the least prestigious; the other reason being that if the woman refuses to marry the man, his deviant act severely affects her status, changing it from donguo to chadwi.

Despite the diversity of marriage forms, there are two features to consider. First, although some marriages are more prestigious than others, all are culturally approved, have equal validity in uniting a man and woman as husband and wife, and legitimate the status of their children. Second, these marriages are more related to the economic status of individuals than to their ritual status as Sapha or Bidin Hod.[10] Although both Sapha and Bidin Hod consider daudo marriage the ideal type, only rich families practice this.[11] In addition, since this marriage requires both the donguo status of the bride and the higher economic status of the bride and groom, its practice is restricted only to those wealthy parents whose daughters are donguo. Since most of the Sunauli Bidin Hod are poor, they do not have daudo rituals even for their donguo daughters.

Brideprice is an integral part of all the above marriages. None of these marriages is negotiated or considered complete without this payment. The brideprice payment (*baha sohan*) is also a ritual complete in itself. It is culturally approved and validates the status of a couple as husband and wife, making them eligible to live together and have children. However, since baha sohan is related to one's lower economic status, it is widely practiced by the poor Hod. Figures 1 and 2 show that more than half of the Sunauli Hod, both male and female, had only baha sohan to legitimize their unions as husbands and wives.[12]

Marriage with Bride-Service

As mentioned earlier, the ghardi jawae (son-in-law at residence)[13] demands uxorilocality as postmarital residence. It reverses the procedure of the brideprice payment, creating a marriage union different from those designed simply to unite a woman and man as wife and husband. Thus, it reveals the distinctiveness of the Hod as a group, separate from their caste neighbors. Although in some cases among the local caste people, sons-in-law do live with parents-in-law, there is no marriage ritual among them—as among the Hod—that creates such residential change. The Hod's ghardi jawae rituals require a change in postmarital residence from virilocal to uxorilocal, and, thereby, give cultural approval to this type of marriage.

The practice of ghardi jawae marriage, however, is limited among the Hod, primarily because it is practiced only by those Hod who have older daughters and much younger sons, or only daughters. By bringing a son-in-law to live with them, Hod parents exercise their rights over their daughter and her husband's domestic services and children. This form of marriage, therefore, requires bride-service in lieu of brideprice.

Bride-service is a contract between the bride's parents and their son-in-law. The contract is for a minimum period of five years and can be renewed. During these years, a ghardi jawae lives with his wife's parents in their household and contributes his labor to the household economy. Upon termination of the contract, he receives a pair of oxen and 160 kilograms of grain (rice and/or wheat). If his parents-in-law are rich, he may also receive a small amount of land and a house. If they are too poor to complete the contract, he may live longer with them, awaiting the contract's completion.

The ghardi jawae marriage, therefore, reverses the postmarital residence of the Hod. As mentioned earlier, the Hod have an ideal of patrilineal virilocal organization. In most cases, postmarital residence follows this rule. A couple with daughters, however, will practice uxorilocality or serial uxorilocality. During both periods of my fieldwork, there was only one case of serial uxorilocality. This occurred in a neighboring village in the family of a rich Bidin Hod couple who had six daughters. In 1985, they were enjoying the bride-service of their youngest son-in-law. Upon termination of the contract, the couple renewed the ghardi jawae contract of one of their other sons-in-law.

The correlation between ghardi jawae marriage and one's economic status deeply affects the identities of the spouses. Since virilocality is the norm, the residential arrangement created by this marriage bestows a certain degree of shame on a man. Although no social stigma is attached to this marriage form, it reveals his lower economic status and demands his subordination to his parents-in-law. As a result, no man wants to have a uxorilocal residence unless he is very poor and sees some prospects in living with his parents-in-law.

A Hod man also loses much of his freedom by being a ghardi jawae. In the beginning, he is a stranger in the village. Furthermore, no matter how long he lives in the village, he is expected to behave in a formal and reserved manner with his parents-in-law and elder members of the village. Although a woman goes through a similar situation in a patrilineal virilocal marriages, it may be more unpleasant for a Hod man because his behavior contradicts cultural norms. Such a situation leads him to feel tension and conflict and pushes him to finish his contract quickly.

In addition, despite his long residence with his in-laws, a ghardi jawae has no inheritance rights in their property. Only his sons can inherit from his wife's parents; he cannot. He does, however, retain rights in his own parents' property.

Although a ghardi jawae recruits his children into his clan, he may not fully exercise his rights over them. This restriction on his rights is evident in the Hod naming system. Hod work with only a few names. Each Hod gets two names in the *nimdak* (name-giving) ritual; one is the name of address, and the other is a ritual name—a name of one of the child's male or female ancestors *(bonga)*. In some cases, the ritual name is also used for addressing individuals, but mostly it is kept secret and used only for referring to the child's bonga. Although the names of the ancestors are passed on to members of descending generations, this practice does not lead to the creation of a long-term genealogy. In fact, the Hod naming practice discourages the preservation of any such knowledge. Hod generally cannot recall the names of their deceased kin beyond the third ascending generation. This is mainly because the names of address as well as the ritual names are repeated in every alternate generation.

This naming pattern first allows an equal distribution of the names of both sexes of the ascending generations, which, in turn, indicates that the patrilineal system of the Hod recognizes women as ancestral bonga and does not downplay their role as such. Second, the naming pattern shows that it is not important for

Hod to know much detail about their remote ancestors. The repetition of names contributes to erasing knowledge of previous generations and puts emphasis on one's immediate ancestors/ancestresses, especially one's parent's siblings and one's grandparents. These relatives are most important to Hod because they often know them personally, spending most of their childhood with them and sharing moments of both happiness and sorrow. Whenever needed, these are the bonga who come to one's rescue. Finally, the Hod naming practice allows grandparents and grandchildren to identify and form an intimate bond with each other since they both share the same name. This tie is further strengthened through a joking relationship that exists between these two generations.

Hod names follow different patterns in virilocal and uxorilocal arrangements. In virilocal residence, the first two children receive their personal names from their patrikin, especially their father's father and father's mother. The next two children are named after their matrikin, and the fifth and the sixth after their patrikin again. This pattern of naming is reversed in uxorilocal residence. Here, the first two children acquire their personal identities from their matrikin, particularly from their mother's father and mother's mother. The next two children receive their names from their patrikin, and the fifth and the sixth from their matrikin again.

Although the egalitarianism of the Hod requires equal distribution of names among the third descending generation of children, uxorilocality encourages distribution of matrikin names over those of the patrikin. Such a pattern responds to different social expectations. It creates a special attachment between children and their matrikin and encourages the children to look after their matrikin—especially their mother's father and mother's mother—and their household property. This bond is further strengthened through jural and legal rights. For example, if a woman does not have any male siblings, her male children will inherit from her parents.

These practices of naming and inheritance weaken the status of a ghardi jawae, but enhance the status of his wife, the daughter of the household. Although the patrilineal organization of the Hod does not allow a woman to inherit property from her parents in the presence of any of her eligible male lineage members, it does allow her to enjoy long-term economic security. This security stems from an inheritance pattern where male children inherit from her parents, and she becomes their guardian until they reach adulthood. Furthermore, uxorilocality reveals her higher economic status vis-à-vis her husband, and, since a woman continues to stay in her natal household, it gives a woman more autonomy in maintaining her ritual status of Sapha Hod versus Bidin Hod. For example, a Sapha Hod woman married to a Bidin Hod ghardi jawae may continue her Sapha Hod rituals. She may also encourage and influence her husband and children to participate in these rituals to become Sapha Hod. Through this residential arrangement, a woman can change the ritual identity of her husband from Bidin Hod to Sapha Hod.[14]

Thus, a ghardi jawae arrangement is highly beneficial for a woman. It allows her to enjoy various statuses—jural, economic, and ritual—and, therefore, challenges the internal contradiction inherent in Hod life: while their ideology theorizes that all Hod are equal, in practice, women are accorded lower status. Hod women's lower status is evident from the characterization of them as potential witches who cannot be trusted because they are capable of hurting and endangering others. Furthermore, as potential witches, Hod women are prohibited from attending or participating in any religious rituals or political gatherings, thus lacking opportunities to make decisions at the village level. The lower status of women is also acknowledged verbally through referring to them as *murkha*, meaning ignorant and/or stupid.

Although a ghardi jawae arrangement does not eliminate these cultural beliefs regarding women, it does counteract the inequalities in status and opportunities by making women visible as social actors and allowing them to exert power over several domains. In this process, it also enables women to challenge the patrilineal ideology without directly confronting men.

Such indirect and subtle confrontation (Dirks 1992; Haynes and Prakash 1992) responds to a particular situation and permits both men and women to pursue different strategies to structure social relations. As we anthropologists know, individual behavior is not always determined by social norms (see Connell 1987). Uxorilocal residence reveals how Hod display choices through acknowledging, yet ignoring the norms, and employing a range of marriage and inheritance patterns to construct meaningful relations.

Furthermore, uxorilocal residence—together with the absence of the practice of tracing genealogy and Hod women's overlapping membership in both their husband's and father's groups (which I explain later in this chapter)—raises some important questions and calls for reexamining the patrilineal organization of the Hod; this is similar to what Barnes (1962) and Geertz and Geertz (1975) have done in probing the relevance of African models in the context of New Guinea and Bali, respectively.

Marriage with Groom-Price

The other marriage form that does not require brideprice or demand any brideservice is jawae kirinok. As with other Hod marriages, this one also legitimizes the status of the children. But jawae kirinok marriage stands out as distinct and unique because it is not necessarily concerned with uniting a man and a woman as husband and wife. It is related mainly to the issue of paternity and the social status of unborn children. In the rituals associated with this marriage type, parents "buy" a father for their pregnant daughter's unborn child if she is unable to name the father, if the genitor denies paternity, or if the father is from a different cultural group. The genitor could be Hod or non-Hod, but the "purchased" father must be Hod so that he can give his clan name to the unborn child. By "buying" the child—recruiting the child into her social father's clan and making her Hod—the child's social status is legitimated. Failing to "acquire" a father makes one an outcast. Since such buying rituals are performed only when Hod are afraid of losing one of their group members, and because such occurrences are rare, there are only a few cases of jawae kirinok marriages. During 1978–79, there were no such marriages in Sunauli (see Figures 1 and 2). The degree of shame and humiliation experienced by the pregnant mother and her guardians may have kept people from even discussing this ritual during this period. In 1985, however, Sunauli had one such marriage, which will be examined below.

The distinctiveness of the jawae kirinok marriage becomes more obvious when compared to similar situations arising from premarital pregnancies among local caste people, who condemn premarital pregnancies and make every effort to ostracize the pregnant mother and her child from the village. When such a child is born, the mother and the child are considered outcasts and, supported by the cultural ideology of pure/impure, a lower ritual status is assigned to them. The Hod, however, deal with such a situation differently. Although they do not encourage premarital pregnancies or pregnancies by someone other than a woman's husband, when such a situation does occur, they have provisions to incorporate the mother and child into their ethnic group. It is in situations like these that the jawae kirinok ritual becomes meaningful.

This ritual is primarily concerned with the strict observance and reinforcement of the rules of incest, clan exogamy, and group endogamy. In the Hod social system, a clan does not play any political role in the organization of Hod activities (Kochar 1970; Somers 1977; Troisi 1979). However, as I discuss below, clans do play a crucial role in maintaining and asserting a Hod's natal, social, and ethnic identities. To understand the meanings of jawae kirinok marriage, implications of clan identity must first be examined.

Clan identity is important for both men and women. In his study of the Santal of Kuapara, India, Kochar notes that "at the time of marriage a female loses the clan name of the father and acquires the clan name of her husband" (1970:43). My research, however, shows that a Hod woman keeps her natal clan identity even after she has married. One of the ways her affiliation with her patrilineal clan is symbolized is through her continued use of her father's clan name as her family name, even after marriage. Hod believe that those who share the same clan name are either siblings or father and child, but never a husband and wife or a mother and child.

By keeping her father's clan, a Hod woman maintains her natal identity even after she is married and/or a brideprice is paid for her. While the brideprice extends her husband's right over her sexual, domestic, and reproductive services, and allows her to be a bonga of her husband's lineage and clan after her death, the continuation of the natal identity symbolizes her relationship to her own ancestral bonga.[15] Such affiliation is symbolically acknowledged when she visits her natal home during the festivals of Soharai and Baha, bringing rice-beer and puffed or flattened rice. The food, especially the rice-beer, is first offered to her ancestral bonga who reside in her natal household, and then is distributed among her hosts and their guests. This ritual indicates the autonomy that a Hod woman has vis-à-vis her husband's group and her continued membership in her natal household.

Clan identity also validates a Hod's social and ethnic status. In the Hod social system, everyone must have a clan name to be a member of the ethnic group. Failure to have a clan name for a child means failure to legitimize the child, which leads to exclusion from the group. As mentioned earlier, in cases of unknown or unacknowledged paternity, fathers are bought from within the Hod group to legitimize the clan and ethnic statuses of the unborn children. As I demonstrate later, failure to do so results in ostracism of the individuals involved: parents, guardians of parents, and the child.

A Hod's clan identity, thus, has far-reaching implications. In the absence of clan identity, status is not validated and a Hod does not acquire ethnic membership. A woman cannot get married within the ethnic group and cannot have proper funeral rites. In such a case, the person is not offered food after her death by her descendants and, therefore, ceases to be their ancestral bonga. A Hod virtually ceases to be a Hod in the absence of clan identity, and is then considered to be a *bitlaha.*

Bitlaha can be literally translated as dangerous, disorder, outcast, impure, or polluted. It is a temporary state that affects both the village and its members.[16] A village becomes bitlaha during birth and death, and an individual becomes bitlaha when he or she violates certain shared norms, such as those of endogamy and clan exogamy. Furthermore, bitlaha is contagious, affecting a bitlaha's parents, guardians, and the village as a whole.

A bitlaha virtually ceases to be a member of the ethnic group. He or she is, however, given an opportunity by the *pancha* (the male representatives of the Hod political office)[17] to regain his or her ethnicity by paying a heavy penalty. Until this penalty is paid, the entire village remains bitlaha, and no festivals, life-cycle rites or other religious rituals can be performed. In addition, other Hod stop interacting with the bitlaha and his guardians, and ignore his presence in all formal and informal contexts. Such a situation brings shame to individuals who act against group norms, and forces them to leave the village, staying outside until they pay the proper penalty for their improper acts.

Bitlaha individuals may choose not to come back, but as my research shows, in most cases, they do return to their villages. This is because of their kinship network and strong interpersonal bonds. To decide to remain a bitlaha means to break these ties and to live in isolation in a non-Hod community. Such a situation brings "social death" to a Hod and, therefore, discourages her from permanently moving out of her group and being treated as an outcast by members of the larger group. I argue that such a simple, but highly valued code of morality, embedded in the notion of bitlaha, helps the Hod remain within their ethnic boundaries. The following case studies illustrate this.

Case Studies

1. In 1978, a twenty-two-year-old Hod woman, Hapan Mai, eloped with a Mohali caste man named Jayaraj. Both of them were from Sunauli. Jayaraj was already married and had been living with his second wife, an eight-year-old daughter from his first wife, and his parents. After eloping, Hapan Mai and Jayaraj lived in India for ten months. Since Hapan Mai had violated the norm of endogamy, her parents had become bitlaha immediately following her elopement. The Mohali also became outcast as far as the Hod were concerned, although the Mohali themselves did not think so. To remove the disorder caused by this elopement, formal political meetings were held by the Hod pancha, and both the Mohali and Hod families were asked to pay a heavy penalty in cash and kind. In the beginning, the Mohali family refused to abide by Hod rules. But when its members suffered the consequences of being isolated and excluded from all village activities, they agreed to play by the rules and paid a heavy penalty to the Hod village council for their son's breaking Hod norms of endogamy. The Hod family also paid an equal amount of money for their daughter's deviant act. In addition, since this act was a matter of great shame for them, Hapan Mai's father left Sunauli "to save face" and lived in India for almost five years. Following the payment by both parties, the village of Sunauli did not remain bitlaha any longer, but when Hapan Mai and Jayaraj came back to Sunauli after ten months, they were not welcomed by either of their families. Both families had suffered enough and were not willing to take any more risk. Such a situation forced the couple to break their relationship. By 1984, Hapan Mai was married to a Hod from a neighboring village. In the meantime, Jayaraj had rejoined his second wife in Sunauli, and moved to live with her in her natal village ten miles from Sunauli.

2. Twenty-three-year-old Baha was mute. She lived with her mother and brother in one part of her mother's brother's household compound. One day they learned that Baha had become pregnant. No one knew who the father of the child was. Although Baha could not speak, she could have pointed her finger at the man who was responsible for her pregnancy. She described the man in the beginning, but was forced to keep quiet by her mother because it seemed that the man was no other than her own mother's brother, a person with whom sexual relationship is taboo. Villagers waited until the fifth month of Baha's pregnancy before suggesting to her mother, directly and indirectly, that if it were not possible to identify the father, she should think of buying one through jawae kirinok rituals so that the ethnic status of the unborn child could be validated. But Baha's mother did not buy a pater. She said she was too poor to afford one. So slowly villagers withdrew from her family. Baha's mother understood she had become bitlaha and that she could no longer live there. She left the village one day with Baha, but both of them came back after two months. Baha was "clean" by then. We were told that she had a miscarriage. Both of them became a part of the village once again.

3. The third incident involved Maili, a twenty-five-year-old female. Maili was

married twice to Hod men and had two children from her second husband. In 1985 she was single and living with her mother and stepfather in their household. During one harvest season, while working in Biratnagar, she conceived a child from a caste man of India. When Maili saw the caste man leaving her in that situation, she returned to her parents in Sunauli. Since Maili had broken the rule of endogamy, she and her parents had become bitlaha. Her parents were already suffering the consequences of their daughter's actions. So, after Maili returned, they called the pancha to remove the state of bitlaha, and paid a penalty for Maili's act. This transaction was completed with the pancha's acceptance of cooked rice from Maili. Following this, Maili's and her parents' ethnicity was reconfirmed.

Maili's pregnancy complicated this case further. Since it is against ethnic law to abort a child, the pancha allowed her to keep the baby on the condition that it would have a clan identity. Maili's parents then arranged a jawae kirinok marriage for their daughter and "bought" a father for her unborn child. This father was about sixty years old, was Maili's mother's father's kin and, therefore, belonged to a clan different from Maili's. He gave his clan name to the child, collected his fee, and left the village. The child's clan and ethnic identities were symbolized in the same ritual mentioned above. Since the genitor of the child was a caste man from India and no one knew him well, they did not file any charges against him.

Discussion

These case studies illustrate the reinforcement of the moral codes of bitlaha and the rules of endogamy and clan exogamy. Hapan Mai's case shows that a Hod-caste union is not viewed by the Hod as having any kind of validity. To be a Hod, one must marry a Hod. When this rule is violated, one becomes an outcast. Maili's case explains how contact situations often make a Hod-caste union unavoidable. This type of union shakes their value system and poses an immediate threat to the Hod. It also means the loss of an ethnic member. Such loss would indicate weak bonds and possible future disintegration of the group. The jawae kirinok ritual functions in a distinctive way in such situations by allowing those who deviate from the rules to be a part of their group again and reassert their own and their unborn childrens' ethnicity. This ritual, thus, rules out the possibility of a Hod child being illegitimate and outcast. Both cases also reveal how the cultural norms of endogamy and bitlaha control the sexual relationship between Hod and non-Hod and work as mechanisms for maintaining ethnic identities.

Although Maili and Baha were both pregnant, Baha's case led to a different outcome. Both their parents were given the option of buying fathers for their daughters' unborn children. Maili's parents did so, but Baha's mother did not. She did not even consider this option. It is important here to understand why Baha's mother chose to act this way. It all relates to the rules of incest. If there had been a sexual act between Baha and her mother's brother and if it had been confirmed in the public meeting to acknowledge the paternity of the unborn child, it would have further complicated the issue. First, since any sexual relationship between a woman and her mother's brother is incestuous, it would have brought great shame to both parties. Second, the penalties for both would, then, have been much higher. And finally at that point, perhaps it would not have been possible at all to buy a father for that particular child, especially because of such an incestuous act. So, in this case, the reason for not buying a father for Baha's unborn child did not simply rest on financial matters. Meanings went much deeper here: relations were threatened and permanent exclusion of both parties from the group was inevitable.

Two points of theoretical interest emerge from these cases. One relates to social versus biological paternity and the other to the status of children of mixed unions. Both Baha's and Maili's cases illustrate the practice of social and biological paternity among the Hod. African ethnography has provided cases of such paternity for a long time (Evans-Pritchard 1951; Kriege 1974; Obolor 1980). The Hod view of such paternity is not unique in South Asia either. The Nayar of India illustrate this. As Gough (1959) notes, the Nayar acknowledge the supremacy and importance of the pater (social father who is a Nambudiri Brahman) as against the genitor (biological father who is a Nayar). However, they recruit the offspring of Nayar-Nambudiri unions through their matrilineal descent rules. Thus, each generation produced by a Nayar woman and a Nambudiri man becomes a Nayar and not a separate caste of mixed union.

Such cultural separation of paternity indicates, as Shapiro demonstrates in the context of woman-woman marriage, that filiation does not "rest on beliefs about the physical transmission of substance from parent to child. Nor does the filiation tie between a man and his children necessarily involve a man's having some significant set of rights over or obligation to his children..." (1981:8). This concept of two paternities can be extended to the Hod. Ideally, a Hod genitor should acknowledge his paternity and carry out his responsibilities (Kochar 1970:28–29). But sometimes, as I observed, due to incest or other reasons, the genitor may not acknowledge his paternity. Even when he acknowledges it in order to validate the ethnic status of the child, he may not fulfill his paternal responsibilities. The pater, however, will acknowledge his paternity by "selling" his clan name to the unborn child. This acknowledgment, however, does not necessarily mean that a pater will accept any further responsibility for that child or the child's mother, such as living with the child's mother, marrying her, and extending his rights over the reproductive or domestic services of the child or its mother. Here social paternity neither implies sexual relationship with the mother of the child nor an economic relationship with her. The sexual and domestic services of a woman may be enjoyed by different men at different times. She may marry one of these men and bring all her children with her to live with him in his household.

As mentioned earlier, the goal of social paternity among the Hod is to validate the social status of those children who are conceived by a woman prior to her marriage. A Hod, simply by being a genitor, does not play any role in validating the social status of his children. He does this simply through the payment of brideprice before the child is born. The genitor who fails to go through this ritual threatens the social status of the child by denying it its paternity and its ethnicity as a Hod. The illegitimate status of the unborn child, in return, makes a village bitlaha whereby no rituals can be performed in the village. And this is when the rituals of jawae kirinok appear crucial.

Such practice of social paternity relates to the second point of theoretical interest, which raises the issue of the status of offspring of mixed unions in the caste societies of South Asia. Some studies examine the reasons underlying caste-ethnic or intercaste marriages and ethnic or ritual statuses of the children born from such marriages (Caplan 1970; Levine 1987). Some others, looking at such marriages in terms of upward or downward mobility, explore the implications of hypergamous and hypogamous marriages (within a caste group or between different caste groups) on the ritual statuses of the children born from such marriages (Barth 1960; Buhler 1886; Fürer-Haimendorf 1966; Gough 1960; Inden 1976; Tambiah 1973).

Many of the above studies also illustrate the purpose of such marriages in cultural terms, that is, by gaining or maximizing status. Also implicit in these studies is the viewing of mixed marriages as maintaining a logical social link between members of ethnic and lower ritual statuses and upper-caste society.

I argue that a Hod-caste union means neither "dying out"—by replacing ethnic identity with caste identity—nor increasing the purity level of the Hod. Neither does it create a social link. Since the Hod, including the Sapha Hod, deny being a part of the caste system, they do not rank the children of mixed unions on the basis of the pure/impure ideology. Furthermore, since Hod social organization gives importance to the mother's ethnic status as opposed to the genitor's (who may be a Hod or a non-Hod) in recruiting the children of mixed unions, it allows the pregnant mother to buy a pater for her unborn child from within the Hod group, whereby the child becomes a member of its pater's clan. Such a cultural practice of social paternity cuts off the social link between the Hod and caste people. It also works as a mechanism to recruit the child of a mixed union into the Hod group. As a result, this child "becomes" Hod, and not a separate category of Hod-caste union. When such buying is not done, the unborn child, its mother and her guardians become outcast.

Here the Hod-Mohali—a cultural group—can be taken as an example to illustrate the notion of "social link." During both periods of my fieldwork, there were no Hod-Mohali in or around Sunauli. They were, and still are, mostly found in the Bihar state of India. Although this group originated from the union of Hod and Mohali couples, today the Hod-Mohali is an endogamous group.

There is no ethnographic data to inform us of the Hod-Mohali's own sense of their ethnic identity, but we can discuss how the Hod and Mohali regard them. The Mohali, who are full-time basket makers, think of the Hod-Mohali as a separate caste group, having a lower ritual status than their own. From their perspective, a Hod-caste union is possible and acceptable. They accept a Hod woman as a wife of a caste man, but assign a lower ritual status to her and her children born from that union; their hierarchical ideology allows them to do so. Such grading adds to the existing hierarchical groups or categories of the caste system and helps sustain the system as a whole.

Hod's perception of the Hod-Mohali is different. They do not think of the Hod-Mohali as Hod, or even "half-Hod." According to the Hod, by marrying the Mohali, Hod ancestors and ancestresses of the Hod-Mohali acted against the norms of endogamy. So they had become bitlaha and had chosen to remain that way. Following this logic, the Hod consider the Hod-Mohali as bitlaha and, therefore, as non-Hod.

From the Hod's point of view, then, a Hod-caste union is neither preferred nor acceptable. It does not have any validity at all. If such a relationship does occur, it goes against the shared norms of endogamy and, therefore, must be broken. Hapan Mai's case exemplifies this. If the union is not broken, the concerned individual becomes bitlaha. For the Hod one is either inside the group or outside. There are no in-between or lower categories created for such individuals or their offspring within the Hod group.

Conclusion

Although all Hod marriages contribute to maintaining and perpetuating cultural identity, I have argued that the ghardi jawae and the jawae kirinok marriage rituals function in special ways. Even though uxorilocality goes against the patrilineal norms of the Hod, it places individuals within the social system by redefining their identities. It also sets a different pattern in constructing the personal identities of the children. The primacy given in bestowing names of the matrikin over those of the patrikin has deeper implications, all of which lead to the weakening of patrilineal bonds without, however, placing anyone outside the Hod social system.

The jawae kirinok marriage relates to the violation of certain crucial norms, such as incest rules, clan exogamy, and group endogamy. It also relates to situations arising from the Hod's participation in a wider caste culture and interactions with caste people. Such interaction often makes a Hod-caste union unavoidable. However, when children are born from these mixed unions, the jawae kirinok ritual enables the Hod to validate the status of these children as Hod. Such practice further illustrates how the Hod resist being a part of caste society. Instead of merging with the caste system by "becoming" members of a caste, with the help of the children of Hod-caste union, Hod not only remain within their ethnic boundaries, but also recruit the children of mixed unions into their ethnic group. As a result, every generation produced by Hod unions or by Hod and non-Hod unions becomes Hod. Even the breach of endogamy does not permeate the ethnic boundaries of Hod and caste groups.

Notes

1. See Levine (1987) on the politics, formation, and overlapping of ethnicity in Nepal.

2. The Hod are known as Satar in Nepal and Santal in India. They, however, call themselves Hod, meaning "human beings." To acknowledge and respect their sense of self-identification, I have adopted the term Hod.

3. The Sunauli Hindu caste groups are Nunia, Gangai, Kiyat, Kevarat, Sonar, Dhanuk, Chamar, Mohali, Teli, and Halwai.

4. Fuchs (1973) distinguishes between "scheduled tribe" and "scheduled caste." According to him, "for a caste to be 'scheduled,' it has to be economically and culturally backward, exploited by the people of superior culture and treated as socially inferior" (1973:24–25). Furthermore, although these "scheduled" caste people share many aspects of Hinduism, they are often kept apart and treated as untouchable. In contrast, as Fuchs continues, the "scheduled tribes," though "often backward and exploited, are rarely socially degraded" (1973:24–25). Unlike the "scheduled" caste people, most of these tribal people have a distinct tradition of their own of which they are very proud.

5. In today's context, diku as an ethnic category represents Indians and Nepalis who speak various Indian languages, such as Bengali, Punjabi, Marwadi, and Maithili. Mundo means "mountain dwellers," and includes all Nepali-speaking caste people and ethnic groups whose members may or may not speak Nepali as their mother tongue, such as the Sherpa, Tharu, Dhimal, Rai, Limbu, Gurung, Tamang, and Newar.

6. This is similar to the Tamang's attitude towards the Bahun (Holmberg 1989).

7. For other criteria suggested as markers of ethnicity, see Ameisen (1990), Baldinger (1990), Ballard and Ballard (1977), Berreman (1975), and Obeyesekere (1975).

8. For more information on Hod marriages, see Archer (1944, 1974), Bodding (1935, 1942), Chowdhury (1952), Kochar (1970), Mukherjea (1962), and Troisi (1979).

9. The caste people's concept of *kunwārī* (*kumārī* in Nepali) is similar to this concept. Similar to a donguo, a kunwārī does not use vermilion powder on her head. A kunwārī, however, has not yet had sexual intercourse with a man, while this may not be the situation for a donguo. In both cultural groups, however, vermilion powder functions to change a woman's status from unmarried to married. Given the dominance of the caste system in South Asia, it is tempting to speculate that the Hod have borrowed the use of this powder from the caste people. However, we can also speculate that the caste people borrowed it from the Hod (Orans 1965:96). The long, complex, and diverse history of South Asian cultural groups, interaction between the Hod and the caste groups, and the crucial role of vermilion powder in the Hod culture support this assumption, yet I agree with Troisi (1979:253) in viewing this "as a case of cultural similarity," rather than of cultural borrowing.

10. In Sunauli, wealthy people own both land and cattle, and they never work for wages. Those without land and cattle define themselves as poor, and work for their neighbors, whom they call malik (master), as tenants or for daily wages.

11. Between the Bidin and the Sapha Hod, the Sapha Hod highly value the donguo status of women, and take great pride in bringing in a donguo and marrying one out. They

do so because the daudo marriage has deeper meanings for them. It functions as a strategy to display their Hod ethnicity on the one hand, and class and ritual statuses on the other. Such a display of ethnicity, class, and caste allows them to be a part of two cultures, Hod and caste, simultaneously.

12. Many of these Satar women did not use vermilion powder on their heads. They thought the application of such powder required the daudo rituals, which would be performed when their husbands were ready to pay the proper brideprice. However, some of these women who had baha sohan rituals did not use the vermilion powder when visiting town because they did not want to be mistaken as unmarried by the town caste people.

13. Ghardi jawae refers both to a marriage form and to a person.

14. There was one such case in Sunauli where a Bidin Hod, who was a ghardi jawae of a Sapha Hod, identified himself as a Bidin Hod while continuing to participate in the Sapha Hod rituals. His wife and children, however, defined themselves as Sapha Hod even after he established his own household, after completing his ghardi jawae contract.

15. Srinivas (1952:54), in his study of the Coorgs of India, examines such affiliation with one lineage while still continuing the membership in another as "double membership." Kochar (1970:81) applies this concept in his study of Hod women and explains that because of such membership, a Hod woman does not enjoy "full jural and ritual status in either of the groups." I argue that "double membership" does not connote the liminal status of Hod women. It rather reveals the multiple extensions of their power and authority in both groups. Further research is needed to explore this.

16. For more information on bitlaha, see Chaudhury (1961), Sachchidananda (1955, 1965), and Somers (1977:187–188).

17. These seven administrative positions are of *majhi* (headman), *jog majhi* (representative of the headman in his absence), *paranik* (the first assistant of the headman), *jog paranik* (the second assistant of the headman), *naeke* (the village priest), *kudum naeke* (the assistant priest), and *godet* (the village messenger). Although the Hod of each village recognize these positions, these may not be necessarily represented by seven individuals. For example, in Sunauli, the office of the majhi was represented by a Sapha Hod, and the offices of the naeke and paranik by another Sapha Hod. One Bidin Hod did the work of both the jog majhi and godet, and another Bidin Hod represented the kudum naeke and jog paranik.

References

Ameisen, Elizabeth R. 1990. Exclusivity in an Ethnic Elite: Racial Prejudice as Boundary Maintenance. *In* Encounters with American Ethnic Cultures. P. Kilbride, J. Goodale, and E. R. Ameisen, eds. Pp. 24–76. Tuscaloosa: University of Alabama Press.

Archer, W. G. 1944. The Illegitimate Child in Santal Society. Man in India 24(3):28–48.

———. 1974. The Hill of Flutes: Life, Love and Poetry in Tribal India—A Portrait of the Santals. London: George Allen and Unwin.

Bailey, F. G. 1968. Parapolitical System. *In* Local Level Politics: Social and Cultural Perspectives. Marc J. Swartz, ed. Pp. 281–294. Chicago: Aldine Publishing Co.

Baldinger, Phillip. 1990. Equality Does Not Mean Sameness: The Role of Women Within the Lubavitcher Marriage. *In* Encounters with American Ethnic Cultures. P. Kilbride, J. Goodale, and E. R. Ameisen, eds. Pp. 151–178. Tuscaloosa: The University of Alabama Press.

Ballard, Roger, and C. Ballard. 1977. The Sikhs: The Development of South Asian Settlements in Britain. *In* Between Two Cultures. James L. Watson, ed. Pp. 21–56. Oxford: Basil Blackwell.

Barnes, J. A. 1962. African Models in the New Guinea Highlands. Man 62:5–9.

Barth, Frederik. 1960. The System of Social Stratification in Swat, North Pakistan. *In* Aspects of Caste in South India. E. Leach, ed. Pp. 113–148. London: Cambridge University Press.

————. 1969. Pathan Identity and Its Maintenance. *In* Ethnic Groups and Boundaries. F. Barth, ed. Pp. 117–134. Boston: Little, Brown and Co.

Basu, K. K. 1944. Missionary Education in the Sonthal Parganas. Journal of the Bihar Research Society 30(2):178–183.

Bennett, J. W., ed. 1975. The New Ethnicity: Perspectives from Ethnology. Boston: West Publishing.

Berreman, Gerald. 1975. Bazar Behavior: Social Identity and Social Interaction in Urban India. *In* Ethnic Identity: Cultural Continuities and Change. C. De Vos and L. Ramanucci-Ross, eds. Pp. 71–105. Palo Alto: Mayfield Publishing Co.

Bodding, Paul Olaf. 1921. The Kharwar Movements among the Santals. Man in India 1(3):222–232.

————. 1935. Notes on the Santals. *In* Ethnographic Notes by Various Authors, Census of India 1931, Vol. 1(3). J. H. Hutton, ed. Pp. 98–107. Simla: Government of India Press.

————. 1942. Traditions and Institutions of the Santals. Oslo: A. W. Broggers Boktrykkeri.

Buhler, George. 1886. The Laws of Manu. *In* Sacred Books of the East. F. Max Muller, ed. Vol. 25. Oxford: Clarendon Press.

Caplan, Lionel. 1970. Land and Social Change in East Nepal: A Study of Hindu-Tribal Relations. Berkeley: University of California Press.

Chaudhury, P. C. 1961. Bitlaha: A Santal Ritual. The Quarterly Journal of the Mythic Society 52(1):1–5.

Chowdhury, Uma. 1952. Marriage Customs of the Santals. Bulletin of the Department of Anthropology 1(1):86–116.

Cohen, Abner P., ed. 1981. Variables in Ethnicity. *In* Ethnic Change. Charles P. Keyes, ed. Pp. 307–331. Seattle: University of Washington Press.

Cohen, Ronald. 1978. Ethnicity, Problem and Focus in Anthropology. Annual Review of Anthropology 7:379–403.

Connell, Robert W. 1987. Gender and Power: Society, the Person and Sexual Politics. Stanford: Stanford University Press.

Culshaw, W. J. 1949. Tribal Heritage: A Study of the Santals. London: Lutterworth Place.

Datta, Kalikinkar. 1940. The Santal Insurrection of 1855–1857. Calcutta: University of Calcutta Press.

Derne, Steve. 1991. Purifying Movements and Syncretic Religious Movements: Religious Changes and the 19th Century Munda and Santal Peasant Revolts. Man in India 71(1&2): 139–149.

Dirks, Nicholas. 1992. Ritual and Resistance: Subversion as a Social Fact. *In* Contesting Power: Resistance and Everyday Social Relations in South Asia. Douglas Haynes and Gyan Prakash eds. Pp. 213–238. Berkeley: University of California Press.

Dube, S. C, ed. 1977. Tribal Heritage of India (Vol. I): Ethnicity, Identity and Interaction. New Delhi: Vikas Publishing House.

Dumont, Louis. 1980. Homo Hierarchicus: The Caste System and Its Implications. Complete Revised English Edition. Chicago: University of Chicago Press.

Evans-Pritchard, E. E 1951. Kinship and Marriage among the Nuer. London: Oxford University Press.

Fuchs, Stephen. 1965. Rebellious Prophets: A Study of Messianic Movements in India. Bombay: Asia Publishing House.

————. 1973. The Aboriginal Tribes of India. Delhi: The Macmillan Co. of India.

Geertz, Hildred, and Clifford Geertz. 1975. Kinship in Bali. Chicago: The University of Chicago Press.

Ghimire, Premalata. 1989. Boundary Dynamics of Sapha Hod Identity. Himalayan Research Bulletin 9(3):1–10.

————. 1990. The Individual and Group Identity of the Sapha Hod. *In* Himalaya Past and Present. M. P. Joshi, A. C. Fanger, and C. W. Brown, eds. Pp. 66–91. Almora: Shree Almora Book Depot.

————. 1992. Alternatives and Choices of a Minority Group: A Case of the Satar. The Proceedings of the National Convention of Nepalese and Friends of Nepal in North America.

Ghurye, G. S. 1963. The Scheduled Tribes. Bombay: Popular Book Depot.

Gough, Kathleen. 1959. The Nayars and the Definition of Marriage. Journal of the Royal Anthropological Institute 89(1):23–34.

————. 1960. Caste in a Tanjore Village. *In* Aspects of Caste in South India, Ceylon and North-West Pakistan. E. R. Leach, ed. Pp. 11–60. Cambridge Papers in Social Anthropology, no. 2. Cambridge University Press.

Haynes, Douglas, and Gyan Prakash, eds. 1992. Contesting Power: Resistance and Everyday Social Relations in South Asia. Berkeley: University of California Press.

Holmberg, David H. 1989. Order in Paradox: Myth, Ritual and Exchange among Nepal's Tamang. Ithaca: Cornell University Press.

Inden, Ronald B. 1976. Marriage and Rank in Bengali Culture: A History of Caste and Clan in Middle Period Bengal. Berkeley: University of California Press.

Jay, Edward. 1964. Revitalization Movements in Tribal India. *In* Aspects of Religion in Indian Society. L. P. Vidyarthi, ed. Pp. 282–315. Meerut: Kedarnath Amarnath.

Keyes, Charles F. 1976. Towards a New Formulation of the Concept of Ethnic Group. Ethnicity 3:202–213.

Kilbride, Philip, Jane C. Goodale, and E. R. Ameisen, eds. 1990. Encounters with American Ethnic Cultures. Tuscaloosa: The University of Alabama Press.

Kochar, Vijay K. 1970. Social Organization among the Santal. Calcutta: Editions Indian.

Kriege, E. Jensen. 1974. Women Marriage with Special Reference to the Lovedu: Its Significance for the Definition of Marriage. Africa 44:11–37.

Levine, Nancy E. 1987. Caste, State and Ethnic Boundaries in Nepal. Journal of Asian Studies 46(1):71–88.

Mukherjea, Charulal. 1962. The Santals. Calcutta: A Mukherjea and Co. Pvt. Ltd.

Narroll, R. 1964. Ethnic Unit Classification. Current Anthropology 5(4):283–312.

Obeyesekere, Gananath. 1975. Sinhalese-Buddhist Identity in Ceylon. *In* Ethnic Identity: Cultural Continuity and Change. C. De Vos and L. Ramanucci-Ross, eds. Pp. 231–258. Palo Alto: Mayfield Publishing Co.

Obolor, Regina S. 1980. Is the Female Husband a Man? Woman-Woman Marriage among the Nandi of Kenya. Ethnology 9(1): 69–88.

Orans, Martin. 1965. The Santal: A Tribe in Search of a Great Tradition. Detroit: Wayne State University Press.

Prasad, Saileshwar. 1971. Modern Education among the Tribals of Bihar in the Second Half of the 19th Century. Man in India 51(4):364–393.

Regmi, Mahesh C. 1976. Landownership in Nepal. Berkeley: University of California Press.

Sachchidananda. 1955. Bitlaha. The Eastern Anthropologist 9(1):42–47.

———. 1965. Profiles of Tribal Culture in Bihar. Calcutta: Firma K. L. Mukhopadhayay.

Shapiro, Judith. 1981. Marriage as a Comparative Concept. Unpublished manuscript. Bryn Mawr College.

Sinha, S. P. 1961. Kharwar Movement in Hazaribagh District. Vanyajati 9(3):98–103.

Skrefsrud, Lars Olsen. 1873. A Grammar of the Santali Language. Benares: Medical Hall Express.

Somers, George E. 1977. The Dynamics of Santal Traditions in a Peasant Society. New Delhi: Abhinava Publications.

Srinivas, M. N. 1952. Religion and Society among the Coorgs of South India. Oxford: Oxford University Press.

Stock, Eugene. 1899. The History of the Church Missionary Society. Its Environment, its Men and its Work. London: Church Missionary Society, Vol. 2.

Tambiah, S. J. 1973. From Varna to Caste through Mixed Unions. *In* The Character of Kinship. Jack Goody, ed. Pp. 191–229. London: Cambridge University Press.

Troisi, J. 1979. Tribal Religion: Religious Beliefs and Practices among the Santals. New Delhi: Manohar Publications.

von Fürer-Haimendorf, C. 1966. Unity and Diversity in the Chetri Caste of Nepal. *In* Caste and Kin in Nepal, India and Ceylon. C. von Fürer-Haimendorf, ed. Pp. 11–67. New York: Asia Publishing House.

Chapter 10 _____

Engendered Bodies, Embodied Genders

Kathryn S. March

ara Suleri, in the opening sentences of the first chapter (called "Excellent things in women") to her bicultural introspection, *Meatless Days*, writes:

> Leaving Pakistan was, of course, tantamount to giving up the company of women....My reference is to a place where the concept of woman was not really part of an available vocabulary: we were too busy for that, just living, and conducting precise negotiations with what it meant to be a sister or a wife or a mother or a servant...yes, once in a while, we naturally thought of ourselves as women, but only in some perfunctory biological way that we happened on perchance. Or else it was a hugely practical joke, we thought, hidden somewhere among our clothes. But formulating that definition is about as impossible as attempting to locate the luminous qualities of an Islamic landscape...(1989:1–2)

My concerns in this paper are not about Pakistan, nor about Islam, but rather about definitions—"hidden somewhere among our clothes"—of how meanings of femaleness (in relation to maleness), gender, and bodies illuminate a Tamang landscape of personal and social identities.

Theorizing the Body

Theorizing the body I take for granted some initial assertions about bodies and their significance. I propose that we lightly abuse Geertz and think of the body as a cultural system, according to which the human body is, like religion:

(1) a system of symbols which acts to (2) establish powerful, pervasive, and long-lasting moods and motivations in men [sic] by (3) formulating conceptions of a general order of existence and (4) clothing these conceptions with such an aura of factuality that (5) the moods and motivations seem uniquely realistic. (1973:90)

The examples of culturally inscribed bodies are too numerous even to do the usual academic citational tour.[1] There are bodies negotiated in exotic rites of passage and bodies shaped by fashion; bodies born, buried, and reborn; bodies constituted whole and body parts; bodies controlled and resistant bodies; bodies observed and represented; bodies constructed and deconstructed; bodies politic, social bodies, celestial bodies, and so forth, being, as bodies are, fruitful and multiplying.

But it is the everyday facticity of the body that gives it its unique realism. Bodies are not only conceptual frameworks, but are pivotal transformative gateways of practical understandings and personal experience. In this way the body, like Bourdieu's linguistic habitus, becomes a bodily hexis—"political mythology realized, em-bodied, turned into a permanent disposition, a durable manner of standing, speaking, and thereby feeling and thinking" (1990:69–70). Thus, the body is the ultimate sense organ in "all its senses, that is to say, not only the traditional five senses...but also...[a plethora of senses and sensibilities including]...sense of direction and the sense of reality, the sense of balance and the sense of beauty, common sense...the sense of humor...and so on" (1977:124). Overall, when we reexamine what was previously concealed from us as the unexamined everyday nature of our bodies, we find we must figure our bodies simultaneously as the locus of our selfhood (as a thinking subject) and of our personhood (as the morally constituted object of wider relations). The body, in Jean Comaroff's clear (if not, as she herself concurs, "novel") observation, mediates all action upon the world and simultaneously constitutes both the self and the universe of social and natural relations of which it is a part" (1985:6–7). There are many interesting speculations to explore in Tamang talk about, as well as physical manipulations of, the human body, but first I must, briefly, situate the Tamang.

The Tamang

"The" Tamang today live in the middle of the physical geography of Nepal: latitudinally, longitudinally, and altitudinally. They inhabit the regions surrounding

Kathmandu like a doughnut (or *sel roti*[2] to use a more properly Nepali metaphor) and at elevations between approximately 4,000 to 10,000 feet. They are peasant farmers growing rice, maize, millet, and potato; herders; and increasingly frequent wage laborers in the most arduous jobs of porter, rickshaw pedaler, and construction worker. But to say that they live in the middle is not to say that they are at the heart of Nepali society, unless it is a vanquished heart. The forebears of peoples today known as Tamang lived directly in the path of conquest of Prithvi Narayan Shah, first nationalist monarch and unifier of modern Nepal. As he built the state of Nepal, he did so literally on the backs of Tamang, who were then, as they were described by Landon in 1928, "hewers of wood and drawers of water, coolies by heritage [doing] much of the menial work in the Valley of Kathmandu" (1987[1928]:246). A complex system of tenurial rights and rents on land, myriad other taxations in kind, a discriminatory legal code based upon caste, and, especially, elaborate corvée labor obligations, all set "the" Tamang apart and further entrenched them in an identity, with related ritual and other practices, including Buddhism, cross-cousin marriage, relative equality between the sexes and general nonobservance of caste dietary and other rules that, while originally derived from Tibet in language and culture, became, as David Holmberg has shown (1989), increasingly subordinated to Kathmandu and increasingly involuted.

Buddhism and Bodies

Buddhism and bodies interact in contemporary Tamang constructions of their bodies: there is, above all, an overarching—and characteristically Buddhist—ambivalence about corporeal reality. The aim of Buddhist moral vectors is to point the way out of this world of suffering and rebirths, until it would literally be "emptied out" of bodies. This Buddhist body—whether the voluntarily and compassionately engaged bodies of the bodhisattvas, or the more witless, lustful, and hotheaded run-of-the-mill human and animal bodies—is at once the root of attachment to the physical world and, at the same time, the potential site of inspiration to action out of this world. Tamang discursions on the body construe not only a moral body capable of significant action, but an immoral one, a daily lesson in the physical ties that bind bodies into painful and recurrent lives.

But if sensory attachment is the root of all rebirths, and, hence, a thing to be stilled, Tamang constructions of the body, too, and the physical senses suggest that it is not just body that must be quieted, but that thing Western dualisms call mind which must also "empty out." For there are not five, but six, named senses: sight, smell, taste, touch, sound, and "mind." Elaborated Buddhist meditative and ritual practice regularly invokes all six. In common speech, as well, the bodily seat of feeling and awareness is the *sem*, the "heart-and-mind"—a consciousness that is simultaneously emotive and cognitive, felt and thought (see also McHugh 1989).

This paper embeds gendered bodies and the question of whether there are sex-distinctive vantages on experience or identity within these more encompassing Tamang ideas about bodies. It is a distinctively personal pleasure for me to embark on these musings; prior to fieldwork, I had titled my research project "With nothing but the body of a woman." The phrase comes from Stephen Beyer's translation of the origin myth of Tara, the most luminous female celestial body in the Himalayan Buddhist pantheistic skies. When, after numberless rebirths of effort, Tara reached enlightenment, the monks are said to have told her to use her new powers to transform herself into a man. She replied:

> Since there is no such thing as a "man" or a "woman" (and no such thing as "self" or "person" or "awareness") this bondage to male and female is hollow....And this is the earnest wish she made: Those who wish to attain supreme enlightenment in a man's body are many, but those who wish to serve the aims of beings in a woman's body are few indeed; therefore, may I, until this world is emptied out, serve the aims of beings with nothing but the body of a woman. (Beyer 1973:64–5)

The elegance of Tara's double gesture moved me then, as it continues to move me now: first, in rejecting hollow bondage to the monks' hierarchical definition of sexual difference and, then, in reclaiming its distinctiveness as integral to her own special efficacy. But these were not the female bodies I found in my fieldwork with (and it is no insult to call them so) less enlightened contemporary Tamang beings.

Tamang gendered bodies were rather more like those described by Suleri: precise negotiations about daughter- and sonhood or wife- and husbandhood. Two Tamang tropes of gendered bodies were especially salient and encompassing: about (1) sibling/sister/brotherhood, on the one hand, and (2) parent/mother/fatherhood, on the other. Both as sibling and as parent, Tamang women and men embody comparably and contrapuntally positioned agents in what Bourdieu has called "generative schemes and practical logic" (1977:96–158). Initially, we might understand the contrast between parent and sibling (in their respective male and female forms) as corresponding to two complementary aspects to identity, not unlike "the complementary opposition of patrilineal descent and matrilateral filiation" of Fortes's Tallensi (1973:297). But, in addition to these more symmetrical Tamang meanings of bodily gender, there is another more distinctively female one; that is, human (in this case Tamang Buddhist) suffering is embodied by women—as both mothers and sisters—to constitute a distinctively female body. Moreover, these distinctively female meanings are not for women alone; female engendered bodies embody very personal and palpable meanings for people who inhabit male ones as well. But I am getting ahead of myself in this story.

Father-bodies and mother-bodies are where I want to begin, with the making of bodies, baby bodies, and the question of gendering baby bodies. Western Tamang, in my experience of highland Nepal, are clear that it takes two kinds of parental bodies—the father's and the mother's—to begin the making of a baby body. As in classical Tibetan tradition, the father's bodily contribution is bone. Not perhaps surprisingly the word for "bone" is also the word for patrilineal clan. Both are unchanging, well-bounded, enduring aspects to bodily and personal identity among Tamang. Mothers' input is more fluid. From the mother's body and into the child's go blood and milk to produce the fleshy, perishable, but more individually distinctive features of identity. With typical Tamang gendered symmetry (and mountain imagery), both the "bone trail" and the "milk trail" remain vitally important throughout one's life. From this perspective the interplay of mothers and fathers is carefully balanced. In this balance, it resembles the gender-parallel invocations that initiate almost all culturally and ritually significant Tamang activity: to the *tsawai lama*, on the one hand, and *dinjen phamo*, on the other.

Dinjen (or *hrangki*) *tsau* are one's revered own patrilineal ancestors. People have particularly honored lamas associated with their ancestral patriline (their tsawai lama) who have important roles at the beginning and end of their lives: as the *syimdembi tsawai lama*, who perform the mortuary chanting at funerals and death ceremonies for one's own patrikin, and the *dinjen tsawai lama*, who do one's afterbirth rituals. In some recitations or songs, these ancestral lamas may be named, or semi-mythically named, such as *Dorje Lopon* ("the thunderbolt teacher"). In all their roles, these special lamas manage important transitions regulating membership, even perhaps identity, in one's own patriline. The unbroken line of lamas is a spiritual patriline presumptively extending back to the mythic times of the primordial Buddhas and may itself symbolize the aspirations for permanence sought after by more mortal human patrilines.

Dinjen phamo, on the other hand, is widely understood as the most honorific way to refer to one's own actual birth mother. More generally *phamo* are honored, divine, female beings to whom both shamans and lamas attribute much of their esoteric knowledge. *Din* in a few contexts (e.g., dinjen tsawai lama) is said by contemporary northwestern Tamang to refer to birth pollution,[3] but in most others it refers to a special kind of birth debt (e.g., *āmā-i din*). Whatever the exact etymology, locals today say that dinjen, in the expression dinjen phamo, identifies the pollution and other dangers mothers risk and thus their unselfish beneficence; it evokes a sense of reverent gratitude for life and identity given.[4] Stupahill Tamang[5] see birth as a time of great danger and suffering. They emphasize the eternal debt of gratitude that children owe the women who physically bore and cared for them.

Moreover, Tamang readily detail a wide array of "mothers" who contribute physically to their children's well-being by depleting their own. First are the separately named, and possibly separately embodied, two kinds of human "mothers": the "birth mother" (*yangbi āmā*) the "mother who bore" (or more literally "found") you," and those who gave of their own vitality to nourish you (*nghyé tungbi āmā*) or "nursing mother." In addition, Tamang "mothers" have spirit assistants, or *kalé āmā* (and there are nine kalé āmā): the "body-making mother," "body-assigning mother," "body-binding (by/in oaths) mother," "breath-making mother," "umbilical cord-making mother," and so on and so forth, codifying female "mother" forces of creation, each of which creates a different physical aspect of the child. Invocations of spirit "mothers" like these culminate ultimately in the *sabsyi āmā*, "the mother of the earth." This Earth Mother gave birth to all creation, in love and pain. She is honored in one of the most eloquent of Tamang songs about the mythic creation of the universe, the "Mother Earth Song"; as seen in the song verses below, her fertility underlies everything.

Specifically maternal bodies shift the initial apparent symmetry of fathers and mothers in the making of babies away from the idea of bones on the one hand and fluids equally on the other, to one which catalogs the fluid, fleshing, and organic constituent parts of the mother's contributions in far greater detail, and with far more emotion, than the father's. Birth and milk mothers are, like bone fathers, people whose bodies contributed half of what made up your body; but mothers, unlike fathers, are, as well, people whose own bodies suffered greatly to effect those creations and hence whose maternal bodies embody the very paradigm of generative compassionate suffering.

To explore some of these images—of bodies, mothers, and human suffering— I want to turn to a genre of Tamang song known as *bomsang*. Bomsang are personal laments: they are composed by identifiable people as they approach and contemplate their old age and death; they are highly crafted—carefully composed, practiced, and reworked; they are evaluated (at least in part) in terms of their ability to make listeners cry. The sixth-born lama's older brother's bomsang[6] tells the story of his life, from his "birthing time" to his anticipated death. He begins with the poignant (and gender-paralleled) invocation:

> The skills of heart-and-mind [are from] Dorje Lopon[7];
> The making of the body [is from] Dinjen Phamo.[8]
> Sit down and listen, sons and daughters, boys and girls.
> Sit down and listen, sons and daughters, my children.
>
> Hey, hai! The orphaned bird hears the crying of the world.
> But, is anyone aware when I, an orphan, too, cry?

The symmetry of mother and father expressed above soon gives way to a more emotive meditation of the maternal body:

> Mother of earth, sacred mother; father of sky, sacred father.
> For what reason have I come to birth in this life form?
> Why did I survive?
> Oh! My Own Mother! Oh! To be born was My Own Mother born.
> Is it only to survive that my body has survived?
> As my body survived, so supreme sorrow was born.
> Oh! My Own Mother!

Thinking about being born, he thinks about dying, and in thinking about both he develops a very precise cartography of mother (Tamang: *āmā*) bodies which ultimately encompass all of creation:

> The heart-and-mind doesn't realize it is born; the body doesn't realize it will die.
> If knowledge of dying were known, why be born?
> Like human men and women,[9] I was said to be born to the supreme happiness,
> But is it not birth to burdens of sorrow?
> Everyone realizes when the fire burns in the forest;
> When fire burns in my orphan's heart, who realizes?

> To be born, in order to be born, it seems, oh! sending my mother to a special
>   place [came] *Kalé Amā*,[10] oh!
> Kalé Amā, *Sem chung Rani*, Kalé Amā, *Patsong Rani...*[11]
> In the heart of Kalé Amā [is] the fragrance of flowers.
> In Péma Debke's place, in Péma Gyésreé's place, Kalé Amā's coming to rest,
> Gyésré's incarnation's coming to rest, after the *brégyul* flower,
>   Kalé Amā, Brégyul Rani came to rest.
> The rhododendron flower's fragrance came to rest, then Kalé Amā,
>   Bell Rani, come sit down, accept this offering, Kalé Amā!
> Breath-making Kalé Amā, stem- and spine-making Kalé Amā!
> I, as a heart-and-mind knowing life form,[12] was born!
> Oh! be wise, Kalé Amā!

> Know this: all came into being through Phamo! In the primordial age, all
>   came to rest!
> The villages and otherworldly realms came into being in the lap of
>   Mother Earth.
> The villages came to rest in her lap.
> Her foot holds up her menstrual napkins playfully.
> By her here, the flowering of her menstrual blood came to rest.
> Time after time, in giving birth, mother mixes menstrual blood and semen in
>   the uterus; from time to time, Mother Earth came to rest.
> Assorted grains came to rest.
> Food, milk, prosperity survive...the mounded hill.
> A puddle collects into a lake, coming to rest:
>   stay in our hearts, Mother Earth!

His own birth, however, is documented not only as an example of this cosmological play of mother creations, but also as a moment of pain and, specifically, the pain of separation:

> A small larva, a week or month after the small larva was born,
> My Own Mother was not yet aware of it.

[next verse incomprehensible]

After six months that little larva was going to be born in My Own
    Mother's body.

After nine months, it came out; it was born from My Own Mother!

It emerged, its birthing time was after nine months.

As it emerged, during its birthing time, oh, My Own Mother,

A 100–1000 thoughts came to My Own Mother's heart-and-mind!

When those 100–1000 thoughts heated up in My Own Mother's heart-and-
    mind, she felt the pain of separation.

Her heart-and-mind boiled and bubbled. Boiling and bubbling like that,
    she was the Bubble-Bubble Queen!

It seems animals were born to Mother Earth!

In Mother Earth, in the heart-and-mind of this birthing Queen,
    [were thoughts:] "Will I die?" or "Won't I die?"

I came to rest after nine months in mother's body;

From mother's body this body [of mine] was taken and differentiated.

...The reason[13] my orphan's eyes cannot see is because of my unendurable
    burden of greatest sorrow arising from the pain of separation.

My heart-and-mind imagines 100–1000 thoughts:

It seems the pain of separation came from uphill and from down below.

Why was I born in this my own life form?

Why, oh, My Own Mother, for what reason was I born in this unbearably
    suffering sundered life form?

The "pain of separation" of which he sings is *gyurba*. Gyurba in its various verbal
forms evokes the feelings of loss caused by being separated from something dear:
in everyday language, people apply this most to things that have been sold off
(and are gone, even though the money received cannot really recompense). In the
lines above and the following lines of this bomsang there are endless plays on the
idea of the "pain of separation," as parturition (from one's birth mother), as parting
(from a beloved), as partition (among brothers of the family estate), and, ultimately,
of course, as death.

The reason my strength is no longer is because of all this tripping and
    tumbling after jewelry.

...In the time of my tenderly sprouting flesh and blood,[14]

Splitting from my brothers, we divided the estate.

I felt the pain of partition.

...In the time of my birthing, it seems I suffered the pain of being orphaned
    from both above and below.[15]

No matter what food is eaten, no matter what is drunk, no matter the life form,
All life forms that come to birth suffer the pain of death.
All suffer the pain of decrepit bodies.
No matter what is drunk, no matter what food is eaten, no matter the clothing
    that is worn,
It seems there will be the unendurably hard burdensome pain of separation.
When enduring such burdensome suffering, is human life a hell of great pain
    and separation or not?
When will my time for separating from this life form be fulfilled?
To die is a cruel cutting off; to live, still surviving, can I ever cut off the great
    hardships of this life form?

I want to highlight at this point that Tamang imagery of birth, suffering, and the maternal body creates highly specific images of the "pain of separation." This is a very elaborate construct for Tamang, with several different verbs exploring its aspects. The most common is gyurba: gyurba here means "to hurt" or "to suffer," but in the sense of "to suffer a loss," "to feel bad at having lost something." Gyurba is a visceral sense, and it is embodied in women.

Women's bodies are intrinsic (in Tamang constructions) sites for gyurba, for feeling the "pain of separation." This happens to women as mothers, not only in children's births, but also in their deaths—from whence come a variety of extremely emotional "orphan" images in Tamang narrative and song. Other smaller life events lead to gyurba, too: working to build up jewelry, then losing it; working to build up household wealth, then watching brother-sons fight over it; and, above all, working to raise daughters, who move to their husbands' houses and communities after marriage. This movement of brides has two saliencies: for parents (and parents-in-law) and for young people (brides, grooms, brothers, and sisters).

For Tamang parents it is hard to know that daughters will move away, even though the loss is only partial. Since Tamang marry their cross-cousins, a daughter will go to live with someone the parents call "brother" or "sister." This means that brothers and sisters become parents-in-law to each other's children. Children's marriages are not, then, the simple loss of daughters or gain of daughters-in-law, although the imagery of the "pain of separation" a woman feels when she must move away from her natal home is, along with childbirth, one of the most common Tamang meditations on gyurba. In addition, when children begin to marry, their parents must once again think of themselves not just as parents, but also as siblings. For the young people themselves, marrying means breaking their own brother-sister sibling ties by reinforcing their parents' sibling ties. Both Tamang brothers and sisters openly lament the fact that they cannot live out their patrilineal and childhood unity forever, but they see the "pain of separation" caused by marriage as being carried bodily by outmarrying sisters.

Sister-bodies and brother-bodies are, then, the other major forms Tamang gendered bodies take. Like the father and mother, the sister and brother are a cross-gender pair. Like the father/mother pair, sister and brother are interdependent, affectionate, and generative. But what they produce are not children's bodies,[16] but a social body. And for northwestern Tamang, the social body is an exchanging body. Brothers and sisters exchange: they exchange ritually significant tokens throughout their lives. But, of course, what they ultimately exchange are marrying children, and their marital exchanges create the whole of the Tamang social fabric. I choose the expression "fabric" advisedly (or ill-advisedly, depending upon whether this reads as a pun or something more profound), since I mean the great cycles of affinal exchange that have enchanted anthropologists and the Tamang long before either knew of the other. But, for Tamang, these exchanges take form around textiles: the production and exchange of cloth literally weaves marriage and the widest social and ritual relations found among Tamang. Moreover, it is both literally and figuratively a female production.

Weaving and writing are central images in the construction of Tamang gender, and indeed, in the construction of the pivotal cultural gendered antinomy (March 1984). They juxtapose, in permanent rivalrous collaboration, two different ways of imagining (Tamang) life. One—the male—emphasizes lineal continuity, fixity, and moral determinacy; it is associated with patrilines (whether lay or lamaic) and patrilocales (whether domestic or divine). The other—female—is both more problematic and more productive. It attempts to embrace and indenture both humanity and divinity into ever more widely ramifying circles of prosperous exchange, at the same time that its reliance upon the efficacy of exchange to produce profit or growth is its limitation. It is difficult to know when someone improperly socialized is going to make off with gifts or when a daughter/sister is going to resist proper marriage.

Women's weaving, and their roles in related hospitality exchanges, have, then, both productive and problematic faces. If these exchanges are successful, then Tamang life grows and prospers, but they are often fragile and too often broken. For me, this is exemplified nowhere so well as in the mythic original tale of the *tsen*. Tsen are (today) spirit females, important divine tutelaries for shamans but regarded as a kind of lesser nonhuman malevolency by lamas. This origin story (see also Holmberg 1989:171–172), however, is about a time before humans and divinities were differentiated, in a time when those who became Tsen and those who became human were like clans, and capable of exchanging in marriage.

> A tsen woman was married to a human man. That man and her tsen brother went hunting one day. After much effort they succeeded in killing one bird. Although the story describes it as a small sparrow-like bird, the tsen brother insists that a portion be carried back to his sister by the human husband, saying that he (the tsen brother) has not forgotten the affection he has for his sister. When the husband returns home, he finds his tsen wife sitting in a crossroads weaving at her loom. He is scornful of this apparently insignificant sibling gift and throws it down

into his wife's lap. It breaks her leg. She gets up, leaves her loom and husband, and walks away, over nine ridges, to be precise. After each ridge, she becomes progressively less visible to her human husband; after the ninth, she is no longer human. Thereafter, humans and nonhumans cannot marry. And humans who wish to receive superhuman blessings (like meat that magically increases), must address themselves, through women and tsen to the spirit universe (March, Fieldnotes 1977).

But even as Tamang worry about the possibilities that exchange with women might collapse, they turn to all kinds of strategies to try to ensure that it won't. Successful female-mediated exchanges in the human realm create marriage and maritally exchanging society. Moreover, femaleness mediates exchange in most interactions with Tamang divinity, too. Many of these strategies simultaneously deploy the bodies of women, especially in all their beauty as sisters about to become wives.

In the song *Om sangla mané padmé hum,* the parsed beauty of women and their bodily ornamentation becomes the metaphoric vehicle of all beauteous religiosity. Just as devotees are instructed in the mantra-based refrain to:

Offer music of all kinds of instruments to the ear.
Offer suitable/pleasing flowers to the Book.
[the mantra] Om mani padmé hum hri!
Om sangla mané padmé hum!

they are also instructed, verse by verse to:

Offer the head ornaments
That suit/please the daughter-women of our place to the Book.
...Offer the earrings
That suit/please the daughter-women of our place to the Book.
...Offer the black eye make-up
That suits/pleases the daughter-women of our place to the Book.
...Offer the nose ornaments
That suit/please the daughter-women of our place to the Book.

The verses of the song continue to cite all the traditional ornaments of Tamang feminine beauty thought to suit *nangsa-la bomo.* Nangsa-la bomo are, literally *"bomo* of our own place"; bomo is an honorific term for "woman," in her identity as "of" one's own lineage, clan, or village. It is in this sense of belonging that I gloss it here as "daughter-woman." The ornaments that suit and please the ear, nose, eye, forehead, and so forth, of the "daughter-women of our place" are situated in this popular dancing and devotional song parallel to the other essential (six sensory) offerings made to the Buddhist scripture and its wisdom. All are defined as suitable and pleasing, to daughter-women and as offerings to the divine. In the

Tamang practical logic of reciprocity, suitably pleased divinities are presumably more inclined to bestow their beneficence.

These symbolic associations between women and exchange, especially exchanges of hospitable generosity (March 1987) also define the bodies of women, especially the sororal body of women-as-sisters, as generators of prosperous exchange, growth, and increase. If the womb is the "flower" (and the metaphor is Tamang) of the maternal body, the hand is the outstanding feature of the sister's body. The sister-woman's hand at the loom, like her hand and beauty in hospitable exchange, ultimately creates Tamang society, not in the sense of birth-origin elaborated upon in images of the maternal (even Earth Mother) body, but in another sisterly and (to our sensibilities) more elusive sense.

There are many examples of the importance of the woman's hand in Tamang hospitality and in the ability of hospitable offerings placed lovingly by a woman's hand to create the ambiance of obligation essential to produce a reciprocal return. The hand and body that place these offerings are not "servile." They make ambitious gestures, both invitations and demands, to involve recipients—whether other human beings or divinities—in a return round of exchanges. And they are so invested in the "hand of beloved women" that few people can even talk about the processes of making offerings or of offering hospitality without also making the proper female hand gestures.

But the most elaborate example is in the *hya hwai*, fittingly, "The Hand Song."[17] The Hand Song is one of the most powerful of Tamang mythic songs: like the "Mother Earth Song," it is literally (about) the creation of the world. But from it emanates a differently female body (part).

> I don't know; I don't know.[18]
> The moon may know; the sun may know.
> *Déné laso.*[19]
> [Refrain]: *Hya hwai! Hya hwai!*[20]
> Hand song! Hand song!
>
> ...The beautiful mistress of the house[21]
> places[22] a golden winnowing tray[23] in front of her.[24]
> ...The beautiful mistress of the house then
> places her request with respectful hand gestures.[25]
> ...The beautiful mistress of the house requests by
> placing a snack to go with the liquor.[26]
> ...The beautiful mistress of the house requests by
> placing pine resin incense.
> ...The affection in the hearts of our beloved women is supreme.[27]
> ...[They] place [their] requests with affection in [their] hands.
> ...The affection in [their] hearts is supreme.
> *Déné laso.*

Hya hwai! Hya hwai!
Hand song! Hand song!

And so, with hand and heart properly prepared, these primordial women figures begin to make offerings:

The beautiful mistress of the house requests by
placing an assortment of grains.
...A pure butter lamp is placed on top of[28] the assortment of grains.
...Coins of gold are placed after the pure butter lamp.
...[There was] the beautiful mistress of the house, and then,[29]
the affection of [her] heart is supreme.
Déné laso.
Hya hwai! Hya hwai!
Hand song! Hand song!

Once the offerings have all been placed, by these loving female hands, the whole of creation unfolds. The bulk of the song details the Tamang creation myth.

Long ago, long ago,[30] the spot of dirt [that became] the nucleus of the earth
did not exist.
This was a time when the patches of blue [that became] the sky did not exist.
...After [there were] patches of blue in the sky,[31] furrows of clouds spread out.
...After those furrows of clouds [came into being], rain and hail fell.
...After rain and hail [fell], a lake of water formed.[32]
...After rain and hail [fell], a whirlwind formed.[33]
...Long, long ago, the dust of the earth did not exist. It was a time when the
blue of the sky did not exist either.[34]
...After the blue of the sky [came into being], a small rock came to rest.[35]
...After a small rock [came into being], a great mound of earth came to rest.
...After a great mound of earth [came into being], [both] small and large
rocks came to rest.
...After [both] small and large rocks [came into being], a supreme rock came
to rest.
...After a supreme rock [came into being], the earth's foundation came to rest.
...After the earth's foundation [came into being], meadow and forest came to rest.
...After meadow and forest [came into being], the moon and the sun came to rest.
...After the moon and the sun [came into being], duba grass came to rest.
...After duba grass [came into being], a great hill came to rest.
...After a great hill [came into being], the nucleus[36] of the earth came to rest.
...After the nucleus of the earth [came into being], the tale[37] of the nucleus[38]
of the sky was told.
...After the nucleus of the sky [came into being], all kinds of things came

to birth.
Déné laso.
Hya hwai! Hya hwai!
Hand song! Hand song!

And so on throughout an even more lengthy song recitation about the origins of plants, animals, the cycle of years, houses and all their contents—in short, everything from the blue of the sky and the light of the moon to the pollen of flowers and the smallest of soup ladles. All this from the hand, the hand of "the beautiful mistress of the house," "our beloved women" who "place requests with affection in [their] hands." It is a vision which startles twice. It stands contrary, first, to the textual frameworks of high religion (Buddhist, Christian, and others) that assert the priority of the "word" as primordial creative force. But, second, it also poses a different kind of female reply. In this Tamang song of beginnings, there was first a woman, but not offering the fertility of her womb; it begins, rather, with the fruitfulness of her hands, beautiful mistressly Tamang hands.

Concluding Remarks

Tamang female mothers' and sisters' bodies are at first paired with male fathers' and brothers' bodies. But, then, they are set apart from their male counterparts by maternal blood and milk, and by sisterly hands. In one sense, the symmetry is subtle and strong, as parents of both genders contribute in tandem to new baby bodies, and as hospitable hostesses *and* hosts may jointly embody cultural impulses to exchange profitably. But this symmetry redoubles back upon itself since ultimately sisters and brothers (not mothers and fathers) share in the regeneration of the patrilineal identity, while mothers and fathers become again brothers and sisters as their children extend and carry on cycles of affinal exchange.

In this framework of doubles, pairs, and opposites, the female body—as both sister and mother—emerges as an elaborate reflection upon its very corporeality. At each contrastive turning with the male, the female is more emphatically embodied, and embodied, embodies suffering. And the suffering female bodies engender is, from one perspective, unique: as maternal bodies they suffer the attachment and severing of their children's natality; as sororal bodies they suffer the attachment and severing of their identity as children. In their personal identities, mothers and sisters who become mistresses in their own dominions embody intermediacy, exchange, increase (whether by birth, weaving, or hospitality), and suffering. As morally embodied persons, they occupy junctures between birth and death, and between marrying affines.

But from another, wider Tamang Buddhist perspective, the "pain of separation" is no more the mother's than it is that of the "orphaned child," male or female; it is no more the sister-bride's than the brother's left behind. As people and self-reflective selves, both women and men find meaning in the symbolic hands and wombs of female-engendered bodily experience. As symbols around which to orient selfhood, the female body need not be personally experienced to be meaningful. Whether as painful presentation of possible reality (as the Tamang maternal or sororal bodies displayed here) or Suleri's "hugely practical joke," the meanings under women's skirts are not the personal property of people who inhabit female bodies.

And so the apparently esoteric Buddhist speculations about the nature of human life as suffering because embodied, and embodied, attached, come full circle. If, as scripture teaches both Tamang laity and lama alike, suffering comes from attachment, the "pain of separation" is quintessential pain, and not the experiential property of either sex, even if it is the symbolic corporeal capital more of one than the other. Tara was perhaps both right, and relevant to Tamang after all, in her conviction that there was nothing different between the spiritual potential of men's and women's bodies, and at the same time that there was something special about finding enlightened release in a female body.

Notes

1. I recommend Jean Comaroff's introduction (1985) as among the best of such tours de force.

2. These *sel rotī* (Nepali) are fried doughnuts of mashed bananas and rice flour. Words in italics are drawn from Tamang, unless otherwise indicated. These are spelled to facilitate approximately accurate pronunciation by English speakers, not in accordance with any precise phonemic or tonal orthography.

3. People know about ideas of birth pollution, but it is relatively unmarked in Tamang practice, except for those births that Tamang classify as illegitimate.

4. In dictionaries of modern Tibetan, some of this complexity is recorded. Jaeschke (1972: 262), having translated *din* as "kindness, favor, grace" and *dintsen* as "kind, gracious, benevolent," gives examples (usually drawn from the religious texts his dictionary was primarily designed to assist in reading): *mai din*, "the benefits conferred by a mother," and *tshe di-la din tse-shos rang-gi ma yin*, "the greatest benefactress for this life is one's own mother." Contemporary Tamang did not use the word to convey ordinary courtesy, but drew associations between *din* and *dim* (or *Dip*; terms for various kinds of pollution, including birth pollution). More at stake here, of course, are contemporary Tamang meanings rather than classical Tibetan ones, although the connections are always intriguing.

5. Stupahill refers to the area in which I did research; I refer to the Tamang who lived there as Stupahill Tamang.

6. Recorded by David Holmberg and Surya Man Tamang in 1976.

7. The primordial lamaic teacher.

8. The primordial mother; the honorific and mystical referent for one's own birth mother; hereafter in this bomsang, it is rendered "My Own Mother."

9. The tape and meaning, here, are not clear.

10. A force/spirit who forms children in their mothers' bodies.

11. Ritual and religious figures or divinities, called "queens."

12. That is, sentient.

13. Literally, the "trail by which..."

14. A common poetic reference, literally "flesh-tendrils blood-tendrils," to the physical fleshy robustness of a human body in its youth.

15. Including the prosaic up the mountain and down the valleys, i.e., all alone, but also meaning to be cut off from both heaven and hell.

16. Except, of course, in wondrous mythic incestuous relations.

17. This version was led by the Syé Pompo and recorded by David Holmberg and Surya Man Tamang on October 25, 1976.

18. Not an exact repetition in the Tamang: *asyé,* "I don't know" (in its usual negative verb form); *masyé,* "I don't know."

19. Tibetan-sounding (to the Tamang ear) words of generic affirmation (e.g., "oh, yes"); here they mark the end of the song specialist's verse and signal the audience to sing the refrain.

20. Hya hwai literally means "hand song."

21. This *némo sangbo* ("beautiful mistress of the house") is a central image throughout. *Namo,* like *damo* (also "mistress of a house"), occurs frequently as part of a pair: *némo-nébo* (or *népo*) and *damo-dabo.* The former pair (némo-nébo) appears to have something more of the connotation of "hostess and host," while dabo-damo refers to the more permanent (especially in ritual and or political contexts) head man and woman of a household.

22. Throughout this song, the verb tense is to me somewhat equivocal. Insofar as many of the constructions have a mythical root, these actions—especially the "placing of requests"—occurred in the distant potent past, but the exact form of the verb is not that of the usual mythical past tense. Instead, it has overtones of a possible present or future action, e.g., "might place" or "will perhaps place."

23. Religious offerings are typically carried and place upon a winnowing tray, albeit typically of bamboo, not gold.

24. This "in front of" is somewhat problematic. In the simplest sense, it means spatial: she places offerings in front of her. As she is presumably facing the altar or guest, this means they get placed "in front of" the desired recipient as well. But the term *khalam* also has meanings of "on top of" or "after" (see below), not unlike the English double entendre "she placed the offerings before her." Here, the implication would be that the beautiful mistress of the house existed before the offerings, that she was their foundation, and that they came to rest "on top" or "after" her.

25. *Tschatang shyésa shyubam* refers to the placement of offerings (which are a request) with the proper hand gestures, namely with the right hand palm up and with the left touching the right elbow. No request or social interaction in Tamang life can proceed far without this gesture: it is simultaneously the hand of generosity proffering the best the (mistress of the) house has to offer; and it is the hand of supplication asking for a return on (potentially even greater than) whatever is offered. This image presumably underlies the very name of this song, as the song itself is seen as an offering and supplication, placed

respectfully in this way.

26. Tamang hospitality—both secular and sacred—revolves around the offering of fermented and/or distilled liquors. Furthermore, these cannot be offered without accompaniment, usually a spicy bean or meat snack.

27. All of the word choices in this verse come from the most respectful register possible.

28. Here and below the "on top of" has the simultaneous meanings of literally "on top" (such as would be done to construct an offering mandala of things piled on top of a grain foundation), but also "after" (as in a ritually ordered sequence).

29. Here is one of the most complex usages of khalam: in a simple translation, this verse is about the "affection of house mistresses," but the imagery is one overlaid with both temporality (first came the mistress, then came affection) and spatiality (the mistress is the foundation upon which the affection is layered).

30. The term for this "long ago" (*dangbo*) refers to that mythical time when, as Tamang say, all things were coming into being, to their first rebirth.

31. That is, after they came into being.

32. Literally, "expanded."

33. Literally, a "wheel of wind expanded."

34. The Tamang for this verse is the same as that more literally translated above.

35. This *tschapa* ("to come to rest") is one of several verbs Tamang use to describe the beginning of the world. *Thungpa* has more distinct connotations of "to come to (re)birth." *Shéngpa* is the more mundane "to make." *Dipa* seems to be "to arrange or set into place." *Syerppa* seems to be "to grow or increase," and *syongpa* and *khilpa* "to spread out, expand or rebound."

36. A *téwa* is the ball-bearing-like stone lying at the center of a hand grain-grinding mill.

37. *Namtar* (tale) are multiply-told tales or histories, usually of the origin of things.

38. Here, *kawa*, stands in the same relation to the sky that téwa has with the earth.

References

Beyer, Stephen. 1973. The Cult of Tara: Magic and Ritual in Tibet. Berkeley: University of California Press.

Bourdieu, Pierre. 1977. Outline of a Theory of Practice. Cambridge: Cambridge University Press.

———. 1990. The Logic of Practice. Stanford: Stanford University Press.

Comaroff, Jean. 1985. Body of Power, Spirit of Resistance: The Culture and History of a South African People. Chicago: University of Chicago Press.

Fortes, Meyer. 1973. On the Concept of the Person among the Tallensi. *In* La notion de personne en Afrique noire: Colloques internationaux du Centre National de la Recherche Scientifique 544:283–319.

Geertz, Clifford. 1973. Religion as a Cultural System. *In* The Interpretation of Cultures. New York: Basic Books.

Holmberg, David. 1989. Order in Paradox: Myth, Ritual and Exchange among Nepal's Tamang. Ithaca, NY: Cornell University Press.

Jaeschke, H. A. 1972 [1881]. A Tibetan-English Dictionary. London: Routledge and Kegan Paul.

Landon, P. (1987 [1928]) Nepal. (2 volumes) Kathmandu: Ratna Pustak Bhandar.

March, Kathryn. 1984. Weaving, Writing and Gender. Man 18:729–44.

————. 1987. Hospitality, Women and the Efficacy of Beer. Food and Foodways 1:352–87.

McHugh, Ernestine. 1989. Concepts of the Person among Gurungs of Nepal. American Ethnologist 16(1):75–86.

Suleri, Sara. 1989. Meatless Days. Chicago: University of Chicago Press.

Part Three _____

Politicized Selves

Chapter 11 _____

The Case of the Disappearing Shamans, or No Individualism, No Relationalism

Sherry B. Ortner

I n the fall of 1966 I sallied forth from graduate school to study the relationship between shamanism and Buddhism among the Sherpas of Nepal.[1] This turned out not to be feasible for the simple reason that there were no longer any practicing shamans in the Solu area in which I settled, or at least none who would admit to practicing the traditional rites. There were, however, five ex-shamans within a two-hour radius of my village. I interviewed all of them and also raised the subject of shamanism with monks, village ritual specialists (*lama*), and laypeople. I collected a fair amount of data, both on the general configuration of the traditional system and on people's notions about the relationship between shamanism and Buddhism.

Nonetheless it seemed to me that I could not write a dissertation on something that I could not actually observe, and so I shelved the project. Instead I wrote a thesis (Ortner 1970) on food symbolism and hospitality among the Sherpas, and then a monograph (Ortner 1978a) on the relationship between village religious rituals and the strains of village social life. But the case of the disappearing shamans had lodged itself in the back of my mind.

Before getting into the problem, however, a few quick words on the Sherpas.[2] The Sherpas are an ethnically Tibetan people living at high altitudes in a relatively remote area of northeastern Nepal bordering on Tibet. Their traditional economy combines agriculture, dairy herding, and long-distance trade. Over the course of the 20th century, they have also become internationally famous as guides and porters for Himalayan mountaineering expeditions. Within their home area, in the general environs of Mt. Everest, they live in small villages, in nuclear family households, and property in both land and animals is privately owned by families.

The Sherpas belong to the oldest unreformed sect of Tibetan Buddhism, which adopted celibate monasticism relatively late in its history, but which also continued to allow certain religious specialists, called lamas, to marry and remain in the villages, conducting village rituals. In addition, among the Sherpas, as in Tibet, there were shamans who practiced curing through trance.[3] Shamans are not classified as religious specialists, but rather are simply persons with a specialized ability. It should be noted that the religious specialists—the monks and the married lamas—also do curing work, although they do not use trance for diagnosis as shamans do.

In the late 1970s, I decided to put together the material I had on Sherpa shamanism and to try to arrive at some sense of why it had declined (Ortner 1978b). I suppose I had been assuming that the major factors behind the decline were the standard modernization phenomena—the availability of modern medicine, the availability of novel role choices, the transition to a cash economy, and so forth. It seemed a matter of rounding up the usual suspects. My fieldnotes, however, told a different story. As far as everyone—shamans, religious specialists, and laypeople alike—was concerned, the main force putting the shamans out of business was pressure emanating from the religious establishment. The monks and lamas had let it be known that they considered shaman work to be unreliable, ineffective, and sinful. Many of the laypeople accepted this and stopped calling the shamans; many of the shamans accepted it and stopped practicing their rituals. A few laypeople continued to want shamanistic curing, but they were forced to call in non-Sherpa curers (I did see a few curing rituals performed for Sherpa patients by shamans from other ethnic groups). And a few shamans told me they were still willing to practice. By and large, however, the pressure from the religious establishment had clearly been effective. The most powerful and charismatic shaman of the area had formally sworn off his practice, performing a ritual to prevent his tutelary deities from visiting him, and selling off all his equipment. Moreover, he and two other former shamans had actually taken up formal, if low-level, religious training, such that they were qualified to participate in certain village rituals along with the village lamas.

Conflict between Buddhism and shamanism is not by any means new to the Tibetan Buddhist tradition. The religion established itself in Tibet in the first place (in the eighth century), according to both internal and external history, by "defeating" shamanism and establishing superiority over it. Subsequently, in both Tibet and among the Sherpas, lamas and shamans coexisted in a peaceful asymmetry, but with this history always in the background, in the form of tales of contests between shamans and lamas of old, with the lamas always victorious. Here is one example, told to me by a village lama:

> There was once a competition between a great lama and a shaman. They both flew to the sky, and both came out the same. This went on for a long time. No matter what the lama did, the shaman matched him. They both made rocks soft. They both made footprints in the rock. Then the lama suggested mountain climbing. The shaman started climbing, but the lama went to sleep. The lama's servants kept trying to wake him, but he kept saying, "Don't worry," and kept on sleeping. The lama said, every time they tried to wake him, "Did the sun rise yet?" They admitted that it hadn't. "Well, then, don't bother me," he said. Finally the sun rose to find the shaman singing and dancing just below the summit, thinking he had won, when the lama came running up the sun rays to the top and won the contest. Then the shaman was humiliated, and hid behind his drum. But the lama said, "Don't worry, don't be ashamed," and he gave him some snow from the mountain, which is why that mountain now has a crimp near its summit. Previously shamans had refused to pay obeisance to lamas, but since then they always do.

This story was part of a rich and apparently very old and widespread stock of Tibetan Buddhist ideology concerning the inferiority of shamanism.[4] The problem was thus not one of understanding where the ideology was coming from—it had been around since at least the entry of Buddhism into Tibet—but rather the specifically historical question of what had suddenly revitalized the ideology, and with such dramatic results—the precipitous decline of Sherpa shamanism.[5]

Part of the answer, after I thought of it, was obvious. I had known at the time of my first fieldwork that all the Sherpa monasteries had been founded in the 20th century. That is, I had known this in the way people know something they learn for an exam—it was a meaningless piece of data. Now, however, it became enormously meaningful, since it occurred to me that the decline of Sherpa shamanism, under the pressure of religious specialists, must have been related to the rise of the monasteries. I went back to the field to find out whether this had indeed been the case, and more generally to get a broader picture of the religious transformation surrounding the rise of monasticism. As the reader might guess, the decline of shamanism turned out to be only one chapter of a much longer story.

The first part of this story concerns the events and processes leading up to the founding of the monasteries themselves. In the latter half of the 19th century, certain major changes were taking place on the peripheries of the Sherpa area. In

Kathmandu, the capital of Nepal, there was a political coup, the main impact of which, as far as the Sherpas were concerned, was an expansion of the taxation system, and an upgrading of its efficiency. More tax collectors were appointed and endowed with more powers. In north India, on the other edge of the Sherpa map, the British were moving into high gear with large-scale programs of road and railroad building. For this they required not only native labor, but native contractors to organize that labor. Certain Sherpas capitalized on both of these developments and became quite wealthy as a result. One man, a village lama and a successful long-distance trader, brought himself to the attention of the Kathmandu authorities and was appointed head tax collector for the region. The post subsequently passed to his son who, through continuing cultivation of government contacts, made a great deal of money. A second son made a fortune as a labor contractor for the British in Darjeeling, and later returned to the Sherpa area to take over the head tax collector post himself. The first son, together with two other men (both successful long-distance traders, one of them a tax collector as well), sponsored the building of the first Sherpa monastery in 1916. The second son, entirely out of his own resources, sponsored the building of the second in 1924. (All of this has been summarized from Ortner 1989a.)

The monasteries in turn embarked on an extraordinary campaign of religious upgrading, which constitutes the second part of the story,[6] and which includes the campaign against shamanism. This campaign, however, was only one of a large number of changes consciously and intentionally wrought by the monks on Sherpa religion. One household ritual, involving a Hindu Nepalese god who required animal sacrifice, was prohibited altogether. The annual village temple festival was purged of a number of bawdy scenes, and was eventually taken out of the hands of the married lamas to be performed henceforth by the monks.[7] Two new rituals, proclaiming the value of the monks to the community, and the superiority of monastic values, were inserted into the annual calendar. The local village lamas as well as the shamans were denigrated, and the monks put themselves forth as the only proper embodiments of the ideals of Sherpa Buddhism. And as all this was going on, new monasteries continued to be built, to a total of 14 in the region in the space of about 50 years.

This article is concerned with one strand of this broad set of changes—the campaign against Sherpa shamanism. For the first half, I will focus on the following questions: What was at stake in the monastic campaign? What, both from the monks' point of view, and analytically, was "wrong" with shamanism and the other aspects of popular Sherpa religion that the monks felt had to be cleaned up? And what was the relationship between the monks' religious purification campaign and what I earlier called "the usual suspects"—money, Western medicine, and sustained participation in Western forms of labor and sociability? In the second half of the paper, however, I shall question the answers of the first half, and of some recent work which links up with it.

The Monastic Critique of Shamanism

Sherpa shamans were individuals who fell ill with some kind of "madness" or delirium in their youth, during which time they acquired one or more tutelary gods who taught them the skills of shamanistic curing. It was a point of pride that they learned their skills directly from the gods and not from other human shamans (as among most other ethnic groups in Nepal) or from books (like monks and lamas among the Sherpas).

The basic shamanic practice among the Sherpas may be briefly described. Called in the case of illness, he performed a *hlabeu* (trance divination): he would enter into a trance, and the spirits who caused the illness would speak through his mouth, voicing their grievances and demands. Often, a series of gods (including his tutelary) would then speak through the shaman. The gods would be given offerings (on the model of human hospitality[8]) and requested to control the spirits, or asked for advice on what needed to be done to control the spirits. Then, when the shaman came out of trance, he would assist the patient's family in preparing the required offerings to placate the spirits and get rid of them.

From the outset, the newborn monastic establishment had little good to say about shamanism. It was a fundamental premise that shamanism and religion (*cho*) "don't mix" or "don't get along" (*mutunmu*). Perhaps the best place to start in understanding the monastic establishment's critique of shamanism is with a myth volunteered by a lama when I asked him what was wrong with shamanism. The myth contains and interrelates all three of the issues that people tended to invoke on the subject: sin, weakness and pollution, and falsehood.

> Once there was a king whose servant was dying. The king called both the lama and the shaman. The shaman, shaking and speaking in his trance, seemed to know everything, but actually he was possessed by a demon [*du*], and the demon knew everything the servant did. [Here the lama-informant added an aside: "Demons inform shamans; that's how they know everything."] Then the king said, "This is much better than the lamas, the lamas only read religious texts." But then Guru Rimpoche [the culture hero] said, "No, lamas are greater, this shaman is possessed by a demon, which is evil." And Guru Rimpoche put his golden thunderbolt [*dorje*, a weapon against demons] up the king's sleeve, and said, "Now go back and see if the shaman speaks so well." He told the king to ask the shaman, "What do we do during [a certain ritual] in the temple?" and similar questions, and the shaman wouldn't know, because during such rituals the demon has been thrown a decoy offering [*gyek*] that has carried him far away to his distant land, so he never sees the ritual. Also, he'll be afraid of the *dorje*. [And everything the Guru Rimpoche said came to pass.]

Now let me pull out some of the threads. The suggestion that shamans are allied with the demons proposes, first, an alliance with evil and sin, for the demons are pure antireligion. Few people, in fact, imagine shamans to be in league with demons and with absolute evil, but there are a variety of ways in which shamanism is thought to be sinful. For one thing, it was said that shamans practiced black magic on behalf of clients, to harm the clients' enemies. It was also said that shamans, in attempting to control witches, physically harmed the persons whom they identified, rightly or wrongly, as the human vehicles of the witches. And it was noted that, by publicly providing the information by which people could identify witches and thieves, the shaman sowed conflict and discord within the community.[9] The obvious point that a shaman gains much merit from curing sick people, and that such merit might actually outweigh any sins committed in the process, was almost never volunteered by informants, and was shrugged off as not to the point when I raised it myself.[10]

The second charge signaled by the myth, and to some extent more salient for both shamans and laypeople if not for lamas, is the issue of the shamans' vulnerability to losing their powers. In the myth the trick is accomplished by decoying away the demons, thus cutting the shaman off from his supposed source of knowledge. In reality, however, the greatest threat is the loss of shamanic powers through pollution.[11] There is a cultural notion that prolonged contact with illness in others is polluting. Pollution, in turn, makes ordinary people ill and causes people with any extraordinary powers to lose those powers. While both shamans and lamas would be affected in curing by the pollutions of illness, lamas have ritual means of purifying themselves that shamans do not have. Thus a shaman's powers have a built-in potential for declining, while a lama's are capable of restoration.

Closely related to this charge is the third one, that of the deceptiveness and unreliability of shamans, in that they claim a certain sort of access to truth and knowledge that in fact (according to the myth) they do not have. One reincarnate lama went so far as to say that shamans are "all liars." Others—lamas and laypeople—were more moderate, saying simply that shamans may sometimes fake their trances and their communications with the supernatural. Religious specialists, in contrast, do it all from books, and there is no risk of fakery. When I pressed one man on whether a nun, as a woman, would be as effective as a monk or a lama, he said yes, because it's all in the book and not in the person.

In thinking about how to interpret the monastic critique of shamanism, one needs to consider not only what was said but what was not said. For upon reflection one realizes that the criticisms of shamanism just discussed are couched in terms of established religious values, that religion essentially controls the discourse and provides the yardstick against which shamanism is being measured. Religion, in these accounts, is simply more moral, more powerful, and more reliable, in terms that it has already defined, which are the only terms available to be applied. This is a nice illustration of a hegemonic process, in which one sector is perforce compelled to speak in the idiom of another, within which it cannot possibly emerge in a superior position. The possibility that shamanism is not simply less good, true, and potent than Buddhism, but actually might embody a different, and noncommensurable, view of the world, is obscured, and must be retrieved through alternative lines of interpretation.

Shamanism Versus Buddhism: "Deeper Meanings"

The deeper contrast between shamanism and Buddhism can be approached in a variety of ways. For present purposes, however, I will pursue the question through a comparison of the different types of spirits dealt with by shamans on the one hand, and monks and (married) lamas[12] on the other.

The central focus of shamanistic practice is a set of beings called *pem*, or witches, and *nerpa*, or ghosts, often referred to as a hyphenated unit—*pem-nerpa*. These beings, along with *lu*, locality spirits, are the major causes of illness in secular village life.[13] When a shaman is called upon to diagnose an illness, with very few exceptions these are the spirits he will discover to have been at work, and with which he will deal with in his ritual. Buddhist ideology and ritual, on the other hand, highlights a class of threatening beings which I will gloss as *demons*. While demons of various kinds were attended to in certain Sherpa ritual contexts before the rise of the monasteries, they were given a big boost after the foundings, since a major demon-exorcism ritual, Mani-Rimdu, was established in each of the monasteries shortly after its founding.[14] There is no generic term for *demons*, but I use the term here to refer to a wide range of creatures (in my locality, *du, de, dirnbu*, and *simbu* were the most prominent members of the set) who are postulated by Buddhist ideology and who—unlike witches, ghosts, and lu, have no "history," as it were, in local life. I will say much more about the distinction below. The point here is that shamans never deal with demons, who in any event are almost never involved in actual known cases of illness. Monks, in turn, are very explicit about never having anything to do with witches and ghosts. Let us look more closely at these different kinds of forces of misfortune.

Witches, or pem, first, are forces embodied in living members of the community.[15] The pem becomes activated through envy—primarily through seeing others' good food, or in some cases fine clothes or other wealth—and strikes the victim with illness, generally stomach and digestive disorders. The pem who makes one ill may well be a kinsperson, although there is no special kin relationship that systematically produces pem activity, and often there is no kin relationship between pem and victim at all, but simply close contact.

Nerpa are ghosts of deceased persons, and the nerpa who regularly cause illness in any given community are almost always ghosts of individuals who are still personally remembered. Some have died in accidents, while others have died natural deaths, but either way they have failed to end their social relationships satisfactorily, and remain attached to and dependent on their former world. Nerpas' chief characteristic is that they are miserable—homeless, hungry, and thirsty, wandering about striking people with illness as a way of expressing their need for food and drink. In some cases the nerpa is kin of the victim, in others not. Even when it is not, however, it is always identified in terms of its former kin ties with some other living member of the community: father of so-and-so, older brother of so-and-so.

And then there are the demons, whose existence is assumed by Tibetan Buddhist myth, and one or another of which is the focus of the major monastic rituals, particularly those staged for the public. Demons are inherently greedy, vicious, cannibalistic beings, ever hungry for flesh, blood, food, and wealth, who will cause general chaos unless kept under control by duly ordained religious specialists. Tibetan Buddhism's central claim to people's allegiance is that it protects people from the demons, and the demons reciprocate with special hatred for the religion as an institution, in addition to their posited aggression against humanity. There are no theories of the origins of the demons, as there are for pem and nerpa; where pem-nerpa arise from human experience and derive from actual human beings, demons existed before the human race came into being, and have gone around eating people ever since.

From these brief sketches, several important points of contrast may be drawn. The first is that, whereas pem and nerpa derive from known members of the actual on-the-ground social community, with whom everyone has (or had, in the case of nerpa) direct acquaintance and personal ties, nothing of the sort is true of demons, who are utterly socially decontextualized.

Second, if we consider the sorts of motivations upon which the two types are assumed to act, we see a radical difference: pem-nerpa are motivated by what may be called relational emotions, whereas demons are motivated by what in modern parlance would be called "drives." Let me expand upon this point.

As noted above, the motivating force of pem is envy—she is roused to activity by seeing the good food or other good things of others. Envy thus depends upon the *relative* well-being of self and other, and is evoked in an interaction in which relative disparities are experienced. As for nerpa, they are propelled by their hunger and thirst, which are absolutes, but note that the primary response they provoke in the living community is what the Sherpas call *nyingje*, pity or compassion, for their sad plight.[16] Thus when nerpa express themselves through shamans, pitifully whining again and again, "I'm hungry, I'm thirsty," the faces of the audience take on pained, empathetic expressions, and murmurs of nyingje can be heard throughout the group. I suggest that pity or compassion is, like envy, a relational sentiment, and indeed is the positive reciprocal of envy—where envy is evoked by the other's being better off than oneself, pity is evoked by the other's being worse off. In both cases the sentiment is dependent on social context and has to do with the relative situations of self and other.

The case of demons is radically different. Demons are motivated by what we would call drives—pure greed and aggression. Where relational emotions are by definition evoked only in relative contrast to the state of others, a drive such as greed may be defined as an essential force pressuring the person or being from within. Greed and aggression are postulated as essences or attributes of the demons themselves, impelling them to act as they do regardless of context. As the demons have come from nowhere, being uncreated existents, so their motivating drives are "natural," essential, and self-generated.

I take this interpretation to reveal a—if not the—fundamental difference, and source of antagonism, between the Buddhist and the shamanistic worldviews. The religious promotion of the demons as the dominant threat to human security represents the promotion of forms of social relations, emotional experience, and selfhood at odds with the local ties, transactional emotions, and relational selves expressed and evoked by pem-nerpa. The demons in the monastic context seem intended to represent, evoke, and contribute to the formation of an altered sort of personhood, socially decontextualized, mobile and uncommitted in terms of social relationships, and "psychologized"—composed of internal drives for the expression or repression or sublimation of which only the individual is responsible.

In support of this argument, we may consider the practice of Buddhist monasticism among the Sherpas, and the attitudes of Sherpa monks toward pem and nerpa. Sherpa monasticism (like much of Tibetan Buddhist monasticism) is a highly individualized affair. Each monk lives, eats, and studies in his privately owned house on the monastery grounds. Aside from specific collective rituals, the monk is there to pursue his personal salvation. In contrast to some Christian traditions, the monastery is not viewed as either a "brotherhood" or a communal entity; a monk is connected to the monastery via his relationship to the head lama, and not via his relationship to the other monks. (See Paul 1970 for more on the organization and practice of Sherpa monasticism.)

In taking vows, a monk has specifically left the ties and bonds and demands of lay life in the villages. This is what enables him to concentrate on his spiritual development. And this is what establishes his views of, among many other things, pem-nerpa and the practice of shamanism. A large number of monks with whom I spoke said that, having become a monk, one is no longer subject to attack by pem-nerpa, that pem-nerpa no longer "bother" them; and indeed, that that was one of the many benefits of monkhood. Pem-nerpa were said to operate only down in the villages, being considered essentially spirits of secular life. Virtually all monks claimed that they would not call a shaman if they became ill, in part because (as noted earlier) shamanism and religion "do not get along," but more importantly because it was unlikely that the illness was caused by pem-nerpa, against which a shaman would be effective.

What the monks are saying, in effect, is that pem and nerpa are no longer relevant or meaningful to them. In renouncing social ties, and the material goods whose significance, beyond sheer survival, is as a medium of those ties, the monk has been rendered a nonrelational individual, that is, a person whose orientation to the world is largely independent of social context, and whose fate is no longer felt to be bound up with the fates of others. While monks are not forbidden to interact with laypeople, even with women, there are a variety of rules and practices designed to render them nondependent upon interpersonal relationships for material and emotional support. They may not exchange material goods, for although they may accept charity, they must not by definition reciprocate, or they would negate the meritoriousness of the act for the giver. They also of course do not marry, and sometimes they also renounce speech. And emotionally or psychologically, they must come to assume very profoundly the doctrine of personal fault and personal responsibility, in which one's thoughts and actions are assumed to arise entirely from psychic forces (such as greed and aggression) residing within one, and are controllable only by one's own mental and spiritual efforts.[17]

The monk is thus in many ways the reciprocal of the demons. Although demons ceaselessly prey upon others, and although the monk in principle demands literally nothing from others, both stand in contrast to the normally exchanging social person. And whereas the demons are inherently greedy and aggressive, and although the monk must "conquer" greed and aggression, both assume greed and aggression as natural and essential drives. Thus demons "make sense" to monks, while pem-nerpa no longer do, they no longer "bother" them. The relationally defined motives of pem-nerpa, and of the layperson—and the shaman—to whom pem-nerpa makes sense, have been rejected and/or superseded.[18]

Finally, it should be noted that this interpretation finds echoes within village discourse. While Sherpas do not operate with a Western category of individualism, they are in general sensitive to selfishness in individuals, and they particularly notice it in monks and nuns, since these people are supposed to have learned to overcome it. Thus for example, I have heard married lamas say that they should get more religious merit than monks, because married lamas remain in the villages and help people, while the monks go off to the monasteries and pursue only their own salvation. Similarly, I overheard a conversation between two laymen in which they were discussing borrowing a pair of cymbals from a monk for a wedding. One was dubious about borrowing from the monk, saying that he would worry about the cymbals cracking. The other agreed saying, "Yes, monks (and women) have 'small hearts.'" And one more example: I had a conversation with a young layman about a nun who had come to the house begging. I gave her some food, but then somewhat to my surprise she went around the house, poking into the shelves and asking for things beyond what I had given her. The man remarked that, although monks and nuns were trained to want less than laypeople, in fact they seemed to come out even greedier than everyone else.

Sherpas respect their monastic community, up to a point. That is, they are convinced that the disciplines of monasticism produce a more powerful kind of religious practice, bringing greater supernatural protection and higher levels of spiritual merit to the world. This does not prevent them, however, from sizing up the monks as persons vis-à-vis the community, and recognizing that monasticism may foster some of the very problems (of selfishness, egotism, etc.) that it seeks to overcome. Although village life has many problems, it presumes a world in which people are interconnected and have ongoing obligations to one another. The theory of illness and curing embodied in shamanism shares those ("relational") assumptions.[19] Buddhist monasticism, in contrast, is both socially and psychologically "individualistic." It encourages a rupturing of social obligations and the renunciation of a subjectivity which finds those obligations compelling.

A Second Look

With only minor changes, the above discussion was drafted in the mid-seventies.[20] Since that time, several important works on shamanism in Nepal have appeared with variants of the same argument. In an elegant book on Tibetan lamas and Gurung shamans in north central Nepal, for example, Stanley Mumford (1989) adapts arguments from Mikhail Bakhtin to the effect that shamanism, or more generally "the shamanic world view," is part of an "ancient matrix" in which "personal identity is relational, defined in terms of connections between persons" and in which "everything acts and takes part in the unified life of the whole"(1989:16). Buddhism (and Christianity), in contrast, offer worldviews in which "the individual life sequence" embodies "a new feeling of interior time, 'sealed off' from other subjectivities. It promotes a directional identity of 'individual becoming' that seeks extrication from the world matrix" (Mumford 1989:16). Mumford's discussion is much more nuanced and sophisticated than a simple oppositional argument, particularly insofar as he argues that these two strands coexist and "interilluminate" one another, thereby producing an "emergent tradition" that is neither the one nor the other (1989:17, 23). Nonetheless, at the base of the argument is a fairly straightforward alignment of shamanism with relationalism, and Buddhism with individualism.[21]

In a study of shamanism among the Yolmo wa, a group in north central Nepal related to the Solu-Khumbu Sherpas, Robert Desjarlais similarly aligns shamanism with "an embedded communality [that] fosters what may best be called a 'relational self'—a sense of personhood...conceived and experienced through social relations" (1992:54). He does not develop this point at great length, but it threads its way through the discussion as a theme. For example, a central category of illness for the Yolmo wa is "soul-loss," and Desjarlais equates the current prominence of soul loss illness with the "dispersion and fragmentation" characteristic of more modern modes of life in Nepal, which threaten the "relational" solidarity of the Yolmo world (1992:155). In addition, one extended discussion of a particular case of illness hinges on providing a patient with some "individuality" in the face of excessive relational demands of in-laws (1992:191). And at the end of the book Desjarlais returns to the point that the shaman's rites among the Yolmo wa "address these larger historical tendencies" of "fission, fragmentation, and dispersal" which threaten their "corporate ways of life" (1992:243).

Finally, among the Sherpas of Solu-Khumbu, Vincanne Adams (1992) also studied the relationship between shamanism and Buddhism, and included as well Western biomedicine. Again the discussion is nuanced, sophisticated, and complex—and often very illuminating. In particular she argues, and I agree, that Buddhism did not entirely succeed in establishing its individualizing agenda among the Sherpas who, as often as not, reconverted individualizing Buddhist practices—such as "disinterested" alms giving—into reciprocity-engendering acts. Yet the argument is built on the familiar basis equating, on the one hand, shamanism and a social self founded in exchange and reciprocity and, on the other hand, Buddhism and an individualized self founded in self-scrutiny and self-regulation.

Only one recent work on shamanism and Buddhism in Nepal avoids casting its argument in terms of some form of the relationalism/individualism contrast: David Holmberg's *Order in Paradox: Myth, Ritual, and Exchange among Nepal's Tamang* (1989). Holmberg sees shamanism as inherently ambiguous and, as it were, disorderly. It exists in counterpoint to the religious specialists' alignment with "order," and stands as a recognition that order itself is shaky and fleeting (1989:169–70). Holmberg's arguments recall Robert Paul's discussion of Buddhism and shamanism among the Sherpas, in which Buddhism is aligned with rules, order, death, as against the shaman's association with "life" and "vital natural energy" (1976:149). But perhaps because Tamang religion was momentarily in a relatively static phase, Holmberg is less concerned with seeing the relationship between shamanism and lamaism as a forced march toward modernity, in which Buddhism/individualism is eclipsing shamanism/relationalism. Instead, he focuses on elucidating the complex existential counterpoint between the two ritual perspectives, as a meditation on order and disorder—a counterpoint as much present in "traditional" as in "modern" society.

The reader may guess where this is all going. I did not publish the 1978 paper in part because, as I said earlier, I felt I needed to know more about the rise of monasticism among the Sherpas and the range of its effects. But more generally I had an obscure discomfort about the argument itself, and particularly about the simple opposition between individualism and relationalism.

Yet it was hard at that time to shake that opposition, for at least two reasons. One was that the opposition was embedded in the powerful modernization narrative: traditional people are relational, modern people are individualistic. The modernization narrative certainly held sway at the time of the first drafting of that paper, and still prevails in many quarters today. The second was that dualistic interpretation per se was very much in vogue in that era: bringing to light (I suppose that should be in quotes) binary oppositions was felt to be clarifying, illuminating, revealing of the underlying logic and order at work. In retrospect, indeed, one can recognize the way in which the two theoretical moves were mutually sustaining—oppositions such as traditional/modern, nature/culture, and relational/individual were embedded in the modernization narrative itself (Fabian 1983; Rosaldo 1980). With respect to South Asian societies in particular, Louis Dumont (1960, 1970) had articulated in that same era his structuralist inspired arguments about the shift from Hinduism to Buddhism around the opposition between "holism" and individualism, and between the "individual-in-the-world" and "out-of-the-world" (see also Carrithers 1985)—variants of the relationalism/individualism opposition.

Theoretical arguments over the past decade or so, however, have radically questioned the modernization narrative (and indeed all "grand narratives") and have particularly insisted on examining individualism as an ideological formation rather than an ontological object (Heller et al. 1986). What I want to do in the second half of this article, then, is to take apart the arguments of the first half, but in a particular way. I do not want to say they are wrong, for I do not think they are, exactly, and I would not have wasted the reader's time with them if I thought they were. But I want to say, and show, that they are too simple, and that this simplicity is dangerous in all the ways that postmodern anthropology has recently brought to light: it feeds into a discourse of otherness in which the Other is either inferior or romantic, but either way excluded from equality of intercourse with us.

The individualism/relationalism opposition is situated in a discursive field that also contrasts the West and the Rest, the Modern and the Traditional, the Male and the Female, and the Adult and the Child. It is not wrong to say that shamanism in some of its forms (particularly when it is up against an aggressively expanding higher Buddhism) is—or becomes—more relational than individualistic, and that Buddhism in some of its forms is just the reverse. But it is wrong to align the shamanism/Buddhism opposition permanently and completely with the relationalism/individualism opposition; in fact as I will try to show, the two can as easily change places for certain purposes, or in certain contexts, or from certain points of view. Moreover, it is wrong to link those alignments permanently and completely with tradition/modernity; while it is probably true that modernity is more individualistic than relational, and that tradition is rather more the reverse, the simple opposition hides at least as much as it reveals about both traditional and modern societies.

The following arguments, then, are meant to both problematize the oppositions and to disrupt the alignments. The discussion follows the lead of earlier, especially feminist, attempts to challenge binary thinking by showing that, while it is always "sort of right," it is nonetheless dangerously misleading (Rosaldo 1980; Strathern 1980). Michelle Rosaldo in particular argued that a focus on oppositions encourages analysis in terms of "essences" of the categories, rather than analysis in terms of the politics of the construction and deployment of the categories. It also follows the lead of recent arguments by Ernestine McHugh (1989) and Akhil Gupta (1992), both of whom pursue very similar interpretive strategies concerning these kinds of dualisms in South Asian societies.

Thus I will argue that we can say that shamanism is relational only if we are prepared to also see the ways it is not; and only if we are prepared to see the historicity of its being this way, and only if we are prepared to realize that its classification in these terms—whether by us, or by Sherpa villagers, or by Buddhist monks—is always ideological in some sense. Indeed, if postmodern theorizing has any meaning at all (and one sometimes wonders), it means this endless hedging of seemingly simple truths—this endless "yes, but" that plays with prior arguments, turns them inside out, roots out their ideological implications, demands historical specificity, and leaves them standing (if at all) only in the most provisional way.

Deconstructing the Oppositions[22]

Was Premonastic Sherpa Society Relational?

The answer to this, I would have to say, is almost perfectly ambiguous. Premonastic Sherpa society (that is, the society that would have been described as predominantly "relational," and upon which the monasteries worked their "individualizing" agenda) can be described in such a way as to have it appear either predominantly relational or predominantly individualistic.

I have thus far avoided defining these terms, largely because they are so large and slippery within Western and/or academic usage. Each of the terms has multiple dimensions/referents/connotations. *Relationalism* may encompass, minimally and among other things, implications of corporateness; of social obligations given by relationships; of statuses given by relationships; of many relationships given by birth or styled on a kinship model; and so forth. With respect to painting a relational picture of Sherpa society, then, one could emphasize the virtually total corporateness of the nuclear family, the obligatory participation in mutual exchange groups, the determination of status by lineage membership and birth order, hereditary attachment to particular temples and to particular "headmen" (*pembu*) and more.

Individualism is of course an even vaster term (see Dumont 1986; Lukes 1973; Macpherson 1962; Riesman 1954; Shanahan 1992; Williams 1973, 1976). Minimally, however, it may encompass notions of personal "ownership"; of obligations generated by agreement ("contract") rather than by relationship; of the social and conceptual autonomy of the skin-bound person; of the creation of status through achievement as a result of personal qualities; and so forth. With respect to painting an individualistic picture of Sherpa society, then, one could emphasize private property and individual inheritance; the centrality of monetarized trade in the Sherpa economy; the acceptability of bachelorhood and spinsterhood and of living alone; the value on personal independence and on the capacity to take on solitary activities (like tending herds alone at high pasture for long periods of time); along with this, the respect for hermits and for solitary meditation even before the founding of the monasteries;[23] the respect for highly individualistic/charismatic (*tsachermu*) lamas; and more.

Any given characterization of Sherpa society could highlight one dimension or the other; this is part of the reason the picture drawn of the Sherpas in the ethnographies of von Fürer-Haimendorf (1964) and Thompson (1982), on the one hand, and Ortner (1978a) and March (1979) on the other, look so different.[24] But it is also the case that the Sherpas themselves can and do play games with these possibilities, emphasizing the selfishness of their covillagers for some purposes, and the solidarity and supportiveness of family and village life—especially when they are away from it—for others.

This, really, is the point. The ontological reality is so slippery and relativistic as to allow for virtually any characterization. Within the region, Sherpas appear more "individualistic" than their Hindu Nepali neighbors (von Fürer-Haimendorf 1964), and indeed than most other groups in Nepal (March 1979). More generally, most Tibetan-related groups (including Sherpas) appear more "individualistic" than the Indians on one side of them and the Chinese on the other (Goldstein 1968:130–131, 185; Samuel 1993:146). Yet compared to "us," Sherpa village life was very "relational," and indeed it also even appears that way to Sherpas in the urban context of Kathmandu. The binary discourse of relationalism and individualism (or some locally or temporally specific variant thereof) was and is an always available discourse, a source of word games and of critical categorizations available to lay Sherpas, outside observers, and Buddhist monks alike.[25]

My argument here is similar to those made by Ernestine McHugh (1989), based on her work among the Gurung of Nepal, and Akhil Gupta (1992), based on his work in rural India. McHugh specifically addresses a version of the relationalism/individualism opposition. Questioning whether "the difference between Western and other concepts of person has been overdrawn" (1989:75), she proposes that "while relatedness is of central importance in South Asia, this does not eliminate the concept of the individual. Concepts of both individuality and relatedness exist, and the ways in which they are articulated and reconciled express tensions inherent in South Asian social life" (1989:77). Gupta (1992) addresses questions of time rather than person, but uses a similar interpretive strategy. Arguing against the notion that the West has linear time while the Rest have cyclical or reversible time, he shows that cyclical and reversible forms of time are strewn across the landscape of Western discourse, but are suppressed in the face of an us : them :: linear : cyclical logic. Both McHugh and Gupta then attempt to disrupt these oppositions (and the modernization narrative within which they are embedded) by showing the presence of the suppressed category where it has been representationally excluded, as I am trying to do in this and the following sections.

Was Sherpa Shamanism "Relational"?

If Sherpa society as a whole, then, cannot be clearly characterized as either relational or individualistic, the same must be true of Sherpa shamanism. Earlier I showed the strong ways in which shamanism could be aligned with relationalism. I also noted that Sherpa villagers (both laypersons and married lamas) seemed to recognize the individualistic tendencies of Buddhist monasticism that can be brought to light analytically. What needs to be shown now is how the whole thing can be turned around. For if one listens carefully to other strands of discourse in Sherpa society, one will hear that it is shamanism, not Buddhism, that is charged with being individualistic. For example, one of the charges heard from laypeople is that shamanism only helps the individual patient, while lama curing rituals (*kurim*) bring benefits to the entire household.

Another line of disparaging comments links shamanism with a kind of impersonal "business" orientation. Thus one lay informant commented that shamans,
in contrast to lamas, bargain over their fees. I do not think this is actually the case,
though I do not have hard data on the point. But I definitely had the impression
that this charge had arisen before. Thus when I asked one shaman what he charged
for his services, he said rather truculently that there was no fixed rate, that he
didn't sell his services "like a Nepali at the bazaar."

A third linkage between shamanism and individualism lies in the area of sor-
cery/black magic.[26] I noted earlier that shamans are accused of performing sorcery or harmful magic (*zingchang*, said to be a corruption of *zhinsek*, a Buddhist
ritual for casting out evil), and that this is one of the charges against them. In
point of fact, lamas also know, and are known to know, black magic rituals. The
difference between the two is said to lie in the fact that the shaman would perform
such rituals for the private gain of a client, while the lama would only perform
them for the good of the larger community.[27]

And one more point: I discussed earlier the fact that it is monastic Buddhism
rather than shamanism that traffics heavily in demons. Most Buddhist rituals are
designed to defeat demons—usually du—who prey upon humanity not because
of violations of relationship but because of their intrinsically evil nature. Most
shamanic rituals, in contrast, are designed to deal with witches (pem), ghosts
(nerpa), and locality spirits (lu) who make people sick because of neglect or abuse
of obligations to them. Yet in fact the monks (and wider Tibetan Buddhist ideology) link shamans, not monks, with demons. Thus we saw earlier that one of the
myths told against the shamans proposes that their information is false and unreliable because it comes not from gods (as shamans claim) but from demons. And
I also argued earlier that demons (along with other aspects of Buddhist philosophy) signal the notion of an interiorized psyche full of naturalized drives (such as
greed and aggression), features of an autonomous self.

Each of these points adds to a picture of shamans, not monks, as individualistic. Treating the patient and not the household; acting like a contractual businessman; doing sorcery for private gain rather than for the benefit of the community;
gaining knowledge from the viciously a-relational demons: each of these practices either elevates the individual above the group or presumes a universe of
autonomous selves/beings in the first place.

With these points higher Buddhism thus reverses the charges of individualism
against itself and turns them against the seemingly relational shaman. How can
we understand this reversal? In the first place we are reminded that, if individualism is a thing, it is equally or more a label, a critical charge that any sector can
level at any other. With a moment's reflection we realize that we should not be
surprised to hear that Buddhist ideology in particular charges shamanism with
individualism, since individualism is available in Buddhist thought as a generalized category of negativity, a category that summarizes much of what is wrong
with the world. In point of fact, Buddhist ideology can and does charge shaman-

ism with *both* relationalism (trafficking in pem-nerpa who do not "bother" the socially detached monk) *and* individualism, and in a sense it does not matter, for both relationalism ("attachments") and individualism ("egotism") block the way to universal compassion and ultimate transcendence.

Additionally, however, the relational/individual reversal with respect to shamanism returns us to the pitfalls of trying to fix Sherpa society as a whole within the opposition. That is, we can only understand how shamanism can appear as both relational and individualistic if we abandon the notion that Sherpa society as a whole was, in its "premodern" state, essentially relational. In fact, as we have seen, both tendencies were deeply intermixed (along with other patterns and tendencies that have not even been discussed).

The tense mixture of the two meant, in turn, that neither could be viewed except in contrast to the other. Against a background of relationalism, individualism was always threatening to some degree. The unconditioned individual could go out of control: the tsachermu lama, magically powerful and ideally operating on behalf of the community, could become the *ongchermu* bully or strongman, relying on threats of physical force and operating purely for his own benefit (Ortner 1989a). Unbridled greed and self interest could be acted out in the lethal forms of sorcery and poisoning.[28] And perhaps most likely and threatening, self-interested individuals could simply become unavailable, so that there was nowhere to turn for help. This in fact seems to have been the most salient (and threatening) aspect of individualism in the premonastic context, for the most prominent images of unconditioned individuals were, after all, the gods. The gods "need nothing" and their primary threat is withdrawal; the religion of the temples and the village lamas is centrally concerned with keeping them *in relationship* with humans, calling them, feeding them, flattering them so that they will help (Ortner 1978a).

At the same time, against a background of individualism, relationalism could seem cloying and demanding. Kin, neighbors, and family members could make demands from which there was no escape. If the strongest image of the ills of individualism in Sherpa society is that of the gods, threatening to withdraw, the strongest image of the ills of relationalism is the witches, ghosts, and lu with their whining needs or angry tempers predicated on violations of relationship with them. And if village temple religion, in the hands of the married lamas, is in part concerned to counter the problematic potentials of individualism (always put as "getting the gods to help"), shamanistic practice is clearly concerned with countering the problematic tendencies of relationalism (pacifying former kin [ghosts], fellow villagers [witches], and nonhuman neighbors [lu] with food and kind words *so that they will leave one alone*). But this is precisely what gives credibility to the monks' charge that shamanism is individualistic. Because while shamans at one level *presume* a relational world, they also help people to push back against the especially importuning aspect of that world.

Deconstructing the Question: What Does It Mean to Investigate "The Decline of Shamanism"?

I began this article by describing how, when I first got to the field, I could not find the shamans I had proposed to study. The project then became one of studying what had caused shamanism to go into decline. I first answered that question in terms of the rise of monasticism among the Sherpas, and with it the rise of a kind of individualism that was hostile to the relationalism reflected in (among other things) shamanic thought and practice. I then spent some time deconstructing the relationalism/individualism opposition, as it applies to both Sherpa society in general and shamanism versus Buddhism in particular. At this point we need to go further with deconstruction: we need to ask whether the question was posed adequately in the first place. I will phrase the problem as follows: In what sense did Sherpa shamanism "decline"?

Local Variation and the Wider Field of Religious Politics

The decline of Sherpa shamanism turned out, first of all, to be regionally variable. While it was almost completely extinct in my original field area, Solu, it persisted much longer in Khumbu. At the time of my first fieldwork, one well-established shaman in Khumbu was still practicing regularly, and at least one other still considered himself available to practice.

The differential survival of shamanism in the two regions may be addressed from a number of points of view. For one thing, the presence of a Western-style medical clinic in the largest Khumbu village may have paradoxically kept shamanism alive. My data indicate that the Western doctors who staffed the hospital viewed the shamans as useful for certain kinds of ("psychosomatic") cases not amenable to Western medicine, and routinely referred patients back to the shamans.[29]

More generally, however, the survival of shamanism in Khumbu needs to be put in the context of a larger politics of supernatural influence operating between monks, married lamas, and shamans. In particular one must look at the fate of the married lamas, who were in many ways at least as much disparaged by the monks as the shamans, sometimes more so. The charges against the married lamas were different from those against the shamans, focusing on how the distractions of lay life—wives, children, work, drink, village sociability—undermined the married lamas' abilities to develop and maintain their religious and ritual expertise and powers. In any event, for reasons I have discussed elsewhere from another angle (Ortner 1989b), although the shamans went into more severe decline in Solu, the married lamas went into more severe decline in Khumbu. At the time of my first fieldwork, most of the married lamas in Solu were genuine *gyudpi* lamas, that is, descended from married lama lineages, while most of the married lamas in Khumbu were fallen monks.

This little historical excursus illustrates precisely the arguments made by Michelle Rosaldo (1980) in her attack on dualistic analysis. For if one looks at the simple opposition, shamanism/monasticism, one almost inevitably comes out with a modernization narrative based on the "essential qualities" of the two types of practitioners. But if one looks at the larger political field, one realizes that the qualities are not *essences* of the categories, but *charges* that are up for grabs and that can be leveled by any sector against any other. There *are* such things in the world as relationalism and individualism, or tradition and modernity, but no one group permanently owns one or the other of these terms, for better or for worse. Rather these are large-scale forces around which every group divides and unites in an unending political process. The ideological move comes from pretending (whether in Sherpa life or academic journals) that certain alignments are essential to certain groups.

What Did the Absence of Shamanism Mean? The Ambiguity of "Decline"

Insofar as we are deconstructing oppositions, we even need to deconstruct the simple contrast between presence and absence of shamanism. Even where shamanism was gone, not being practiced, its absence had various meanings.

At one end of the spectrum, the not-practicing of shamanism was relatively clearly and unambiguously related to an acceptance of monastic ideology. This was the case for both some shamans and some laypersons. Take the case of Upa Gyaldzeu (Father-of-Gyaldzen from Upa), who had been, by all accounts, including his own, the most famous and powerful shaman in Solu.[30] He had suffered a series of personal misfortunes—several of his children died, one in a bizarre accident—and the lamas persuaded him that it was because he was committing sin in his shaman work. He formally swore off shamanistic practice, doing a ritual to get his tutelary gods to release him and selling off all his equipment. After renouncing shaman work, he took up religious training, and at the time of the field-work was performing lama divination-cum-textual curing rituals if called. But he would not diagnose through trance.[31]

A similarly dramatic story comes from a layman whom I knew very well. Dawa (not his real name) told me about the time he was living in Darjeeling, doing expedition work, and became ill. He was a devotee of both the Western medicine available on mountaineering expeditions, and the higher Buddhism of the monasteries. In a letter to his sister back in Khumbu, he mentioned that he was sick. His sister called in a shaman to her home in Khumbu, and the shaman performed a trance divination (hlabeu) in which he diagnosed that the problem was an angry lu spirit who lived under a certain large rock near Khumjung village. Dawa's sister went and made offerings to the lu, and—although the chronology is not clear here—Dawa did get well. He did not know about his sister's calling the shaman and making offerings to the lu until some time later when he visited her in Khumjung and she told him what she had done. He became extremely angry, since he had renounced his belief in shamanism, and evidently in lu spirits as well. He went to the rock where the lu was supposed to live, took down his pants, and shat on the rock. Moreover, he pointed out, he did not get sick after doing that.

But most cases were much less clear cut. Starting with the shamans themselves, it was not even clear whether some of them were still practicing or not, nor—since they didn't appear to be—why they weren't if they weren't. Upa Gyaldzeu's younger brother was said by many to still practice hlabeu, but he denied it to me, and was said to have refused to perform it or anything else in my presence, when asked by a family during my stay. People said he was probably "ashamed," a category that covers a multitude of feelings; the suggestion in his case was that he feared he would be seen as unmodern.[32] Hlakpa, the only woman, was said to have been quite powerful, and she did not deny that she still practiced hlabeu curing. But the one time a family in my village engaged her, partly at my prodding, to come and do a cure, she didn't come (according to them) because her husband wouldn't let her go.[33] Purbu, finally, was fairly old, and lived furthest from my village; it seemed that people simply didn't call upon him anymore, and one man said, when another (at my suggestion) thought about calling him, that Purbu had lost most of his powers through pollution. Purbu was the one who said he didn't go around knocking on doors to drum up trade, "like a Nepali at the bazaar."

If we turn then to the lay villagers, we get a similarly confused and ambivalent situation. At one end of the spectrum I heard a good bit of support for shamans. Some people were still prepared to argue that shamanism was the most effective mode of curing, especially in the case of serious illness. Their reasoning was that both lamas and Western medicine only medicate symptoms, while shamans really get to the deeper causes—they grapple with the spirits behind the whole thing. Others took a more moderate position, arguing that curing by lama, shaman, and Western medicine each had its sphere of effectiveness, that which one chose depended on what one's problem was, and that in effect shamanism was as valid as the others.

Similarly, there was practical evidence, regardless of what people said, that many people still wanted the shamans' services. Thus two cases of trance curing by Sherpa shamans were said to have taken place shortly before I came to the field (one possibly when I was actually there, early in my stay), and in two cases people claimed to have invited Sherpa shamans for trance curing while I was there (once at my urging), but the shaman failed to materialize. And in two cases families invited non-Sherpa shamans (a Chhetri man, and a Newar woman, the latter from another village) to perform, although both of these situations were clearly last resorts, and the patients died shortly afterwards.

More in the middle of the spectrum were the cases in which people toyed with the idea of calling a shaman, or said they were planning to call a shaman, but then never did. Too much, probably, should not be made of this—people drag their feet about going to the doctor in our own culture, and it does not necessarily signal any deep ambivalence about the whole medical system. Yet it seems worthy of note in this context, where shamanism seems as it were half in and half out of the culture. One presumes that people's ambivalence about calling shamans articulates with the shamans' ambivalence about practicing: people might have called the shamans more if the shamans had exhibited more commitment to their practice, but the shamans might have been more enthusiastic about practicing (and more resistant to the monks' point of view) had they not perceived a withdrawal of lay support.

The ambiguity of the whole situation is perhaps caught up in an ironic Sherpa saying: "The lama's wife gets sin, the shaman's wife gets merit." The literal meaning of the saying is that the lama's wife hopes the patient will die, so that her husband will get the money for making the funeral, while the shaman's wife hopes the patient will get better, so that shaman's reputation will grow, he will get more calls for curing rites, and he will make more money. At one level the saying is ironic, even silly, since "everyone knows" that lama work is more meritorious than shaman work (see Paul 1976). The silly and immoral position—hoping the patient will die—is attributed to a woman (the lama's wife, not the lama himself) who, because of women's culturally assumed greater greediness (see Ortner 1983), will violate the hegemonic valuation of lama over shamanistic curing. But another reading seems equally possible—that the women in the saying are serving as mouthpieces for a wider cultural ambivalence about the religious charges against shamanism, and express a fairly substantial skepticism about exactly who is more greedy and selfish than whom. Essentially, the religious reversal is reversed— whereas shamanism seems from one point of view largely relational and relatively selfless, the religious establishment reverses the point and highlights its more individualistic and selfish aspects. But the folk saying reverses the religious position and places the more harmful greed on the side of the religion—the lama's wife hopes the patient will die.

Even When It's Gone It May Not Be Gone

The deconstructive move may be pushed yet one step further: even though shamanism seems no longer to exist, it may yet still exist in other forms. In part this point is a simple recognition of the fact that Sherpas will still use shamans from other ethnic groups when their own shamans are not—for whatever reason— available. I noted earlier that there were several instances in the village of Sherpa families calling non-Sherpa shamans. This is even more common in Kathmandu, where it seems that Sherpa shamans have never practiced (see Adams n.d.). Sherpas pointed out that if one gets sick in Kathmandu one is likely to have been attacked by the local Nepali witches and ghosts, against which the local shamans (*dhami*) are assumed to be more effective in any event.

But the point that shamanism in some sense lives on even when it appears to have disappeared may be taken to a different level. I refer here to the popularity of reincarnate lamas among the Sherpas, and to the arguments made by others (Aziz 1976; Paul 1976) that the reincarnate lama, or *tulku*, is in effect a religious version of the shaman. A tulku is a mortal human body permanently possessed, as the shaman is occasionally possessed, by a god (or in some cases by a nearly divine soul on its way to godhood). The figure of the reincarnate lama in Tibetan Buddhism is a literalized version of the Mahayana notion of the bodhisattva renouncing nirvana to save all sentient beings. Among contemporary Sherpas, some tulku, being gods incarnate themselves, were said to be able to commune directly with the world of the gods as a shaman does.

Tulku are expected by the Sherpas to be extremely benevolent figures, no doubt because of the bodhisattva association. Although not every single tulku is in fact highly benevolent (and everyone will have his or her favorite counterexample), my perception is that a surprising number of tulku are in fact strikingly warm, kindly, and caring. (Anyone who has had a chance to observe the Dalai Lama in action, perhaps in a film, will have seen a bit of this style of personhood.) In other words, many tulku actively enact nyingje (compassion) not only for "all sentient beings" in some abstract sense, but for the many specific, real persons with whom they come in contact.

Tulku, then, not only formally appear as a shamanic analogue (a god in a body), but also evince a kind of reversibility of the individual/relational modalities that—in a very different way—is also true of the shaman. At one level the tulku is highly individualized: he is first of all a monk, cut off from normal social exchange like any other monk, and is additionally defined as a very unique and individually powerful and charismatic person. Yet at the same time his normatively expected and frequently manifested nyingje transcends the selfishness that often seems to go with the basic monastic orientation.

As I will discuss at length in another context (Ortner n.d.), Sherpa monasticism itself may be declining (if one dares use that term, very provisionally, for the moment) in the late 20th century. Despite this, however, Sherpa respect and affection for tulku is very clearly going strong. Indeed, there seems to be something of a cult of tulku going on in both the villages and Kathmandu. But insofar as tulku are really upgraded shamans, it may not be going too far to say that shamanism is, after all, alive and well among the Sherpas.

Conclusion: What's Left?

The point of this paper has been to try to figure out what is right and what is wrong with a certain kind of argument about shamanism that has been made by myself and others, and more generally what is right and what is wrong with a certain style of argumentation. Shamanism has been interpreted as embodying a relational orientation, as opposed to a more individualistic orientation embodied in Buddhism or modernity or both. I argued that while this may be true in some sense, we needed to follow the lead of feminist and postmodern theorists and be suspicious of both binary oppositions in general and the modernization narrative in which this opposition is embedded in particular.

I pursued several strategies for enacting this suspicion. In the first place I tried to show that shamanism could analytically appear individualistic as well as relational, and, moreover, that these categories were as much part of a politics of labeling as they were labels for real things in Sherpa society. That was why, whatever was "really" the case, both shamans and monks could in effect call *each other* "individualistic." The point here, which is important enough to repeat at the risk of offending the reader with redundancy, is that while an opposition between some phenomena in the world called relationalism and individualism might be real enough, the way in which these terms are attached to (or separated from) persons, or categories of persons, is almost invariably ideological. The analytic endeavor, then, was not only to problematize the oppositions—to show that shamanism as well as Buddhism is individualistic as well as relational—but to attend to the politics of the construction and distribution of the categories, and to disrupt any permanent set of alignments between any given set of terms. Shamanism may be opposed to Buddhism as relationalism is to individualism in some contexts, or for some purposes, or within some ideological framework, but we must never imagine that shamanism is essentially and eternally relational, or that Buddhism is essentially and eternally individualistic.

The individualism/relationalism opposition, in turn, is normally embedded in the narrative of modernization, the bleak march of individualism and commodity fetishism before which "relational" institutions like shamanism are destined to fall. My strategy for disrupting the modernization narrative in turn was to question the way the problem was framed in the first place—the problem of "the decline of shamanism." Of course, the phrase "the decline of shamanism" referred to some real thing in the world—five ex-shamans in Solu no longer practicing trance diagnosis, as well as a lot of attitudes in people's heads. Yet the phrase could be picked apart quite productively in several different ways: that shamanism didn't "decline" in the same way in Khumbu as in Solu; that even where it was gone, this absence meant different things to different people; and that there was even a sense in which, even where it was gone, its spirit, as it were, lived on rather vigorously in other forms. This section thus attempted to deconstruct the opposition "presence/absence (of shamanism)" itself, on which one version of the modernization narrative, for the Sherpas, depends.

Each of its subsections, in turn, opened up the possibility of illustrating some other points—the survival of shamanism in Khumbu as against the decline of the married lamas in that region allowed us to see how the shamanism/Buddhism opposition was just too simple (at the very least we were really dealing with a three-part structure of monks, shamans, and married lamas, as Holmberg [1989] well argued); the multiple meanings of the absence of shamanism even in Solu—

from active renunciation, to passive neglect, to (perhaps) pretending not to practice because one does not like the anthropologist's gaze—showed us just how crude the category of "decline" is even where it most appears to refer to something in the real world; and the argument for Sherpa shamanism's survival within the healing practices of other groups, and within the tulku's role, allowed us to see once again how something such as relationalism moves around in a large political field, and how the analytic focus must precisely be on the shifting alignments of this field, rather than on the essences of Buddhism and shamanism.

Yet finally we must return to the historical question. Academics can deconstruct anything; that is their business. But is one really saying that nothing has happened? That there is no such thing as a "modernity" different from, say, a "traditional" Sherpa culture within which shamanism thrived? To ask the questions *in these forms* is to fall once again into the dualistic trap. The challenge today is to do history or other forms of social science without the master narrative of modernization, that is, the narrative in which "they" become more like "us" by shedding "traditional" institutions. The challenge is rather to see how people construct multiple histories including their own forms of modernity, and the interesting questions lie both in the specificities of those histories and in the processes by which they are made. Sherpa shamanism may well have declined, as I originally argued, under the twin impact of Buddhist monasticism and Western labor. It would be silly to deny that something like this was going on. But what makes the Sherpas more like "us" is not the absence of an unmodern shamanism, but the fact that Sherpas, like anyone else, struggle to make a world for themselves in a world they did not make.

Notes

The title of this article is a tribute to Marilyn Strathern's elegant paper, "No Nature, No Culture: The Hagen Case" (1980). For extremely helpful comments on the present article, I would like to thank Vincanne Adams, Joyce Marcus, Al Pach, Robert A. Paul, Stacy Leigh Pigg, David Scobey, Marilyn Strathern, Tim Taylor, and Harriet Whitehead.

1. The first field trip was supported by a National Institute of Mental Health predoctoral fellowship and a National Science Foundation dissertation research grant. Subsequent fieldwork among the Sherpas, all of which enters into this article, was supported by Granada Television, the National Science Foundation, and the Rackham School of Graduate Studies of the University of Michigan. Write-up time in 1989–90, specifically for the component of the long-term work that includes this article, was supported by the National Endowment for the Humanities. I am deeply grateful to all these agencies.

2. Basic sources (book-length only) on the Sherpas include Adams (1996); Brower (1991); Fisher (1990); Funke (1969); Jerstad (1969); Kunwar (1989); Oppitz (1968); Ortner (1970, 1978a, 1989a); Paul (1970, 1982); Sangye Tenzing (1971); Stevens (1993); von Fürer-Haimendorf (1964, 1984).

3. The shamans are Buddhist like everyone else.

4. See Holmberg (1989:218–219) for a Tamang version. See also Heissig (1980) for the Mongolian case of suppression of shamanism.

5. Shamanism persisted to some extent in the Khumbu region; see below.

6. Currently being written (Ortner n.d.).

7. This was true in Khumbu. In Solu the married lamas successfully resisted. See Ortner (1989b).

8. For the importance of the hospitality model in Sherpa life, see Ortner (1978a).

9. On the importance of not naming names and sowing discord, see Paul (1977).

10. Again, the situation in Khumbu is somewhat different. See below and Ortner (1989b).

11. On Sherpa notions of pollution and purity, see Ortner (1973).

12. The married lamas are actually a complex intermediate category, who sometimes appear as more similar to the shamans, and sometimes as more similar to monks. They will be dealt with more fully in Ortner (n.d.).

13. In the interests of space, I will not discuss lu and their "husbands," *sabtak*, at length in this article. Often described as "nature spirits," lu and sabtak get angry when people defile the streams, trees, and so forth, that lu and sabek live in. In all other respects, however, these spirits have very similar characteristics to pem and nerpa, in the sense that they live in close proximity to humans, have prior and ongoing relationships with them, and make regular demands upon them for care and feeding. The interpretation developed here for pem-nerpa would thus apply fully to lu/sabtak as well.

14. We have dates for the establishment of Mani-Rimdu at Tengboche (1930) and Thami (1940). See Ortner (1989a).

15. They happen to be mostly women, but I will not pursue the gender aspects in the present interpretation. See Ortner (1983) and (n.d.).

16. Nyingje is also a major category in Buddhist ideology. In the context of Buddhist philosophy, however, it takes on different, more impersonal, meanings.

17. See Dumont (1960) and Carrithers (1985) for similar arguments about the "individualism" of Buddhism. Conze (1975 [1951]) and others would agree that Buddhism is individualistic but would confine the charge to Theravada Buddhism. Collins (1982) argues that the "compassion" of Mahayanism was latently present even in the Theravada. In any event, the ideology of compassion, while countering "selfishness," does not necessarily counter "individualism"—the two are not always coterminous.

18. There are other ways of pulling the relationalism/individualism contrast out of shamanism and Buddhism. If one translates the terms into a personal/impersonal opposition, for example, and if one looks at the kinds of causality the two groups invoke in illness diagnosis, one notes that for shamans, the illness-causing agents are always other beings— witches, ghosts, lu, and so on—beings with intentions, desires, agency in some sense. When monks do illness diagnosis (which in any event is only a minor part of their role), the problems they uncover usually derive from completely agentless processes, the operations of mechanical laws such as *le* (past sins, bad karma), and violations of horoscopic indexes.

19. There were also herbal medicines (*men*) in the traditional system, and these partook of a "relational" logic. On the one hand they only worked when administered by specific persons who had specific abilities to "activate" them. On the other hand they had to be paid for (in some modest or token way) or they would not "detach" from the healer and do their work for the patient.

20. The paper circulated in unpublished form (Ortner 1978b), and is cited in Adams (1996), Holmberg (1989), and Mumford (1989).

21. Although the thrust of Samuel's (1993:447, 449) argument is somewhat different, he picks up Mumford's language.

22. By now *deconstructing* has entered common analytic language as simply meaning "dismantling" or "taking apart." That is how I use it here. The term is very useful since it carries a connotation not just of dismissing a category but testing out its underlying ideological baggage in the process.

23. See Paul (1991) on the psychology of solitude in Tibetan Buddhism.

24. See also Ortner (1989b) for a discussion of other, regional and historical, reasons for these differences.

25. One is reminded here of Raymond Williams's discussion of similar issues in *The Country and the City* (1973). No matter how far back one goes in Western literature, one finds a sense that some form of individualism is emerging and eclipsing an older relationalism.

26. The Sherpas have no "white magic"—that is, love or fertility magic—although they believe the Indians practice the former and claim that the Nepalis practice the latter.

27. I heard rumors of at least one lama—very tsachermu (magically powerful)—sending sorcery against a personal enemy with whom he had a property boundary dispute. Although in theory lamas do not use sorcery for private gain, people fear that they do.

28. Sorcery (zingchang) as noted earlier is usually performed by shamans for private clients for gain or for revenge. Poisoning (*tuk terup*) is thought to be done by women in order to enrich their households. The poison is given to strangers in the guise of hospitality; when the stranger dies the poisoner somehow gains his or her wealth. Certain women and certain villages have the reputation for being poisoners, and travelers will avoid taking hospitality from them.

29. More recent studies have found more shamans in Khumbu (Adams 1996; Draper 1988). It is not clear whether the differences represent, as Draper suggests, normal fluctuations, or whether shamanism is actually on the increase in Khumbu, possibly because of the Kunde doctors' practices just mentioned.

30. For a full discussion of Upa Gyaldzeu's career, see Paul (1988).

31. A very similar case was Mingmar, in his thirties the youngest of the five shamans in Solu. Mingmar said that he had, over years of contact with sick people, been polluted, such that he gradually lost his shamanistic powers; like Gyaldzeu he had shifted over to a more orthodox Buddhist mode, and now performed lama divinations and textual curing rituals.

32. See especially Pigg (n.d.) on shamanism's place in an explicit Nepali national modernity discourse.

33. At the time I met her, she dressed in a manner vaguely suggestive of a nun: her hair was cut short, and she wore a long-sleeved robe (not specifically a clerical garment, but almost never worn by secular women in this warmer Solu region). This suggested that she was coming under the monastic logic about shamanism.

References

Adams, Vincanne. 1992. The Production of Self and Body in Sherpa-Tibetan Society. *In* Anthropological Approaches to the Study of Ethnomedicine. M. Nichter, ed. Switzerland: Gordon and Breach.

———. 1996. Tigers of the Snow and Other Virtual Sherpas. Princeton: Princeton University Press.

Aziz, Barbara. 1976. Reincarnation Reconsidered: Or the Reincarnate Lama as Shaman. *In* Spirit Possession in the Nepal Himalayas. J. Hitchcock and R. Jones, eds. Pp. 343–360. New Delhi: Vikas.

Brower, Barbara. 1991. Sherpas of Khumbu: People, Livestock, and Landscape. Delhi: Oxford University Press.

Carrithers, Michael. 1985. An Alternative Social History of the Self. *In* The Category of the Person: Anthropology, Philosophy, History. M. Carrithers, S. Collins, and S. Lukes, eds. Pp. 234–256. Cambridge: Cambridge University Press.

Collins, Steven. 1982. Selfless Persons: Imagery and Thought in Theravada Buddhism. Cambridge: Cambridge University Press.

Conze, Edward. 1975 [1951]. Buddhism: Its Essence and Development. New York: Harper and Row.

Desjarlais, Robert R. 1992. Body and Emotion: The Aesthetics of Illness and Healing in the Nepal Himalayas. Philadelphia: University of Pennsylvania Press.

Draper, John. 1988. The Sherpas Transformed: Towards a Power-Centred View of Change in the Khumbu. Contributions to Nepalese Studies 15(2):139–162.

Dumont, Louis. 1960. World Renunciation in Indian Religions. Contributions to Indian Sociology 4:33–62.

———. 1970. Homo Hierarchicus: The Caste System and its Implications. M. Sainsbury, trans. Chicago: University of Chicago Press.

———. 1986. Essays on Individualism: Modern Ideology in Anthropological Perspective. Chicago: University of Chicago Press.

Fabian, Johannes. 1983. Time and the Other: How Anthropology Makes Its Object. New York: Columbia University Press.

Fisher, James F. 1990. Sherpas: Reflections on Change in Himalayan Nepal. Berkeley: University of California Press.

Funke, F. W. 1969. Religiöses Leben der Sherpa. Innsbruck and Munich: Universitätsverlag Wagner.

Goldstein, Melvin C. 1968. An Anthropological Study of the Tibetan Political System. Unpublished Ph.D. dissertation, Department of Anthropology, University of Washington, Seattle.

Gupta, Akhil. 1992. The Reincarnation of Souls and the Rebirth of Commodities: Representations of Time in "East" and "West." Cultural Critique 22:187–211.

Heissig, Walther. 1980. The Religions of Mongolia. G. Samuel, trans. Berkeley: University of California Press.

Heller, Thomas C., Morton Sosna, and David E Wellbery, eds. 1986. Reconstructing Individualism: Autonomy, Individuality, and the Self in Western Thought. Stanford, CA: Stanford University Press.

Holmberg, David H. 1989. Order in Paradox: Myth, Ritual, and Exchange among Nepal's Tamang. Ithaca, NY: Cornell University Press.

Jerstad, Lute. 1969. Mani-Rimdu, Sherpa Dance Drama. Seattle: University of Washington Press.

Kunwar, Ramesh Raj. 1989. Fire of Himal: An Anthropological Study of the Sherpas of Nepal Himalayan Region. Jaipur and New Delhi: Nirala Publications.

Lukes, Steven. 1973. Individualism. Oxford: Basil Blackwell.

Macpherson, C. B. 1962. The Political Theory of Possessive Individualism: Hobbes to Locke. London: Oxford University Press.

March, Kathryn. 1979. The Intermediacy of Women: Female Gender Symbolism and the Social Position of Women among Tamangs and Sherpas of Highland Nepal. Ph.D. dissertation, Department of Anthropology, Cornell University.

McHugh, Ernestine L. 1989. Concepts of the Person among the Gurungs of Nepal. American Ethnologist 16(1):75-86.

Mumford, Stan Royal. 1989. Himalayan Dialogue: Tibetan Lamas and Gurung Shamans in Nepal. Madison: University of Wisconsin Press.

Oppitz, Michael. 1968. Geschichte und Sozialordnung der Sherpa. (Student translation, name lost, files of the author.) Innsbruck and Munich: Universitätsverlag Wagner.

Ortner, Sherry B. 1970. Food for Thought: A Key Symbol in Sherpa Culture. Ph.D. dissertation, Department of Anthropology, University of Chicago.

————. 1973. Sherpa Purity. American Anthropologist 75(1):49–63.

————. 1978a. Sherpas through Their Rituals. Cambridge and New York: Cambridge University Press.

————. 1978b. The Decline of Sherpa Shamanism: On the Role of Meaning in History. Unpublished manuscript.

————. 1983. The Founding of the First Sherpa Nunnery, and the Problem of "Women" as an Analytic Category. In Feminist Revisions: What Has Been and Might Be. V. Patraka and L. Tilly, eds. Pp. 93–134. Ann Arbor: University of Michigan Women's Studies Program.

————. 1989a. High Religion: A Cultural and Political History of Sherpa Buddhism. Princeton: Princeton University Press.

————. 1989b. Cultural Politics: Religious Activism and Ideological Transformation among 20th Century Sherpas. Dialectical Anthropology 14(3):197–211.

————. n.d. Sex and Death on Mount Everest: A Double Historical Ethnography. Manuscript in preparation.

Paul, Robert A. 1970. Sherpas and their Religion. Ph.D. dissertation, Department of Anthropology, University of Chicago.

————. 1976. Some Observations on Sherpa Shamanism. In Spirit Possession in the Nepal Himalayas. J. Hitchcock and R. Jones, eds. Pp. 141–152. New Delhi: Vikas.

————. 1977. The Place of Truth in Sherpa Law and Religion. Journal of Anthropological Research 33(2):167–84.

————. 1982. The Tibetan Symbolic World: Psychoanalytic Explorations. Chicago: University of Chicago Press.

————. 1988. Fire and Ice: The Psychology of a Sherpa Shaman. *In* The Psychoanalytic Study of Society. Vol. 13. S. A. Grolnick and L. B. Boyer, eds. Hillsdale, NJ: The Analytic Press.

————. 1991. Fare Lonely as Rhinoceros: Solitude as a Positive Goal in Buddhism. Unpublished manuscript.

Pigg, Stacy Leigh. n.d. The Credible and the Credulous: Shamans in the Politics of Culture. Unpublished manuscript.

Riesman, David. 1954. Selected Essays from Individualism Reconsidered. Garden City, NY: Doubleday.

Rosaldo, Michelle Z. 1980. The Use and Abuse of Anthropology: Reflections on Feminism and Cross-Cultural Understanding. Signs 5(3):389–417.

Samuel, Geoffrey. 1993. Civilized Shamans: Buddhism in Tibetan Societies. Washington, DC, and London: Smithsonian Institution Press.

Sangye Tenzing (sang-rgyas bstan-'dzin). 1971. Shar-pa'i chos-byung sngon med tshangs-pa'i dbu-gu. (The Unprecendented Holy Scepter: A Religious History of the Sherpa People.) Junbesi (Nepal) and Paris/Nanterre (France). (P. Pranke and C. Huntington, trans.) Translation in files of the author.

Shanahan, Daniel. 1992. Toward a Genealogy of Individualism. Amherst: University of Massachussetts Press.

Stevens, Stanley F. 1993. Claiming the High Ground: Sherpas, Subsistence, and Environmental Change in the Highest Himalaya. Berkeley: University of California Press.

Strathern, Marilyn. 1980. No Nature, No Culture: The Hagen Case. *In* Nature, Culture and Gender. C. MacCormack and M. Strathern, eds. Pp. 174–222. Cambridge: Cambridge University Press.

Thompson, Mike. 1982. The Problem of the Centre: An Autonomous Cosmology. *In* Essays in the Sociology of Perception. M. Douglas, ed. Pp. 302–327. London: Routledge and Kegan Paul.

von Fürer-Haimendorf, Christoph. 1964. The Sherpas of Nepal. London: J. Murray.

————. 1984. The Sherpas Transformed. New Delhi: Sterling.

Williams, Raymond. 1973. The Country and the City. New York: Oxford University Press.

————. 1976. "Individualism." *In* Keywords: A Vocabulary of Culture and Society. Pp. 161–165. New York: Oxford University Press.

Chapter 12

Imagined Sisters: The Ambiguities of Women's Poetics and Collective Actions

Elizabeth Enslin

Rise up, sisters! Rise up!
To claim our rights, let's keep moving on
We don't know how the world has changed
And still we don't have our rights.

They say we have no rights because we're women
Let's pursue our rights with unity
With unity, we will overcome
In the women's world, we'll plant a new tree.

The above song was written by Bhavani Bhandari, a young, unmarried Bahun (Brahman) woman of Gunjanagar village in Chitwan District, Nepal. She was admired among her friends for her prolific writing of songs and poetry. During the spring of 1988, while many of her friends began organizing to establish a women's center in Gunjanagar, Bhavani hanged herself from the rafters of her parents' house. Upon discovering Bhavani's body, her mother and father burned her songs and poems. Friends of Bhavani's, many of whom were also activists in the campaign to establish a women's center, found a copy of one of Bhavani's songs. They submitted it in Bhavani's name in the Mahilā Kabitā Utsav (Women's Poetry Festival) sponsored by Nārī Jāgarān Samiti (Women's Awareness Organization) in Gunjanagar in 1990.

Recent studies show "everyday forms of resistance" as a set of practices with multiple, ambiguous, and sometimes contradictory intentions and consequences (e.g., Haynes and Prakash 1991; Ortner 1996).[1] Following this trend in the study of resistance, I consider the ambiguities in content and local historical context of high-caste women's songs such as Bhavani's presented during the 1990 Mahilā Kabitā Utsav as well as those shared during literacy classes in Gunjanagar and other villages of western Chitwan District between 1987 and 1992. But rather than reading these songs as *ambiguous expressions* of resistance, I read them as expressions of women's *ambiguous positions* in middle-class social reform in Nepal. Resistance is not, I argue, an unmediated activity of oppressed people, but is tied in complex ways with the construction of individual and collective identities in relation to social inequalities of class, gender, ethnicity, and caste.

Why do I begin this analysis of women's resistance with the account of a woman songwriter's suicide? I do so partly because the pain and despair of women in western Chitwan who have committed suicide or who have been beaten, raped, or murdered have been haunting my own writing about women's resistance. As I began writing this essay while in Nepal during the heavy monsoon rains of 1993, I heard about the deaths of two other women in western Chitwan. In August 1993, the plastic sandals and hair ribbon of a seventeen-year-old Bahun woman were found on the banks of the Narayani River in Gunjanagar. Her family and other villagers presumed that she took her life by throwing herself from a high bank into the rain-swollen river. The woman's mother had committed suicide the previous year by swallowing poison. The story circulating in Gunjanagar at the time was that the young woman could no longer bear the daily verbal (and perhaps physical) abuse meted out by her brother and father. Such abuse was what some said drove her mother to suicide as well. This was the fifth suicide case (including Bhavani's) of a woman in Gunjanagar (a village of about 9,000 people) over the previous six years.

In May 1993, the body of another seventeen-year-old Bahun woman was discovered on the bank of the Rapti River in nearby Gitanagar. Investigations led to the popular consensus that after three months of marriage, the woman was strangled to death through the cooperative effort of her husband, his mother, father, and brother after her parents refused demands to give a television and (some say) a motorcycle in dowry. This pattern of dowry murder has been well documented in India (e.g., Kishwar and Vanita 1984), but is only recently coming to light in Nepal.[2] Local people said that while husbands have certainly killed their wives before for various reasons, the Gitanagar incident was the first explicit (or perhaps the first publicized) case of dowry murder in Chitwan. Until 1993, dowry murder was something that happened "elsewhere"—in India or in areas of Nepal that border India.

As I have thought more about such forms of violence suffered by women in western Chitwan, I recognize that while not my primary analytical focus, they are not events that happen in an analytical "elsewhere," outside the realm of resistance. They are the more horrible aspect of the ambiguous terrain of women's resistance that I am trying to elucidate: the area between the ideal of Pure Resistance and the monolith of Pure Power, between critical discourses and everyday practice, and between agency and victimization. At the very least, they suggest the need to be cautious in analyzing the connections between resistance, oral expression, collective action, and everyday life. I have often been seduced myself by what Abu-Lughod (1990) calls "the romance of resistance," emphasizing and celebrating the creative, everyday ways in which people, especially women, defy and subvert various cultural norms. I have highlighted women's agency in western Chitwan in resisting dominant gender ideologies and relations through work practices, rituals, oral expressions, everyday mobility, appropriations of space, and collective action (Enslin 1992, 1990, n.d.; Parajuli and Enslin 1990). Yet as O'Hanlon reminds us, "the mere celebration of what look like autonomous defiances may do grave disservice to those who refuse to conform themselves, in underestimating the actual weight and harsh social cost entailed in contesting authority" (1991:104).

More importantly, I see how forms of violence, such as beating, rape, murder, and suicide sit uneasily alongside the construction of women's critical discourses and oppositional activities in western Chitwan.[3] They form part of the experience and subjectivity of high-caste Bahun and Chetri women who while projecting themselves as agents of social reform and modernity also recognize that they, their daughters, sisters, mothers, grandmothers, daughters-in-law, mothers-in-law, friends, or neighbors might fall victim to specific forms of violence, pain, and despair. And at the same time, the formation of a middle-class, high-caste women's identity rests on middle-class, Hindu reformist, and modernist notions of women's endurance and strength, class mobility, and the amelioration of suffering through progress that tend to displace pain and suffering to some "elsewhere" of culture, class, or nation. Thus just as stories of pain are produced and shared in creating a collective women's identity, they also become strangely silenced in the politics that emerge from that identity.

While my emphasis on the class basis of Bahun and Chetri women's critical songs in this essay mediates the celebration of resistance as an expression of the purely oppressed, an insistence on women's pain, even though somewhat anecdotal, mediates the portrayal of women as self-sufficient, autonomous agents. Women, whether they "resist" or not (however resistance might be defined), are subject to specific forms of pain and victimization. The importance of bringing pain into discussions of women's agency and subjectivity is made clear in Rajeswari

Sunder Rajan's (1993) discussion of contemporary practices and representations of sati in India. She argues against seeing "helpless victim" and "self-sufficient agent" as exclusive and opposing categories. By making "pain" the basis for the subjectivity of "victim," she attempts to make possible a politics of feminist empathy and intervention (a move towards no pain) while avoiding portrayals of Third World women as pure victims.

While Sunder Rajan invokes a specific understanding of bodily pain in her analysis of sati, I consider here a more general notion, *dukha*—a Nepali word that refers to diverse experiences of pain, suffering, hardship, and sorrow. It is frequently invoked by high-caste women in everyday conversation, in speeches, and in song to characterize their lives. As one Bahun woman's song explains: "Men and women are equal by birth, yet women face more dukha than men on this earth" (*Puruṣa nārī samāna huncha garbha ko driṣṭima; puruṣalāi bhandā dukha cha dherai nārīlāi sṛṣṭimā*)."[4] The dukha of a high-caste woman's life is certainly related to the despair that might drive some to commit suicide. It is also a general complex of gender oppression that sometimes takes the form of violence—beatings, rape, or murder, experienced as bodily pain by women.

In western Chitwan, Bahun and Chetri women's oppositional practices have been motivated by specific social relations and cultural practices that create dukha for women. But in attempting to live up to the ideals of middle-class social reform and constructing individual and collective identities as agents of change, Bahun and Chetri women in western Chitwan simultaneously distance their politics from such dukha.

The Emergence of Nārī Jāgarān Samiti in Western Chitwan

Nārī Jāgarān Samiti (hereafter NJS) emerged out of a complex convergence of events and forces that crystallized in 1988.[5] The organization involves communities scattered throughout the western region of Chitwan District, but is centered in Gunjanagar village in Chitwan District.[6] Chitwan District encompasses a large valley at the base of the Himalayan foothills in Nepal's central *tarai* (plains). Over the last forty years, Chitwan has been transformed from a dense jungle, sparsely populated by indigenous Tharus and numerous wild animals, such as rhinoceros and tigers, into a largely deforested, heavily populated, and developed region.[7] With assistance from His Majesty's Government and the World Health Organization's malaria eradication campaign in the 1950s, settlers of various *jāti* (caste/ethnic groups) from Nepal's hill regions began deforesting and cultivating the fertile soil of Chitwan Valley. The settlement of such hill-dwellers along with the building of roads, schools, college campuses, and the establishment of development infrastructure, such as agricultural development banks and various planned social change programs, have made Chitwan one of the most prosperous, "developed," and politically active regions of Nepal.

As I have described elsewhere, NJS took shape in association with literacy classes begun by popular educator Pramod Parajuli.[8] Drawing on Freirian methods of teaching literacy and numeracy through discussion and phonics, literacy classes have provided a crucial forum for women in some villages of western Chitwan to discuss, critique, and affirm various aspects of their everyday life (Freire 1972; see also Parajuli 1986, 1990). In the first literacy class, for instance, organized in 1987 primarily for *sukumbāsi* (land-poor) women, participants explored the difficulties of collecting firewood and fodder, the problems of men's gambling, drinking, and wife-beating, the lack of safe spaces in which women could meet, the pros and cons of smoking, and notions of women's versus men's work (Parajuli and Enslin 1990).

Pramod began these classes against the backdrop of political opposition in villages in Chitwan, which has in many ways played a greater role in determining the direction of NJS than Pramod or literacy classes have. Chitwan District was one of the key centers of organized political opposition to the authoritarian Panchayat system, which was finally overthrown by a popular democratic movement in April 1990 (see FOPHUR 1990). In 1987 when Pramod began literacy classes, many women and men had long been active in both underground and collaborative opposition politics, working along respective party lines—democratic socialism or communism—to end the Panchayat system. Many of the men and women already active, or at the very least, sympathetic to the opposition, saw in the successful literacy classes a means for mobilizing a constituency of women for their various party goals.

At the first ever International Women's Day celebration in Gunjanagar (organized by Panchayat leaders), some women, led by a well-known Nepali Congress leader, built on enthusiasm generated by literacy classes and publicly challenged village leaders (also sympathetic to the Congress Party) to donate a plot of village land for a women's center.[9] Between March and June 1988, at least one hundred women from Gunjanagar and some neighboring villages met every few weeks to develop strategies for gaining land for a *mahilā kendra* (women's center) and to discuss other areas of women's concern. Leaders filed petitions, met with male Panchayat leaders, and held public rallies, giving speeches expressing the importance of having a women's center. In the process of organizing to claim land for a meeting center, women also began reclaiming other public spaces. As women became increasingly discouraged by legal means (i.e., submitting petitions to the Panchayat requesting a plot of public land), they became more confrontational. At the same time, they found themselves excluded or harassed in public places that they considered partly theirs (see Enslin 1990,1992, n.d.).

By March 1989, women finally won a plot of land next to the administrative buildings and Ram Mandir in Gunjanagar in the name of NJS. They registered with the government as an official organization, after the "democratic" revolution of 1990 that brought multiparty democracy, some forms of free speech, and greater rights of association to citizens of Nepal. By December, 1990, women activists completed construction of a two-room, cement building, Nārī Jāgarān

Kendra, to serve as a center for activities that are still being determined through discussion and internal struggle.

The campaign for a meeting center included women of various jāti, reflecting the cultural diversity of western Chitwan District.[10] Bahun and Chetri women from *hukumbāsi* (landowning) families dominated the women's campaign. Low-caste Damai, Sarki, and Kami women, mostly sukumbāsi who worked as agricultural laborers, as well as some Tamangs, Magars, Gurungs, and indigenous Tharus also attended meetings and rallies, although few gave speeches. Bahun and Chetri women dominated general meetings and rallies, but some Tamang, Magar, Gurung, and Tharu women were active in initiating and running literacy classes in their respective hamlets.

The Middleness of Middle-Class Women in Rural Chitwan

Political action and expression in Chitwan District are shaped by the growth of the rural middle class. The place of the middle class in social reform in South Asia has been explored by Chatterjee (1992). Although applied to a colonial situation, Chatterjee's notion of "middleness" in relation to social reform and the normalization of a middle-class culture resonates with the kinds of contradictions I see in NJS and the cultural production of songs associated with it. With reference to colonial Calcutta's middle class, Chatterjee shows that the main feature of this class was its "middleness" so that it was "simultaneously placed in a position of subordination in one relation (colonialism) and a position of dominance in another (leadership of the indigenous masses)" (1992:41). Chatterjee notes that the contestation of relations of domination from this position of middleness is premised upon the cultural leadership of subordinates, and concludes that the nationalist project led by this middle class in colonial Calcutta was "in principle a hegemonic project" (1992:41).

Key leaders as well as some (although not all members) and supporters of NJS are part of the rural literati in Chitwan—educated small holder farmers whose family members have salaried positions (*jāgir*) in teaching, industry, or government service. Some are schoolteachers and/or wives and mothers of men with landholdings and salaries. While in contemporary rural Chitwan there are clear disparities in landownership resulting from initial inequalities in distribution or from family partition, sale, and debt; the disparities run along a continuum, with a majority of Chitwan residents cultivating small to medium-sized farms for subsistence and the sale of small surpluses. This contrasts with other regions of Nepal's Tarai, characterized by large estates owned by absentee landlords and cultivated by large populations of landless tenants. Among those with land in Chitwan, it is access to nonagricultural income that marks sharp breaks among farmers. Such income comes from a wide variety of sources, including clerical work, schoolteaching, construction contracting and labor, security and police work, petty trade, army service and pensions (Nepali, Indian, and British), transportation, entrepreneurship, and employment in the Royal Chitwan National Park. Some factory work is also available in the major towns of Chitwan, such as Narayangarh, Bharatpur, and Tandi Bazaar. Many young men work in India, and increasing numbers are migrating temporarily to earn money in the Middle East or in East Asian countries. Those with higher education and perhaps political connections have high prestige jobs in Kathmandu, in European countries, or in the United States. The expansion of such employment opportunities within Chitwan and their extension to urban centers and other countries, primarily for the educated, has provided cash incomes for growing numbers of rural families. This contributes to some of the most visible aspects of the emerging rural middle class: the increasing consumption of market commodities (purchased food items, clothing, radios, bicycles, motorcycles, televisions, refrigerators, etc.) and the burgeoning construction of cement and brick houses to replace older wood and mud plaster ones, making rural Chitwan look more and more like a sprawling extension of its central towns, Narayangarh and Bharatpur.

At the local level, the dynamics of land, income, and class relations are expressed by the two semantic oppositions: sukumbāsi/hukumbāsi and *garib* (poor)/ *dhani* (rich). In both scholarly and popular language, sukumbāsi is usually defined as "landless," but has come to acquire a more complex meaning in the context of land settlement politics in the Tarai. Sukumbāsi refers to illegal occupants of public land who are seeking (and have in some cases secured) legal rights to the land that they currently cultivate (see Ghimire 1992; Kaplan and Shrestha 1982; Shrestha 1990).[11] Sukumbāsi in western Chitwan disparagingly refer to those with legal rights to land as hukumbāsi, which literally means those who live in a place from which they can give orders (from *hukum*, order or royal degree; and *bāsi*, inhabitant). Yet both sukumbāsi and many hukumbāsi often refer to themselves as garib in contrast to *dhaniharu* (rich people). While the opposition between sukumbāsi and hukumbāsi refers to differences in landholdings, that between rich and poor refers more broadly to income-earning capacities. Thus many sukumbāsi, such as those with male members working in relatively high-paying construction or carpentry work, may be more dhani than hukumbāsi families with no off-farm income. The boundaries between rich and poor are thus highly contested; a woman might refer to herself and her family as poor, while others might call her rich. In this context, wealth and poverty become situationally defined, reflecting, I would venture, the "middleness" of many Chitwan farming families in relation to various others.[12] There are then in Chitwan a majority of people in the "middle," who are primarily hukumbāsi but who are neither excessively rich, nor poor. They have begun to share in some of the benefits promised by "development," such as mechanization, fertilizers, pesticides, agricultural credit, roads, and consumer commodities. This rural middle class, connected in varying degrees through patronage and sometimes kinship to national-level politicians, plays important leadership roles in social welfare activities, such as NJS, as well as local party and community politics.

For many women leaders and participants of NJS, the local contestation of women's oppression is a hegemonic project as they attempt to take on the leadership of diverse women in Chitwan. Middle-class leaders and many participants of

NJS are at once subordinated as women to various men: husbands, fathers, brothers and to wealthier rural households, urban merchants, bosses, regional and national political leaders, and government officials in relations of labor, exchange, and political patronage. They are also marginalized by being rural and outside of the political center of Kathmandu. Thus while many middle-class, high-caste women and men may see themselves as vastly superior to others around them, such as sukumbāsi or lower castes; they may feel marginalized in a wider political and economic context. Many of those in rural Chitwan with some land, some money, and both economic and political aspirations often express frustration at their distance from social and physical centers of power and education, be it the district headquarters of Bharatpur, the market town of Narayangarh, or the capital of Kathmandu. Both men and women may be anxious to carve out a privileged political space for themselves by showing what contributions they can make to the development of the community, region and nation. Leadership and participation in an organization like NJS become a means of carving out spheres of influence for the emerging middle class.

The Critical Discourse in Women's Songs

Women in Nepal express themselves in various genres of song and poetry, some of which are tied to specific rituals, others not. The themes, rhythms, ritual, and performance aspects of song vary by caste, ethnic group, and region, making any generalization risky. Emerging work is beginning to shed light on women's songs, especially those associated with the annual Tij festival, as an arena of resistance and critical expression (Ahearn 1991; Enslin 1992, 1990, n.d.; Holland and Skinner 1995, 1996; Skinner and Holland, this volume; Skinner, Holland, and Adhikari 1994). Involving women of various jāti in some regions, Tij is an annual women's songfest and has become a significant space of women's cultural production and contestation. Songs about dukha, about the pain and suffering experienced by women in Hindu society, are a significant part of both contemporary and older Tij repertoires in various regions of Nepal (Skinner et al. 1994:265–276).

In this essay, I am primarily concerned with the content of songs and their circulation in the context of NJS rather than on their performance in specific rituals, such as Tij. Most of the songs I discuss here have been widely circulated in writing among friends, in NJS meetings, and in literacy classes, so that they have taken on a life beyond specific oral performances. Most songs reached me already in written form. While I am analyzing women's songs in relation to NJS politics in western Chitwan, many have a much wider circulation, being associated as well with political party organizing. Thus much of what I discuss here is part of a much wider phenomenon of middle-class cultural production in the context of social reform and party politics in Chitwan District and Nepal. I limit my analysis, here, however, to the more narrow context of songs produced and circulated primarily by Bahun and Chetri supporters of NJS.

The songs submitted for the Mahilā Kabitā Utsav (hereafter MKU) sponsored by NJS in 1990 to inaugurate the new Women's Center in Gunjanagar as well as those shared in literacy classes[13] in western Chitwan are representative of the genres and styles of song shared primarily by Bahun and Chetri women who support NJS. Sixty-four songs and poems were submitted for the MKU Festival competition. Out of these, 51 (almost 80 percent) were submitted by Bahun and Chetri women. Six songs were submitted by Tharu women, five by women of artisan castes (two Damai, one Kami, and two Sarki), and two by Magar women.

Over 250 women of various jāti and economic backgrounds as well as some men attended MKU. Songs were judged and ranked by a panel of village leaders, primarily Bahun and Chetri men. The songs that scored highest among the judges were all submitted by Bahun and Chetri women. Songs submitted by women of other jāti scored among the lowest. Some participants later criticized the judging of the songs, especially the jāti and gender bias of the judges.[14]

The songs women presented in MKU and literacy classes have several influences.[15] Some appear to have been produced primarily for the competition itself, for literacy classes, or for school assignments. Some are Tij songs, circulated and performed during the Tij festival. Still others are personal compositions or modified versions of popular songs. Genres of "popular" song inspiring women's oral expression in contemporary Nepal include Hindi and Nepali film and radio songs, played frequently on Radio Nepal and Nepal Television; various kinds of "folk songs" (*lok gīt*); and political party/nationalist songs that are popularized in Chitwan through pamphlets, performances, and picnics. Some women compose their own verses to the tunes of these popular songs and/or borrow catchy phrases.[16]

Almost all of the songs submitted by Bahun and Chetri women in MKU (out of which I share only a few here) describe, evoke, and critique the dukha in women's lives. Some are also calls to action: calls for women to join literacy classes, or to become united to end women's oppression. "Women Should Unite" (*Mahilā Ek Juṭa Hunu Cha*), submitted by Sanumaya in MKU, is one of the most consistently radical questionings of women's dukha and gender subordination that I have yet come across in songs shared among women involved in NJS between 1987 and 1992.

> Sisters! Let's march ahead united
> Subordinated for so long, how can we endure it?
> What is left to bear? We have borne everything
> United, let us end women's oppression
>
> This sinful society does injustice to women,
> Always subordinated, always in sorrow, always in chains
> In our house of birth, brothers remain
> While we leave for another's dominion

For our brothers, our father's wealth
For a daughter, leaving her *māita* (natal home), which house?
Children of the same parents, sons and daughters are the same
But when the daughter goes away the son remains

Like *gāidān* (cow gift), *kanyādān* (virgin gift) is animal-like
Add to that child marriage—curse these customs!
Kanyādān purifies mother and father of sins, or so they say
But see, kanyādān is for their own gain.

This song is a strident call for women's unity and action against an unjust society. Sanumaya's song suggests the hypocrisy of kanyādān—the most orthodox and highly valued form of Hindu marriage—where the parents of a young woman are believed to gain *puṇya* (religious merit) by giving a virgin to the husband's family in marriage. It also ironically highlights the "animal-like" nature of giving virgins, by comparing the practice to gāidān, "the gift of a cow," where the bride's family ceremonially gives a female calf to the groom's family during the wedding. The anthropological literature in Nepal (e.g., Bennett 1983) emphasizes the sacred reproductive symbolism of exchanging cows and virgins between families, but the song demystifies this connection and insists that listeners look at the more beastly aspects of the exchange. The parents gain prestige by giving a virgin-gift and at the same time ensure that they will not lose prestige at some later date if their daughter loses her virginity before marriage. As the song suggests, there is a sinful side to all piety. Isn't there a sin in sending a daughter off to become a laborer and producer of children for another house while the son enjoys the wealth and property of the parents? And can the parents ensure the health, happiness, and safety of the daughter in the new house? Does kanyādān purify the parents of sin, as some contemporary, orthodox Hindu theories would hold? Or does it immerse them in sin, as the song suggests and many women's experiences of harassment at the hands of husbands and in-laws might reveal?

The above song expresses dukha from the performer Sanumaya's own life. She shared it while a student in the first literacy class we began in 1987, while describing her pain over her seventeen-year-old daughter's near death from infection following childbirth. Sanumaya attributed her daughter's illness to mistreatment in her in-law's house following the birth of her second girl. On hearing of the illness, Sanumaya traveled herself to a distant village to fetch her daughter from her *ghar* (married home), take her to Bharatpur hospital, buy antibiotics and iron pills, then bring her back to her *māita* (natal home) to nurse her back to health.

Significantly, Sanumaya's song also clearly locates a material basis for women's oppression in the differential inheritance rights of women and men. While many songs suggest the injustice of treating boys and girls differently, few openly question the customs and laws that deprive women of unconditional rights to parental or marital property. The messages in Sanumaya's songs are fairly unambiguous in analyzing women's dukha. Yet almost all other Bahun and Chetri women's songs presented in MKU or shared during literacy classes send mixed messages about the causes of and solutions to women's dukha. For example, the following song, "Groping in the Darkness" (*Andhakarma Rumalieka*) written by a young, (then unmarried) Bahun woman, Bhagvati Aryal, weaves together the more contradictory messages prevalent in most songs.

> They must find a husband for their daughter
> Where he lives, who he is, she doesn't know
> Does he gamble, smoke, or drink whiskey?
> When his wealth is gone, will he say, "Return to your father"?
>
> Sons and daughters, you grow by sucking mother's milk
> But you are not equal in Hindu society
> How did the gods' drama become a game of creation
> Where women are born, already defeated by fate?
>
> Tears swept the *ṭikā* down your cheeks
> Oppressed women rise up by burning your sorrows
> God, you gave man ten doors open
> Why did you make me oppressed by mistake?
>
> How unjustly men walk off, leaving housework
> While women sit with their thirty-two qualities wrapped in a shawl
> She works her fingers to the bone doing housework
> Seeing this law, her heart breaks and tears overflow
>
> So friends, sisters, listen to what I say
> Let education be the basis of success
> Let's sit down and study when the housework is finished
> If we don't know, friends, let's learn from those who do
>
> Shame is shining just like the water on the leaves
> It's no good unless we succeed
> We're just like prisoners in the jail
> Let's learn two or three words and be wise.

Bhagvati's song, like many others, moves from a scathing critique of the dukha, especially the uncertainty and injustice, in women's lives to a call for women to become educated. Two of the most common themes of MKU songs, songs shared in literacy classes, and also various Tij songs in western Chitwan are the recollection or anticipation of the trauma of marriage into the house of an unknown husband ("where he lives, who he is, she doesn't know") and the descriptions of the hard, daily work that follows ("she works her fingers to the bone doing housework"). A song shared by Royedi Devi Dhakal recounts: "Crying, I went to another's house at age ten...Since age ten, my time is for the broom, the *poto*, and water spring." Many older and even some middle-aged (thirty-five to forty-five-year-old) Bahun and Chetri women became married between the ages of nine and twelve. Nowadays most high-caste women in Chitwan become married between sixteen and twenty, usually just before or after sitting for the School Leaving Certificate Examination (taken after completing tenth grade). Women's everyday life after marriage is evoked in song by key symbols of women's work: *kucho* (broom), *poto* (cloth for plastering with mud and dung), *ḍhiki* (husker), *janto* (grinder), *culo* (stove), *ḍoko* (basket), *ghās* (fodder), *dāura* (firewood), *pādhero* (water spring), and *dhāro* (water tap).

Marriage marks a painful transition between an unfinished childhood and what is perceived as a long life of toil and hardship. Women's songs and stories emphasize the dukha and the monotony of this period of time after marriage, a life dominated, as in a song from Menuka Indu, "in the morning by milling and grinding" (*bihāna uṭhi ḍhiki janto*) and "in the afternoon by field labor"(*diūso melāpat*).[17]

Some songs, like Bhagvati's, also emphasize the everydayness of women's endurance, where men unjustly "walk off leaving housework," while "women sit with their thirty-two qualities wrapped in a shawl." The latter line refers rather ironically to the thirty-two physical and personality traits, such as tolerance, modesty, shapely hands, fingers and feet, pointed nose and fair skin, that should be judged by Hindu families in selecting a bride. But the reference to women's qualities that are hidden, wrapped in a shawl, also implies that certain qualities might make themselves more visible or perhaps even be transformed so that "oppressed women will (one day) rise up by burning their sorrows."

In terms of analyzing gender inequality, one of the most significant aspects of these songs is the refusal to accept women's subordination as natural. It is something that must have had an historical beginning. As Bhagvati's song describes, it is "a game of creation" where one can be "defeated by fate." Sons and daughters, who "grow by sucking (the same) mother's milk," become differentiated by "the game" at some point. Other songs, such as one sung by Sanumaya during Tij, have verses that echo this message of the fundamental biological sameness of women and men: "The son goes from high school to a B. A. pass. But for a daughter of the same womb, only forest, wood and grass" (*Uhī kākhako chorīlāi I. A. bāṭa B. A. pass. Uhī kākhako chorīlāi banko dāura ghās*).[18] Inequality is something that happens after birth. It is not predetermined in the womb but rather is constructed by society. By implication, the system—"the game"—can also be dismantled. In their songs, Bahun and Chetri women identify themselves as beings constructed not by nature, but by culture. There is thus an awareness that, in Simone de Beauvoir's famous words, "one is not born a woman" (1974). One becomes constructed as a woman on being born into a society where a woman is looked upon as being other to man. As Prakash (1990, 1991) argues in reference to bonded laborers in Bihar, India, such a historicization of social inequality is a critical form of resistance, since it fundamentally challenges dominant explanations of the nature of inequality.

In some songs, women take on injustices in more abstract ways. Song after song calls for women to rise up (*didi bahinī uṭha*), to march ahead (*agādi badhaun*), united (*ek juṭa bhayera*), and to seek their rights (*adhikāra khosne*). These phrases form a kind of standardized militancy that women incorporate into their own compositions or their improvisations on popular songs. Some songs reflect a move to globalize as well as localize women's struggles, to relate women's oppression in Nepal to the rest of the world. For example, some popular songs in western Chitwan describe aspects of everyday life, punctuated by the refrain (or variations on it): "Go tell every oppressed sister that Nepali women are oppressed too" (*Gayera bhandeu na soshita piḍita nārīlāi, sarhai nai thico mico cha Nepāli nārilāi*). The chorus derives from a popular leftist song, but some women in western Chitwan make up their own verses to match the chorus. Women may also vary the chorus by calling on women to "go tell the silent sisters..." or "to go tell the village sisters...."[19] These variations redirect the "universal" message of women's liberation to the local level where it may reach the "silent, village sisters." There is thus a simultaneous globalization and localization, a rhetorical attempt to create a sisterhood, an "imagined community" of women, united by common oppression and struggle, within and outside Nepal.[20] As I will show below, this universalizing discourse is predicated on the emergence of a particular community of women to the exclusion of others.

The various issues that women raise, especially the militant rhetoric of rising up, burning the system, and ending oppression are part of a popular discourse on women's rights and responsibilities in projects of social reform and modernization. Much of it has been inspired by communist and social democratic (Nepali Congress) organizing in Nepal. The latter emerged in concert with struggles against colonialism in India and shares a strong current of Gandhian-inspired, Hindu reformism. Gandhi projected a pivotal role for women in nationalist struggles and social change in India, but viewed women's leadership primarily in reference to motherhood, marriage, and family (Kishwar 1985; Visweswaran 1994). In Nepal, the previous Panchayat and current Congress regimes' focus on "integrating women into development" also contributes to the production of a popular discourse on the rights and responsibilities of women. From various political perspectives, women are thus told that they are agents of social change; the country, community, and family cannot move ahead without them. They must come together and march forward to bring development and modernization to the country. In speeches, songs, and pamphlets addressed to women, communist parties have brought attention to the injustice of inheritance laws, dowry-giving, and women's heavy work burdens.

Political parties often organize special events, such as picnics for women in western Chitwan. There women listen to speeches, watch dramas, and listen to songs, thereby learning the party line on the liberation of women. Many women also organize their own less formal picnics where they sing various kinds of popular, political, and individually composed or improvised songs. Political party activists also publish Tij songs every year and sell them in book and music stalls throughout Chitwan (as well as other areas of Nepal), attempting to appropriate women's voices to sing their analyses of the year's events and issues.[21] Many of these Tij songs are written by male party activists (e.g., Dinabandhu 1993; Gautam 1993; Gharti-Chetri 1991).

Critical Discourse as Middle-Class Consciousness

I have looked at how various themes such as universalized analyses of women's oppression, calls for equality and women's unity, and expressions of women's everyday suffering are woven into various songs that Bahun women have shared in NJS events between 1987 and 1992. These songs create critical discourses, thus contributing to a sense among some women of their shared subordination and the need to transcend party, caste, and class differences to mobilize to end women's oppression. Yet as powerful as it is, the critical rhetoric that runs through a wide variety of Bahun women's songs is mediated by other themes. It is difficult, in fact, to find many songs that throughout express a coherent critique of social relations. Like Bhagvati's song, they present fragments of critique laced with ambiguities. Running through various songs is also a discourse on class, ethnicity, and modernity. While women's oppression is sometimes attributed to "this sinful society," to material inequalities, or to particular practices (such as kanyādān or the giving of dowry), it is just as often linked to women's illiteracy, ignorance, backwardness, and lack of education. While Bhagvati's song begins with a moving account of the injustice of women's lives and a radical call for women to "rise up" and "burn their sorrows," it ends, like most other songs, with a more domesticated call for women to become educated.[22] They must remove the shame of ignorance, "shining like water on the leaves and learn two or three words." While previous lines of Bhagvati's song pointed out the injustice of leaving all the housework to women, the last part calls on women not to leave their housework to come study, but to come to study only after finishing their housework. Education will be the way to move forward and succeed but not at the expense of domestic duties. These seeming contradictions and ambiguities reveal more than a mere lack of theoretical cohesion: what Gramsci calls "contradictory consciousness" (1971:333). Rather, I suggest, they reflect what I have been emphasizing as the "middleness" of many women activists and supporters in NJS, who are situated rather tenuously between classes and between various men.

Literacy, in general, and education and knowledge of English, in particular, are one of the means for both class mobility within Nepal and national mobility in the hierarchy of nations. In contemporary Nepal, notions of women's political activism and agency become cast as a woman's duty to become educated. Many songs contrast the darkness and backwardness of illiteracy to the light and progress of literacy. Such contrasts are common in state "development" speeches, pamphlets, Radio Nepal, Nepal Television, educational materials used in primary and secondary schools, and in political party rhetoric as a means of promoting the ideal Nepali citizen: a modern, urban, literate, high-caste person (Enslin 1992; Pigg 1992; Skinner and Holland 1996). Such a citizen is contrasted to the "underdeveloped" villager. In much of this rhetoric, women—especially illiterate, low-caste, rural women—are represented as the most undeveloped of the underdeveloped (Enslin 1992). This official discourse on social hierarchy finds its way into popular expressions, including women's songs.

Of course, in western Chitwan, the concern with women's literacy and education grows partly out of NJS's focus on literacy. Many of the songs submitted for MKU or shared in literacy classes are celebrations of literacy or meant to appeal to what women might assume to be the primary concern of their sponsors (such as Pramod Parajuli or myself). However, I would argue that the centrality of literacy and class as a theme in popular songs predates the emergence of NJS in western Chitwan. Indeed, it is probably the increasing valuation of literacy that compelled many women to participate in literacy classes and NJS rather than vice versa. For example, literacy is a theme found in Tij songs that circulate not only in western Chitwan, but in other regions of Nepal as well (Holland and Skinner 1995; Skinner et al. 1994). The songs are a general expression of the ways in which literacy and education have come to be symbols of progress, modernity, and class mobility, not only in Nepal but worldwide. The need to eradicate illiteracy overrides questions of what literacy is for and whom it serves (Parajuli 1990). Women's "need" to become literate is thus partly imposed by a new world order that equates knowledge with literacy and progress with education.

For women in western Chitwan, the desire to become literate or more broadly "educated" is tied to class aspirations, achieved primarily through marriage. A generation ago, women in higher castes with little education might have become married to reasonably educated men with some promise of salaried careers in government service, such as teaching. However, nowadays most high-caste women of the younger generation in Chitwan, where schools and colleges are numerous, are expected to be educated. And the stakes are becoming increasingly high. For a family to gain a college-educated man as a son-in-law, with some hope of having a salaried job, their daughter must have at least a School Leaving Certificate (SLC) and preferably also an Intermediate Certificate and several years of college education. Families with a daughter who has not yet passed the SLC level, will have a hard time finding an educated man who has hopes of moving ahead, unless the daughter has some other bargaining points (exceptional beauty, promise of a large dowry).

Related to the concern for class mobility is a less direct discourse on jāti. This comes out most clearly in women's songs as well as speeches that condemn the brewing and drinking of alcohol.

> The Thakali woman distilled whiskey
> Tasting it in a bowl (she beckons)
> "Come, come Bahun
> Take off your sacred thread to drink whiskey."[23]

Other lines of this song make fun of the Bahun man who falls into the dangers of whiskey drinking, can't stand up, and loses his clothes. Yet the temptress is clearly the Thakali woman who urges him to forget his caste (symbolized by his sacred thread) and imbibe. Thakalis are one of many ethnic/caste groups in Nepal who produce liquor for their own use and for sale. In Chitwan, liquor-making remains an important aspect of household production in Gurung, Magar, Tamang, Thakali, Newar, Tharu, as well as in low-caste Hindu households. It is integral to economic, social, and ritual life in these jāti. Thakali women are especially renowned for running tea shops that serve food and liquor. Bahun women in NJS frequently focus on liquor production and drinking as a source of various social evils (e.g., laziness, violence, social backwardness) and sometimes call on women of liquor-drinking jāti to join them in temperance. This call, often couched in rhetoric for purifying society or ending male violence, reinforces the dominant Hindu discourses where liquor drinking as well as meat eating are taken as "natural causes" for impurity and lower social status (Höfer 1979). Bahun women thus distance themselves from the dukha—wife beating and gambling—that they associate primarily with alcohol and low-class, low-caste behavior. Significantly, my own interviews with composers and performers of such songs reveal that in contrast to songs mentioned earlier, they reflect little of Bahun and Chetri women's personal, everyday experiences of dukha, but are observations and interpretations of the lives of cultural "others." Moreover, when questioned directly, many women can relate more actual tales of male violence in their own or other families than they can of violence in other jāti. And such violence may have nothing to do with alcohol (Enslin 1990).

Given the priority of "development" in Nepal, the improvement of women through temperance, education, and the increase of wealth is not only a matter of individual concern but becomes a moral duty to home, village, and nation. Some lines from a song illustrate this common theme:

> Let's increase the beauty and wealth of our house
> Manage and develop the village and house
> Children in our laps, let's teach them *"ka-kha"*[24]
> Let's build the foundation for the country
> If the house and the society improve, the country improves
> For all this, moving united, women have the power.[25]

These lines envision a progressive Nepal, moving steadily along the path to improvement or "development." As the reproducers of the emerging middle class, women will play an important role in this "developing" nation, providing the building blocks of home upon which the country can realize its wealth and beauty. Children in our lap, let's teach them "ka-kha": this is a powerful image of women as mothers of Nepal's literate "citizens" of tomorrow. Women share a moral imperative to become educated in order to serve their husbands and children and by implication, all children of mother Nepal. In other historical and cultural contexts, such notions of domesticity and bourgeois motherhood have accompanied the emergence of a middle class (e.g., Banerjee 1990; Beneria and Sen 1981; Chatterjee 1990; Rapp 1982; Scott 1988; Young 1981). Women gradually withdraw from field or factory labor and take up their "proper" occupations as wives and mothers. "Appropriate" forms of education are the means of cultivating women's proper occupations while women's education and reform become a major task of nationalism (Banerjee 1990, Chatterjee 1990). The songs of Bahun and Chetri women active in NJS are a call to duty for women to join in the task of modernity. These duties include educating themselves and their children, improving the moral fiber of society, and sanitizing popular culture of vulgarities, such as liquor drinking.[26] Just as Bahun and Chetri men present themselves as leaders in education, social reform, party politics, and Hinduism, so too Bahun and Chetri women often cast themselves as leaders in these areas.

Gender, Class, and Collective Action

The militant rhetoric of Bahun and Chetri women's songs is mediated not only by recurring themes of class, caste, and ethnic inequality but also by the practical, collective actions of NJS. The songs of Bahun and Chetri women associated with NJS reflect a concern for women's *dukha* and a critical analysis of gender subordination. Yet the practical actions of NJS seem to be more in tune with the carving out of a sphere of political influence for certain middle-class women than with the more radical call to "burn the system" (*śasān jalāun*).

NJS activists and leaders were sporadically involved in various projects between 1987 and 1993, such as running literacy classes, providing legal aid, establishing tree nurseries, distributing saplings, and training. However, according to some participants and observers, there has been an overall lack of focus and direction in the organization. This is partly due to political party conflicts, which divide leaders and members alike and make coming to an agreement on any proposal or project nearly impossible. But the lack of clear focus is also partly due, I argue, to the "middleness" of many leaders and members, who while challenging their own subordination in gender, class, urban-rural, and regional relations are also casting for themselves the role of leading the women of rural Chitwan (and by extension all Nepali women). A description of two arenas of NJS activity will illustrate some of the gaps between leading and serving women in their everyday concerns and carving out a middle-class women's sphere.

Each year NJS receives petitions from community women requesting intervention in domestic disputes and legal cases (*muddā*). These include requests for helping *sautā* (co-wives) claim their inheritance, pressing men to marry women they have made pregnant, preventing child marriage, and resolving disputes between mothers and daughters-in-law. Although petitions have come both from poor and middle-class women of various jāti, NJS has seriously intervened only in cases involving middle-class, Bahun women in Gunjanagar. I have heard complaints that although lower-caste women sometimes bring cases forward, they receive little attention. The dominant Congress leadership also shows less enthusiasm for cases occurring in communist-dominated hamlets.

Domestic cases are dealt with in circumscribed ways that do not usually challenge women leaders' influence in local community politics or their positions as respected wives of male leaders. For example, in one case, a co-wife in a wealthy Bahun family approached NJS to support her in separating from her husband and claiming her legal share of the property. She has one daughter, who has many serious illnesses. Under Nepali law, she may seek separation and is entitled to a share of land equal to that of her husband and her co-wife since she has been married for fifteen years and has reached the age of thirty-five (Bennett with Singh 1979; Gilbert 1992; New Era 1988).[27] In 1992, she lived in a small hut next to her co-wife's large, cement house and complained of trouble making ends meet and buying medicine for her daughter. She was often verbally humiliated and sometimes beaten by her husband and the adult sons of his second wife. Leaders in NJS agreed to support her inheritance claim and called a meeting with her husband and other village leaders. But, as she complained, during this meeting NJS leaders backed down from supporting her legal rights. After much heated discussion, the husband and his supporters (locally prominent Nepali Congress leaders) agreed that the woman had no right to property, but the right only to material maintenance, with special consideration for the daughter's education and medical fees. NJS leaders who were present at the meeting were also Nepali Congress supporters, and rather than alienating their male counterparts they agreed that material maintenance was sufficient as long as the husband fulfilled his duties. They compelled the husband and wife to sign a contract agreeing to the terms. Fortunately, the contract she signed then was legally nonbinding. She has since gone on to seek better legal counsel and taken her case to the district court, where she hopes to be awarded her share of property and thus provide for herself and her daughter independently of her husband's whims or the politics of NJS.

NJS's most recent efforts have focused on skills training. In June 1993, the organization completed its first training in weaving for twenty-five women, with teachers and looms provided by His Majesty's Government Department of Cottage Industries. This program caused substantial resentment among sukumbāsi who live near the NJS building in Gunjanagar, where the training was held. NJS leaders signed up hukumbāsi women, many of whom are known by local standards to be economically well-off or *dhani*. There was some attempt to have caste diversity with a few Tamang, Magar, and Tharu women participating. Most participants were, however, Bahun and Chetri. There were no lower-caste women. As one sukumbāsi

Tamang woman said to me, "Nārī Jāgarān only wants us sukumbāsi when there's work to be done. But when there's something to be gained, then they call on the hukumbāsi." Many sukumbāsi women have over the years helped to dig holes and carry manure for planting trees around NJK and beginning a nursery, so they express deep resentment that they were not included in the first training program. While some sukumbāsi and low-caste women gave their support to NJS in initial phases of mobilization in 1988, some even offering to take land for the center by force, their concerns have since been marginalized in NJS activities.

Shared aspirations for "development" and also for gaining women's space are what motivated women of many different jāti to participate in NJS, at least in the beginning. Literacy classes have been the most inclusive and perhaps most successful of NJS's efforts.[28] In other activities, NJS has done little to address the kinds of everyday issues or the specific kinds of oppression raised in song. Like the rhetoric of "development" and progress in Nepal more generally, the emergence of NJS has mostly raised expectations for class mobility among many women.

The campaign for a women's center in western Chitwan and the various activities carried out in its name have thus become "a hegemonic project" of the middle class. As Chatterjee suggests, "the construction of hegemonic ideologies typically involves the cultural efforts of classes placed precisely in such (middle) situations" (1992:41). In western Chitwan, Nārī Jāgarān has become what Sangari and Vaid would call a movement "to modernize patriarchal modes of regulating women" (1990:19). It can be contrasted to other kinds of social movements that attempt to democratize gender relations both in the home and the workplace. The latter kinds of movements actually attempt to challenge inequalities in everyday social relations while the former tend to provide a more liberal space for middle-class women.

> The historical role of the modernizing movements was that of "recasting" women for companionate marital relationships and attendant family duties as well as of enabling middle-class women to enter the professions and participate in political movements in a limited way. (Sangari and Vaid 1990:20)

As with the emergence of reformist women's movements elsewhere, that of NJS accompanies the formation of a middle-class "public sphere" as separate from the home.[29] Women's political activism, while often highly visible and rhetorically radical, allows the "homes" of the rural middle class to be relatively free from challenges to male authority. Women may "rise up" and "burn their sorrows" elsewhere, but at home they should remain with their "thirty-two qualities wrapped in a shawl." They may go to study and make speeches after their work is finished. As Sangari and Vaid argue, "It is this guarantee that will ease the access of women to the middle-class public sphere as both reformed women and as women reformers" (1990:12).[30]

Conclusion

Bahun and Chetri women's songs in western Chitwan create a sense of shared experience and bring women together under the unifying theme of dukha. Yet in calls for women to become educated, modernized, and developed as well as in the practical collective actions of middle-class, Bahun and Chetri women in organizations such as NJS distance the imagined sisterhood from the everyday dukha of women's lives. Critical consciousness is constructed within the context of class and jāti differentiation. As Bahun and Chetri women read against the grain of dominant constructions of gender, they also form their own notion of "woman" as an individual and "women" as a social group capable of collective action. These categories are formed in opposition to other women and exclude certain categories of experience as constitutive of ideal womanhood.[31]

A popular Nepali saying has become the motto of NJS and is written on the front of the pamphlets they circulate. "Women and men are two wheels of the cart" (nārī ra puruṣa ekai rathaka dui pāṅgra hun). This is a telling representation of women's agency in the middle class. Both wheels—man and woman—are, indeed, necessary for the cart to move forward, and they must work together. But wheels are only an instrument of mediation, reducing friction between the cart and the road. The cart cannot move forward without the labor of the bullocks and must be given direction by the driver. Middle-class women in western Chitwan, like the wheels of a cart, have the illusion of moving things forward, but must also carry a heavy burden under the direction of others. As studies from around the world show, middle-class womanhood is not an escape from male domination (e.g., Beneria and Sen 1981; Rapp 1982). NJS leaders, although able to carve out a local sphere of influence, are still subject to multiple relations of domination. While their education and social service work may enhance their family's class position, they remain economically dependent on fathers, husbands, brothers, and sons. For women, the "middle" is fraught with insecurity, ambivalence, and tension. The escalating economic and cultural demands of the middle class also exacerbate practices that are commonly associated with the dukha in Bahun women's lives in Nepal: early marriage, dowry, the consolidation of property in patrilines, household duties, material insecurity and lack of social support especially in the early years of marriage, and lack of mobility. And gender oppression takes specific forms, such as dowry murders, as men and women struggle to attain the material trappings of a middle-class lifestyle, such as televisions, motorcycles, refrigerators, and so forth. The middle class perpetuates old and creates new pressures for women. According to the demands of Hindu reformism, nationalism, and modernity, middle-class women must carry the multiple burdens of maintaining family prestige and financial security and carrying the family, community, and nation forward on the road to progress.

I began this discussion of women's critical expressions, resistance, everyday life, and collective action with accounts of women's suicides and murders. I also end by discussing women's pain to remind myself and my readers that the underside to women's resistance and critical expression are forms of suffering and pain specific to women's subjectivity in various times and places. While women's critical expressions and political action currently abound in places like western Chitwan and are tied to class and caste relations, some women like Bhavani Bhandari will continue to take their lives for whatever complex reasons while others live through the terror of rape, die in the horror of murder, or endure frequent beatings, psychological humiliation, and/or sexual abuse from husbands, brothers, fathers, mothers-in-law, sisters-in-law, or others.

What seemed heartening to me as I began writing about women's poetics and resistance in western Chitwan in 1988 was that women's dukha did not remain hidden in local discourses. It is becoming increasingly documented and historicized in various expressions, especially songs throughout the region. For example, songs documenting the first dowry death in Chitwan in May 1993 (discussed earlier) hit the bookshops in published book form and the music shops on recorded cassettes in August 1993. They were sung throughout Chitwan District (and perhaps elsewhere) for the women's Tij festival in 1993, four months after the tragic event. Yet this popular documentation also displaces the "subaltern who cannot speak" and appropriates her voice to construct the kind of normalized critical discourse on women that I have discussed here (see Spivak 1988). Similarly, the publicization of some women's voices marginalizes others by creating a limited notion of what women and women's public voice can be. The critical discourse in some women's songs in contemporary western Chitwan is connected to the projection of a modern Nepali woman, based on a Brahmanical, middle-class ideal. This excludes a vast diversity of women in Chitwan and Nepal, differentiated by caste, ethnicity, religion, regional languages, sexual practices (i.e., prostitution), and political pursuits, and the specific kinds of dukha that they suffer as well.

My conclusions raise a number of disturbing questions for which I have neither the research material nor the space to consider fully here. I make some of these questions explicit in the hopes that they might motivate more serious consideration among scholars and activists of Nepal. I have shown that while the content of women's songs reflects attempts to understand the dukha in women's lives, the political and economic context in which the songs are produced and circulated limit both individual and collective attempts to change the underlying conditions that bring about forms of dukha specific to women. But I wonder to what extent high-caste, middle-class women (and middle-class men—the other wheels of the cart) more *actively* distance themselves from everyday experiences of dukha through the rhetoric of cultural or class superiority. Do middle-class movements for social reform build their appeals not only on the sanitization and elimination of such signs of backwardness and vulgarity as illiteracy, ignorance, and the drinking of alcohol but also on the displacement of specific forms of pain and suffering? After all, class mobility is supposed to be about leaving hardship behind in the pursuit of happiness. Might not the experience of certain kinds of pain and suffering (i.e., the kind of bodily pain associated with suicide, rape, beatings, murder) in Nepal be considered low-class, backward, and uncultured— something that happens elsewhere, in other families, classes, castes, ethnic groups, or countries? I have certainly heard Bahun and Chetri men in western Chitwan circumvent serious debates about women's oppression in Nepal by pointing to the much greater violence and injustice, such as dowry murder, in India. And because Bahun and Chetri women activists in western Chitwan associate men's violence with alcohol, then women suffering such violence are, in their eyes, likely to be of the lower castes—those among whom drinking is legitimate cultural practice. I have even heard some Bahun and Chetri women activists in NJS shrug off or laugh about rapes or violence against low-caste women as not being worthy of intervention because they are thought to be so "common" in the sense of being both frequent and vulgar. Such violence is simply part of what makes lower-caste people lower caste. And if Bahun women do suffer certain kinds of violence, they are often spoken of as inviting it by belonging to "bad" families or having "bad" reputations themselves (implying improper sexual conduct). Certain kinds of dukha may then be "other" to or a deviation from respectable high-caste Hindu or middle-class behavior, rather than being a central part of it. To what extent then are women's identities as political activists in Nepal dependent upon an understanding of women's agency and power through their roles as good wives and good mothers, who endure pain and suffering with bravery? Such understandings have been crucial to women's participation in various social movements in India (e.g., Kishwar 1985).

If women's practices of resistance are constructed through a partial erasure or displacement of women's victimization and suffering (as well as women's participation in perpetuating such hardship), then we scholars and activists need to reconsider how we conceptualize them. In my ethnographic research in Nepal, I have always avoided emphasizing the horrors of women's lives so as not to construct women in "other" cultures as victims. Yet I have more recently come to believe that while being careful not to construct a politics of intervention and solidarity based on portrayals of purely victimized women in stereotyped Third World patriarchies, we must find a way to connect our understanding of everyday resistance with empathy for everyday suffering, pain, and despair. I have tried to make those connections here only in an insufficient, anecdotal way precisely because the sufferings and violence that nag at my analysis, insistently reminding me that I have not painted a full picture, also defy it. They just don't fit in. Perhaps novelists and short-story writers are more successful than ethnographers at evoking those murky, unsettling spaces between subversion and suffering and defiance and despair (e.g., Allison 1992; Dangarembga 1988; Devi 1987, 1990; Walker 1982, 1992). Yet in analyzing resistance, we must attend to those spaces even if we cannot fully illuminate them.

Notes

I am grateful to women of Nārī Jāgarān Samiti and western Chitwan District, who have since 1986 been sharing their songs, lives, and politics with me. I am especially indebted to Parvati Parajuli and Pramila Parajuli who have given me so much insight into the politics of NJS and gender relations in Nepal. I am grateful to Anil Bhattarai for his help in translating and interpreting all of the songs included here. I also thank Anil, Pramod Parajuli, Debra Skinner, Al Pach, and anonymous readers who provided helpful comments for revision. I have received financial support for various phases of research and writing from the following: the Wenner-Gren Foundation for Anthropological Research; the Institute for International Studies, Stanford University; the Rockefeller Residency Fellowship in the Humanities at the Women's Studies Program, University of Iowa; the Social Science Research Council; and the John D. and Catherine T. MacArthur Foundation, Grants for Research and Writing on International Peace and Cooperation.

1. The notion of "everyday resistance" has become popular in many fields for describing various practices and expressions of subordinated peoples. Early work on resistance, such as that of Scott (1985) or Genovese (1972) uncovered the many ways in which oppressed peoples subvert or reject dominant ideologies and elude demands on their labor and deference. This opened up new areas of research and analysis, especially in anthropology and social history. Such work largely depicted "Resistance" as an autonomous or semiautonomous domain of practice in opposition to "Power." More recent work, inspired primarily by Foucault (especially 1978, 1983) and Gramsci (1971), emphasizes the ambiguous and multidimensional intentions and consequences of resistance played out in complex fields of power (e.g., Haynes and Prakash 1991; Kondo 1990; Ortner 1996). It is becoming increasingly difficult to conceive of an autonomous domain of "pure" Resistance opposed to a monolithic Power. There are many resistances dispersed in intersecting fields of power. These resistances are rarely total escapes from domination; they are themselves shaped in the play of power.

2. For further documentation of dowry murder in India, see also articles in various issues of *Manushi: Journal of Women in Culture and Society*. In Nepal, various atrocities committed against women, including wife beating, murder, police torture, and rape are being documented in various districts of Nepal through the work of the Informal Service Centre (INSEC). This organization appears to be making a special effort to expand the understanding of human rights beyond state repression and torture by including documentation of more silent and hidden kinds of violence, such as wife beating and murder, bonded labor, forced prostitution, development and environmental degradation, and occupational hazards (e.g., INSEC 1992, 1993).

3. What is written here is not intended to explain the causes of Bhavani's suicide (or the suicides of other young women in western Chitwan). Her friend, Pramila Parajuli, told me that Bhavani suffered from frequent depressions and seemed to have "no will to live" (*bacne man thiena*). Bhavani's words, which might have given more clues into both her defiance and her despair, were destroyed.

4. Indira Subedi, "Women's Lament" (*Nārīko Bilāunā*), submitted to Mahilā Kabitā Utsav, Gunjanagar, Chitwan, 1990. Hereafter, unless otherwise cited in the text or footnotes, each MKU song will be referenced by the name of the woman who submitted it and the title, if any.

5. I do not have space here to do full justice to the complexity of the phenomena, which involve my own, Pramod Parajuli's, and his family's work as well as local and national politics. I discuss the emergence and institutionalization of NJS in order to provide the context for a fuller discussion of songs and activities associated with the organization and its supporters.

6. It is important to clarify the meaning of "village" in contemporary Nepal. *Gāū Vikās Samiti* (Village Development Organization) is an administrative unit previously known as the *Gāū Pancāyat* (Village Panchayat). Such administrative divisions were formed under the national Panchayat system, which gained its ideological impetus from the historical legacy of panchayats, various systems of village councils in precolonial South Asia. In Nepal, what was once a local and varied form of governance became elevated between 1961 and 1990 to a national system of authoritarian rule, Panchayat Raj, legitimized by the rhetoric of promoting local democracy (see Borgström 1980; Rose 1970). In Chitwan, each "village" has from 8,000 to 10,000 people. The bureaucratically defined "villages" of western Chitwan have become especially important in connecting citizens to the state since they demarcate populations eligible to vote and to receive development funds. Yet an outsider traveling through Chitwan finds no discernible boundaries to differentiate the "village" of Gunjanagar from neighboring "villages" of Saradanagar or Mangalpur. Each village contains within it many hamlets (*ṭol*), which are clusters of households organized with varying degrees of cohesion along ethnic, economic, residential, and/or political party lines. For further discussion of the diverse and politically loaded meanings of "village" in Nepal, see Pigg (1992).

7. Chitwan became an integral part of the Nepal state's visions for political and economic development during the 1950s. With the help from the United States Agency for International Development (USAID) and the World Health Organization, the royal government of Nepal began in the mid-1950s a campaign to resettle thousands of hill dwellers in Chitwan Valley (Ojha 1983). Settlers attempted to gain their land through various means (i.e., direct application to the resettlement office, purchase from speculators, self-occupation) and with varying degrees of success depending on their jāti, their kin, their wealth, and their political connections (Shrestha 1990:196–204).

8. Both Pramod Parajuli and I have played important, but not determinant roles, in sponsoring and running literacy classes, gaining land for a meeting center between 1988 and 1990, linking the organization with funding agencies, and opening up debate on women's issues in western Chitwan. We are currently less involved than we have been in the past, partly because of the contradictions discussed in this essay. A full discussion and self-critique of our involvement requires a separate essay. I address some aspects of our, especially my, participation in Enslin (1994).

9. Even though political parties were officially banned until 1990 under the Panchayat system, they operated fairly openly in regions such as Chitwan, which had strong opposition

politics. Thus the affiliation of various leaders and their followers was well-known, although not spoken of directly.

10. Residents of Chitwan District commonly use the term jāti to refer to different ethnic and caste groups. I follow such usage here, but also refer more generally at times to "high castes" (*māthillo jāti*) and "low castes" (*tallo jāti*) to refer to those clustered at either end of the caste hierarchy. I use ethnic names (Gurung, Magar, Tharu, Tamang) for those in the middle since such groups identify more strongly with ethnicity than caste. Under Hindu ideology imposed for at least 200 years, especially in central Nepal, different jati are arranged in a hierarchy of varna. The hierarchy appears relatively clear for the Upadhyaya Bahun on the top but becomes more contested in the middle and the bottom, with some jāti not fully internalizing a few of themselves as inferior to those higher up, but still seeing those below as such. Those highest in the hierarchy are *tāgādhāri*, literally "wearers of the sacred thread." These "twice-borns" include Bahun, Chetri, and Thakuri of Indo-Aryan origin. The next category is *matwāli* (literally, "liquor-drinkers"), who are considered by tāgādhāri to be "touchable, but impure." This category is broad and includes most Tibeto-Burman language speakers (Magar, Tamang, Gurung, Rai, Limbu) as well as Tharu, the people indigenous to Chitwan District. Some of these groups are developing strong ethnic and religious identities and may contest their place in the caste hierarchy formerly imposed by national law and currently upheld by social practice and ideology. Some are Buddhists or practice various local religions. As Holmberg (1989) points out, the ethnic identity of groups, such as the Tamang, is fairly recent and partially constructed by state policies. At the bottom of the hierarchy are *pāni na calne*, literally, "those from whom water cannot be taken." They are considered "untouchable and impure" by matwāli and tāgādhāri, and include occupational groups, such as Kami (Blacksmith), Damai (Tailor), Sarki (Cobbler) and Sunar (Goldsmith). Newars, the urbanized inhabitants of the Kathmandu Valley and various bazaar towns of Nepal (many of whom have also migrated to Chitwan), include both Hindus and Buddhists and have their own internal jāti with even more differentiation among "untouchable" occupational groups. Bhojpuri- and Maithili-speaking Hindus who straddle the India-Nepal border in Tarai regions also have different jāti names and parallel, but different varna rankings from those of *pahādi* (hill-dwelling) Hindus.

11. Turner defines sukumbāsi as a person "remaining without work or food" (1980:611) and Pokhrel et al. as a "subject without land and other properties" (1983:1355) (cited in Ghimire 1992:21). As Ghimire (1992:21) points out in his study of sukumbāsi politics in Nawalparasi District, the above definitions are inadequate since they imply that sukumbāsi have neither shelter, productive land, nor livelihood. In contemporary times, sukumbāsi have tenuous rights to land and shelter and are involved in various kinds of agricultural and nonagricultural labor. I use the word sukumbāsi here, rather than the impoverished translation, "landless," in order to capture the dynamic politics of land settlement in the Tarai.

12. Published studies of the historical process of class formation remain relatively rare in Nepal. Works that discuss some aspects of class from various theoretical viewpoints include Blaikie, Cameron, and Seddon (1980), Caplan (1970), Ghimire (1992), Kaplan

and Shrestha (1982), Shrestha (1990). I am not aware of any scholarly study of the middle class in Nepal or of gender and class formation.

13. There is a great deal of overlap since many of the songs that I first heard in literacy classes in 1987–88 were later submitted in written form for the poetry festival.

14. Although I focus on Bahun and Chetri women's songs here, I emphasize that women of other jāti also produce and perform songs, including Tij songs, in Nepali and vernacular languages. I am concerned here, however, with a very specific aspect of song as it becomes a vehicle for middle-class, social reform movements. Since Bahun and Chetri women's songs dominate this movement in western Chitwan, I focus on them here. Songs of women of other jāti have not been circulated to the extent that Bahun and Chetri women's songs have in association with NJS. Indeed, in MKU, they were actively marginalized. Although not a topic of this essay, it would be interesting to explore the extent to which the songs of women of other jāti might create a counter-discourse to Bahun women's songs.

15. Most of the compositions submitted in the festival were songs that would be easily accessible both in meaning, rhythm, and style to women of all castes, educational and economic backgrounds. There were, however, also two lengthy poems submitted by Bahun women, written in classical metric forms on abstract philosophical and cultural themes. They would have appealed more to an elite, educated audience. They were rather anomalous both in style and theme, so I do not consider them here.

16. Authorship of songs and poems is a murky area. Women frequently claim to have written or composed songs that are known to be freely circulating "folk" songs. This may mean that they have altered some verses, or it may simply mean that they heard a song somewhere and wrote it down. However, some women, like Bhavani Bhandari or my mother-in-law, Parvati Parajuli, do write mostly "original" songs and poems. I have not tried to investigate the authenticity of authorship claims here, but instead speak rather ambiguously of women having "shared," "submitted," "performed," or "sung" a song.

17. Menuka Indu, "The Inequality of Daughters and Sons" (*Chorī ra Chorāmā Asmāntā*).

18. See Skinner et al. (1994) for examples of similar Tij songs.

19. Indu Adhikari, "Oppressed Sisters" (*Piḍit Didi Bahinī*).

20. Benedict Anderson's (1983) term "imagined community" is useful in capturing the constructed and contingent nature of a collective identity, such as "nation," or in this case, "women."

21. One of the published leftist Tij songs that caught my eye in 1993 is entitled, "Don't Give Your Daughter to Congress (*Congresslāi Chorī Nadinu*)." It neatly weaves more traditional Tij themes of anxieties about marriage with the party rivalry so characteristic of contemporary Nepal (Timilsina 1993).

22. Of course, demands for education in Nepal also have multiple meanings as pointed out by Skinner and Holland (1996). They might be calls to consciousness in struggles for change or discourses on social difference. My point here is to examine some of these ambiguities by showing how critical discourses on gender difference are tied to a domesticating discourse on social improvement (through education and development) that

reproduces and exacerbates class, caste, and ethnic difference. It is important to keep in mind, however, that one could trace similar contradictory intentions and consequences in student movements or in demands for educational change.

23. Recorded as sung by Rita and Manu Pokharel, March 1992, Gunjanagar.

24. The beginning of the Nepali alphabet, equivalent to "ABC's."

25. Sita Gautam, "Women's Shakti" (*Nārīko śakti*).

26. See also Chatterjee (1991) and Banerjee (1990) on the sanitizing tendencies in middle-class movements in colonial Bengal.

27. This provision existed under Panchayat law. For a discussion of recent changes in inheritance laws and their social implications in Nepal, see Gilbert (1992).

28. Participation in literacy classes reflects greater caste and class diversity than that of NJS leadership. Thirteen literacy classes were completed by mid-1992. Graduates to date total approximately 300. Some graduates and supporters of classes in various hamlets of western Chitwan have formed strong local women's committees that operate somewhat independently of NJS. Some are more closely affiliated with local units of the various communist parties or the ruling Nepali Congress party. Some of these local groups are more active and effective than NJS in addressing women's diverse concerns.

29. Various ethnographies of women in Nepal have taken the separation of public and private spheres to be a cultural given, determining women's status in particular ethnic groups (see esp. Bennett 1979, 1983). I see the separation of private and public as both a historical process and cultural ideology associated with the rise of capitalism and class relations. This process occurs unevenly, affecting women in various classes, castes, nations, and ethnic groups differently.

30. Having emphasized the hegemonic tendencies of NJS as a modernizing movement, I must also point out there is still a great deal of contestation going on between its leaders, particularly between Congress, Communist, and a few activists who seek a nonparty women's movement. Democratizing tendencies, as well as some lower-class interests, have also existed at various stages and still erupt at various times on the fringes. At some future point, these tendencies may coalesce into an alternative movement. Currently, such tendencies have mostly been overwhelmed by a discourse on women's upliftment and duties, constructing the qualities of modern womanhood in Nepal. Moreover, since the advent of multi-party democracy in 1990, the terrain of contestation is currently limited to a struggle over political predominance, with each party promising the fastest route to modernity and women's liberation. Party politics have currently divided local leaders, like their national counterparts, to such an extent that unified mobilization on any issue of common interest is almost impossible.

31. Cultural and class conflicts in women's movements are, of course, by no means unique to Nepal (nor to women's movements, for that matter). For discussions of racism and classism in U.S. feminist movements, see hooks (1981), Hull et al. (1982), Lorde (1984), Mohanty (1991), Moraga and Anzaldúa (1983).

References

Abu-Lughod, Lila (1990). The Romance of Resistance: Tracing Transformations of Power through Bedouin Women. American Ethnologist 17(1):41–55.

Ahearn, Laura. 1991. The Emergence of Cultural Meaning in a Nepali Women's Songfest. Paper presented at South Asia Annual Meeting, Madison, WI.

Allison, Dorothy. 1992. Bastard Out of Carolina. New York: Dutton.

Anderson, Benedict. 1983. Imagined Communities: Reflections on the Origin and Spread of Nationalism. New York: Verso Press.

Banerjee, Sumanta. 1990. Marginalization of Women's Popular Culture in Nineteenth Century Bengal. *In* Recasting Women: Essays in Indian Colonial History. K. Sangari and S. Vaid, eds. Pp. 127–179. New Brunswick, NJ: Rutgers University Press.

Beneria, Lourdes, and Gita Sen. 1981. Accumulation, Reproduction and Women's Role in Economic Development: Boserup Revisited. Signs 7:279–98.

Bennett, Lynn. 1979. Tradition and Change in the Legal Status of Nepalese Women. The Status of Women in Nepal: Background Report. Vol 1, part 2. Kathmandu: Centre for Economic Development and Administration.

———. 1983. Dangerous Wives and Sacred Sisters: Social and Symbolic Roles of High Caste Women in Nepal. New York: Columbia University Press.

Blaikie, Piers, John Cameron, and David Seddon. 1980. Nepal in Crisis: Growth and Stagnation at the Periphery. New Delhi: Oxford University Press.

Borgström, Bengt-Erik. 1980. The Patron and the Panca: Village Values and Panchayat Democracy in Nepal. New Delhi: Vikas.

Caplan, Lionel. 1970. Land and Social Change in East Nepal. Berkeley: University of California Press.

Chatterjee, Partha. 1990. The Nationalist Resolution of the Women's Question. *In* Recasting Women: Essays in Indian Colonial History. K. Sangari and S. Vaid, eds. Pp. 233–253. New Brunswick, N.J.: Rutgers University Press.

———. 1992. A Religion of Urban Domesticity: Sri Ramakrishna and the Calcutta Middle Class. *In* Subaltern Studies VII: Writings on South Asian History and Society. Partha Chatterjee and Gyanendra Pandey, eds. Pp. 40–68. Delhi: Oxford University Press.

Dangarembga, Tsitsi. 1988. Nervous Conditions. Seattle: The Seal Press.

de Beauvoir, Simone. 1974. The Second Sex. Harmondsworth: Penguin.

Devi, Mahasweta. 1987. "Draupadi" and "Breastgiver." *In* Other Worlds: Essays in Cultural Politics. Gayatri Chakravorty Spivak, trans. Pp. 187–196, 222–240. New York: Methuen.

———. 1990. Giribala. Of Women, Outcastes, Peasants, and Rebels: A Selection of Bengali Short Stories. Kalpana Bardhan, ed. and trans. Pp. 272–289. Berkeley: University of California Press.

Dinabandhu. 1993 (2050). Nirmam Hatya ra Charchit Ghatana: Tijko Git. Narayangarh: Joshila Prakashan.

Enslin, Elizabeth. n.d. From Tactics of Space to Strategies of Place: Women's Resistance and Collective Action in Nepal. Unpublished manuscript.

———. 1990. The Dynamics of Gender, Class and Caste in a Women's Movement in Rural Nepal. Ph.D. dissertation, Department of Anthropology, Stanford University.

———. 1991. Women, the State, and the Politics of Development in Nepal. Paper presented at the South Asia Annual Meetings, Madison, WI.

————. 1992. Collective Powers in Common Places: The Politics of Gender and Space in a Women's Struggle for a Meeting Center in Chitwan, Nepal. Himalayan Research Bulletin 12(1-2):11–25.

————. 1994. Beyond Writing: Feminist Practice and the Limitations of Ethnography. Cultural Anthropology 9(4):537–568.

FOPHUR (Forum for Protection of Democracy and Human Rights). 1990. Dawn of Democracy: People's Power in Nepal. Kathmandu: Forum for Protection of Democracy and Human Rights.

Foucault, Michel. 1978. The History of Sexuality. Vol. 1, An Introduction. Robert Hurley, trans. New York: Vintage/Random House.

————. 1983. Afterword. *In* Michel Foucault: Beyond Structuralism and Hermeneutics. H. L. Dreyfus and P. Rabinow, eds. Pp. 208–264. Chicago: University of Chicago Press.

Freire, Paulo. 1972. Pedagogy of the Oppressed. M. B. Ramos, trans. New York: Penguin.

Gautam, Narayan Ajadi. 1993. Tijko Git. Bharatpur.

Genovese, Eugene. 1972. Roll, Jordan, Roll: The World the Slaves Made. New York: Vintage Books.

Gharti-Chhetri, Jhapendra. 1991 (2048). Tij Git Mala. Lumbini, Nepal: Lok Sahitya Prakashan.

Ghimire, Krishna. 1992. Forest or Farm? The Politics of Poverty and Land Hunger in Nepal. Delhi: Oxford University Press.

Gilbert, Kate. 1992. Women and Family Law in Modern Nepal: Statutory Rights and Social Implications. Journal of International Law and Politics 24:729–758.

Gramsci, Antonio. 1971. Selections from the Prison Notebooks. Q. Hoare and G. Nowell Smith, eds. and trans. New York: International Publishers.

Haynes, Douglas, and Gyan Prakash, eds. 1991. Contesting Power: Resistance and Everyday Social Relations in South Asia. Berkeley: University of California Press.

Höfer, András. 1979. The Caste Hierarchy and the State in Nepal: A Study of the Muluki Ain of 1854. Innsbruck: Universitätsverlag Wagner.

Holland, Dorothy, and Debra Skinner. 1995. Contested Ritual, Contested Femininities: (Re)forming Self and Society in a Nepali Women's Festival. American Ethnologist 22(2):279–305.

————. 1996. The Co-Development of Identity, Agency, and Lived Worlds. *In* Comparisons in Human Development: Understanding Time and Context. J. Tudge, M. Shanahan, and J. Valsiner, eds. Pp. 193–221. Cambridge: Cambridge University Press.

Holmberg, David H. 1989. Order in Paradox: Myth, Ritual, and Exchange among Nepal's Tamang. Ithaca, NY: Cornell University Press.

hooks, bell. 1981. Ain't I a Woman? Black Women and Feminism. Boston: South End Press.

Hull, Gloria T., Patricia Scott, and Barbara Smith, eds. 1982. All the Women Are White, All the Blacks Are Men, But Some of Us Are Brave: Black Women's Studies. Old Westbury, New York: The Feminist Press.

INSEC (Informal Sector Service Centre). 1992. Bonded Labour in Nepal Under Kamaiya System. Kathmandu.

————. 1993. Women's Initiation to Fight Against Women's Victimization: A Report of Victim Women's Forum (Feb 12–15, Nepalgunj). Kathmandu.

Kaplan, Paul F., and Nanda Shrestha. 1982. The Sukumbasi Movement in Nepal: The Fire From Below. Journal of Contemporary Asia 12(1):75–89.

Kishwar, Madhu. 1985. Gandhi on Women. Economic and Political Weekly 20(40 & 41).
Kishwar, Madhu, and Ruth Vanita. 1984. In Search of Answers: Indian Women's Voices from Manushi. London: Zed Press.
Kondo, Dorinne K. 1990. Crafting Selves: Power, Gender, and Discourses of Identity in a Japanese Workplace. Chicago: University of Chicago Press.
Lorde, Audre. 1984. Open Letter to Mary Daly. *In* Sister/Outsider: Essay and Speeches. Trumansburg, NY: Crossing Press.
Mohanty, Chandra Talpade. 1991. Cartographies of Struggle: Third World Women and the Politics of Feminism. *In* Third World Women and the Politics of Feminism. C. T. Mohanty, A. Russo, and L. Torres, eds. Pp. 1–47. Bloomington: University of Indiana Press.
Moraga, Cherríe, and Gloria Anzaldúa. 1983. This Bridge Called My Back: Writings by Radical Women of Color. Kitchen Table Press.
New Era. 1988. A Study of the Legal System and Legal Situation in Rural Areas of the Kingdom of Nepal. Kathmandu: New Era/Friedrich Naumann Foundation.
O'Hanlon, Rosalind. 1991. Issues of Widowhood: Gender and Resistance in Colonial Western India. *In* Contesting Power: Resistance and Everyday Social Relations in South Asia. D. Haynes and G. Prakash, eds. Pp. 62–108. Berkeley: University of California Press.
Ojha, Durga P. 1983. History of Land Settlement in Nepal Tarai. Contributions to Nepalese Studies 11(1):21–44.
Ortner, Sherry B. 1996. Resistance: Some Theoretical Problems in Anthropological History and Historical Anthropology. *In* The Historic Turn in the Human Sciences. Terrence J. McDonald, ed. Pp. 173–193. Ann Arbor: University of Michigan Press.
Parajuli, Pramod. 1986. Discourse in Development, Grassroots Movements and Popular Education. Convergence 19(2):29–40.
———. 1990. Politics of Knowledge, Models of Development, and Literacy. Prospect 20(3):289–98.
Parajuli, Pramod, and Elizabeth Enslin. 1990. From Learning Literacy to Regenerating Women's Spaces: A Story of Women's Empowerment in Nepal. Convergence 23(1):44–56.
Pigg, Stacy Leigh. 1992. Inventing Social Categories Through Place: Social Representations and Development in Nepal. Society for Comparative Study of Society and History 34(3):491–513.
Pokhrel, B. K. (1983). Nepali Brihat Shabdakosh. Kathmandu: Nepal Royal Academy.
Prakash, Gyan. 1990. Bonded Histories: Genealogies of Labor Servitude in Colonial India. Cambridge: Cambridge University Press.
———. 1991. Becoming a Bhuinya: Oral Traditions and Contested Domination in Eastern India. *In* Contesting Power: Resistance and Everyday Social Relations in South Asia. D. Haynes and G. Prakash, eds. Pp. 145–174. Berkeley: University of California Press.
Rajan, Rajeswari Sunder. 1993. Real and Imagined Women. New York: Routledge.
Rapp, Rayna. 1982. Family and Class in Contemporary America. *In* Rethinking the Family. B. Thorne and I. Yalom, eds. Pp. 168–187. New York: Longman.
Regmi, Mahesh C. 1978. Thatched Huts and Stucco Palaces: Peasants and Landlords in 19th Century Nepal. New Delhi: Vikas Publishing House.
Rose, Leo, and James Fisher. 1970. The Politics of Nepal: Persistence and Change in an Asian Monarchy. Ithaca: Cornell University Press.

Sangari, Kumkum, and Sudesh Vaid. 1990. Recasting Women: An Introduction. *In* Recasting Women: Essays in Indian Colonial History. K. Sangari and S. Vaid, eds. Pp. 1–26. New Brunswick, NJ: Rutgers University Press.

Scott, James. 1985. The Weapons of the Weak: Everyday Forms of Peasant Resistance. New Haven: Yale University Press.

Scott, Joan Wallach. 1988. Gender and the Politics of History. New York: Columbia University Press.

Shrestha, Nanda. 1990. Landlessness and Migration in Nepal. Boulder: Westview Press.

Skinner, Debra, and Dorothy Holland. 1996. Schools and the Cultural Production of the Educated Person in a Nepalese Hill Community in Nepal. *In* B. A. Levinson, D. E. Foley, and D. C. Holland, eds. The Cultural Production of the Educated Person: Critical Ethnographies of Schooling and Local Practice, Pp. 273–299. Albany: SUNY Press.

Skinner, Debra, Dorothy Holland, and G. B. Adhikari. 1994. The Songs of Tij: A Genre of Critical Commentary for Women in Nepal. Asian Folklore Studies 53(2):259–305.

Spivak, Gayatri Chakravorty. 1988. Can the Subaltern Speak? *In* Marxism and the Interpretation of Cultures. C. Nelson and L. Grossberg, eds. Pp. 271–316. Urbana: University of Illinois Press.

Timilsina, Parvati. 1993 (2050). Tijka Githaru. Gitanagar.

Turner, R. C. 1980. A Comparative and Etymological Dictionary of the Nepalese Language. London: Routledge and Kegan Paul.

Visweswaran, Kamala. 1994. Betrayal: An Analysis in Three Acts. In Scattered Hegemonies: Postmodernity and Transnational Feminist Practices. I. Grewal and C. Kaplan, eds. Pp. 90–109. Minneapolis: University of Minnesota Press.

Walker, Alice. 1982. The Color Purple. New York: Washington Square Press.

———. 1992. Possessing the Secret of Joy. New York: Pocket Books/Washington Square Press.

Young, Iris. 1981. Beyond the Unhappy Marriage: A Critique of Dual Systems Theory. *In* Women and Revolution, Lydia Sargent, ed. Pp. 43–69. Boston: South End Press.

Chapter 13 _____

Growing Up Newar Buddhist: Chittadhar Hridaya's *Jhī Macā* and Its Context

Todd Lewis

Mother and Child
> One day, the child sat in his mother's room with a book. His mother asked him, "Do you know our [Newari] script yet?" Having shown his book to her, the child said, "Why, I do not know it. Are not all these our letters?" The mother made him understand: "This indeed is not our writing. This is in fact *devanāgarī* script. Do you see the large letters in your other book?"
> Child: "Yes, yes. There are many round vowels in them, are there not?"
> Mother: "Indeed, that is our writing…"

This passage is from *Jhī Macā*, a short book published in 1947 by Chittadhar Hridaya, a Newar of Kathmandu, Nepal. Its Newari title—"Our Child"—conveys the author's intention that it serve as a cultural guidebook for Newar parents in their home teaching and as a first reader for their children (Hridaya 1947). In addition to providing a renowned poet's intimate appreciation of Newar childhood, this work can also be read to understand other areas of the modern Newar experience of ethnic identity. After introducing the text, its author, and the

Nepalese context from the Kathmandu Newar perspective,[1] I will discuss a series of issues *Jhī Macā* raises about the ongoing struggle to reconstruct Newar Buddhist identity in modern multi-ethnic Nepal.

In many studies across the Himalayan region, scholars have devoted special attention to the issue of ethnicity, group interaction, and the problem of defining and maintaining group boundaries utilizing cultural symbols (e.g., Barth 1956, 1969; Berreman 1960, 1963; Burghart 1984; Gellner 1986; Levine 1987). This paper focuses upon an influential Newari literary source, *Jhī Macā*, and its community context to examine these themes.[2]

The Text

A 32-page pamphlet-sized work, one among thousands in the Kathmandu Valley's vibrant Newari literary tradition, *Jhī Macā* takes the reader through a series of sixteen family vignettes, interweaving episodes of maturation—from infancy to early school-age—simultaneously with typical daily actions in the life of the Newar market. *Jhī Macā* teaches core vocabulary, nursery rhymes, family customs, and religious attitudes to Newar children. The book naturally focuses on language, closing with the already cited instructions on writing in the distinctly Newar script, *rañjanā* (Slusser 1982).

The children's stories from *Jhī Macā* convey the author's intimate poetic appreciation of the Newar market and its vibrant urban lifestyle. Having lived in the Kathmandu bazaar of Asan Tol for a number of years, I can testify to the authenticity of Hridaya's "child's eye" renditions of omnipresent pigeons, swooping swallows, and thieving crows, as well as to his evocations of the mice and feral cats that prowl the rooftops. Anyone who has walked the bylanes of the old Newar towns will recognize the author's graceful imagery of festivals that crowd the streets and of children looking out upper-story windows at passing cows, sheep, and processions. Subsequent generations of Newar youth up to the present have read this book, and its popularity led Chittadhar to compose a sequel. Both have been reprinted several times.

The Author

Chittadhar Hridaya is recognized today as one of the great literary figures of modern Nepal and the preeminent Newar poet of this century. A childless widower at an early age, he devoted his life to writing in Newari and participating in the vigorous intellectual life that evolved in post-Rana Kathmandu. During the last years of Rana rule, Chittadhar defied the prime minister's prohibition against publishing Newari language materials in Nepal; while jailed for attempting this, he wrote *Jhī Macā* and his great poetic masterpiece, *Sugat Saurabh*, the life of Sakyamuni Buddha, in Newari. With the coming of greater press freedoms after the fall of the Ranas, Chittadhar became a leading author and a renowned cultural figure. Besides his poetry, he published several novels and was a significant scholar in his own right, also writing articles and books on a variety of historical subjects. His prolific literary career continued until his death in 1982. A local newspaper eulogized him in these terms:

> ...[Chittadhar] consecrated all his life without frustration to the cause he was committed to. He even gave all his material possessions for the promotion of literature... and accepted the hardship a writer is supposed to face in a poor and undeveloped country. The life he lived should continue to be a source of inspiration to those who have taken to writing as a serious pursuit.

Chittadhar remains an icon of Newar cultural revival. Since his death, books of reminiscence have appeared (e.g., Karmacarya and Vajracarya 1983) and almost all his major works have been reissued.

Newar Buddhists and Buddhism in the Modern Nepalese Context

A Tibeto-Burman language-speaking ethnic group unique for its urban culture and a remarkable level of artistic achievement, the Newars have shaped life in the Kathmandu Valley for at least a millennium. Protected from colonization by the lowland malarial zones and the high Himalayan barrier, the Newars created a civilization adapted in their own style from the cultures of north India. Living traditions of ancient Indic art, architecture, texts, rituals, and festival celebration endure in great multiplicity. Newar Buddhism is perhaps the most notable Indic cultural survival (Lienhard 1984) as it has remained a separate tradition adhered to by distinct Newar castes, primarily in the largest cities (Gellner 1992). Newar Buddhists have long lived alongside other Newars practicing Shaiva and Vaiṣṇava forms of Hinduism.[3]

Once the Newar line of Malla kings was deposed in 1769 by the Shah dynasty of Gorkha, the country's new elite emerged: Pahari (or Parbatiya) Brahmans and Chetris, along with their allies from various ethnic groups.[4] Other (mostly Hinduized) peoples from the Himalayan mid-hills subsequently migrated into the Valley to work as laborers, start businesses, or to take posts in the new government enclaves close to the capital. Today roughly one-half of the Valley's population is non-Newar, and royal rule by the Shahs endures.

From its inception, the modern state has been staunchly Hindu in character and dominated by high-caste elites. Shah and Rana governments have sought to unify the many non-Indic peoples across the modern state by promoting Nepali as the national language, implementing a legal system based upon ancient Hindu lawbooks (the *Dharmashastra*), and maintaining the Hindu customs of *Kshatriya* (Nep. Chetri) royalty. I will return to specific aspects of modern Nepal's policies of unification shortly.

The Hindu-Buddhist admixture makes the pluralism and cultural complexity of Kathmandu, modern Nepal's capital, especially striking. Through increasing Tarai-Valley and hills-Valley migration into the old town and suburbs, urban

Kathmandu now mirrors the immense sociocultural pluralism of the nation. Ethnic boundaries, caste distinctions, and class stand in high relief as both rich and poor migrants from the periphery have settled around the capital. Their presence and patronage have both intensified and complicated the Hindu-Buddhist cultural interaction in the Kathmandu Valley. For Newars, their ethnicity and caste remain important social markers, and in many domains the rich and varied traditions in the Valley reflect the long-standing Newar need to assert hierarchical separation from neighbors and vis-à-vis other ethnic groups.

With their home territory conquered and occupied by the new royal court, Kathmandu Newars have responded variously to the new state's formation and development since 1770. Some became involved as officials and businessmen in alliance with the Shahs in the unification process that created the modern state of Nepal. Entire lineages left the Kathmandu Valley to pursue business opportunities across the mid-hills, dependent upon the new state's contracts and protection (English 1985; Lewis and Shakya 1988). Other Newars were removed from former positions of influence and had their lands confiscated. The intra-Newar variance is striking: the influential Buddhist Newar merchants who traded with Lhasa even welcomed the Shah restoration of trans-Himalayan trade (Stiller 1973), and the state's subsequent support (throughout the Rana period) of their lucrative ventures (Lewis 1993a).

Although increasingly inundated by migrants and encircled by state offices, hotels, and burgeoning suburbs, the old core areas of Kathmandu, Patan, and Bhaktapur retain their Newar character. Social divisions shaped during the Malla era also endure: the Newar community remains divided into over 100 castes and fissured further according to strong loyalties to localities and subcastes. To the outsider, Kathmandu Newars may seem unified by a common language, history, urban lifestyle, and religion, but in fact dialects divide Newar localities (Genetti 1988) and each settlement has its own history. Cultural traditions among Newars do vary quite dramatically.[5] Status competition between castes and subcastes is a feature of Newar life, with Hindu and Buddhist factions prominent at the pinnacles of Kathmandu's social pyramid.

Since the Valley's conquest over two hundred years ago, almost all socio-religious institutions in Newar communities have declined. Early Shah and Rana elites used legal legerdemain or seized outright temple and monastery lands (Regmi 1971, 1976), depriving these institutions and the Newar priesthoods (both Hindu and Buddhist) of their former endowment incomes. Myriad *guṭhis*, committees of devotees dedicated to some religious practice (and many also with land endowments), were likewise dispossessed, undermining the social institutions developed in the Malla era to support the performance of many religious practices. At the same time, the new rulers heavily patronized Hindu temples and priests, while promoting Brahmans as government officials. All of these factors realigned the standards of social, economic, and political advancement toward those practicing Hinduism. In so doing, the state supported high-caste authority and privilege, rewarding those who gained alliances with the Pahari elite, especially those connected with the Shah palace (Rose 1970).

In the later years of the Rana era, these efforts were pushed to excess, especially through the state instituting coercive measures against non-Parbatiya ethnic groups, actions that created a strong dialectic of increasing resistance. In 1905 when the Ranas prohibited the public use of non-Nepali tongues and the printing of literary works in Newari, they created among a large portion of the Newar community the conviction that the state was against them.[6] These actions by the state continued even after the Shah restoration (1950), especially in the 1964 Panchayat decree which eliminated any radio programming in Newari or other non-Nepali tongues. Only since the 1991 Revolution has the media broadcast policy been broadened. Even today, when educated Newars hear the term "national unification," many associate that call with state policy aimed at weakening their culture.

When Rana statutes were aimed against Newars, it was the Buddhist Newars who were especially targeted. Nowhere was this more evident than in the case of the sumptuary laws enacted in 1947—the year of *Jhī Macā*'s publication—that specifically delimited Urāy[7] Buddhist ritual observances. These widely publicized laws enacted by the Rana government[8] set very specific limits on the cultural celebrations that punctuate the Newar Buddhist year and life cycle. They sought to scale back drastically the size of offerings, the number of people in processions, the gifts that could be exchanged, the magnitude of feasts, and so forth. As the statute reads:

> Performance of rites and social functions may be in accordance with the rules stated above or in a much simpler scale but without breaking the traditional rules. Those rites not covered by the rules may be performed in accordance with custom but as economically as possible.

Some old customs were banned outright, such as community-wide meetings held once each year at the rotation of guṭhi responsibilities (Toffin 1975b). For example, Rule 38 sought to outlaw the caste-wide feasts showing recognition of the senior guṭhi leader:

> 38. While celebrating *Thakali Luye*,...the married-out daughters and in-laws may bring besides the *sagaṃ* tray a headdress of cotton for the father, a blouse for the mother. Other persons including the married daughters of sons and nephews may not bring gifts of any sort. Nor may any other persons be invited.

The 1947 statute cited *fifty-one* customary rituals, from birth to death, as falling under state supervision, with each very specifically listed and with threat of fines and punishments standing behind the regulations if limits were breached.[9]

These regulations did not exist merely on the books, but were aggressively publicized right into the neighborhoods and the households of prominent Newar Buddhist citizens. (Such laws, by the way, existed until at least 1982, although I know of no efforts to enforce them in Kathmandu.) As the 1947 Promulgation concludes:

For facilitating strict enforcement, these rules are to be printed at the Government press and distributed to the people of the Uray caste residing in Kathmandu, Bhaktapur, and Lalitpur. Emissaries may be sent by the Police Office to each neighborhood of these cities to announce publicly these rules. Urāys of each household may be called in person to sign a statement that he is prepared to accept these rules and act accordingly.

Thus, through language policy and sumptuary laws, the state provided a common Valley-wide experience that Newars themselves had traditionally lacked: state-sponsored discrimination aimed at their mother tongue and their venerable religious practices. In this repressive climate, Newar activists from formerly rival caste groups and city-states found the basis to unite in organizations to promote communal uplift, language education, cultural recognition, and political change.

This heavy-handed attempt at national unification, polarizing communities that unite in resistance, has, of course, been a mistake repeated again and again by South Asian states. If exchange is the basis of social life (Murphy 1971), state laws limiting exchange represent an intrusive attempt to weaken social groups and undermine their culture. I have emphasized these laws to convey vividly the setting of *Jhī Macā* and the Buddhist Newar sense of suffering special discrimination at the hands of the Hindu state.

Textual Analysis:
Jhī Macā's Definition of Newar Ethnicity

In other writings, Chittadhar held that loyalty to one's artistic traditions could effectively undermine growing social division in the Newar community and reverse the trend toward cultural disintegration. For him, this was to be a long process that must go forward with hope, even in the face of government hostility. So suggests Chittadhar's "Entrance," the lead poem from one of Chittadhar's most celebrated poetry collections:

> O Seedling, a day will come when you will also get your turn.
> Yes, the field has dried without sufficient rain
> And is doubly ruined for want of proper care.
> Moreover, it is encroached upon by others
> For want of embankments to mark its boundary.
> Bear it, remembering well the well-known saying,
> "Endurance is equal to a thousand virtues."
> The future understands the value of time
> And surely come to look for you also.
> O Seedling, a day will come when you will get your turn. (Hridaya 1976:v)

Underlying most of Chittadhar's writings is the social activist's commitment to Newar culture. Born 130 years after the Newar kingdoms fell, the author saw dramatic indications of cultural decline over his lifetime: many temples were nearly in ruins and their sculpture was being looted; old customs were declining, even, as we have seen, by state decree. Since the government also allowed only Nepali as the national school and state administrative language, Newars were giving up the use of their mother tongue. Most discouraging to Chittadhar, Newars by the end of the Rana period did little to resist, as their own factionalism impaired attempts at unified response. Thus, many Newars were intimidated, reduced to despair or co-optation.

Jhī Macā itself represented Chittadhar's own literary response to resist these trends. In the narrative, the author draws upon important personal relationships and activities to define the paradigmatic Newar urban experience. Several other selections from the text give the flavor of Chittadhar's book:

Episode 4. On the Balcony
From the balcony, the sun was still not visible. The child sat on the small woven rice-stalk mat and began eating the flattened rice. While eating, the boy felt chilly, but when the first sun rays of the day finally arrived, he made a *namaskār*[10] to the sun and said:

Come on, come on Sunlight!
Lock it! Lock it! At mirrors, windows bowing
I beg the sun-giving deity for sun
And bow to Jana Bāhā deity's[11] two feet.

Episode 6. At the Window
One day in the afternoon, the boy was sitting at the window and looking down. His mother was standing behind him. In the street below, a herd of cows was coming. The child looked around, held onto the mother's shawl, and asked, "O Mother, where are all of these cows going?" Stroking the child's head, she answered, "Yes, they are coming to browse in a distant field"...Soon thereafter came a flock of sheep led by a Tibetan hollering "*gyū, gyū*" at them. The sheep jumped along and ran ahead, baaing. The child held on to the window bar and said, "Here they come! Oh how many sheep!" as he was jumping up and down excitedly. Pointing at the sheep, the mother said, "Yes, Yes, many have come. And can you count them? How many sheep are there?" The child counted, "One, two, three, four, five, six, seven, eight, nine, ten...oh ho, there are so many more. I cannot count them all! Where are they all coming from? Oh, so many sheep!"

Episode 7. Saturday
One day while sitting in a room, mother was grooming herself. The child came up from behind and crowded her while she was looking in the mirror. The mother nudged the child aside and said, "Go off now, it is late. Why are you getting in the way?" The child moved off a little and asked his mother, "Where are you going now, mother?" [The mother said] "Today is Saturday, isn't it? I am going to do *pūjā*.[12] Stay with your father today." Scratching his temples with both hands, the child continued to pester her and said, "I will

also come along." The mother replied: "I cannot carry you. You are to walk now." The child laughed and replied, "Yes I will walk."

Episode 8. In the Garden

...In the meantime a very beautiful butterfly came and landed on the fragrant flower. The child ran over in order to catch it. The butterfly flitted over to another flower. The child again went after it but could not catch it. Then he went running over to his mother and said, "Mother, give one butterfly to me." While still picking flowers, the mother said, "Son, we should not catch butterflies. If we catch it, it will die. Just watch it as it goes from place to place. Look at how beautiful its wings are! While looking at it, how much it seems like a flower itself." The child said, "Um," and held on to his mother's shawl. Then a sparrow came there and captured the butterfly. The butterfly struggled and its wings were torn off. The child took the wings and showed them to his mother: "Look mother! Here are its wings." Mother: "Gha, tisk, tisk. This evil sparrow has killed such a beautiful butterfly. Look, I say we should not capture them. Let's go now, it is done."

Episode 13. In the Morning

One day in the morning, the child heard the sound of the *bājan*, stood up unsteadily, and looked out. Looking from the window, he heard from a distance the sound of drums, a clarinet, and a trumpet. He then went inside to his mother and asked, "Today where has the bājan gone?" The mother replied, "Yes, from today and throughout [the month of], it will go to Svayambhū[13] to do a pūjā and come back."

Child: "What is *Gumlā*?"
Mother: " Gumlā is a month and thirty days make up this month."
Child: "What are the months, mother?"

Episode 14. *Saunti*[14]

During this festival, lamps were lit in all places. Seeing them, the child with some pastry in his hand felt very happy. His mother called for him many times but he never heard her. With his neighborhood friends he was singing loudly:

Come, come Lakṣmī, come to our place!
Do not go there, to another place.
Jhili-mili, jhili-mili go the burning lamps Come right here to our dwelling's special room; Mother will feed you a good feast indeed.
(Lewis 1989a:199–208)

We now turn to the linguistic and religious themes in the text by which the author defines essential Newar culture and group boundaries.[15]

Language and Identity

In the *Jhī Macā* vignettes, the author eschews using fancy Sanskrit vocabulary terms—"spicing" literature with Sanskrit is a sign of erudition in Kathmandu—because this little book was intended to be as fully "Newar" as possible.[16] The author wanted this work to be a specimen of authentic *Newa: bhāy*[17] (Newari language) for school-age children who could only study Nepali in school, but also were in need of learning to read and write Newari. Above all else, Chittadhar's *Jhī Macā* wants Newar children to use Newar terms, not Nepali or Sanskrit loan words, to refer to kin, units of time, to count, and to identify the deities that inspire enduring loyalty. He also espoused the revival of *rañjanā*, one of fourteen old Newar textual scripts. This last aspect of his work still continues in the educational groups and literary societies promoting Newar cultural revival.

Kinship

It will surprise no anthropologist who has worked in Newar society that one episode finds the mother teaching her child kinship terms (Episode 2). These complex ties dominate Newar social life (Toffin 1975a), and so the text. Newar society is patrilineal in the north Indian style, with preference for patrilocal marriage and large, extended family households dominated by the eldest males (Quigley 1986). The bond between a mother and her sons—who live under the same roof all their lives—is understandably the chief narrative presented in *Jhī Macā*. The text often testifies to the Newars' love for their children. This is touchingly conveyed in Episode 1, when the author writes of a father observing his baby breast-feeding. Also interwoven in the text is a sense of the dual membership of Newar women, who readily move back and forth between their natal and husbands' homes throughout their lives, creating a distinctive caste-wide sense of support and dependence. Every child likewise maintains enduring and loving bonds with the mother's brothers, the *pāju*s; the latter also have ritual obligations to fulfill throughout the child's life.

Religion

The child is taught the months largely in terms of a shorthand outline of major religious festivals.[18] The choices again underline how Chittadhar saw loyalty to traditional family customs as integral to the modern revival of Newar culture. Religious ritual (*pūjā*) is likewise a recurring theme. The many references to sacred observances and morality underline the pervasive presence of Indic traditions, Hindu and Buddhist, in Newar life.

This Hindu-Buddhist coexistence has been rightfully cited as a cultural environment unique in modern South Asia, closest to north India before the Muslim conquests of the twelfth century (Levi 1905–8; Gellner 1992). Some episodes touch upon important common popular traditions shared by all Newars: Sūrdyah, the sun god worshipped every day on the rooftop, merits attention (Episode 4) as does Saunti, the fall festival of lights devoted to Lakṣmī, goddess of fortune (Episode 14). But the Buddhist tradition is especially highlighted: the Mahāyāna Buddhist celestial bodhisattva Avalokiteshvara, the most popular Newar deity (Episode 4), receives devotional chanting.

It is noteworthy how elements in *Jhī Macā* reflect the perspective of the author's own Buddhist merchant caste, the Urāy of Kathmandu. The best example of this are the references made to the *Gum̐lā bājan*, a Buddhist musical procession. For the latter, drummers and other musicians go each day for a month to Svayambhū, the chief Buddhist shrine on a nearby hilltop, and fill the morning market with drumbeats on their return (Lewis 1993b).[19] Chittadhar's choice of the bājan is consistent with his dislike of the Theravāda modernist movement in his midst; he saw the latter as abandoning too much of the Newar cultural heritage orchestrated through Mahāyāna-Vajrayāna ritual (Lewis 1993c) and tainted by moral scandals.

The text also illustrates the enculturation of core ethical viewpoints from the Newar lay Buddhist's perspective. A recurring theme is the moral superiority of *ahimsā*, the abstention from killing any living being. Cats are thought evil for their killing mice (Episode 5), as are the sparrows for catching butterflies (Episode 8). Thus, the ethos of nonviolence is fundamental to Chittadhar's statement of Newar character.[20] In his general approach to defining Newar identity, then, Chittadhar is a traditionalist who holds that the central principle of Newar moral life, *ahimsā*, must be inculcated in childhood.

In *Jhī Macā*, we see, in part, Chittadhar's conviction that Newars must hold fast to their old traditions in response to the threats of state discrimination and modernization. This book directs children to adopt "purely Newar" kin terminologies, learn a Newar script to underline group pride, use the Newari names for months, numbers, and deities, and adhere to the norms of nonviolence and ritual celebration that have made the Newars unique in ethnic, moral, and devotional terms.

It is also significant to note how the author's subject choices in several places delimited his audience to Kathmandu Buddhists of high caste. The specific content of the text itself implies a limited audience: the literate urban sector of Newars in the Buddhist community. This is true in its depiction of Svayambhū, the Gumlā bājan, script instruction, and so forth. Thus, the ideal lifestyle in *Jhī Macā* could not naturally resonate far beyond the high-caste Buddhist communities. This may have been intentional: perhaps Chittadhar hoped that Newar children from other backgrounds would see the Buddhist customs depicted in *Jhī Macā* as the original Newar culture; if they did not emulate them, at least they could know of the traditions and respect them. The text, thus, can also be read as a celebration of the Urāy lifestyle, a modern "lifestyle account" gifted to his own community though shared with all Newars. This interpretation points to a commonly held Newar Buddhist attitude that Shresthas and other newly Hinduized Newars have abandoned their Buddhist traditions, and so a portion of their true Newar-ness.

Concluding Observations

In the ethnohistorical context of mid-20th century Nepal, author Chittadhar Hridaya responds to the Kathmandu Newar Buddhist middle-upper class's situation: a sense of geographic and political encirclement; Newar disunity with some, mostly Buddhists, who were bitter and unreconciled to the new order while another large subsection of the urban elite, mostly Newar Hindus, were integrally involved in the Shah state apparatus; public schools teaching only Nepali, as many children were abandoning Newari language and culture; Buddhists struggling against forces seeking "national unification" via Hindu laws, high-caste bureaucracy, and Brahmanical ritual; Pahari cultural dominance at the expense of non-Nepali languages, Buddhism, and indigenous legal systems; the decline of Newar Buddhist institutions and the traditional priestly (*vajrācaryā*) elite. Chittadhar Hridaya's literary revivalism represents one of many contending responses to this situation.

Chittadhar was no revolutionary and counseled Newars not to revolt against the Shah state. (He himself accepted awards from King Mahendra.) He had traveled modestly to countries of modernizing Asia and argued that the unification of Nepal was necessary and desirable. His position was that each group should strengthen its culture; like many Kathmandu activists who followed his lead in seeking to revive traditional Newar traditions through literary pursuits, Chittadhar felt that one day the government would see that national integration would be truly possible only when each ethnic group did not feel threatened.

Since Chittadhar's death, the entire question of ethnic culture and national unification has become yet more complex and problematic in urban Kathmandu. The contestation between nationalism and Newar ethnicity continues, with the since-1991 legalized voice of the Congress Party and the myriad-factioned communist parties adding into public discourse further alternative visions of ethnic identity and modernization. Many of these groups are dominated by Newars and have found strong support in the large cities of the Valley.[21]

Another powerful transformative influence has been the introduction (since 1979) of mass video technology and the availability of global television programming via satellite dishes (since 1988). For example, there are now in Kathmandu satellite dish guṭhis that share purchase and maintenance expenses. The expansion of media programming has altered many variables in the process of situating identity along the tradition-modernity axis. A partial listing would include expenditures of patronage funds away from traditional institutions and devotions; choices for the investment of free time; effects of the symbolic content of the programs themselves (Indian TV Hinduism, global news and information, television and movie stereotypes of modern America or Japan).[22] As elsewhere, the Newar literary community of modern Kathmandu is an audience whose understandings of self, kin, community, and world have been transformed and multiplied far from those of Chittadhar's generation.

Ten years after his death, Chittadhar's books are still found among booksellers and still read by Newar youth. Yet there is an anachronistic, romantic sense one gets when talking to young Newars today about what the half-century-old literary culture represented by Chittadhar means to them. Those seeking to sustain Newar culture and identity in modern Nepal still honor the poet's life and many still use *Jhī Macā* with their own children. But they must also contend in a different era, one in which Shah-Newar alliances endure and state discrimination has abated, but in which Nepal's failure to develop its economy, infrastructure, and governmental institutions is now leading to the rapid deterioration of the Kathmandu Valley's ecology. The precipitous decline in urban living standards (water supply, air quality, sanitation, public health facilities) is a problem faced by all Newars, and others, living in Kathmandu. How will the commitment to Newar cultural identity intersect with the call for identification with party programs and alliances in the new political system? For the young, who can say how they will negotiate their commitments and identities vis-à-vis their country's economic stagnation and the multifaceted impact of global mass media?

Notes

An early version of this paper was presented at the 18th Annual Conference on South Asia, University of Wisconsin, Madison, in November 1989. Special thanks go to Nirmal Tuladhar and Subarna Man Tuladhar for guiding me early in my fieldwork to meet Chittadhar and become aware of his work. Some information presented here was derived from interviews with Chittadhar in 1981 and 1982. This article is dedicated to Margaret Mead, an exemplary ethnographer and an inspiring teacher.

1. Scholars who have worked in different Newar communities in the Kathmandu Valley have long recognized the difficulty of generalizing beyond their fieldwork for all Newars. A further complication is that today half of all Newars live outside the Kathmandu Valley (Lewis and Shakya 1988), making any sweeping pan-Newar generalizations difficult to support. Even within the Valley, many Newar groups cultivated discrete community practices in caste-based separation, in large part reflecting the legacy of walled cities being self-enclosed polities (called *desha*, "countries"). Of particular relevance to this paper, note that the religious cultures of Bhaktapur, Patan, and Kathmandu are quite strikingly different. Bhaktapur is predominantly Hindu (Levy 1990; Lewis 1992), while Patan is the most Buddhist city (Gellner 1992). Kathmandu, the focus of this essay, is roughly equally divided along Hindu-Buddhist lines; closest to the centers of state power, it is also the city most affected by state Hinduism, national development initiatives, and other modernizations (Lewis 1986, 1995).

2. A full translation of the book has been published in *Asian Folklore Studies* (Lewis 1989a) and the discussion in this article, of course, will be best comprehended by the reader having familiarity with it. Some points made here found earlier expression in the short introduction to this translation.

3. To treat the subject of Hindu-Buddhist relations in Indo-Nepalese history, belief, and practice would require a lengthy monograph. Many scholars working on Newar Buddhism have entered into the subject (e.g. Gellner 1992:83–104; Lewis 1984:468–481;

Lienhard 1978; Toffin 1984), at least to expose the false impressions conveyed by early European visitors, still endlessly repeated by modern tourist brochures, that these traditions are inextricably intertwined for all Newars.

Until very recently, the Newar Buddhist communities of the Kathmandu Valley successfully reproduced a vital and broad Mahāyāna-Vajrayāna Buddhist culture, with its householder *samgha* of Shākya and Vajrācārya unsurpassed in its translation of Buddhist ideas into domestic and shrine ritualism (Gellner 1988, 1989, 1991; Lewis 1989b, 1993b, 1994a, 1994b). Newar Buddhist tradition until recently cultivated scholar lineages conversant in the high Sanskritic commentarial traditions, as well as meditation masters who have passed down initiation lineages originating from the later Pala era in northeast India (c. 1000 CE). There have also been prominent lay castes in Kathmandu that for centuries patronized and strongly identified with the Buddhist traditions in the Newar cities, with a significant faction that supported the resident Tibetan samghas (Lewis 1989c) and, more recently, the Theravada revival (Kloppenborg 1977; Tewari 1983). If the assertion is made that Hinduism and Buddhism are inextricably blended in the Kathmandu Valley, as has been long suggested, Urāy, Sākya, and Vajrācārya (and doubtless many other) respondents will wax indignant. For them, being Buddhist, not Hindu, has meaning as both spiritual practice and in their self/caste identities.

4. The Pahari (Parbatiya) are speakers of the Indo-European language now called Nepali (also *khas kura* or, more archaically, "Gorkhali") in the modern state. This ethnolinguistic area actually extends across the mid-montane region from Himachal Pradesh across the eastern Himalayas (Berreman 1963). Although likely descended from a group known as the Khas, an Indo-Aryan people cited in ancient sources, Kshatriya elites across this zone have since Mughal times asserted that their origins were among Rajput clans that fled from Muslim rule. This claim has stood behind their allegiance to Hinduism, promoted intergroup solidarity, and justified their predatory dominance over other peoples in the region. Modern Himalayan history was shaped decisively by one Pahari clan from Gorkha that built upon, extended, and finally dominated the petty Kshatriya states across the region (Burghart 1984; Stiller 1973). By 1769, the entire region was conquered and integrated into this new state.

5. Among neighbors in Asan Tol, northeast Kathmandu, we noted fifteen examples of divergent vocabulary terms used for common household items between Hindu Shresthas and Buddhist Tuladhars.

6. The sense of conquest is not gone: for several weeks in 1980, I recorded the life history of an old Newar businessman. One day we sat talking about the Rana period, surrounded by several of his elderly Newar friends who sat looking out over the rooftops of Kathmandu. The Valley foothills and Himalayas were visible in the distance. When the conversation turned to relations with the Paharis, for whom the Newars have the special term "Khem," my informant was silent for a moment, then suddenly volunteered in broken English: "This still our Valley, not theirs." His friends nodded their agreement. (For a corresponding Pahari anecdote, see note 9.)

7. The Urāy caste is composed of eight subcastes, numbering in all several thousand. Predominantly merchants and artisans, and indigenous to Kathmandu city, the Urāy are one of the most important lay Buddhist communities in the Valley. See Lewis (1994) for

an extended discussion of this group and more in-depth consideration of the history of Newar Hindu-Buddhist contestation from the late Malla period onward.

8. The Nepali manuscript consulted was obtained from a private collection, hand copied from the original government printed version (1947). Special thanks go to Subarna Man Tuladhar for bringing this to my attention years ago and for his kind help in translating the Nepali text. (As our copy's Nepali title page has been lost, I can only give the English translation of the title in the bibliography.) Beyond Höfer's work on the *Muluki Ain* of 1856 (1979), I have not been able to research the history of sumptuary laws, or their application (and enforcement) among other Newar Buddhists or other ethnic groups. Such a study of the legal history of state-ethnic group interaction would be invaluable.

9. Why were the Buddhist Newars of Kathmandu singled out? First, the ruling state elite (Rana and Shah) used the claim that Nepal was the world's only remaining "pure Hindu state" to justify its sovereignty (Burghart 1984:115–116). The Buddhist Newars were also quite wealthy and they were right there directly before the palace and the new government. I have had informants cite pre-1950 cases in which Rana family members acted in despotic fashion to take property from wealthy Kathmandu merchants and even seize beautiful young women they espied in state processions through the old town. (The women became their subsidiary wives.) The 1947 sumptuary code in fact does lay the legal basis for the Rana state to fine or confiscate any excessive displays of wealth. The enduring Pahari jealousy about Newar culture and sophistication has been noted in Bista (1991). In support, I can recount a conversation I once had in the United States Marine Bar in Kathmandu with a young man from a prominent, if somewhat dissipated, Chetri family. With feeling, and knowing my research on Newar communities, he volunteered what he said was the Chetri sense of inferiority regarding Newar artistry and tradition. "But," he added, "I will never give up the feeling that we deserve to rule since my ancestors conquered them, created the nation and have set their roots into this Valley." (Fieldnotes, 1987)

10. A gesture of respect with the palms joined at shoulder height. For honoring deities and individuals of higher status, *namaskār* (also called *namaste*) is common across the Indian subcontinent. This is the very first gesture a Newar child is taught.

11. The Buddhist celestial bodhisattva, Avalokiteshvara, who is also called *"Karuṇāmaya"* ("Compassionate-hearted One"). The chief shrine for this deity in Kathmandu city is in a monastic courtyard called *Jana Bāhā*, hence the appellation. See Locke (1980).

12. Pūjā can be defined as "ritual offering" and constitutes any gesture or substance offered to an icon.

13. Svayambhū is the large hilltop Buddhist shrine that is the focus of Newar Buddhist devotionalism. Groups gather to play drums and sing devotional songs there for the entire month. For elaborate notes and documentation on the Gumlā month, see Lewis (1993b).

14. Also called "Tihār" in Nepali and "Dīpāvali" in northern India, devotees celebrate this festival by lighting lamps dedicated to Lakṣmī, goddess of wealth.

15. I want to make it clear before turning to certain themes pertaining to ethnic boundary maintenance, that I do not want to violate the poet's artistry by implying that the "didactic uplift agenda" pervades every episode in the text. There is this element in *Jhī*

Macā—which I will now focus upon— but Hridaya's little book is not one of the heavy-handed works of "Newar nationalism." The poetry of Chittadhar's language makes *Jhī Macā* more than a mere manual. As I have written elsewhere, "It rises to the level of art by its poetic celebration of the Newar lifestyle, enlivened by the author's love of his own culture and its children" (Lewis 1989a:199).

16. For example, the text uses idiomatic onomatopoetic expressions for flittering fireflies (Episode 10) and burning butter lamps (Episode 14).

17. "Newari" is a modern English neologism. There are two emic terms preferred by Newars: the colloquial form as given in the text; or the Sanskritized "Nepāl Bhāṣa" that also expresses the old pre-Shah boundary of "Nepāl" as the Kathmandu Valley only.

18. See the notes in Lewis (1989a) and Lewis (1984) regarding the details of these festival observances. As cited in Episode 9, these are:

Month	Known by:	Tradition or Trait
Bacalā		*mwāli* horn playing and *Digu Pūjā*
Tacalā		hot
Dillā		rice planting
Gumlā		the *bājan*
Yamlā		*Indrajatra* and *Dīpa Pūjā*
Kaulā		*Mohini* (Nep. *Dasain*)
Kachalā		*Mhah Pūjā* (Nep. *Tihar*)
Thinlā		*Yomari* confections
Pohela		Full moon frost
Sillā		*Māhra* festival (Nep. *Shiva Ratri*)
Chilā		*Holi*
Caulā		Bathing at *Lhuti Ajimā*

19. The bājan before 1991 also coordinated various Urāy communities' participation in political protest marches, including the demonstrations each year urging the government to adopt the Newari yearly cycle, Nepal's only indigenous calendar system, as the official standard for the country.

20. Such observations on the natural world are not peripheral to the foundations of Newar moral reckoning. As Parish has noted, "Newars…tend to see morality as an objective part of the world, rather than as a human construction—morality reflects natural or sacred law" (1991:340). This *ahimsā* ideal provides a linkage to the Pahari stereotype of Newars in general: as Prithivi Narayan Shah, the unifier of the country once said, "This three-citied Nepal is a cold stone. It is great only in intrigue. With one who drinks from cisterns [the Newar practice] there is no wisdom; nor is there courage" (quoted in Burghart 1984:111, with my notation). This view is even expressed by Newars themselves in an old verse:

Lvāy he maphu ("Can't fight
Mile naṇ majū Or unite.")

21. The study of the political parties in modern Newar contexts and their views on ethnic identity and religious tradition would be a fascinating and important area for research. Impressionistic observations of Gumlā devotional activities at Svayambhū in 1991 and the 1993 Samyak in Kathmandu suggest to me that the popularity of Marxist-Communist parties in the capital have led to no discernible falling away from festival practices.

22. Kathmandu television owners receive on Star Cable (Hong Kong) CNN, MTV, Asian sports, BBC, and movies. Indian television features government news and many religious series. The government-run Nepal TV features government news and American TV shows (e.g., *Bonanza, The Brady Bunch*).

References

Barth, Fredrik. 1956. Ecological Relationships of Ethnic Groups in Swat, North Pakistan. American Anthropologist 58:1083–1089.
———. 1969. Ethnic Groups and Boundaries. Boston: Little-Brown.
Berreman, Gerald. 1960. Cultural Variability and Drift in the Himalayan Hills. American Anthropologist 62:774–794.
———. 1963. Peoples and Cultures of the Himalayas. Asian Survey 3:289–304.
Bista, Dor Bahadur. 1991. Fatalism and Development. Kathmandu.
Burghart, Richard. 1984. The Formation of the Concept of Nation-State in Nepal. Journal of Asian Studies 44(4):101–125.
English, Richard. 1985. Himalayan State Formation and the Impact of British Rule in the Nineteenth Century. Mountain Research and Development 5:61–78.
Gellner, David N. 1986. Language, Caste, Religion and Territory: Newar Identity Ancient and Modern. European Journal of Sociology 27:102–148.
———. 1988. Monastic Initiation in Newar Buddhism. *In* Oxford University Papers on India. R. F. Gombrich ed. 2(1):42–112.
———. 1989. Monkhood and Priesthood in Newar Buddhism. Purushartha 12:165–191.
———. 1991. Ritualized Devotion, Altruism, and Meditation: The Offering of the Guru Mandala in Newar Buddhism. IndoIranian Journal 34:161–197.
———. 1992. Monk, Householder and Tantric Priest: Newar Buddhism and Its Hierarchy of Ritual. Cambridge: Cambridge University Press.
Gennetti, C. 1988. A Contrastive Study of the Dolakhali and Kathmandu Newari. Cahiers de linguistique Asie-orientale 17:181–204.
H. M. G. 1947. Rules Prohibiting Extravagance in Social Practices. (Original in Nepali). Kathmandu.
Höfer, András. 1979. The Caste Hierarchy and State in Nepal: A Study of the Muluki Ain of 1854. Innsbruck: Universitätsverlag Wagner.
Hridaya, Chittadhar. 1947. Jhi Maca. Varanasi: Dharmodaya Sabha.
———. 1948. Sugat Saurabh. Calcutta: General Printing Works.
———. 1976. Degah/Pagoda. Upendra Man Malla, trans. Kathmandu: Sri Saraswati Mudranalaya.
Karmacarya, Madhava Lal, and Phanindra Ratna Vajracarya. 1983. Chittadhar Hridaya Smriti Grantha. Kathmandu: Nepal Bhasa Parisad.
Kloppenborg, Ria. 1977. Theravada Buddhism in Nepal. Kailash 5(4):301–322.
Levi, Sylvain. 1905–8. Le Népal. 3 Vols. Paris: Leroux.
Levine, Nancy. 1987. Caste, State, and Ethnic Boundaries in Nepal. Journal of Asian Studies 46 (1):71–88.
Levy, Robert I. (with Kedar Rajopadhyaya). 1990. Mesocosm: Hinduism and the Organization of a Traditional Newar City in Nepal. Berkeley: University of California Press.
Lewis, Todd T. 1984. The Tuladhars of Kathmandu: A Study of Buddhist Tradition in a Newar Merchant Community. Ann Arbor: University Microfilms International.

————. 1986. The Anthropology of Development in Nepal. Contributions to Nepalese Studies 13 (2):167–180.

————. 1989a. Childhood and Newar Tradition: Chittadhar Hridaya's Jhi Maca. Asian Folklore Studies 48:195–210.

————. 1989b. Mahayana Vratas in Newar Buddhism. The Journal of the International Association of Buddhist Studies 12(1):109–138.

————. 1989c. Newars and Tibetans in the Kathmandu Valley: Ethnic Boundaries and Religious History. Journal of Asian and African Studies 38:31–57.

————. 1992. Review of Mesocosm. American Anthropologist 94:968–970.

————. 1993a. Himalayan Frontier Trade: Newar Diaspora Merchants and Buddhism. *In* Anthropology of Tibet and the Himalayas. Martin Brauen et al., eds. Pp. 165–178. Zurich: Volkerkundemuseum.

————. 1993b. Contributions to the Study of Popular Buddhism: The Newar Buddhist Festival of Gum.la Dharma. Journal of the International Association of Buddhist Studies 16(2):7–52.

————. 1994a. The Nepal Jana Jivan Kriya Paddhati, a Modern Newar Guide for Vajrayana Life-Cycle Rites. Indo-Iranian Journal 37:1–46.

————. 1994b. Contributions to the History of Buddhist Ritualism: a Mahayana Avadana on Caitya Veneration from the Kathmandu Valley. Journal of Asian History 28(1):1–38.

————. 1995. Buddhist Merchants in Kathmandu: The Asan Tol Market and Uray Social Organization. *In* Contested Hierarchies: A Collaborative Ethnography of Caste among the Newars of the Kathmandu Valley, Nepal. D. Gellner and Quigley, eds. Pp. 38–75. Oxford: Oxford University Press.

Lewis, Todd T., and D. R. Shakya. 1988. Contributions to the History of Nepal: Eastern Newar Diaspora Settlements. Contributions to Nepalese Studies 15(1):25–65.

Lienhard, Siegfried. 1978. Religionssynkretismus in Nepal. *In* Buddhism in Ceylon and Studies on Religious Syncretism in Buddhist Countries. H. Bechert, ed. Pp. 146–177. Gottingen: Vandenhoeck and Ruprecht.

————. 1984. Nepal: The Survival of Indian Buddhism in a Himalayan Kingdom. *In* The World of Buddhism. H. Bechert and R. Gombrich, eds. Pp. 108–114. New York: Facts on File.

Locke, John K. 1980. Karunamaya. Kathmandu: Sahiyogi.

Murphy, Robert F. 1971. The Dialectics of Social Life: Alarms and Excursions in Anthropological Theory. New York: Basic Books.

Parish, Steven M. 1991. The Sacred Mind: Newar Cultural Representations of Mental Life and the Production of Moral Consciousness. Ethos 19(3):313–351.

Quigley, Declan. 1986. Introversion and Isogamy Marriage Patterns of the Newars of Nepal. Contributions to Indian Sociology (N.S.) 20(1):75–95.

Regmi, Mahesh Chandra. 1971. A Study in Nepali Economic History, 1768–1846. New Delhi: Manjusri Publishing House.

————. 1976. Landownership in Nepal. Berkeley: University of California Press.

Rose, Leo E. 1970. Secularization of a Hindu Polity: The Case of a Hindu Polity. *In* Religion and Political Modernization. Donald E. Smith, ed. Pp. 31–48. Princeton: Princeton University Press.

Slusser, Mary. 1982. Nepal Mandala. Princeton University Press.

Stiller, Ludwig J. 1973. The Rise of the House of Gorkha. New Delhi: Manjusri.

Tewari, Ramesh Chandra. 1983. Socio-Cultural Aspects of Theravada Buddhism in Nepal. Journal of the International Association of Buddhist Studies 6(2):67–93.

Toffin, Gerard. 1975a. La terminologie de parente Newar: Analyse descriptive et comparative. L'Homme 15.

————. 1975b. Etudes sur les Newars de la Vallée Kathmandou: Guthi, Funerailles et Castes. L'Ethnographie 2:206–225.

————. 1984. Societe et religion chez les Newar du Nepal. Paris: CNRS.

Afterword

Afterword _____

Selves in Motion

Robert I. Levy

And men, do they profit from experience? They are made like birds who always
let themselves be taken in the same nets where a hundred thousand birds of their
species have already been caught.

Bernard Le Bovier de Fontanelle (1657–1757)

Man alone has made a goddess of *choice* in place of *necessity...*, he can explore
possibilities and choose between alternatives.... Even when he most despicably
abuses his freedom, man is still king. For he can still choose even though he
chooses the worst.

Johann Gottfried von Herder (1744–1803)

The ultimate goal of the human sciences is not to constitute man but to dissolve
him.

Claude Lévi-Strauss (1908–)

"**M**an's" freedom, his agency, his self—heroic navigators of internal and
external seas—are perennially slippery topics. The first two quotations
above assume an internal freedom, a *potential* freedom to choose, to
try. Some commentators, insisting on the force of external pressures and on internal

foolishness and weakness, have always been pessimistic about the realization of that freedom; some have been more optimistic about the possibility of achieving wisdom and ripping through or avoiding the constraining nets. Still others, like Levi-Strauss and his deterministic predecessors and descendants, reject the debate, and write off freedom and agency and optimism and pessimism as illusions, as a "humanistic" mirage.

I wish in this essay to review some positions, mostly recent ones, on self and agency, and argue that the contemporary choices in orientation about self and agency exemplified in those chapters in this collection that are concerned with agency, are not only expressions of contemporary thinking, but arise out of the conditions of present-day Nepal, conditions that are not universal, which make these contemporary orientations about freedom and agency seem, somehow, right.

❖ ❖ ❖

The recent emphasis on agency and on potential freedom is set against powerful modern theoretical attacks debunking or weakening it. In an early modern example, the representative *philosophe* Denis Diderot, in the late 18th century, wrote— visualizing mankind as cogs in a tightly built cosmic clock—that "each of us is imperceptibly carried along by the general current which leads one to glory and another to ignominy." Therefore such "human fancies" as self-respect, a sense of shame, and guilty remorse are "childish notions founded on the ignorance and vanity of a person who takes upon himself the credit or blame for a quite unavoidable moment of evolution" (Diderot 1966:218).

Such "childish notions" of freedom were also questioned in the psychic determinism of Freud, contributing to the "dissolution of man," which Freud felt completed the decentering of mankind started by the Copernican and Darwinian revolutions. Freud, like most people taking positions on determinism and freedom, left a small and problematic opening to the *other* position, in the form of a limited and "strictly relative" degree of freedom to the "ego," the executive "psychic agency" responsible for the interests of the person as a whole, as it mediated creatively between superego, id, and "reality" (Laplanche and Pontalis 1973:130).

Anthropological culture theory had similar implications for the preeminence of non-agent determinism, particularly insofar as it conceived of the constitution of individuals by their cultures and the radical embeddedness of individuals in their cultures. Gregory Bateson, an exemplary figure, summed up the intellectual mood of the advanced thinking of his time. "Freudian psychology expanded the concept of mind inwards to include the whole communication system within the body—the autonomic, the habitual, and the vast range of unconscious process. What I am saying expands mind outwards. And both of these changes reduce the scope of the conscious self." And, thus, he added, echoing Diderot, "a certain humility becomes appropriate, tempered by the dignity or joy of being part of something much bigger" (1972:462f.). Like Freud he doesn't *totally* deconstruct self, person, and agency; he is content to radically reduce their "scope."

Post-structuralism was more intransigent, and more logically consistent. Michel Foucault's aim, like Levi-Strauss's was "the destruction of the subject." "One has to dispense with the constituent subject, and to get rid of the subject itself, that is to say, to arrive at an analysis which can account for the constitution of the subject within a historical framework" (Foucault 1980:117, quoted in Best and Kellner 1991:117). The subject "must be stripped of its creative role and analyzed as a complex and variable function of discourse" (Foucault 1977:138, quoted in Best and Kellner 1991:51). The "creative subject" was rejected as "a humanist fiction, along with the use of the vocabulary of freedom, liberty, and autonomy," all eschewed by Foucault in his role as a "theorist of the death of man" (Best and Kellner 1991:60).

But, once again, the position generated paradoxes. *Who* was meditating on the "death of man," writing books, and hoping to liberate readers? Foucault's late concerns shifted to "the technologies of the self, where *individuals create* their own identities through ethics and forms of self-constitution" (ibid., 60f. emphasis added). Agency seems to be back, man is reborn. As Foucault put it, "If one wants to analyze the genealogy of the subject...one has to take into account not only techniques of domination, but also techniques of the self" (Foucault and Sennett 1982:10). These techniques of the self involve a degree of freedom from or within society, for they "permit individuals to effect by their own means or with the help of others a certain number of operations on their own bodies and souls, thoughts, conduct, and ways of being, so as to transform themselves" (Foucault 1988:18).

The most nearly contemporary trans-individualistic positions have been framed in the conception and politics of "identity," the emphasis on a set of "enclosures," such as race, gender, class, and ethnicity, which were taken to have been neglected in favor of "enclosures ignored by universalist, rationalist and individualist biases of previous generations" (Hollinger 1997:336). But there has here too been a countermovement, reminiscent of late Foucault. "Especially in the 1990s [there has been] a flurry of 'neo-Enlightenment' attempts to prevent the hermeneutics and politics of identity from obscuring the agency of individuals..." (Hollinger 1997:337).

Most of the papers in this volume have this very contemporary "neo-Enlightenment" emphasis on agency, with their moving portrayals of actors doing the best they can in, usually, difficult or complex communal situations. Not only—in close allegiance to contemporary values—is the agent emphasized over the system, but that *actor* is not portrayed as "exotic"; it is the *situation* of, say, local family values that may be strange. The actor turns out to be much like "us," an easy target for moral empathy and political solidarity—"This is what I can imagine myself doing and feeling in such a situation." "Self," which was in the recent past problematic for those obsessed with the *constitution* of actors—whether those obsessions were psychodynamic, cognitive, matters of cultural learning theory, or poststructural, is here generally taken as nonlocal, nonproblematic, universal.

◩ ◩ ◩

There is something special about contemporary Nepal in its contrasts to many other traditional anthropological sites (now mostly vanished) that facilitates this sense of similarity to "us" of selves—for we are dealing with what are, in some dimensions, contemporary-type selves. There are and have been other kinds of places, other kinds of selves, other kinds of relation and balance between "self" and "context," and thus other types, degrees, and limits of "agency."

As most of the chapters in this book emphasize, Nepal is a place of peculiar ethnic and social complexity. This has for many centuries been the case for the complex Kathmandu Valley communities and (since the eighteenth century) of the multi-ethnic nation of Nepal, and has, in recent decades become the rapidly accelerating situation of many once-remote groups. Premalata Ghimire puts the situation and its consequences for our purposes precisely. "In a multi-ethnic community like Nepal, identities are constantly in a state of flux. Individuals are engaged in creating, maintaining, switching, or changing their personal and cultural identities to meet their various needs and life-strategies" (this volume, p. 195). "Individuals" are actively and purposely and necessarily *doing* something with their "identities." One aspect of "self" has become salient, and is acting upon another.

Economic changes, general modernization, and urban migration add to and transform this long-standing ethnic and social structural complexity. As Mark Liechty writes, "In the 1990s members of the city's middle class are forced to negotiate their places in new cultural economies and systems of value" (this volume, p. 132). He argues that "to begin to understand people's behaviors and motivations [in Kathmandu] we have to keep in mind the almost overwhelming sociocultural flux that many people experience" (this volume, p. 137).

Ernestine McHugh argues that in the traditional village context, "a knowledge of alternative worldviews of neighboring ethnic groups provides frames of reference in terms of which the Gurungs orient and judge themselves" (this volume, p. 161). But for Gurungs who have migrated to one of the Nepalese cities (and this applies to all urban immigrants from the various distant rural Nepalese communities), the situation becomes even more complex. Now, for the construction of "honor" and "identity," "one draws from cross-cutting value systems.... Identity is less strongly determined by one's social origins in the new system because there are multiple frames" (this volume, p. 170).

What are the implications of such complexity for "agency" and "self?" (It is important to note that we are talking about a "meaningful complexity" and not chaos and anomie—conditions which have still different implications for self and agency.) In these situations of "multiple frames," "selves" become not only complex but (as Skinner and Holland characterize the situation as manifested in Naudadan songs and discourse) "contradictory and contested" (this volume, p. 104). Parish, writing about low-status people in Bhaktapur's complex caste society, argues that as "inconstant selves in an equivocal world, actors in caste society may shift from resistance to acquiescence, and back again.... An 'inner' politics of self parallels the politics and exigencies of caste life" (this volume, p. 79).

The experience of and navigation in a complex world with its many visible examples of different possible lives has certain consequences. They provide the conditions for the politically pregnant sense of *unfairness*, which many chapters emphasize. "My condition might well have been, might, in fact, well still be, different and better." "Unfairness" is enmeshed with the idea of the *arbitrariness* of one's situation, which can be altered in imagination, and in creative songs and stories, and, ultimately, in personal and political action. In these situations resistance to perceived unfairness as well as the choice of resistance or of willful acquiescence is, as Elizabeth Enslin argues, "tied in complex ways with the construction of individual and collective identities in relation to social inequalities of class, gender, ethnicity, and caste" (this volume, p. 270).

Unfairness, arbitrariness, active construction of collective identities, are related to a certain transformation of consciousness, what the politically committed used to call a "raising" of consciousness. As Parish notes (and I have argued at length, 1990, and elsewhere), the complex caste society of Newar Bhaktapur generates tensions between concrete personal identity and caste-ascribed identity and an unsettling awareness that "the caste system is an *arbitrary* human construction" (this volume, p. 78, emphasis added).

We have in most of the chapters of this book stories of agency, of the freedom of people to strain against locally determined external social bonds, of attempts to put identity and ethnicity to use. But this brings us back in our endless circling of freedom versus constraint to who or what is resisting, navigating, criticizing, being an agent? And what has this to do with the "self"?

❖ ❖ ❖

There have been a multitude of attempts to dissect out an anatomy of self, to cut up and bound "it" in various ways. The Random House dictionary defines self globally (and ethnocentrically and ideologically) as "a person or thing referred to with respect to complete individuality" and adds "a person's nature, character, etc." This is a first and ideal approximation of the "actor," the "agent," set against the external and internal "other," against the inauthentic and the false, against "empty role playing" actions and deluded self-definition. Social science discourse (building on Western and probably more general commonsense perceptions) make some distinctions in this global definition. Anthropology insofar as it has been "person centered" has been variously concerned with issues usually (but not consistently) glossed as "identity," "person," and what we might as well call the "self itself"—but has relatively ignored another "component," which is central to the Nepalese (and modern situation): the "observing and executive 'I'."

"Identity," as used by those influenced directly or indirectly by the work of

Erik Erikson (1950, 1959, 1968) (not quite the same "identity" as in "identity politics") focuses on the way "external" sociocultural elements and "internal" psychological forms are integrated to produce a socially meaningful sense of "who one is." "Person," when it is not used simply as a synonym for "individual," has often been used in a special way related to Mauss's idea of what (a particular) society takes to be the morally (and/or legally) responsible individual (or corporate group) (Carrithers et al. 1985). Like "identity" (although with a very different perspective), "persons" can be taken as "points of intersection between the subjective and the social" (White and Kirkpatrick 1985).

We can for our present purposes take the "self in itself" as the overall "me" that the observing "I" observes, frets about, and tries to control—an aspect of the mind as viewed by another aspect. This "self" has to do with the culturally and individually variable boundaries that set "me" off from "not-me" or "ego alien" aspects of mind (which "contact" the self as dreams, inspiration, hallucinations, possession, emotion, etc.) and of those aspects of body and bodily processes which stand against the "me." This self—in culturally variable ways—also includes or excludes, in a sense, behaviors and aspects of other individuals, and this expanded self is one basis for "corporate" empathy, shame or pride, solidarity and opposition.

Identity, person, and self—constituted by learning and social environment— vary in different settings, and make actors somewhat exotic to each other. But when we turn to that aspect of self, the executive and observing "I" that is the concern of these papers, we (Western intellectuals) find ourselves in less exotic territory—and something different is at play.

This calls for a brief ethnographic excursion into my own impressions of the peculiarities of the self among Newar respondents in Bhaktapur.

◈ ◈ ◈

My own work among Bhaktapur's Newars (see, for example, 1989, 1990, 1996, 1997) supports the images of relational and problematic identity reported for other communities in this book. In a sequence that I have more than once quoted elsewhere because of its eloquence—although many other respondents said something like it—after asking a Newar in Bhaktapur (whom I had been interviewing for several weeks) "Who are you?" he answers that he and his friends talk about that a good deal. He refers me to a remark of the god Krishna that a person is really "everything other." "To a great extent," my respondent goes on, "it seems that I [too] am everything other, because whenever I cook, I am a cook; whenever I love some girl, I am a lover; whenever I have a son or a daughter, I am a parent, I am a father; whenever I am with my father, I am a son; whenever I am alone with a friend, I am a friend; whenever I am with foes, I am an enemy." This is more elegantly put than the remarks on self of many others in Bhaktapur, but the remarks of others consistently tend to suggest, as this quotation does, that identity is something that needs to be thought, talked, and, perhaps, read about, that it is problematic, not a simple given in the world; and that it is in part at least, a shifting function of present significant relationships. The "I" of this man is something that navigates, as it happens effectively and proudly, among these separate situations and separate identities in a situation that is consciously thought about, and employs concrete cultural representations—here the dictum of Krishna—in an effort at clarification. "Who are *you* in all this," I asked him. "I am the one who does these things well," he answered. His "I" is *above*, meta, to these situation-determined shifting identities—which are, although shifting, coherent, it is again essential to note, in some larger picture. His agency is not so much a function of his total self, as of these executive functions of the "I" who manages and transcends his various selves.

This sort of discourse, and the realities it reflects, is not only a direct implication of the speaker's ambient reality, but it is generated in very specific patterns of child socialization (Levy 1996) where children at all status levels in Bhaktapur are vigorously taught (in absolute contrast with, say, children in a Tahitian village) that they are deeply dependent for all learning, proper orientation, and moral integrity on the systematically shifting, but culturally legitimate and ultimately integrated, contexts in which they find themselves.

Are things any different anywhere else? The rural and peripheral Tahitian village that I worked in before working in Nepal, was, in comparison to Nepal, tiny (284 versus some 40,000 people in Bhaktapur) and isolated, and equally coherent as a community—but with a greatly different kind of coherence—a coherence based on the conviction that social reality was an integrated "given," much like the physical world, a conviction generated out of experience and learning, and "sunk" into commonsense. Bhaktapur's coherence lay largely in the use of religion and the sacred to impose an ordering of the greatly *different* "ordinary" and "common sense" experiences of the city's multitude of hierarchically arranged and quite different social units and of each individual's sharply contrasting experiences in the course of a day, and of a life (see Levy 1989, 1990, 1996, 1997).

In two years of working and interviewing in Piri, I found nothing like the kind of discourse and sense of complex and problematic identity that characterized my respondents in Bhaktapur. In Piri people tended to identify themselves by their names, and by a bundle of attributes which defined "who they were" in themselves. The answer to "who are you?" was usually followed by the person's name, "I am Manu," and, after some probing, with the attributes of temperament or character that distinguished him or her from other villagers. Self-definition by some group solidarity and opposition— "we men" (and not women), "we Tahitians" (and not French), were only rarely salient in the conditions of village life at the time. These oppositional identities were minor in the usual conditions of village life. In the course of many lengthy interviews and village observations in the course of which I was able to infer many local qualities of self, identity, and the "I," I found no examples of such matters being consciously problematic, or puzzling, or even interesting to local people. The fact of their self, the self-as-a-whole in our dictionary's sense, seemed no more puzzling to them, than, say, the given fact of their body (Levy 1973).

◈ ◈ ◈

The particular aspect of self that is at issue in those chapters in this book concerned with self is an aspect centrally related to "agency." The agent here is not the self as a whole, which is an agent in the way that the general organization of any living creature acts as an agent in that creature's context. It is the agency of the observing and conscious "I," which has active, executive functions not only in regard to the external context, but in relation to other aspects of the self, and to other parts of the mind.

The conditions of life in Nepal, as the chapters vividly suggest, are the sorts of conditions which cause a kind of hypertrophy of that "I." This contemporary situation of Nepal condenses with contemporary Western intellectual experience and ideological moods. (One might even suggest that the particular individuals picked in these papers as "interesting" and as exemplars are precisely those who are most sensitive to these conditions.) The perceptions, interpretations, and actions of such people are not—in the particular contexts of action at issue in these chapters—determined primarily (as much village Tahitian behavior once was) through "internalized" local forms of identity, cognitive understanding, and qualities of self, which represent the kind of constituting controls that Bateson and mid-career Foucault emphasized. Such "constituting" controls operate in intimate and small contexts in Nepal, as everywhere. But the larger complex and contradictory world, the generation of a sense of paradox, unfairness, and imaginable (if not feasible) choice, impels a transformation of "consciousness," a sense of an "I" which questions and directs and controls its constituted self and its outer world, and which asks, "Why am I what I am? What might I be? What in this world of unfairness and alternate possibilities should I do next?" This all seems familiar, for it is our situation too.

In such conditions the relative force and meaning of both "self" and "culture" are different from what they were in the (for the most part) relatively simpler and more isolated and more imperiously systematic communities that informed much of the empirical component of the classical anthropological imagination. The breaking loose from "culture" (in its narrower anthropological sense), the enhancement of freedom of imagination, moral evaluation and, sometimes, of rebellious action described in these papers tempts communities under stress, and, in particular, states to develop new forms of control—priestly, sanctioned, religious forms; fundamentalist retreats; the transcendent force of laws, police, and armies. The freedom from the tyranny of culture, the efflorescence of agency developing under specific conditions, brings new human crises.

References

Bateson, Gregory. 1972. Steps to an Ecology of Mind. New York: Ballantine.

Best, Steven, and Douglas Kellner. 1991. Postmodern Theory. New York: The Guilford Press.

Carrithers, Michael, Steven Collins, and Steven Lukes, eds. 1985. The Category of the Person: Anthropology, Philosophy, History. Cambridge: Cambridge University Press.

Diderot, Denis. 1966. Rameau's Nephew/D'Alembert's Dream. Leonard Tancock, trans. London: Penguin Books.

Erikson, Erik. 1950. Childhood and Society. New York: W. W. Norton.

———. 1959. Identity and the Life Cycle. *In* Psychological Issues, monograph series, Vol. 1, No. 1. New York: International Universities Press.

———. 1968. Identity: Youth and Crisis. New York: W. W. Norton.

Foucault, Michel. 1977. Language, Counter-Memory, Practice. Ithaca: Cornell University Press.

———. 1980. Power/Knowledge. New York: Pantheon Books.

———. 1988. Technologies of the Self. *In* Technologies of the Self. L. Martin, H. Gutman, and P. Hutton, eds. Amherst: University of Massachusetts Press.

Foucault, Michel, and Sennet, Richard. 1982. Sexuality and Solitude. *In* Humanities in Review. Vol. 1. D. Rieff, ed. London: Cambridge University Press.

Hollinger, David. 1997. The Disciplines and the Identity Debates. Daedalus 126:333–351.

Laplanche, Jean, and J. B. Pontalis. 1973. The Language of Psychoanalysis. New York: Norton

Levy, Robert I. 1973. Tahitians: Mind and Experience in the Society Islands. Chicago: University of Chicago Press.

———. 1989. The Quest for Mind in Different Times and Different Places. *In* Social History and Issues in Human Consciousness. A. Barnes and P. Stearns, eds. New York: New York University Press.

———. 1990. Mesocosm: The Organization of a Hindu Newar City in Nepal. Berkeley: University of California Press.

———. 1996. Essential Contrasts: Differences in Parental Ideas about Learners and Teaching in Tahiti and Nepal. *In* Parents' Cultural Belief Systems. S. Harkness and C. Super, eds. Pp. 123–142. New York: Guilford Press.

———. 1997. The Power of Space in a Traditional Hindu City. International Journal of Hindu Studies 1:55–71.

White, Geoffrey, and John Kirkpatrick, eds. 1985. Person, Self, and Experience: Exploring Pacific Ethnopsychologies. Berkeley: University of California Press.

Index

agency: Gurung women and, 39–40; Tij songs and, 100–02; self and, 321–29
alcohol, songs and, 283–84, 285
Amitabha, 191
apangir marriage, 200, 201
asceticism: Brahmans and, 71–74; untouchables and, 67, 71–77
Atisa, 177

Bahun women, songs of, 269–70, 276–82, 294nn14–16
Bardo guidance, Tibetan Buddhism and, 187–89, 191
Bateson, Gregory, 322, 328
behavioral disorders. *See* madness
Bhaktapur, 325; identity and, 326–28
bitlaha, Hod and, 198, 207–9, 211
bodhisattva level (global identity), 177, 179, 182, 184–85, 189–93
bodies. *See* Tamang, female bodies and
bomsang, Tamang and, 224–27
boys: education and, 94, 96, 97; status of, 97
Brahmans, 53; asceticism and, 71, 72–73, 74; food and, 119, 126n12; ideal women and, 90, *see also* girls, gendered identities in; karmic identity and, 70–71, 177, 179, 180–82, 184, 188, 189–91; narratives of, 57, 59–62, 65–68, 111–28; religious roles of, 54, 71; renouncer and, 74–75; untouchables and, 54, 64, 70, 71, 75–77; women, 42
brideprice, marriage with among Hod,

199–202
bride-service, marriage with among Hod, 199, 200, 202–5, 212
brother-bodies, Tamang and, 228
Buddhism: *Jhī Macā* and, 301–18; Newars and, 303–6, 312n3. *See also* Sherpa shamanism; Tamang, female bodies and; Tibetan Buddhism
buying schemes, of Kathmandu consumers, 144–46. *See also* consumer materialism

capture, marriage by, 200, 201
cash economy, consumer materialism among middle class in Kathmandu and, 131–54
caste system, 325; equality and, 68–70; food and, 53, 54–55, 119, 126n12; Gurungs and, 159–60; Hod and, 196–99, 208, 211–13; mixed, 90; of Newars, 51–85, 81nn1–2; women in, 90, *see also* girls, gendered identities in. *See also* Brahmans; untouchables
Chenresig, 182
Chetri women, songs of, 269–70, 276–82, 294nn14–16
childbearer, women as, 40, 91–92, 97
children: Gurungs and, 21–22, 27, 31, 32, 34–36, 40, 46n25; identities of, 89; *Jhī Macā* for, 301–18. *See also* girls, gendered identities in
Chitwan women, 269–99; *dukha* (suffering) of in songs, 272, 277–80, 282, 284, 285, 289, 290; as middle class,

About the Contributors_____

MARY DES CHENE is an independent researcher affiliated with the Nepal Studies Group, in Kathmandu, Nepal, and coeditor of the journal, *Studies in Nepali History and Society (SINHAS)*. Recent publications on Nepal include the 1996 articles "Ethnography in the Janajati-yug," in *SINHAS* 1(2):97–161; "In the Name of Bikas," in *SINHAS* 1(2):1–10; and "Sabdachitramaa Kathmandu" in *Madhuparka* 29(12):27–31. An essay on historical ethnography, "Locating the Past" appeared in *Anthropological Locations: Boundaries and Grounds of a Field Science*, A. Gupta and J. Ferguson, eds. (University of California Press, 1997). Des Chene is also involved in collaborative translations of Nepali progressive literature and preservation microfilming of Nepali language journals and periodicals.

ELIZABETH ENSLIN received her Ph.D. from Stanford University in 1990. She is currently Assistant Director of the Center for Working Life, a nonprofit organization in Portland, Oregon. Her research in Nepal between 1986 and 1993 focused on women's resistance in Chitwan District. Her articles include "Beyond Writing: Feminist Practice and the Limitations of Ethnography," in *Cultural Anthropology* 9(4):1–32, 1994; and "Collective Powers in Common Places," in the *Himalayan Research Bulletin* 12(1&2):11–25, 1992. She is currently working on a book of essays reflecting on her experiences as an anthropologist giving birth and working with women in Chitwan.

PREMALATA GHIMIRE received her Ph.D. from Bryn Mawr College in 1988. She is now Professor in the Department of Community Medicine at B. P. Koirala Institute of Health Sciences in Dharan, Nepal. Her research and publications have focused on issues of ethnicity and identity among the Hod. One representative article is "The Individual and Group Identities of the Sapha Hod," in *Himalaya Past and Present*, M. P. Joshi, A. C. Fanger, and C. W. Brown, eds. (Almora: Shree Almora Book Depot, 1990). Other research interests include health and illness, ethnic minorities and hierarchical societies, and gender and class identities.

DOROTHY HOLLAND is Professor and Chair of Anthropology at the University of North Carolina, Chapel Hill. Her work in social and cultural anthropology has contributed primarily to theory in cognitive anthropology (see, for example, *Cultural Models in Language and Thought*, D. Holland and N. Quinn, eds. Cambridge University Press, 1987), to the extension of sociohistorical theories of the person (see "Symbols, Cognition, and Vygotsky's Developmental Psychology" in *Ethos* 16(3):247–272, 1988; and *Identity and Agency in Cultural Worlds*, Holland et al., Harvard University Press, in press), and to the social and cultural (re)production of gender in the United States and Nepal (see, for example, *Educated in Romance: Women, Achievement, and College Culture*, D. Holland and M. Eisenhart, University of Chicago Press, 1990; and D. Holland and D. Skinner, "Contested Ritual, Contested Femininities: (Re)forming Self and Society in a Nepali Women's Festival," in *American Ethnologist* 22:279–305, 1995).

Robert I. Levy is currently Research Professor in the Department of Anthropology at Duke University. He retired as Professor of Anthropology from the University of California, San Diego in 1991. He is author of numerous articles in psychological and cultural anthropology. He is also the author of *Tahitians: Mind and Experience in the Society Islands* (University of Chicago Press), a seminal work in person-centered ethnography; and *Mesocosm* (University of California Press, 1990), an encyclopedic ethnography of the role of a traditional Hindu city in the lives of its inhabitants.

Todd Lewis is Associate Professor of World Religions at Holy Cross College in Worcester, Massachusetts. His scholarship has included many works on Himalayan history, Newar Buddhist traditions, and the historical anthropology of Buddhism. His recent publications include *A Syllabus of Himalayan History, Anthropology and Religion* [with Theodore Riccardi, Jr.] (Ann Arbor: Association for Asian Studies Monograph Series, 1995) and "The Anthropological Study of Buddhist Communities: Historical Precedents and Ethnographic Paradigms," in *Shamanism, Altered States, Healing: Essays in the Anthropology of Religion*, Steven Glazier, ed. (Westport: Greenwood Press, 1997). He is also author of *Mahayana Buddhist Texts from Nepal: Narratives and Rituals of Newar Buddhism* (forthcoming from State University of New York Press in 1998).

Mark Liechty is Assistant Professor of Anthropology at the University of California, Santa Barbara. Recent articles include one on middle-class culture youth in Kathmandu in *Youth Cultures*, V. Amit-Talai and H. Wulff, eds. (Routledge, 1995) and another on cultures of space and place in Kathmandu in *The Geography of Identity*, P. Yaeger, ed. (Michigan University Press, 1996). He is working on a book on mass media, consumer culture, and the middle class in Kathmandu.

Kathryn S. March is Associate Professor of Anthropology and Women's Studies at Cornell University. Her work on the cultural and ethnohistorical construction of gender has resulted in several articles and one book, *Women's Informal Associations: Catalysts for Change* [with R. Taqqu] (Westview Press, 1986). She is currently working on a manuscript based on Tamang women's life histories and song compositions. She has worked in Nepal, specifically with Tamang and Sherpa peoples, since 1972. Since 1990, she also has collaborated jointly with Tribhuvan University on the Cornell-Nepal Study Program.

ERNESTINE MCHUGH is Assistant Professor of Anthropology and Religion at the University of Rochester's Eastman School of Music. Her publications include "Concepts of the Person among the Gurungs of Nepal," in *American Ethnologist* 16(1):75–86 (1989), and "Culture and the Transformation of Suffering," in *Anthropology of Tibet and the Himalaya*, C. Ramble and M. Brauen, eds. (Volkerkundemuseum der Universitat Zurich, 1993). Her research interests center on the interplay and mutual shaping of culture and experience.

STAN MUMFORD received his Ph.D. in Anthropology from Princeton University. He was Associate Professor and Chair of the Department of Anthropology and Sociology at Albertson College of Idaho until his death on December 23, 1993. He was a recognized scholar of Tibetan and southeast Asian culture, authoring numerous articles on the interaction of Tibetan Buddhist and Gurung shaman religious traditions. He also authored *Himalayan Dialogue: Tibetan Lamas and Gurung Shamans in Nepal* (University of Wisconsin Press, 1989). An early proponent of the dialogic approach to cultural understanding, Mumford was interested in dialogic encounters between Eastern and Western cultures, conflicts between modernization and preservation, and finding solutions to contemporary global conflicts through dialogue.

SHERRY B. ORTNER is Professor of Anthropology at Columbia University. She is the author of *Sherpas Through Their Rituals* (Cambridge University Press, 1978), *High Religion: A Cultural and Political History of Sherpa Buddhism* (Princeton University Press, 1989), and *Making Gender: The Politics and Erotics of Culture* (Beacon Press, 1996), as well as numerous articles on Sherpas, social and cultural theory, and feminist theory. She is currently completing an intertwined, Sherpa/sahib history of Himalayan mountaineering, tentatively entitled *Sex and Death on Mount Everest*.

ALFRED PACH III is Research Scientist at the National Opinion Research Center, University of Chicago. His research interests include the ethnology of Nepal; psychiatric, drug, and AIDS ethnography and epidemiology; and social networks research. His published articles focus on relations between substance abuse, HIV/AIDS risk behavior, social networks and interventions. Recent publications include the 1997 article "Changes in Network Characteristics and HIV Risk Behavior among Injection Drug Users" [with J. Hoffman and S. Su], in *Alcohol and Drug Dependence* 46:41–51.

STEVEN M. PARISH is Assistant Professor of Anthropology at the University of California, San Diego. He is the author of *Moral Knowing in a Hindu Sacred City* (Columbia University Press, 1994) and *Hierarchy and Its Discontents* (University of Pennsylvania Press, 1996). His research interests include moral and political consciousness, religion, psychological anthropology, and complex societies.

DEBRA SKINNER is Research Investigator at the Frank Porter Graham Child Development Center and Adjunct Associate Professor in the Department of Anthropology at the University of North Carolina at Chapel Hill. She is author and coauthor of numerous articles and chapters on children's emerging identities in sociocultural worlds; women's political culture; the co-development of identity, agency, and cultural worlds; constructions of the educated person; and constructions of disability in the Nepal context. She is coauthor with Dorothy Holland, William Lachicotte, and Carole Cain of *Identity and Agency in Cultural Worlds* (Harvard University Press, in press).